John Marsh

An Epitome of General Ecclesiastical History

From the Earliest Period to the Present Time

John Marsh

An Epitome of General Ecclesiastical History
From the Earliest Period to the Present Time

ISBN/EAN: 9783744733397

Printed in Europe, USA, Canada, Australia, Japan

Cover: Foto ©ninafisch / pixelio.de

More available books at **www.hansebooks.com**

AN

EPITOME OF GENERAL

ECCLESIASTICAL HISTORY

FROM THE EARLIEST PERIOD:

WITH A CONDENSED ACCOUNT OF THE JEWS
SINCE THE DESTRUCTION OF JERUSALEM.

By JOHN MARSH, D. D.

SIXTEENTH EDITION REVISED AND CORRECTED BY THE AUTHOR, AND
BROUGHT DOWN TO THE PRESENT TIME.

"How great are his signs! and how mighty are his wonders! His kingdom is an everlasting kingdom, and his dominion is from generation to generation."

NEW YORK:
A. S. BARNES & Co., 111 & 113 WILLIAM STREET,
(CORNER OF JOHN STREET.)

1867.

Entered according to Act of Congress in the year 1864, by
JOHN MARSH,
In the Clerk's Office of the District Court of the United States for the Southern District of New York.

PREFACE
TO THE FIRST EDITION.

A COMPENDIOUS history of the Church of God, properly executed, cannot fail of being useful in the Christian community.

The inspired history is both true and eminently beautiful: but its leading facts, detailed in the ordinary style, and illustrated and explained, will be perused with profit and pleasure. The period intervening between the Old and New Testament dates, lies hid from the mass of men in the Apocryphal books, in Josephus, and Prideaux's Connexions. And modern ecclesiastical history though ably presented by Mosheim, Milner, Haweis, Gregory, Newton, Neal and others, is extended through many volumes, and accompanied by much dry discussion and minute detail, repulsive to the young. In compiling this work no references are made to authorities, as they would uselessly fill the margin; but the utmost care has been taken that nothing be stated for fact which is not well authenticated. Early notice of errors will be gratefully received. The view given of existing denominations will not probably give universal satisfaction; but the classification of subjects, the attempt to give the history of religious opinions and the rise and fall of the different sects, and the moral and religious reflections will, it is thought, be pleasing to all who "contend earnestly for the faith once delivered to the saints," and profitable to the youthful inquirer after truth.

The work is divided into three Periods. The first extends from the Creation to the Call of Abraham.

The second, from the Call of Abraham to the birth of Christ.

The third, from the birth of Christ to the present time. Occasional notice is taken of false prophets and false systems of religion, and of various providential dealings with the nations of the earth.

The whole is commended to the blessing of God.

ADVERTISEMENT.

Published and for sale by M. W. Dodd, No. 506 Broadway, opposite St. Nicholas Hotel.

QUESTIONS on MARSH'S ECCLESIASTICAL HISTORY, compiled originally by Rev. Joseph Emerson, of Wethersfield, Ct., and long used by him in his Female Seminary; but recently brought out, revised and completed by Dr. Marsh himself, one Vol. 18mo., 134 pp.

To all individuals, families and students, loving thorough mental discipline and seeking an accurate knowledge of dates, events and truths in the history of the Church, these Questions cannot fail to afford both important and valuable assistance.

CONTENTS.

PERIOD I.
FROM THE CREATION TO THE CALL OF ABRAHAM.

CHAPTER I.

Creation, ... 25

CHAPTER II.

Primitive state of man. His trial and apostacy. Promise of a Saviour. Institution of Sacrifices. First fruits of the Spirit, ... 28

CHAPTER III.

Long lives and numbers of the Antediluvians. Preservation of the Church. Her enemies. Their great wickedness. God's care of his people. Deluge, ... 32

CHAPTER IV.

Re-settlement of the Church. Prophecies of Noah. Location of Ararat. Building of Babel. God curtails the future power of the enemies of his church, by the confusion of tongues and shortening men's lives, ... 37

CHAPTER V.

Early defection from the true religion. History of Idolatry, ... 40

PERIOD II.
FROM THE CALL OF ABRAHAM TO THE BIRTH OF CHRIST; EMBRACING 1921 YEARS.

CHAPTER I.

Call of Abraham. Institution of Circumcision, and establishment of the Jewish Church. Destruction of the cities of the plain. State of religion in the world, ... 44

CHAPTER II.

Descent of the Church in the line of Patriarchs. Prophecy respecting Shiloh. Joseph. Residence of the Church in Egypt. Her deliverance from bondage. Plagues of Egypt. Institution of the Passover. Baptism of the Church. Murmurings of the Israelites. Their typical journey, ... 49

CHAPTER III.

Giving of the Law. Moral and Ceremonial. Symbol of the Divine Presence. Tabernacle. Urim and Thummim. Priesthood. Re-institution of the Sabbath. Completion of the Pentateuch. Outpouring of the Spirit. Character of Moses. Two remarkable Prophecies of Christ, ... 56

CONTENTS.

CHAPTER IV.

Entrance of the Church into the promised land. State of the Church from Joshua to Samuel. Schools of the Prophets. Establishment of Monarchy in Israel. David. Solomon. Erection and dedication of the Temple. Prosperous state of the Church. Additions to the sacred Canon, ... 64

CHAPTER V.

Declension of religion in the Jewish nation. God's judgments for it. Precious seasons of the Church of God in the days of Hezekiah and Josiah. History of the Prophets, ... 73

CHAPTER VI.

Babylonish captivity. Ezekiel. Triumphs of faith. Prophecies of Daniel. Providence of God relating to Cyrus. Restoration of the Jews. Temple rebuilt. Preservation of the Church through Esther. Favorable decrees of Artaxerxes to Ezra and Nehemiah. Their labors and success at Jerusalem. The last of the Prophets. Closing of the sacred canon. Zoroaster, ... 81

CHAPTER VII.

Civil government of the Jews. Sanhedrim. Religious order. Degeneracy in piety. Conflicts for the High Priesthood. Joshua slain in the Temple. Destruction of the Persian and erection of the Grecian monarchy. Daniel's vision of the ram and the he goat. Fulfillment of prophecies against Tyre. The Jews favored by Alexander. Course and end of the he goat. Of the four horns which stood up in its place. Death of Simon the Just. Septuagint version of the Scriptures. Ptolemy's violation of the Holy of Holies. The Jews favored by Antiochus the Great, ... 93

CHAPTER VIII.

Desolation of Jerusalem under Antiochus Epiphanes. Jason erects a Gymnasium. Temple shut up for three years. Bold and artful plot of Antiochus to extirpate the Church. The temple consecrated to Jupiter Olympus. Jewish martyrdoms. General revolt under Mattathias. Wars of the Maccabees. Death of Antiochus. Prophecies fulfilled in him. Destruction of the Grecian, and establishment of the Roman empire, the legs and feet of Nebuchadnezzar's image. Prosperous state of the Jews under Jonathan and Simon. Apochryphal books, ... 103

CHAPTER IX.

Prosperous state of the Jews under Hyrcanus. Royalty re-established. Jerusalem taken by the Romans. End of the Asmonean princes. Herod the Great. The Temple repaired and enlarged. Family of Herod. Sceptre departed from Judah. Religious sects among the Jews—Pharisees, Saducees, Essenes, Herodians, Galileans, Karaites. Different orders of men—Scribes, Rabbis, Nazarites. Wickedness of the Jews, and of the Heathen. State of the Civil World. Reflections on the providence of God, 112

PERIOD III.

FROM THE BIRTH OF CHRIST TO THE PRESENT TIME.

CHAPTER I.

Birth of Christ. Jesus circumcised. Welcomed by saints and angels. Worshiped by the wise men. Sought for by Herod. Carried into Egypt. Conversant at twelve years with the Doctors. Lives in retirement until thirty years of age. Birth, character, and work of John the Baptist. Jesus baptised by him, and consecrated to the Priesthood. Christ's ministry. Abolition of the Jewish, and establishment of the Christian Church. Christ's Priesthood. His death, resurrection, and ascension. Jesus, King in Zion. Evidences of his divine mission, ... 126

CONTENTS.

CHAPTER II.

Number and character of Christ's disciples. Death of John the Baptist. The twelve Apostles chosen. The seventy sent. History and character of the twelve. Descent upon them of the Holy Ghost. Outpouring of the Spirit on the day of Pentecost. Three thousand added to the Church. Boldness and success of Peter and John. Holiness and harmony of the Church. Detection of Hypocrisy. Institution of the office of Deacon. Martyrdom of Stephen. Persecution and dispersion of the Church. The gospel carried to the Samaritans and dispersed Jews. Conversion of Saul, . . . 138

CHAPTER III.

The Gospel preached to the Gentiles. Cornelius and his family baptised. Martyrdom of James. Revival at Antioch. Saul and Barnabas ordained missionaries to the Heathen. Ministry of Paul. Constitution of the Christian Church. Its early moral and religious state. Character of the Apostles' preaching. Writers of the New Testament. Firm establishment of the kingdom of Christ. Opposition of the Jews. God's judgment upon them. Destruction of Jerusalem. Dispersion of the Jews. Opposition of the Roman Emperors Nero and Domitian. Martyrdom of Paul and Peter. Early Heresies, ... 152

CHAPTER IV.

General state of the Church from the first century to Constantine. Extension of the Gospel. Change of means. Persecution in Bithynia. Pliny's letter to Trajan. Writings of Clement. Death of Simeon. Martyrdom of Ignatius. Favorable decree of Antoninus Pius. Persecutions under Marcus. Justin Martyr. Polycarp. Persecutions in France. Rest of the Churches under Commodus. Corruptions of the second century. Increase of Rites and Ceremonies. Easter, ... 169

CHAPTER V.

Conduct of the Roman Emperors in the third century. Extension of the Gospel. Decline of Piety. Increase of Useless Rites. Genuine Fruits of the Spirit. Tertullian's account of the conduct of the Christians. His character. Irenens. Origen. Cyprian. Question concerning Infant Baptism. Novatians. Sabellians. Manicheans. Attacks of Heathen Philosophers. Porphyry. First great declension of Christianity. Tremendous Persecution under Diocesian. Elevation of Constantine to the Roman Empire. Abolition of the Ancient Religion of Rome. Establishment of Christianity throughout the Empire, ... 184

CHAPTER VI.

Results of the Revolution under Constantine. Rise of Arianism. Council of Nice. Death of Constantine. Succeeding emperors. Julian's attempt to restore Paganism. His defeat in re-building the Temple at Jerusalem. Persecutions in Persia. Eusebius Basil. Chrysostom. Jerome. Augustine. Pelagianism. Civil revolution in Europe. Daniel's vision of the ten horns. Conversion of the barbarous nations. Franks. Irish. Britons. Progress of error and superstition in the 5th and 6th centuries, ... 198

CHAPTER VII.

Monachism. Its rise and progress. Reflections on its odious character. Mahometanism. Appearance of Mahomet in Arabia. His religion. Extension of the Saracen Empire. Destruction of the Eastern Churches. Present extent of Mahometanism, 214

CHAPTER VIII.

Prophecies relating to the Papacy. Its general rise. Grant of Phocas. Causes of the vast increase of Papal dominion. Ignorance, Superstition, and Corruption of the age. Tradition substitued for the Bible. Subjection of Heathen Nations. Subserviency of the Monks. Papal Rome Idolatrous and a Temporal Power, the Little Horn. Supposed time of her Continuance. Election of Popes. Efforts at Supreme Dominion. Hildebrand's treatment of Henry. Thomas a Becket. Interdiction. The power given to the Beast, ... 223

CONTENTS.

CHAPTER IX.

Measures adopted by the Roman pontiffs to secure their dominion. They fill all important stations. Increase their revenues. Send out Legates. Forbid Marriage to the Clergy. Hold over men the rod of Excommunication. Establish the Inquisition. Strengthen superstition. Canonize Saints. Establish Transubstantiation, Purgatory, Auricular Confession. Worship in an unknown Tongue. Make the Pope infallible. Institute the Crusades, and Military Orders, ... 233

CHAPTER X.

Two Witnesses, predicted by John. Their character. Why said to be two. Their History obscure. Traced out in an age of darkness. Leo and Constantine. Council of Constantinople and Frankfort. Alcuin. Council of Paris. Rabanus *и* Statius. Claudius of Turin. Goteschalcus. Council at Trosly, Athelston, Afric, Arnulphus. Witnesses in France, in England. Waldenses. Peter Waldo. John Wickliff and his followers. William Sautre. John Badby. Lord Cobham. John Huss and Jerome of Prague. Their adherents and followers. The Hussite War. Brethren and Sisters of the Free Spirit, ... 242

CHAPTER XI.

Circumstances in Europe favoring a reformation. Philip's triumph over Boniface. Removal of the Pope to Avignon. Great Western Schism. Mendicants unpopular. General demand for a reform. Council of Constance. Discouragements. Character of the Popes. Their power. Low state of Religion and Learning. Immediate causes. Avarice of the Popes. Sale of Indulgences opposed by Martin Luther. Luther's birth and education. Retires into a Monastery. Rends the scriptures. Made professor at Wittemberg. Opposes Tetzel. Meets with applause. Circumstances favoring his cause. Summoned to Rome. Appears before Cajetan and Miltitz. Disputes with Eckius. Reformation commences in Switzerland. Erasmus. Melancthon. Frederick the Wise. Luther excommunicated. Burns the Pope's bull, and establishes the Lutheran Church. Summoned to the Diet at Worms. His defence and condemnation. Secreted at Wartburg. Re-appears and publishes the New Testament in German. Preaches the Gospel with great success, ... 255

CHAPTER XII.

Reformation spreads. Death of Leo X. Sacramental controversy. War of the Peasants. Death of Frederic. Decision of John. Martyrs. Diet at Spire. Luther marries. Writes, in vain, submissive letters. Publishes his Hymns. An attempt made to poison him. His conflict with Erasmus. Second Diet at Spire. The reformers condemned, and protest. Called Protestants. Diet at Augsburg. Confession of Augsburg. League of Smallkeld. Peace of Nuremberg. Anabaptists. Reformation in England. Conference at Worms. Death of Luther. Council of Trent. Battle of Mukleberg. Interim. Peace of Religion. Reformation in Switzerland. Zuinglius. Calvin. Reformation in Holland and Scotland. John Knox. Sentiments of the reformers. Church Government. Blessings of the Reformation, ... 273

CHAPTER XIII.

Modern Christendom. Roman Church. Her efforts for self-preservation. Order of the Jesuits. Missionary operations and establishments. Persecution of the Protestants. Expulsion of the Moors from Spain. Massacre on St. Bartholomew's day. Edict of Nantez. Its revocation. Inquisition. Auto de fe. Downfall of Popery. Reverses in the East. Disaffections in Europe. Suppression of the Jesuits. French Revolution. Principles and rites of the Roman Church. Character of her Popes and Clergy since the Reformation. Monastic orders. Present state of Popery in the World, . . 289

CHAPTER XIV.

Greek Church. Its history, doctrine, and discipline. Russian Greek Church. Its establishment and separation from the Greek Church. Sect of Isbranki. Efforts of Peter the Great. Doctrines and discipline. Eastern Churches. Ground of their early divisions. Nestorians. Monophysites. Asiatics. Africans. Copts. Abyssinians. Armenians, ... 303

CONTENTS.

CHAPTER XV.

Page

Divisions of the Protestants. Lutherans. Their residence, rise, system of faith, liturgy, government. Persecutions. Internal commotions. Syncrgistical controversy. Attempts at a reconciliation between them and the Calvinists. Syncretistic controversy. Degeneracy of Clergy and Churches. Pietistical controversy. Liberalism. Present state of religion in their Churches. Swedenborgianism. Theological erudition, . . .312

CHAPTER XIV.

Helvetic Churches. Difference between Zuinglius and Calvin. Triumph of Calvinism. Its five points. Genevan Academy. Controversies with the Lutherans. Internal dissensions. Spiritual brethren and sisters. Castalio. Bolsec. Servetus. Persecutions from the Catholics. Rise of Arminianism. Synod of Dort. Decline of Calvinism in Holland, England, France, and Switzerland. Disputes in Holland. Pres ent state of the Reformed Churches. Literature of the Calvinists. Distinguished men. Five points of Arminius. Persecution of his followers. Their restoration and prosperity, ... 318

CHAPTER XVII.

Imperfect character of the Reformation in England. Cranmer made Archbishop of Canterbury. Bible translated and given to the people. Monasteries suppressed. Relics ridiculed. Catholic Rebellion. Henry VIII. excommunicated. His death. Excellent reign of Edward VI. Liturgy and articles introduced. Reign of Mary. Popish persecution. Martyrdom of John Rogers, Saunders, Hooper, Taylor, Bradford, Ridley, and Latimer. Cranmer. Darkness and distress of the period. Death of Mary and accession of Elizabeth. Restoration of the Protestants. Establishment of the English Church, ... 329

CHAPTER XVIII.

Troubles in the English Church. Efforts of the Papists to regain their lost dominion. Rise of the puritans. Acts of Supremacy and Uniformity. Demands of the Puritans. Persecutions of the High Commission Court. The Puritans separate from the establishment. Their character and principles. Conference at Hampton Court, and oppression under James I. Popish powder plot. King James' translation of the Bible. Persecutions by Laud, and overthrow of Episcopacy. Assembly of Divines at Westminister. Irish Massacre. Triumph of the Puritans. Restoration of Monarchy and Episcopacy. Severity towards the Nonconformists. Efforts of Infidelity. New efforts of the Papists. Revolution. Rise of two parties, High and Low Church. Bangorian controversy. Deists. Great excitement from the Methodists. Effects of the French Revolution. Present state of parties. Discipline and Doctrine of the Church of England. Distinguished Divines, ... 340

CHAPTER XIX.

Presbyterian Church of Scotland. First General Assembly. Established by Law, Suppressed by Charles I. Re-established and prosperous during the Protectorate. Solemn league and Covenant. Gains free toleration in the Revolution. Seceders, Burghers, and Anti-Burghers. Glassites. Presbytery of Relief. Scotch character. Presbyterian Discipline.
English Presbyterians and Independents. Early distinguished divines, Baxter, Owen, Flavel, Bates, Howe. Number and state of the Dissenters after the Revolution. Henry, Watts, Doddridge. Spread of Arianism, and decline of Presbyterians. Increase and flourishing state of the Independents, ... 361

CHAPTER XX.

Mr. Robinson's Church. Its emigration to Holland and to New England. Rapid increase of the New England Churches. Character of their first ministers and members. Constitution. Harvard College founded. Roger Williams. Hutchinsonian controversy. Troubles from the Baptists. Cambridge Platform. Disturbances from the Quakers. Hartford controversy. Synod of 1657. Half-way covenant. Synod of 1680. Witchcraft. Yale College. Saybrook Platform. Great Revival. Sandemanian controversy. Demoralizing influence of the French and Revolutionary War. Revival of the Churches. Unitarianism. Theological Institutions. Number and order of the Churches and Ministers. Distinguished Divines, ... 374

CONTENTS.

CHAPTER XXI.

Episcopal, Presbyterian, Dutch, Associate Reformed, German Lutheran, and Reformed Churches in the United States, ... 392

CHAPTER XXII.

Unitarians, Anabaptists or Mennonites. English Baptists, General and Particular. American Baptists. Free Willers. Seventh-day Baptists. Quakers. Shakers, . . 402

CHAPTER XXIII.

Moravians. History and discipline. Methodists. Early labors of Wesley and Whitfield. Their separation. Methodist Episcopal Church. Their order, discipline, and increase in Europe and America. Whitfieldian Methodists. Associated Methodists. Wesleyan Methodists. Swedenborgians. Universalists, ... 416

CHAPTER XXIV.

Protestant Missions. Neglected by the Reformers. First attended to by the Puritans in North America. Eliot. Mayhews. Brainard. Danish Missions. Swartz. Hans Egede. Moravian Missions. Wesleyan Methodist Missions. Baptist. London, Edinburgh, Church Missionary Society. Buchanan. Martyn. American Board. Bible, Tract, and Education Societies. Concluding Remarks, ... 427

APPENDIX.

History of the Jews from the destruction of Jerusalem to the present time . 445

AN EPITOME, &c.

PERIOD I.

FROM THE CREATION TO THE CALL OF ABRAHAM.

CHAPTER I.

Creation.

This WORLD, the theatre of the most wonderful divine operations, has been in existence 5868 years. The learned Greeks were fond of speculating upon the origin of all things Aristotle supposed the world, in its organized form, eternal; and that the Supreme Being put it in motion. Anaxagoras, followed by Socrates and Plato, believed in a Supreme Mind who organized the world out of matter which always existed; yet held to an animating principle in matter which propelled and regulated the organized system. Epicurus, the father of atheism, traced the beautiful order of the earth, and all its inhabitants and productions, to a fortuitous concurrence of atoms. No one in Greece or Rome ever acknowledged a Creator of the world.

The old heathen nations ignorant of their origin, were fond of ascribing to themselves vast antiquity. The Babylonians and Egyptians boasted of their astronomical observations, and counted their dynasties through thirty and forty thousand years. The modern Chinese and Hindoos make similar pretensions.

> " Some drill and bore
> The solid earth, and, from the strata there,
> Extract a register by which they learn
> That He who made it, and revealed its date
> To Moses, was mistaken in its age."

has done, of the manner of execution, and of his benevolent purposes, we cannot fail to exclaim, "O Lord! how manifold are thy works; in wisdom hast thou made them all."

CHAPTER II.

Primitive state of man. His trial and apostacy. Promise of a Saviour. Institution of sacrifices. First fruits of the Spirit.

THE primitive state of man was one of holiness and unmarred felicity. The first exercises of his heart toward God, were love and reverential fear. Between him and the Father of his spirit existed a free and blessed intercourse. His soul was a stranger to selfish and corrupt affections, and was filled with joy in God, and his perfect administration.

As a moral agent, he was subjected to that law which requires all rational beings to love the Lord their God with all their heart, soul, strength and mind, and their neighbor as themselves. To make special trial of the first parents of the human family, God placed Adam and Eve in the garden of Eden, in the midst of all that could gratify the taste or delight the eye; and there, while he gave them the full indulgence of every thing else, forbade their eating of the tree of knowledge of good and evil. As a reward for obedience, he promised them eternal life; everlasting holiness and happiness in his presence. For disobedience, he assured them that *dying, they should die;* that sinning, renounced the dominion of their maker, and departing from all holiness, they should sink for ever under his wrath and curse. The trial, God had a right to make; for he was their creator and lawgiver; and so bountiful had he been to them, so small was the thing denied them, and so great were the motives to entire abstinence, that disobedience would call for the severest judgments. The trial was one of greatest consequence to them and their posterity. In it was involved their eternal well being. They were to secure a state of perpetual holiness, or to reject their Maker and become totally depraved in their moral affections. And, as it had become a law of creation that every thing should bear the likeness of its progenitor, the moral state and character of all future generations depended on the issue.

At this moment of solemn trial, Satan, the chief of those angels who kept not their first estate, but revolted from God,

PROMISE OF A SAVIOUR.

and were cast out of heaven, appeared in the garden of Eden, in the form of a serpent; and full of envy, resentment, pride and malice, sought their ruin. He addressed himself craftily to the mother of men, and endeavored to excite in her mind an unbelief in the threatening as the word of God. Failing in this, he made her a promise of an understanding like that of the gods; excited her curiosity; tempted her appetite, until, impatient of divine restraint, and renouncing her confidence in God, for confidence in the serpent:—

> "She pluck'd; she ate;
> Earth felt the wound, and nature from her seat,
> Gave signs of wo, that all was lost."

Adam soon ventured on the same ground of infidelity, and with his wife, apostatized from God. Their moral character was now wholly changed. They no longer appeared before God in prayer and praise as dear children, but hid themselves from his presence in conscious guilt. And when called to account for their conduct, instead of confessing their sin and imploring pardon, they had the effrontery to charge their sin upon others; yea, indirectly, upon God himself.

This was the moment when angels looked for their immediate destruction. But said God, "Stay them from going down into the pit, for I have found a ransom." A Saviour was promised. A tremendous sentence was pronounced upon the serpent, the animal in which the father of lies approached the innocent pair, that mankind might ever have before their eyes something that would powerfully remind them of this event; but reaching beyond that, even to Satan, the old serpent, the deceiver, insuring his destruction and the destruction of his cause by Jesus Christ, the seed of the woman, the Saviour of sinners. "And I will put enmity between thee and the woman, and between thy seed and her seed; it shall bruise thy head and thou shalt bruise his heel."

This promise was the light and hope of a ruined world. To lead mankind to rest upon it, sacrifices were immediately instituted. Over the blood of beasts, they were to be brought to feel their sinfulness; that there was no access to the Father without an atonement; and to look forward in faith and hope to the Lamb of God that should take away the sin of the world.

The first transgressors were the first fruits of the Spirit

Convinced of sin, terrors took hold on them, and they fled from the presence of the Lord. The voice of mercy melted their hearts. God gave them life. Adam, who had before called his wife Woman, now called her Eve, because she was the mother of all living ; of all, who according to the gracious promise, were to be raised to immortal life : and Eve, at the birth of her first born, (evidently rejoicing in the promise respecting her seed which should bruise the serpent's head,) exclaimed, " I have gotten a man, the Lord" the promised deliverer. With the coats of animals which they no doubt offered in sacrifice to God, they made themselves garments and were clothed.

Thus early did Christ gain a victory over Satan, redeem to himself a peculiar people, and

ESTABLISH A CHURCH IN THE WORLD.

But the race had become rebellious ; and because of the apostacy, God cursed the ground, and drove the transgressors from the beautiful garden, lest, by being suffered to remain there in the enjoyment of their former privileges, they should partake of the tree of life ;—i. e. be insensible to the evil of sin, and fancy that they could gain heaven by their own obedience. They went forth to a world of thorns and briers ; there to beget a race of their own fallen nature ;—a race corrupt ; enemies to God ; who, through voluntary transgression, would bring upon themselves innumerable evils in this life, and become exposed to eternal death.

How many of their offspring were trained up for heaven by their daily sacrifices and instructions, we know not. One interesting, lovely youth in this family, stands on record, " an heir of the righteousness which is by faith." Abel believed in God. In hope of eternal life through the promised seed, he offered a lamb from his flock. The doctrine of the cross was foolishness to Cain. He scorned the thoughts of receiving salvation through the merits of another, and, trusting to his own righteousness, he brought only an offering of the fruit of the ground. The Lord rejected it, but had respect unto that of Abel. Cain's anger rose. He fell upon his brother and slew him. Awful fruit of the apostacy ! Solemn stroke ! The first of unnumbered, that should fall from the hands of wicked men upon the followers of the Lamb. Abel perished ; the first martyr to truth. Heaven's portals opened wide to admit the first of the ransomed of the Lord, who should come to Mount Zion, washed sanctified, and justified in the name of the Lord Jesus, and by the Spirit of God. Him, angels welcomed with joy, as a spectacle never before witnessed in their happy regions; while he, being dead, by his faith yet speaketh to all the children of men, assuring them that a sacrifice, offered with an honest and true heart, a deep sense of the guilt of sin, and a firm reliance on the atonement of Christ, will render sinners acceptable to God, and fit them for glory.

Having laid his body in the grave, his parents returned to their dwelling, cast down, yet not destroyed. They trusted the promise of God, for a righteous seed, and the Lord remembered them in mercy, and sent them another son, whom they called Seth;—manifestly a pious man, for said his mother in holy faith, God hath appointed me another seed instead of Abel.

In their posterity of the third generation, in the days of Enos, they witnessed a general outpouring of the Spirit. "Then," says the inspired historian, "men began to call upon the name of the Lord." Whether we consider these words as denoting that then prayer became a duty of common observance, or that in that age men first erected houses of worship, and assembled for prayer and praise, or entered into covenant with God and professed themselves his people, it is manifest there was a general and great revival of religion; for nothing else could have induced men to do either of these things. This was in about the 235th year of the world, when the church was probably large and many were prepared for heaven.

Of the state of religion in the three succeeding generations we have no account. Probably there was no other outpouring of the Spirit, and the love of many, who had turned to the Lord, had waxed cold. In the seventh generation from Adam, we find Enoch, a man eminently elevated above this world and devoted to God. He was a prophet of the Lord, and uttered a remarkable prophecy of the coming of Christ to take to himself the kingdom and the dominion, and to judge the world. "And Enoch also, the seventh from Adam," says Jude, "prophesied of these, saying, behold the Lord cometh with ten thousand of his saints, to execute judgment upon all, and to convince all that are ungodly among them, of all their ungodly deeds, which they have ungodly committed; and of all their hard speeches which ungodly sinners have spoken against him." What a view does this give us of the wickedness of man at that period! How solemn was that voice echoing through that world of sin and transgression—like the last trump in the morning of the resurrection! If many mocked, with what anguish must they have remembered it in a future age, when the fountains of the great deep were broken up, and the floods came and swept them all away!

Enoch lived a life of faith, maintained holy fellowship and sweet communion with God ; and God testified his delight in him by translating him, soul and body, to heaven, not suffering him to taste death. By this great event also, God gave his church a lively assurance of a future world, and the resurrection of the dead. All who had died were sleeping in their graves. No specific promise had been given that the body should be delivered from the ruins of the fall. Here the saints witnessed a rescue of Enoch from death and the grave, and had a precious intimation of the future entire deliverance of the whole man from the bondage of corruption. One instance God gave to the antediluvian church. One to the church, by Elijah, in succeeding periods, that her faith might be in God ; until Christ should burst the bands of death and ascend a triumphant conqueror—" *the resurrection and the life.*"

CHAPTER III.

Long lives and numbers of the Antediluvians. Preservation of the church. Her enemies. Their great wickedness. God's care of his people. Deluge.

God was pleased to continue the inhabitants of the old world upon earth to an astonishing period. Enoch was taken to heaven in the 365th year of his age ; but the rest of Seth's descendants, of whom we have any account, all lived more than seven centuries. Methuselah attained to the age of 969 years. Many, "not knowing the power of God," have supposed that their years were lunar months : but a moment's consideration will show the absurdity of such a conjecture ; for it would make them parents when mere infants, and reduce the duration of the old world to less than 130 years. By suffering man to remain long upon the earth, God gave him an opportunity to act out the wickedness of his heart, and to show to the universe the malignity and bitterness of sin

Living as they did, through many centuries, the Antediluvians must have been very numerous. When Cain destroyed his brother, they had greatly multiplied, so that he was fearful to go forth, lest any one that met him should kill him. The first generation lived through several successive periods, until the mass of men had accumulated to millions.

Among this vast population we behold the church, small but distinct. Indeed it was the only thing of any worth in the sight of God—the only thing deserving sacred record. He has suffered every thing else—mighty kingdoms, flourishing cities, vast achievements, powerful warriors, and renowned statesmen—all to perish in oblivion; and has told us only of the holy seed, the generation of the righteous, who maintained religion, and who, especially from Enoch to Noah, were doubtless hated of all men. The following is their record:

	Began his birth in the year of the world.	Had his son in the year of his life.	Lived after his son's birth, yrs.	Lived in all, yrs.	Died in the yr. of the world.
Adam, . . .	1	130	800	930	930
Seth, ...	130	105	807	912	1042
Enos, . . .	235	90	815	905	1140
Cainan, . . .	325	70	840	910	1235
Mahaleel, . .	395	65	830	895	1290
Jared, ...	460	162	800	962	1422
Enoch, . . .	622	65	300	365	987
Methuselah, . .	687	187	782	969	1656
Lamech, . . .	874	182	595	777	1651
Noah, ...	1056	500			

The enemies of the church were mighty. Cain was a hardened wretch. He despised the sacrifice which prefigured the atonement, and attempted to please God by his own devices. Angry with Jehovah for exposing the hollowness of his heart, he wreaked his vengeance on his brother Abel. God called him to account, and inquired for Abel; but, in hardened impudence, he said, "Am I my brother's keeper?" The Lord pronounced him cursed, and drove him out, a fugitive and a vagabond on the earth At hearing his sentence, remorse seized his soul; and he exclaimed, "My punishment is greater than I can bear!" What a picture of impenitent misery! God determined he should live, a monument of the Divine abhorrence of his crime; and he set a mark upon him, lest any finding him should kill him. Cain went forth and forsook the presence and ordinances of God—intrenched himself in a city, and became a miserable worldling. His posterity greatly increased and walked in his steps. Of some we read, who were ingenious artificers, but of none who sought the Lord. Lamech took to himself two wives, and introduced to the world the dreadful sin of polygamy.

Not long did the descendants of Cain flourish in the earth, without exercising a baneful influence upon the children of God. These, beholding their beautiful women contracted marriages with them. Their progeny were giants in wickedness. Says the inspired historian, "there were giants in those days; when the sons of God came in unto the daughters of men, and they bear children to them; the same became men of renown;"—no doubt the men of whom Enoch prophesied the Lord would be avenged for "all their ungodly deeds which they had ungodly committed, and all their hard speeches which they had spoken against him." And now the flood-gates of wickedness being open, and the torrents of iniquity overflowing the earth, the Lord sware in his wrath, "My Spirit shall not always strive with man, for that he also is flesh," is corrupt, depraved, has prostituted all his noble powers, before the most debased appetites and passions.

The Spirit of God being withdrawn, the prince of the power of the air, the spirit that worketh in the children of disobedience, had a full triumph. Generation succeeded generation, practising the most open, daring, atrocious wickedness. Violence, murder, war, rapine, and vile idolatry filled the earth. Terrible were the enemies of vital godliness.

But amidst the moral desolations of the old world, the church stood. It was the cause of Jehovah. In the little families of Methuselah and Lamech and Noah it lived; and in the last of these holy men, God designed to carry it through the most awful judgment ever inflicted upon our globe. Upon a view of the horrid impiety which filled the earth, "it repented the Lord that he had made man upon the earth and it grieved him at his heart." Not only had he an extreme abhorrence of the crimes of men and their desperate wickedness, but his soul loathed them— "And the Lord said, I will destroy man whom I have created, from the face of the earth, both man and beast, and every creeping thing, and the fowls of the air, for it repenteth me that I have made them."

Easily indeed, might he have sent forth his Spirit, and converted the hearts of that ungodly generation to himself, and fitted them all for the happiness of heaven; and not less impious men of later ages have had the hardihood to contemn God, because, when it lay in his power, he did not save them and all men. But it pleases Jehovah sometimes to manifest his justice and his wrath, as well as his grace. He would have been righteous in destroying them without warning. But to exhibit further his patience and long suffering, he warned them by the preaching of Noah, for the space of 120 years. In that holy man was the Spirit of Christ; he was full of the Holy Ghost. By this Spirit, says Peter, "he went and preached unto the spirits in prison," (the spirits confined in the time when Peter wrote in the prison of hell, suffering the vengeance of eternal fire,) "which sometimes were disobedient, when once the long suffering of God, waited in the days of Noah."

For the preservation of this holy man and his family, God directed Noah to prepare an ark. It was a strange commission. It was making provision against a calamity which, to the eye of sense and reason, seemed impossible. But Noah believed the word of the Lord. He did not expostulate against the judgment; nor did he decline a labor almost too great for man, and which would expose him to the most cutting ridicule and reproach. But "moved with fear," reverencing Jehovah, he commenced his work; and by his works, warned every beholder to repent of his sins and flee from impending destruction. The world beheld, ridiculed, and mocked; went on eating and drinking, marrying and giving in marriage. No heart relented. No sinner, fearful of the truth, inquired, Where is God my Maker? But the purpose of God was fixed; and he moved on to its accomplishment, glorious in holiness.

At the appointed time, the ark was completed; and Noah and his wife, and his sons and their wives, the LITTLE CHURCH OF GOD, and two of every flying fowl and creeping thing, for their continuance upon the earth, were gathered in. Solemn moment! The door was shut; and the rain **descended, the windows of heaven were opened, and the** fountains of the great deep were broken up, and God had no pity, and man could find no refuge; the tallest trees, the highest mountains were alike covered, and paleness, and horror, and death, seized the vast family of man.

To this great and awful judgment of God upon the enemies of the church, we have evidently some allusion in early writings, and the religious rites of heathen nations, and there are numerous appearances in the earth which clearly indicate that it was once overwhelmed by a deluge of water. Trees, bones of animals, sea-shells, petrified fishes deeply imbedded in the earth, yea, in the hardest strata and on the tops of the highest mountains, are memorials of this dread event. But we believe it chiefly, because God declares it in his holy word. We do not ask how it could be,—we enter into no philosophical discussion, we seek for the intervention of no comet; sufficient for us is it to know that the winds and the waves and the seas obey the Almighty. We learn from it that God abhors the workers of iniquity, and will not let the wicked go unpunished; and we lift up our hearts to God in the heavens and say, Lord, give us grace that we may take warning, and flee from the wrath to come.

The ark consisted of three stories, with one window in the top. It was sufficiently large for the purpose for which it was designed; being 480 feet in length, 81 in breadth, and 41 in height. After floating on the waters 150 days, it rested on one of the mountains of Ararat. Noah and his family continued in it one year and ten days.

The flood took place in the 1656th year of the world; 2348 years before Christ, and 4177 years from the present time.

This flood which cleansed the world was a remarkable type of the redemption by the blood of Christ, which is sealed to us by the baptism of water. These "eight souls were saved by water." "The like figure whereunto" says Peter, " even baptism doth also now save us, (not the putting away the filth of the flesh, but the answer of a good conscience toward God,) by the resurrection of Jesus Christ." And the ark, which was the refuge of the people of Jehovah, amid the storms of divine vengeance, was a type of Christ, the eternal refuge of perishing sinners. "Come thou," says God, in this day of mercy to every sinner, "Come thou and all thy house into the ark."

CHAPTER IV.

Re-settlement of the Church. Prophecies of Noah. Location of Ararat. Building of Babel. God curtails the future power of the enemies of his church, by the confusion of tongues, and shortening men's lives.

WHEN God had fully executed his vengeance on the wicked inhabitants of the old world, he brought forth his little church from the ark, and gave it the earth for a possession. To express the grateful emotions of his heart, Noah built an altar, and offered sacrifices unto the Lord. His offerings were accepted, and God renewed with him and his seed, the covenant of grace, making the rainbow, a thing permanent as light, a token of the covenant; and gave them every moving thing to be meat for them, prohibiting however the eating of blood, because he had appointed the blood to be an atonement for sin. As mankind had no right to eat flesh before the deluge, this grant was a great alleviation of the original curse upon human sustenance; an alleviation, in prophetic view of which, at the birth of Noah, Lamech might well exclaim, " This same shall comfort us concerning our work and toil of our hands, because of the ground which the Lord hath cursed."

" Noah was a just man and perfect in his generation." But " there is not a just man on earth that doeth good and sinneth not;" and such is the fidelity of the scripture historians, that they fail not to record the vices of the holiest men. Noah planted a vineyard, and drank to excess of the fruit of the vine. As he lay inebriated and uncovered in his tent, he was discovered by Ham. his youngest son, who made sport of the humiliating spectacle. But, actuated by a better spirit, Shem and Japheth took a garment and went backward, and decently covered the nakedness of their father. When Noah awoke and was informed of the deeds they had done, he declared, under the influence of the Spirit, the feelings of his soul relating to the future condition of their families.

" Cursed be Canaan!
A servant of servants to his brothers let him be!
Blessed be Jehovah, the God of Shem!
And let Canaan be their servant!
And may God extend Japheth,

And may he dwell in the tents of Shem!
And let Canaan be their servant."

It was a wonderful prophecy, which has been astonishingly fulfilled, first, in the subjection of the Canaanites to the children of Israel, and since, in the more extensive subjection of Africa, (which was settled by Ham,) to the Romans, the Saracens, the Turks, and in the millions on millions who have been carried from that unhappy region into foreign slavery;—in the preservation of the true church in the line of Shem, (from whom Abraham descended,) and the tabernacling of Christ among the Jews; and in the wonderful spread of the posterity of Japheth over all Europe and America, and many parts of Asia, where, especially by Grecian, Roman, and British conquests, they have dwelt in the tents of Shem; and in a still higher sense, in their extensive conversion to the faith of the Gospel, and dwelling in the tents of Shem, the church of the living God.

The Ark rested on one of the mountains of Ararat.—These mountains are commonly supposed to lie in the ancient country of Armenia. Some have conjectured that they were farther East, perhaps on the Hymlaya mountains, the highest in the world; as the journeying of the descendants of Noah towards Shinar, is said to have been from the East, and not as it must have been on the common supposition, from the West; as no mention is ever made of Noah in any account of the Western nations, though he lived 300 years after the flood; as the Hindoo and Chinese are very ancient nations; and Fohi, the reputed founder of the Chinese empire, bears strong resemblance to Noah. But it is most probable that they were not far distant from Shinar, as no motive could have led so early to a distant emigration.

At the close of the first century, after Noah came out of the ark, his descendants, who might already have increased to a million of souls, spread over that beautiful country through which ran the Euphrates.

At this time the whole earth was of one language; that language, no doubt, with which God endued Adam. Had men been uncorrupt, uniformity of speech might have been of the highest utility. But guided by the depraved heart, it had become one of the most powerful instruments of corruption, and was probably one of the chief sources of the abominations and violence of the Antediluvians. One mind powerful in oratory or song, could easily reach the hearts of a world. God therefore resolved to deprive the future enemies of his church of so tremendous an engine. This purpose he executed on beholding them there on the plains of Shinar, combining together and erecting a city and tower which should make them one vast and powerful people. "Go to," said he, "let us go down and confound their language, that they may not understand one another's speech." The builders of Babel were thrown into confusion and scattered abroad, and the little church was left to gather strength, unmolested by so great a weapon.

Another thing, which before the flood, had nearly destroyed the church, was the great age which the wicked were suffered to attain. Worldly power would not be the portion of God's people. Should the wicked therefore, who ordinarily inherit it, be continued again centuries upon earth, and for centuries persecute the church, how could she live? She almost expires in particular provinces, even under the tyranny, for a few years, of some merciless persecutor. God, therefore, out of regard to his church, shortened the lives of men, first to a few centuries; and then to three score and ten years.

Where to look for the church at this period we know not; but it continued in the family of Noah, and in the line of Shem. Shem lived an hundred and fifty years after the birth of Abraham, and must have been venerated for his piety and age, by all about him; but he seems to have been unknown by the family of that pious patriarch. His descendants, however, we soon find in the regions of Chaldea and Assyria; though, by many able and learned writers, it is thought they had no concern in the building of Babel. They feared God. They maintained among them the true religion. They were the branch from which Christ was to come. God was their God, and Christ their Redeemer; and, if they sometimes partook of the general corruption around them, and "served other gods," yet the gates of hell were never suffered to prevail against them.

In the providence of God, the world, which had been in so awful a manner depopulated, was soon filled with inhabitants. Japheth had seven sons. These settled Armenia and Greece, and from them came the present inhabitants of Europe and the United States. Ham had four, whose posterity filled Babylonia and Arabia, Canaan and Egypt. Shem five. From these descended the Assyrians, Persians

Jews, Hindoos, and Chinese, and aborigines of America. These were the sons of Noah, "after their families, after their tongues, in their lands, after their nations; and by these were the nations divided in the earth after the flood."

Some will ever affirm that the Negro, the Chinese, the European, and the American Indian, could not have had a common origin; but the candid inquirer after the truth will receive the testimony of God, and by this be satisfied that all mankind descended from the patriarch who was preserved in the ark.

CHAPTER V.

Early defection from the true religion. History of idolatry.

THE awful judgment of God upon the old world, did not eradicate depravity from the human heart. Even Ham, the youngest son of the patriarch Noah, one who had witnessed all the wonders of the flood, soon exhibited an unnatural and depraved spirit, and went out, like Cain, with his posterity, from the presence of the Lord, an ungodly generation. The Cushites, his immediate descendants, were probably the chief families that were concerned in the building of Babel; but neither were they brought back to the Lord by the new and fearful judgment of heaven inflicted upon them. The whole of that country through which they were dispersed, was, in a few centuries, almost entirely idolatrous; so that even the generation of the righteous, drawn in by the general corruption, were accused of serving " other gods" than Jehovah.

If there were others less vile and ferocious; others, who had a high veneration for Noah, and who would religiously commemorate the deluge and the re-peopling of the earth, still their descendants soon perverted the whole, and canonized and worshipped those memorable incidents. Among all the Eastern nations, therefore, we find many allusions, in religious rites, to Noah and his ark, the dove, the olive branch; indeed, almost a complete mythological history of the deluge.

Having once departed from the living God, the nations multiplied to themselves deities with amazing rapidity. As the most striking objects in nature, and the mediate source of all good to men, the heavenly bodies soon attracted veneration.

Renowned men, who had been the benefactors or scourges of their race, were, in great numbers, enthroned on high. But gods were found in every thing. Egypt, settled by Mizraim, the second son of Ham, was the fruitful mother of abominations. There the earth, sea, hills, rivers, animals, fishes, birds, plants and stones received homage. Later nations deified abstract qualities, fame, piety, truth, and even physical evils, evil fortune; and several, the very vices of men. Some of the gods were supposed to be good, and the authors of happiness; others, cruel and malignant, the authors of all misery. Every nation, city, and family, in time, had its respective deity; and through complaisance, the heathen nations adopted all gods of which they had any knowledge. The Athenians erected an altar to the Unknown God.

The principal heathen deities mentioned in the history of the Jews, are Baal, or the Sun; Astarte or Ashtaroth, the Moon; several Baalim or Lords; as Baal Peor, a god of the Moabites; Baal Berith, or god of the Covenant, a god of the Schechemites; Baal Zebub, a tutelary deity in the city of Ekron, that protected the people from gnats; Moloch, or the planet Saturn, which was worshipped as a god who devoured his own offspring. The statue of Moloch, erected in the valley of Hinnom, was of brass. Its arms were stretched out; upon these, children were placed, and as the arms declined, they rolled off into a furnace of fire, placed below. Dagon, a female deity, the goddess of the Philistines; also Rimmon, an idol of the Assyrians; and Chiun or Saturn, whose tabernacles or small shrines the Israelites carried with them in the wilderness.

Discontented with a pure spiritual worship, men early began to form images of the true God. The Jews made a calf to represent Jehovah, probably because they had seen the Egyptians worship Apis, a bull, as God. Micah had an image of Jehovah. The heathen carried imagery to a great extreme. They worshipped nothing without an image. The images were at first rude blocks of wood or stone. These were afterward carved with care into every form and shape. The Teraphim were images in the human form. Some idols were part man and part beast. Dagon, of the Philistines, had a human body terminating below in a fish. One of the Egyptian deities had the head of a dog; another, the head of a bird. Some of the gods were made of precious metals, or covered with silver or gold, and adorned with the most costly vestments.

As they became precious, slight buildings were erected over them to protect them from the weather. These were soon succeeded by splendid temples. The goddess Diana had a most magnificent temple at Ephesus. Sometimes groves were planted around the temples, especially if the deity was a patron of licentiousness.

The deities it was believed, might be induced to enter the images and grant such favors as were desired, by certain ceremonies, incantations and sacrifices, whence arose a vast multitude of rites and ceremonies; sacrifices; oblations; and an immense priesthood, whose business it was to attend upon them. Their sacrifices were victims, salt cakes, libations, honey, incense. Almost every distinguished god was honored with some great festival, which was the holiday of thousands, and was observed by sports and solemn processions and great feastings. Sacrifices were accompanied with prayers, followed by loud shouting and leaping, and wounds upon the body. These false deities demanded no morality of their worshippers, and even knew none themselves. Often were they supposed guilty of the grossest vices and abominations. And to please them, an imitation of their wickedness formed part of their worship.

Out of idolatry early arose divination and necromancy. Many pretended to an intimacy with the deities; to the power of working miracles and the knowledge of future events. These wonder-workers were held in high esteem in the time of Moses and Belteshazzar. In later periods oracles were established, from which it was pretended that the god spoke; answering the inquiries of mortals. Dreams were thought to come from the gods; and all nations, particularly the Romans, gave much heed to omens and prodigies—such as monsters, comets, eclipses, the flight of birds, and entrails of beasts.

The light of philosophy had, in some measure, opened the eyes of men in civilized Europe to the fooleries of idolatry, when Christ appeared; but it was three centuries before Christianity obtained a triumph over the gods of Rome. But little variation has probably been made in those countries which still remain pagan, from their former state

They have from the days of Nahor, " served other gods,"*
—are " old wastes, the desolations of many generations."
India has her three hundred million deities. Her images
are brass, wood and stone. Her horrid idol Juggernaut is
drawn in a splendid car. Most of the islands of the Pacific
have been, until of late, in the same awful bondage. When,
O when, shall they cast all their gods to the moles and the
bats?

Some would charitably suppose that every idolater is a sincere worshipper of his Creator and Benefactor. But Paul assures us that idolatry originated in the depravity of the heart.
" Because that when they knew God they glorified him not as
God, neither were thankful, but became vain in their imagination, and their foolish heart was darkened. Professing themselves to be wise, they became fools; and changed the glory
of the incorruptible God into an image made like to corruptible
man, and to birds, and four-footed beasts and creeping things."
And the correctness of his declaration is evinced by the
moral character of the whole heathen world. Through every
generation, in every clime, it has been vile and abominable
beyond what language can express. The picture of it in his
day, drawn by Paul in the close of the first chapter of his
Epistle to the Romans, is the best ever presented to the world,
and is a correct representation of heathen immorality in every
period of time. " And even as they did not like to retain God
in their knowledge, God gave them over to a reprobate mind,
to do those things which are not convenient; being filled with
all unrighteousness, fornication, wickedness, covetousness,
maliciousness; full of envy, murder, debate, deceit, malignity;
whisperers, backbiters, despiteful, haters of God, proud, boasters, inventors of evil things, disobedient to parents, without
understanding, covenant breakers, without natural affection,
implacable, unmerciful;—who, knowing the judgment of God,
that they which commit such things are worthy of death, not
only do the same, but have pleasure in them that do them."

---

* From idol worship the Aborigines of America have been remarkably free.

PERIOD II.

FROM THE CALL OF ABRAHAM TO THE BIRTH OF CHRIST;
EMBRACING 1921 YEARS.

CHAPTER I.

Call of Abraham. Institution of Circumcision, and establishment of the Jewish Church. Destruction of the cities of the plain. State of religion in the world.

ABRAHAM was born in the 2008th year of the world; 352 years after the flood, and 1996 years before Christ. He was the son of Terah; and the tenth, in a direct line from Noah. His ancestors lived in Ur of the Chaldees; whence his father came into Mesopotamia, expelled, if we may credit a traditionary account recorded in the book of Judith, by the idolaters, for his worship of the true God. Even they, however, were seduced into the heaven-provoking abomination, and bowed down, to some extent, to idols. "Your father," said God, by Joshua, "dwelt on the other side of the flood (the Euphrates) in old time; even Terah, the father of Abraham and the father of Nahor; and they served other gods." Besides Abraham, Terah had two sons, Nahor and Haran, and one daughter, Sarai, who became Abraham's wife. Though she was his sister, she was of a different mother. Haran was the father of Lot, and died in Ur.

As the nations were becoming corrupt with amazing rapidity, and true religion was in danger of being extinct in the world, God selected this family to be the depository of truth. He appeared to Abraham in the 75th year of his age, directed him to leave his country and his kindred, and go to a land he would show him, and promised that he would bless him and give him a numerous posterity, and that in him all the families of the earth should be blessed. This was the third time that the covenant of grace had been revealed by God to his church. It was first made known to Adam and Eve, when the Lord assured them that the seed of the woman should bruise the serpent's head. It was renewed with Noah and his sons, when they came out of the ark. And now it was presented to Abraham with still greater fullness. Christ was promised from his loins; and in him, it was declared, that all the families of the earth should be blessed. This was a great ERA in the church.

Confiding in the word of the Lord, this pious patriarch took Sarai his wife, and Lot, his brother's son, and all their substance, passed to Sichem, in the land of Canaan, and there built an altar unto the Lord. There again God appeared to him, and renewed covenant. Finding a grievous famine in the land, he went to Egypt, where he came near losing his wife, because she was very beautiful, and was known only as his sister. But God interposed for her rescue, and made his power and his wrath known to the Egyptians. When the famine had ceased, Abraham returned to Canaan, laden with much wealth, and divided the land with Lot. He soon became a man of great substance and strength: having 318 servants in his household, and being able to wage effectual war with the plundering nations around him. God often appeared to him; assuring him that He was his shield and his exceeding great reward; accepting his sacrifices and confirming the promises. On a certain occasion, Melchisedec, king of Salem, a priest of the most high God, met him and blessed him in the name of the most high God, possessor of heaven and earth.

But though Abraham believed the word of the Lord, that in his seed should all the families of the earth be blessed, yet so long was the promised heir delayed, that he foolishly took to himself Hagar, his Egyptian maid; and became the father of a son whom he called Ishmael. But this was not the promised seed. So far were all the nations from being blessed in him, that the angel of the Lord prophesied concerning him, "he will be a wild man, his hand will be against every man, and every man's hand against him." His posterity, the Arabs, have, to this day, been thieves and robbers, unsubdued by any people.

At length, however, when God had well tried the faith of the patriarch, he gave him, in the hundredth year of his age, the promised son; again renewing with him his covenant for an everlasting covenant, promising that he would be a God to him and to his seed after him, and instituting the ordinance of circumcision, which was to seal to them the covenant of grace, and bind them to an observance of all its requisitions.

Hitherto the church had existed in an unembodied state By no token was she distinguished from the world. God was now pleased to give her a visible standing among the nations By the ordinance of circumcision, all his people, with their infant seed, were set apart as the Lord's. Whoever beheld them in successive generations, might know by this sign and seal, that God was their God, and they were his people. From this event, which occurred in the 2108th year of the world, is dated the establishment of the

JEWISH CHURCH.

By two other remarkable events, was the life of this eminently holy man, this head of the church, and father of believers, distinguished.

One was an awful destruction of the ungodly.

The inhabitants of Sodom and Gomorrah, with whom Lot dwelt, were among the most wicked of the posterity of Ham. Their abominations cried aloud to heaven for vengeance: and the Lord God determined to make an "example of them to those that should after live ungodly." His purpose he made known to his favored servant, Abraham; whose humble, fervent intercession for the righteous that might dwell among them, has since greatly endeared him to the people of God. Lot was a righteous man, a member of the true church, the only one that dwelt in the cities of the plain. His righteous soul was vexed from day to day, with the conversation of the wicked, and with their unlawful deeds; yet he remained among them, from an inordinate attachment to the world, and saw all that were dear to him corrupted and destroyed. But Abraham had effectually interceded for him; and the angels said unto him "Escape for thy life." No sooner had he fled, than the Lord rained fire and brimstone from heaven, and the inhabitants were totally destroyed; the whole plain was converted into a vast lake, called the Dead Sea; which still remains a memorial of the vengeance of God. How awful the wrath of an holy Jehovah! This judgment was inflicted in the 2108th year of the world, and 1896 years before Christ.

The other event was a trial of Abraham's faith.

Thirty years had elapsed since the birth of Isaac; the long expected seed, the child of promise, the declared progenitor of Him, in whom "all the families of the earth were to be blessed;" when God said to Abraham, "Take now thy son, thine only son Isaac, whom thou lovest, and get thee into the land of Moriah, and offer him there for a burnt offering on one of the mountains which I will tell thee of." Never was there a command so full of terror! Every word must have wrung the patriarch's heart with anguish. What can we look for but a firm remonstrance against the horrid deed; a plea from the fatal example on the surrounding heathen, the reproach of his piety, and the very promises and covenant of God ratified over and over! But nothing of this. With calm submission and holy confidence in God, he went forward and built the altar, and laid the wood, and bound Isaac his son, and lifted the knife to slay him, when the Angel of the Lord interposed and said, "Now I know thou fearest God, seeing thou hast not withheld thy son, thine only son from me." It was a glorious exhibition of faith; for which God again confirmed to him his exceeding great and precious promises. Having laid Sarah in the grave, and provided a wife for Isaac, from the family of his brother Nahor, in Padanaram, Abraham died in the 175th year of his age.

This eminent patriarch was as distinguished for his piety, as for the remarkable events of his life. In humility, meekness, patience, submission, and unwavering confidence in God, he has been a pattern to all saints of succeeding ages. Like the rest of this fallen world, he was a sinner; he could not be justified by works; he had nothing whereof to glory. But he saw Christ's day afar off, and was glad. He believed in God—rejoiced in a Saviour to come, and his faith was counted for righteousness. His faith was a vital principle. "It wrought with his works, and by works was his faith made perfect; and he was called the FRIEND OF GOD."

The age of Abraham was one of great declension. It was the age of Sodom and Gomorrah. But it was not the period, when in one of the capital cities of the world, an altar should be erected "To the Unknown God." Mankind had not as yet lost the knowledge of Jehovah. Some who came out of the ark with their immediate descendants, were still living. A knowledge of that dread event, and of the power and holiness of God which occasioned it, must therefore have existed among all people, while not a few were to be found of sincere and fervent piety. The Persians were the descendants of Shem, by his son Elam, as Abraham and his descendants were by Arphaxad; and continued, probably for a considerable period, to walk in the way of their fathers. The Chaldeans, the descendants of Ham, were so far corrupt, as to expel the father of Abraham for his religion, from their country. Among them, therefore, we may look in vain for any true religion.

The Arabians retained the knowledge and worship of the God of heaven, until after the days of Moses. Among them we find in this far distant age, Job. He dwelt in that part of Arabia Petrea, which was called Edom, and bordered upon the tribe of Judah to the south. His origin is uncertain; and the exact period in which he lived cannot well be determined. His years were more than 200—the age of man before the days of the patriarchs. In his writings are mentioned only the most ancient species of idolatry, the worship of the sun and moon; and his riches are reckoned by his cattle. If he lived after the days of Abraham, and as some suppose, as late as Moses, still he appears to have known nothing of that eminent patriarch, or of the wanderings of the children of Israel. His knowledge of God was evidently handed down to him from Noah; but was greatly increased by intimate communion with heaven. The book which bears his name, and gives an account of the wonderful dealings of God with him, has been ascribed to Moses, to Solomon, to Isaiah, and Ezra, but it is evidently the work of Job himself. Its style is sublime and lofty; full of figure, and corresponds to the genius of the Arabic language. It every where abounds with religious instruction, and the noblest sentiments of piety; and, with inimitable majesty, proclaims the Almighty power and unsearchable wisdom of the Maker of the universe.

With all his faults, Job was a man of deep humility and exalted piety. Through traditional religion and the suggestions and influences of the Holy Spirit, he disclaimed all hope of justification from his own righteousness; placed his confidence in the great Redeemer, and looked forward with joyful hope to a resurrection and future judgment. Such a man must have been a light in the world. His book conveyer truths to mankind which unassisted reason had never learned and powerfully refuted the erroneous views which were fas/ spreading in the earth, of the moral government of God When it was admitted into the sacred cannon we know not; but it is cited as inspired by the Apostles, and was universally received as canonical by the early Christians.

Among the Canaanites, Abraham lived as those who were

well acquainted with Jehovah. He even there found a king, Melchisedec, who ruled his people in righteousness and peace, and officiated at the altar, as priest of the most high God ; a man who, on both these accounts, was a remarkable type of Christ. Abraham honored him for his rank and piety, and priestly character, and received as a distinguished favor, his blessing.

Over Gerar in Philistia, reigned Abimelech, an upright man, who acknowledged and feared Jehovah. All these nations must have been solemnly impressed with the majesty and holiness of God, in the destruction of Sodom and Gomorrah.

The Egyptians early fell into idolatry, but the God of Abraham was terrible among them. And in subsequent ages, he must have been extensively known by the piety of Joseph, the religion of the Hebrews, and more especially, by the plagues upon Pharaoh and the nation, in the days of Moses.

It may be inquired why, if there was so much knowledge of the true God in the world, was Abraham called ? It was no doubt in part perspective. The clouds of pagan darkness were fast overshadowing the earth. In a little time, the knowledge of Jehovah, of his name, his worship and his laws, would be banished from among men, without some special provision for its preservation, and the earth would be in complete subjection to the prince of darkness.

CHAPTER II.

Descent of the Church in the line of Patriarchs. Prophecy respecting Shiloh. Joseph. Residence of the church in Egypt. Her deliverance from bondage. Plagues of Egypt. Institution of the Passover. Baptism of the church. Murmurings of the Israelites. Their typical journey.

IF there was true piety elsewhere in the earth, still we are now to contemplate the Church of God embodied in the family of Abraham, and sealed with the seal of circumcision. God confirmed to Isaac the promises made to his father, " in thy seed shall all the families of the earth be blessed." In his youth, Esau sold his birthright for a trifle to Jacob his younger brother ; thus, in the freedom and wickedness of his own heart, accomplishing, though he meant not so, a purpose of divine sovereignty; "For the children, being not yet born, neither having done any good or evil, that the purpose of God, according to election, might stand, not of works, but of him that calleth; it was said unto her, (Rebecca) the elder shall serve the younger." Zealous for the execution of the divine purpose thus revealed to her;— revealed, no doubt, that it might be accomplished, his mother craftily diverted the blessing from Esau to Jacob. Esau having in the folly and wickedness of his heart, cast away his birthright, was angry with Jacob, and sought to kill him; but Jacob fled into Mesopotamia, to his mother's relatives. Driven from his home, a lone wanderer, night overtook him without a shelter or a friend, and he laid himself down in the open air, with a stone for his pillow. But God was there. In a dream, he saw a ladder standing on the earth and reaching unto heaven, on which the angels of God ascended and descended. Above it stood the Lord God, who assured him that he was the God of his fathers, and would give him and his seed the land of Canaan, and that in him all the nations of the earth should be blessed. In this manner did God exhibit to him his providence, administered by angels, and renew the covenant containing the precious promises. When Jacob awoke, his soul was deeply impressed with the presence of God, and he said, "Surely the Lord is in this place, and I knew it not. How dreadful is this place! this is none other but the house of God! and this is the gate of heaven." He erected his pillow for a monument, and sealed himself to be the Lord's.

Jacob was worthy of the sacred trust. He was a man of prayer. He wrestled with Christ, the angel of the covenant. He vowed unto the Lord, and performed his oaths. His blessings and his trials were uncommonly great; but in the height of prosperity, while master of two bands, he was meek, humble, and grateful; and, when all things went against him, and he seemed about to be stripped of all his heart held dear, he was patient and submissive, and committed himself to Him who judgeth righteously in the earth.

From Jacob descended twelve sons, who, by a mysterious providence, were removed, according to the revelation of God made to Abraham, to Egypt; there to reside in bondage many years. Before the venerable man died, he uttered a more remarkable prophecy of Christ than any the church had as yet received—a prophecy in which not only the line was pointed out in which Messiah should come, but the time of his appearance was marked with great precision. "Judah," said he, in blessing his sons, "is a lion's whelp; from the prey, my son, thou art gone up; he stooped down, he couched as a lion, and as an old lion, who shall rouse him? The sceptre shall not depart from Judah; nor a lawgiver from between his feet, until Shiloh come, and unto him shall the gathering of the people be." In conformity with this prediction and promise, Judah was never without a ruler and lawgiver, until subdued by the Romans, when Shiloh or Christ came; and when Jesus Christ appeared in Judah, then departed ruler and lawgiver; and these have never since been known in her borders.

Jacob was born in the year of the world 2168. He was 75 years of age when he fled into Mesopotamia. He came into Egypt in 2298, and died 17 years after, being 147 years of age. When he came into Egypt, the visible church of God consisted of 70 souls.

A single instance of humble piety in that distant age of the world, even in the most retired walks of life, is refreshing to the soul. But we have exhibited to us a lovely youth, who, in the providence of God, was exalted almost to royalty, and became a father to his people; who feared God; resisted the most powerful allurements to sin; kept his garments white amid an adulterous generation, and stands forth an illustrious monument of the power of divine grace. This was Joseph, the eleventh son of Jacob. Moved with envy, his brethren sold him for a slave. But he became the deliverer of his people and temporal saviour of the Egyptian nation. His history is one of the most beautiful, pathetic, interesting and instructive tales which was ever written, and remarkably exhibits the overruling providence of God. His envious brethren sold him; but it was God who carried him into Egypt for the execution of his purposes.

During their long residence in Egypt, the chosen people of God multiplied astonishingly, though oppressed by a most cruel bondage; but having no religious ordinances, Sabbaths, or instruction, they in a great measure lost the true religion, and polluted themselves "with the idols of Egypt."

Their bondage was a lively picture of the natural state of the true Israel; who were bond servants to sin, and in bondage to the law as a covenant of works.

The church was suffered to decline, that the seed of the woman might gain the more illustrious victory over the prince of darkness. The children of Israel, having served a heathen prince more than 200 years, until they had increased to two millions of souls, God determined to bring them out of bondage, in fulfillment of his promise to Abraham, with a high hand, and a strong arm, amid many signs and wonders, and to magnify himself before all people.

The instrument by which he resolved to effect this deliverance was Moses, the son of a Hebrew woman, who, to avoid destruction by the Egyptians, was hid by his mother in an ark in the bulrushes, by the river's brink; where he was discovered by Pharaoh's daughter as she came to bathe, and adopted by her as her own son. In the court of Pharaoh, he was trained up in all the learning of the Egyptians; and if we may credit Josephus, was made a general in their armies, fought many battles, and was considered heir to the crown. But " by faith he refused to be called the son of Pharaoh's daughter; choosing rather to suffer affliction with the people of God, than to enjoy the pleasures of sin for a season; esteeming the reproach of Christ greater riches than the treasures of Egypt, for he had respect unto the recompense of the reward." He had a holy confidence in the promises of God, and he turned his eye and heart from the crown of Egypt, to the deliverance of his brethren from their cruel bondage. Failing in some premature efforts to accomplish this, he fled to Midian, to Jethro, a priest, whose daughter he married, and with whom he lived forty years. Here he might have remained till death, had not Almighty God spoken to him out of the burning bush, and assured him of his design to deliver the Israelites by his hand. Obedient to the heavenly command, he left Jethro; and taking with him Aaron his brother, he appeared before Pharaoh, and demanded the release of the children of Israel. That haughty monarch repulsed him with scorn. Then ensued such a series of judgments, as no nation before or since ever knew. Their river was turned into blood. Frogs, and lice, and flies filled all their habitations. Murrain was on all their cattle. Boils covered man and beast. Rain and hail mingled with fire, descended upon their land. Devouring locusts rested on all their coasts. A supernatural darkness that might be felt, overspread the earth. And last and heaviest of all, the first born, " from the first born of Pharaoh, that sat upon the throne, to the first born of the maid that was behind the mill," became in one night, cold and silent corpses.

The Egyptians were accustomed to divination. They had their diviners, enchanters, witches, charmers, wizards and necromancers. These were called in to confront Moses; and, as they pretended by their magical arts to perform the same wonders, the heart of Pharaoh was more and more hardened against the Lord. But God moved on to the accomplishment of his purposes. The church was his, and he would redeem it from the iron furnace.

On an ever memorable night, the Passover was instituted. It was then to be celebrated by the Israelites, as a token, or means of their deliverance, and afterward, as a memorial of the power and love of God in their redemption, and a prefiguration of Christ our Passover. Scarce had they eaten the paschal lamb, when there was a cry made throughout all the land of Egypt; for it was the moment of the execution of the last and heaviest of God's judgments. And the Egyptians pressed them to depart, for they said, "we be all dead men." They arose and went, for the Lord was their helper. But no sooner was their departure known to Pharaoh, than he pursued them with all his hosts, and overtook them as they were encamped on the banks of the Red Sea. It was a dreadful moment. The sea before and the Egyptians behind, no chance of escape appeared; and they said unto Moses, " Because there were no graves in the land of Egypt, hast thou brought us here to die in the wilderness?" But Moses said, " Stand still and see the salvation of the Lord." And he stretched out his hand over the sea, and the sea divided, and the children of Israel passed through on dry ground; the Lord going before them in a pillar of fire and of cloud. The presumptuous Egyptians pressed after; but the Lord caused the waters to enclose and cover them; and there they slept the sleep of death.

The exit of the children of Israel from Egypt, took place in the 2513th year of the world, 1491 years before the birth of Christ, 430 years from Abraham's coming into Canaan, and 215 from Jacob's descent into Egypt. Their number was about three millions. It was an event typical of the redemption of the church from the bondage of sin and death, and must have deeply and solemnly impressed the surrounding nations, with the majesty, power, holiness, and wrath of God, and the value he placed on his chosen people.

The Apostle Paul remarks, that all the Israelites were baptized unto Moses in the cloud and in the sea. They were literally so, from the drops of water which were sprinkled upon them from the overshadowing cloud and from the sea, which stood in heaps beside them. This was a baptism unto Moses, as a typical mediator, by which they were bound to submit to that covenant which he, as the minister of God, was to reveal to them; but it was especially a type of the later initiating seal of the covenant of grace;—rather, a type of the washing of regeneration and sprinkling of the blood of Jesus, of which baptism is only the sign.

On the completion of this wonderful deliverance, Moses composed a song, which he and the children of Israel sung unto the Lord; to which responses were made by Miriam the prophetess, accompanied by timbrels and dances. No doubt among that vast multitude there were many sincerely pious people, who from the heart, extolled God for his wonderful works. There was the true church. But all were not Israel, who were of Israel. Indeed the greater part of that generation which came out of Egypt were unsanctified men, and exceedingly perverse. God delivered them from bondage for "his name's sake, and that he might make his power known." And if they united in the song of Moses, it was in the triumphs of victory. They sang his praise, but his loving kindness was soon obliterated from their minds. Forty years they wandered in the wilderness, but they were years of constant murmurings and rebellions. Before they crossed the Red Sea, they spake contemptuously to Moses. And within three days after they had sung the praises of the Lord, they murmured at the waters of Marah, because they were bitter. Then in a short period, they murmured for bread, looking back with bitter regret to the day when they "sat by the flesh pots, and did eat bread to the full." God gave them bread from heaven, but "their soul loathed that light bread." Next they murmured for flesh. They were jealous of the honor conferred on Moses and Aaron. They made them a molten calf in imitation of the Egyptian god Apis, and were afterward joined to Baalpeor· did eat the sacrifices of the dead, and committed abomination with the daughters of Moab. Their whole life was a continued scene of rebellion. "Forty years long," said God, "was I grieved with this generation." And though he did not destroy them utterly, he sometimes caused them to feel the power of his indignation. At one time three and twenty thousand were destroyed in a day. At another, the Lord sent among them fiery flying serpents which bit them, so that many of the people died. At another, three rebellious families were swallowed up in the earth for their sins, and 14,700 persons were suddenly cut off by a plague for murmuring against it. Such was their perverseness, that God sware in his wrath that none save Caleb and Joshua, of that generation, should enter the promised land.

Yet for their father's sake, God was kind and compassionate towards them. Oft he forgave them at the intercession of Moses, when provoked to destroy them. He went before them in a pillar of cloud by day and pillar of fire by night, and protected them by the angel of his presence. He gave them day by day, manna from heaven, and quails for flesh. He caused water to flow out in abundance from the rock. He raised in the wilderness a brazen serpent upon a pole when the people were bitten by the fiery flying serpents, that whosoever looked upon it should be healed. He gave them power over their enemies, and wrought for them the most wonderful victories.

"All these things happened unto them for ensamples, and they are written for our admonition upon whom the ends of the world are come." Their whole journey toward the promised land was typical of the journey of the true Israel toward the heavenly Canaan. They were indeed the true Israel. The true church was among them; though the great mass of the people were wicked and rebellious. Were they brought through the depths of the sea? So all the children of God are born of water and the Spirit. Were they baptized by sprinkling, from the cloud and the sea, unto Moses? So are we baptized into Jesus Christ, "buried with him by baptism into death—that we may walk in newness of life." Were they to live by faith, as to their daily support, in the wilderness? So are we. Were they fed by manna and did they drink of water from the rock? So are we fed by "that bread which cometh down from heaven" in the dispensation of the word, and our souls are refreshed from the fountain of life. They "did all eat the same spiritual meat and all drank the same spiritual drink, for they drank of that spiritual rock that followed them, and that rock was Christ." Were they guilty of much murmuring and rebellion? Did they disbelieve the promises? and was their soul discouraged because of the way? It was but a type of the imperfection, stupidity, disbelief and backsliding of saints, Did the anger of the Lord burn against them, and did his judgments destroy them? We may behold in this a lively representation of his grief and indignation at the misconduct of saints, and of his judgments upon them; though these judgments under the new dispensation are marked with far less severity. Did he, at the intercession of Moses, oft forgive their sins, and extend to them his pardoning and saving mercy? So at the intercession of Christ, he pardons the iniquities of his people, and will acquit them in the judgment. Did Moses lift up the serpent in the wilderness, that whoso looked on it should be healed? So was the Son of man lifted up, that "whosoever believeth in him should not perish, but might have everlasting life." And did God, finally, bring his ancient Israel into the land of promise, through the waters of Jordon, by his servant Joshua? So does he conduct his saints, through death, by Jesus, the great captain of their salvation, to a better country, which is the desire of their souls, even a heavenly. "The ransomed of the Lord shall return and come to Zion with songs and with everlasting joy upon their heads; they shall obtain joy and gladness, and sorrow and sighing shall flee away."

CHAPTER III.

Giving of the Law. Moral and Ceremonial. Symbol of the Divine Presence. Tabernacle. Urim and Thummim. Priesthood. Re-institution of the Sabbath Completion of the Pentateuch. Outpouring of the Spirit. Character of Moses. Two remarkable Prophecies of Christ.

During the wanderings of the church in the wilderness, four remarkable events occurred which claim particular notice. THE GIVING OF THE LAW. THE RE-INSTITUTION OF THE SABBATH. THE COMPLETION OF THE PENTATEUCH, AND AN EXTENSIVE OUTPOURING OF THE HOLY SPIRIT.

For 2500 years, the church had enjoyed much precious intercourse with heaven. Christ, the angel of the covenant, had appeared to Adam, to Noah, to Abraham, Isaac and Jacob, and established with them the covenant of grace, but she had no written law. On the tenth of the third month after leaving Egypt, the Israelites pitched their camp at the foot of Mount

Sinai. There they remained a year. On the morning of the third day of their encampment, the mount was in a smoke and there were thunders and lightnings and a thick cloud upon the mount, for the Lord descended upon it in fire. Such was the majesty of the scene, that the people trembled and stood afar off, and said unto Moses, " Speak thou with us, and we will hear ; but let not God speak with us lest we die. And Moses went up to God in the mount."

The Ten Commandments were first given. To express their importance and perpetuity, they were written by the finger of God, on tables of stone. These commandments have their foundation in the nature of God and man, and in the relations which men bear to God and to one another. They contain the primary principles of all law. They are obligatory upon all men to the end of time.

Next, God gave to Moses the political and ceremonial law of Israel. He had set apart this nation for himself. Its government was to be a Theocracy. God was to be its King. He therefore gave his statutes for the regulation of the commonwealth.

It was also to form his visible church ; and he prescribed such ceremonial observances as would maintain the knowledge of the true Jehovah ; keep the Jews separate from the heathen; and, by lively types and shadows, prefigure the Gospel dispensation.

Under this divine constitution, the worship of Israel consisted much in sacrifices and offerings ; in presenting to God slain animals and the fruits of the earth.

Sacrifices had been offered by the pious from the promise of a Saviour. They were doubtless of divine origin. They were now reduced to a regular system. God prescribed three kinds for the Jewish nation ; the whole burnt offering, the sacrifice, and the thank offering. The first was the most ancient and excellent. It was expiatory. The whole victim, whether a bullock, a lamb, a turtle dove or young pigeon, was burnt; and a libation of wine was poured out upon the altar. The second was a sin offering or trespass offering, made on account of legal pollutions, or sins of ignorance. The third was an expression of gratitude for mercies received. The slain animals were accompanied with unleavened cakes ; and most of the animal and the cakes were converted by the person offering, into an entertainment for the poor. All these sacrifices were so many symbols, corresponding with the several branches of piety. In the expiatory sacrifice, the offerer came before God confessing that he was a sinner, and that he deserved to die, as the animal died. The acceptance of the sacrifice on the part of God, was a confirmation of the divine promises of pardon to the penitent. But this sacrifice was chiefly figurative of our Lord Jesus Christ, our true substitute; the Lamb of God which taketh away the sins of the world. If any trusted to a fancied efficacy in the sacrifices themselves, and to the multitude of victims, they drew upon them the divine anger.

That the Israelites might have a fixed place where they should offer their sacrifices, worship, and receive communications from heaven, God commanded Moses to build a tabernacle. Noah and the patriarchs had erected altars. As yet, temples were unknown among the people of God. The tabernacle was a movable tent, made of the most costly materials. Before it was the court, 150 feet in length, and 75 in breadth, and enclosed by curtains made of linen. In the centre of the court stood the altar for sacrifice, and on one side the laver, with water. The tabernacle was West of the Court. It was thirty cubits from West to East, and ten from North to South, and was divided into two apartments. The outer was called the holy place; the inner, the Holy of Holies. In the former, on the North side, was the table of show bread. On this were placed twelve loaves of unleavened bread, sprinkled over with frankincense; and wine in bowls. On the South side was the golden candlestick, in which seven lamps burned by night, and three by day. In the middle, was the altar on which incense was offered daily, morning and evening. In the inner room, from which was excluded the light of day, was the ark of the covenant—a small box covered with pure gold. In this was deposited the two tables of stone, on which were written the ten commandments. The lid or cover of the ark was called the mercy seat. On the ends of this seat were placed two cherubims, with their faces inclined toward each other, and toward the mercy seat, and their wings stretched out so as to overshadow it. These wings formed the throne of God, while the ark was his footstool. By the side of the ark, in a golden vase, was kept some of the manna, Aaron's rod, and the books of Moses.

"Here," said God to Moses, from between these cherubims, "I will meet with thee and commune with thee." Here was seen a cloud of glory, the visible symbol of Jeho-

CHAPTER 3.] REINSTITUTION OF THE SABBATH. 59

vah, which became bright and shining, when God there revealed his will by an audible voice. Such an emblem of Jehovah's presence, accompanied with frequent communications from him, caused the Israelites to feel that he was near; gave them a deep sense of the Unity of the Godhead, and kept them from the worship of the heavenly luminaries.

Of the seasons of worship, the first was the Sabbath. This was instituted at the close of the creation, and was doubtless observed by the pious both before the flood and after, according to their knowledge and opportunity. In the books of Moses, such observance is not indeed mentioned, nor was there any special occasion for the notice. But expressions exist, implying such observance, and which cannot well be accounted for without it. Time was divided into weeks of seven days* both before the flood and after. Probably the children of Israel were made incessantly to labor in Egypt; but no sooner were they released than they observed the Sabbath, before the promulgation of the law, as a day they felt to be holy.† God, in the fourth commandment, speaks of the Sabbath not in a way which he would if instituted for the first time, but as an old institution, which they were required to remember and keep holy. The Sabbath was now reinstituted with peculiar solemnity, and its observance was placed in the moral code, among the ten commandments. But it is probable that the day of its observance was changed. For the day first marked out for the Jewish Sabbath by the manna's not falling upon it, was the twenty-second of the second month; and counting backward seven days, we find the people performing, by divine direction, a long and wearisome march. The original Sabbath, consecrated by the heathen to the Sun, may have been set aside, and that day made holy on which the Jews came out of Egypt. Of that event, the Sabbath now became a special memorial. He who is Lord of the Sabbath has a right to alter the day of its observance. He did alter it at a subsequent period, to commemorate his own resurrection. And if the Sabbath was then put back one day, as has been computed by some learned men, we have now the original Sabbath, and do commemorate both the creation and redemption of man.

As standing memorials of the goodness of Jehovah, and

---

* Gen. xxix. 27. her week. Heb. her seven. Gen. iv. 7.   † Exodus xvi. 22—30

the truth of the Mosaic religion, three great Festivals were instituted;—the Feast of the Passover, of Pentecost, and of Tabernacles. The first was a memorial of the deliverance from Egypt. It was celebrated for seven days, from the 15th to the 21st of the month Nisan (April.) The second called Pentecost, because it was celebrated the fiftieth day from the Passover, was the feast of harvest and of the first fruits, and was a solemn acknowledgment of the divine goodness and their dependence and obligations. The third was a solemn thanksgiving for all the bounties of the year; and a memorial of the goodness of God to them when they dwelt in the tabernacles in the wilderness. These festivals were always celebrated at Jerusalem. All who could, attended them. They greatly promoted social affection, and kept the people from intercourse with foreign nations and idol festivals.

Besides the worship of the Sabbath and these festivals, the Hebrew ritual prescribed the daily sacrifice, offered morning and evening for the whole congregation;—a religious service consisting of animal and vegetable offerings, on the appearance of the new moon, that the Israelites might be kept from the superstitious worship of that heavenly body; an annual service on the commencement of the seventh month, the beginning of the Jewish civil year;—a Sabbatical year, a rest every seventh year from the cultivation of the earth, which was also a year of unusual attention to religion and the release of poor debtors from their creditors; and the year of Jubilee, wh ch took place every fiftieth year or after every seven sabbaths of years. This was ushered in by the sound of a trumpet, and restored every native Israelite to his original property and freedom.

To perfect the Jewish worship, God instituted an order of priests. In the patriarchal ages, the father of a family exercised the priestly office. This descended to the first born. The whole tribe of Levi was now set apart to attend upon the service of the sanctuary. Aaron and the first born of every generation descending from him, were consecrated to the high priesthood; his other sons to be priests. The rest of the Levites performed the inferior services of the Temple. All the priests and Levites were solemnly consecrated by purification and atonement, were maintained by the nation, and treated with great respect. The priests had the superintendence of the ceremonies of religion, and presented the victims for sacrifice. The High Priest alone appeared before God on the day of atonement in the Holy of Holies, and consulted the divine oracle.

The dress of the High Priest was very splendid. In his breast plate was the Urim and Thummim, i. e. *light and justice*. This is supposed to have been three precious stones, on one of which was written Yes, on the other No. The third was without writing. These stones were carried in the lining of the breast plate. When the High Priest would obtain an answer from God, he appeared before the Holy of Holies, and proposing his question, took a stone from the breast plate. If he drew out the one with no inscription, no answer was to be given. Never was this oracle to be consulted for any private person, but only for the king, or general of the army.

All the instructions and institutions of Moses had an high moral tendency. They led the children of Israel to love the Lord their God with all their heart, and their neighbor as themselves, and trained up many of the greatest ornaments of antiquity. The worship he prescribed was eminently typical of the worship of the New Testament church; and in the High Priest was beautifully shadowed forth the Lord Jesus Christ, our great High Priest, who neither by the blood of goats and calves, but by his own blood, entered in once into the holy place—into heaven itself, now to appear in the presence of God for us. During the abode of the church in the wilderness, Moses wrote the Pentateuch, comprising Genesis, Exodus, Leviticus, Numbers and Deuteronomy. It was deposited in the tabernacle, and preserved with the greatest vigilance. It was read every Sabbath day in the Synagogue, and through at the feast of Tabernacles, every Sabbatical year. The Prince was required to copy it, and the people were commanded to teach it to their children, and to wear it as "signs on their hands, and frontlets between their eyes." It is the only history we have of the creation, the antediluvian nations, the flood, and the re-settlement of the earth. Without it the first two thousand years of our race would be entirely hidden from us. It was written in Hebrew in one continued work, by inspiration of God, and was divided into books, probably by Ezra, or at the formation of the Septuagint version.*

---

* Many are the conjectures of the philosophical and the curious, respecting tne antiquity of the art of writing. Some suppose that symbolical represen-

The generation that came out of Egypt was, as has been remarked, very froward and perverse. They had been corrupted by the idols of Egypt. God was angry with them, and swore they should not enter the promised land. Their carcasses fell in the wilderness—all but Caleb and Joshua. But on their children he poured out his Holy Spirit. They became eminently devoted to God. "I remember thee," says he, in later ages of the church, "the kindness of thy youth, the love of thine espousals, when thou wentest after me in the wilderness. Israel was holiness to the Lord and the first fruits of his increase." With them God solemnly renewed his covenant. They stood all of them at Shechem before the Lord their God, the captains of the tribes, their elders, their officers, all the men of Israel; their little ones, their wives, and the stranger that was among them, and entered into covenant with God and into his oath. It was a day of deep and awful solemnity, a day of great glory to the church.

Moses was born in the 2432d year of the world, and died in the 120th year of his age. "His eye was not dim, nor was his natural force abated." The place of his death was mount Pisgah; from whence he had a view of the promised land, which he was not permitted to enter because of transgression. His sepulchre was miraculously concealed to prevent idolatrous veneration.

God had endowed him with wonderful wisdom, prudence and integrity, and placed him in a situation where he was enabled to exhibit unparalleled legislation and government. Almost every action of his life we can love and approve, while many traits in his character command our highest admiration. Whether we look at him leaving the court of Pharaoh, choosing to suffer affliction with the people of God; or at the burning bush, sacrificing diffidence to duty; or behold him in the presence of Pharaoh, wielding the most awful engines of terror; or at the Red Sea, dividing the water; or see him ascending amid the thunders of Sinai, to converse with the Almighty; or trace him through forty years of toil and trial, unmoved by homage, unawed by faction, undaunted by danger,

---

tations were first used; then hieroglyphics; then alphabetical writing But perhaps men were never strangers to letters. Books and writings were common in the time of Moses. Written genealogies were kept in the days of the patriarchs. What was known before the flood would be handed down through Noah. The Hebrew is generally supposed to have been the original language, and the root of all other languages.

unaltered by distress; or contemplate him, the great historian, poet, orator, lawgiver, the wonderful deliverer of his nation, the greatest of prophets, who conversed with God face to face, meek and humble beyond all men, we may well believe that he was very great in the land of Egypt, in the sight of Pharaoh's servants, and in the sight of the people; we must pronounce him the most exalted man that ever appeared on this stage of action.

In this period of the history of the church, we have two remarkable prophecies of Christ. The first was by Balaam, a diviner or magician of great renown; a wicked man, whom God employed for the benefit of his people, " I shall see him, but not now; I shall behold·him but not nigh; there shall come a star out of Jacob, and a sceptre shall arise out of Israel, and shall smite the corners of Moab, and destroy (rule over) all the children of Sheth."* In a subordinate sense, David may have been pointed out in this prediction, but it manifestly has its full accomplishment in the exalted kingdom and spiritual victories of Christ, who will destroy the enemies of the church, and gain dominion from the river to the ends of the earth. From this prophecy, a star was the known emblem of the Messiah; and it doubtless prepared the wise men in the East to follow the star which actually appeared at his birth.

The other is a prophecy by Moses; which, in a very particular manner, reveals the prophetic character of Christ. " The Lord thy God will raise up unto thee a prophet from the midst of thee, of thy brethren, like unto me; unto him ye shall hearken. And it shall come to pass, that whosoever will not hearken unto my words which he shall speak in my name, I will require it of him."† Among all the eminent prophets who appeared between Moses and Christ, none were like him; none were lawgivers to mankind; none conversed with God face to face; none performed such signs and wonders; but in these and other respects, Christ was like Moses, though vastly superior. It is clear, therefore, that if, as some suppose, Moses here predicted Joshua, or a succession of prophets, who should speak to the church in the name of the Lord, yet this prediction had special reference to our blessed Redeemer.

---

* Numbers xxiv. 17.   † Deuteronomy xviii. 15.

Before his death, also, Moses most accurately predicted* all the great and terrible judgments which God would in after ages bring upon the Jews for their disobedience; their captivity by the Chaldeans, a nation of fierce countenance; their subsequent or present dispersion, when they should become "an astonishment, a proverb, and a by-word among all nations," and† the calling in of the Gentiles in their stead, "provoking them to jealousy by them which are not a people."

CHAPTER IV.

Entrance of the church into the promised land. State of the church from Joshua to Samuel. Schools of the Prophets. Establishment of monarchy in Israel. David. Solomon. Erection and dedication of the Temple. Prosperous state of the church. Additions to the sacred Canon.

The church passed into the promised land through the waters of Jordon, divided by Almighty power, A. M. 2554. Its leader was Joshua, the son of Nun, a man of great courage and deep piety; and, in this transaction, an eminent type of the Lord Jesus Christ, the great Captain of our salvation, who conducts the invisible church into the Canaan of endless felicity. But it was composed of very different members from those who came out of Egypt; for God sware in his wrath that none of that rebellious generation, save Caleb and Joshua, should enter the promised land. The millions who now formed the church, were their children, and were " holiness to the Lord."

Having planted his people in that land, which 430 years before he had promised to Abraham for a possession, God directed every male to be sealed with the seal of circumcision. This sacred rite had been neglected during their wanderings in the wilderness. It was now imposed on the whole nation, and the Passover was solemnly celebrated.

The Canaanites were an exceedingly wicked people. Their abominations cried to heaven for vengeance; and God made his people the rod of his anger. He gave them power over his enemies. By the most simple instruments as well as by fire and sword, they exterminated thousands and millions, and took possession of the land.

---

* Deuteronomy xxviii. † Deuteronomy xxxii. 21, compared with Rom. x. 19.

This was divided among them for an inheritance. Here the Tabernacle was set up in Shiloh; and the Israelites with God for their king, commenced their national existence under the best political and ceremonial institutions. But alas! they were surrounded by enemies who perpetually sought their destruction. They retained among them many of the Canaanites, who were "scourges in their sides, and thorns in their eyes," and "snares and traps," seducing them to idolatry. They wandered from God; and the first 300 years of their history, was a period of darkness and trouble.

A little before the death of Joshua, the whole church solemnly renewed covenant with God at Shechem; which was a most affecting transaction. But after his decease, the Israelites had no regularly appointed governor, and appear to have acted in separate tribes. They soon fell into a state of anarchy and forgetfulness of God, for which they were delivered over, first to eight years bondage to Cushan, king of Mesopotamia; and afterward to the Moabites; the Canaanites; the Midianites; the Ammonites, and the Philistines. When they were sufficiently chastened and humbled, "the Lord repented himself for his servants," and raised up Judges to deliver them and guide them. Illustrious were their exploits. God was with them; and we behold in this conflict between the church and the world many striking exhibitions of divine justice and mercy. But this long period is one on which the eye dwells with little complacency. The people were ignorant and vicious. "The highways were unoccupied, and the travelers walked through by-paths." Few prophets were appointed to guide the people. "Every one did that which was right in his own eyes." Yet, in the darkest seasons, Christ had a seed to serve him. In the characters of Gideon, Barak, Samson, and Jepthah,* we have illustrious examples of faith. Enlightened by the Gospel, we may see in them many imperfections, but theirs was a holy confidence

---

* Infidel writers have considered the story of Jepthah's sacrificing his daughter, as an indelible blot on the Jewish religion, and utterly inconsistent with his being a good man. But for such a sacrifice the Jewish religion is not answerable, for it did not warrant it, but pointedly condemned it. His vow was rash; and if he acted conscientiously, his conscience was erroneous, through ignorance of the law of God, and too much intimacy with heathen customs. On conviction of sin, he might like David, have become a true penitent. To this event may be traced the heathen story of Iphigenia sacrificed by her father Agamemnon.

in God; and they "subdued kingdoms, wrought righteousness, obtained promises," and went triumphant to the rewards of heaven.

In the early part of this period, the book of Joshua was written by Joshua himself, and subjoined by him to the law of God.

It is worthy of remark, that during this dark period, though idolatry was prevalent, it never extended to the demolition of the Tabernacle; for it was never, as in later ages, commanded by the rulers.

In the 2868th year of the world, Samuel was born; and dedicated by his mother to the service of God. He became a faithful servant of Jehovah, Supreme Judge in the land, and was eminently endowed with the spirit of prophecy. He was much feared and respected by the whole nation, and was a great blessing to the church. He doubtless wrote the book of Ruth, and the greater part of the first book which bears his name. It is supposed he died about the 98th year of his age.

The most remarkable event in his life, connected with the history of the church, was the establishment of the School of the Prophets.

Prophecy, or the power of foretelling future events, belongs solely to God. The government of the universe is in his hands. He determines in his own infinite mind, what shall be, he has control of the volitions and actions of men; and he only therefore can tell what will come to pass. The accomplishment of prophecy is one of the most striking proofs of the divine unity, and of the inspiration of the Scriptures of the Old and New Testament. The heathen nations have ever been filled with diviners, who have professed to derive from their gods a knowledge of futurity; and who have, in this way, been the chief supporters of pagan idolatry. But their whole system has been a system of lies; an abominable imposition upon the ignorance and credulity of mankind.

By dreams, by flights of birds, by the entrails of beasts, by throwing dice, did the Grecian oracles, the most cunning the world ever saw, give their answers; and these were always so ambiguous as to admit of different interpretations, and save their credit if they failed of the truth.

We have seen that divine revelations were made to mankind in the earliest periods; and that, through Enoch, and Noah, and Abraham, and Jacob, God was pleased, from time to time, to foretell future events. We have also contemplated

Moses as a prophet, whom the Lord knew face to face. But no regular order of men, bearing the prophetic office, existed in the church until this period. We now find schools of them established at Bethel, Gilgal, Najoth, Jericho, and Jerusalem, and " Samuel standing as appointed over them." In these schools of the prophets, young men of piety were collected, who were instructed by some eminent teacher in divine things, and fitted for the high stations of prophets, as God should call them. Their dress was plain and coarse; their food, pottage and herbs. They were designed to reprove, rebuke, and reform a stupid and backsliding nation; and, by lively admonitions of impending judgments, by bold predictions of future events, to cause kings and priests and people, to turn with fasting and mourning to the Lord. Many of them may have risen no higher than the business of composing and singing hymns to the divine honor, and instructing the people in the common principles of religion; but some of them were exalted to the very highest rank in the nation, and made the most powerful princes tremble before them.

Their predictions were not confined to the Jewish nation, but extended to the rise and fall of all the great empires of the earth, and constantly directed the church to Him who was to redeem her by his blood; overturn all the kingdoms of men; and establish a spiritual dominion which should never be destroyed. These extraordinary men continued in the church from the days of Samuel to Malachi—a period of about 700 years, when the prophetic spirit was withdrawn for about 400 years, until John the Baptist, the last of the prophets in the Jewish dispensation.

The Israelites having departed from God, demanded of Samuel a king, that they might be like the nations around them. Such ingratitude to Him, who for centuries, had been their Sovereign, and had kindly directed all their concerns, might well have provoked immediate destruction; but, for his promise to their fathers, he bore with them and gave them Saul. About 2923 A. M. the monarch was publicly crowned, and God endued him with suitable qualifications for government. But he soon departed from the Lord, and showed himself unworthy of his exalted station. God therefore determined to dethrone him and his family; and, since the Hebrews would have a king to reign over them, he was pleased to advance the work of redemption and exalt the church by raising that family to the throne from which the

5*

Messiah, the promised seed, should descend. David, the youngest son, was selected, and anointed by Samuel to succeed to the government, and be the distinguished ancestor and type of Christ. God brought him to the notice of the nation, to influence and royalty by a series of wonderful providences. He sanctified him early by his Holy Spirit; endued him with the power of prophecy; and excited him to celebrate in a vast variety of beautiful songs, the Divine character and government, and the glorious scheme of redemption by Jesus Christ.

David was the man after God's own heart. But, in common with all of the ransomed of the Lord in this world, he was far from perfection. He sinned in numbering the people. He was guilty also of a gross violation of the sixth and seventh commandments. That sin was of a scarlet dye and crimson hue;—most offensive to God, and injurious to his own soul, and has been the sport of thousands of mockers and scoffers, from that day to this. His heart too was greatly hardened. No man dared directly tell him his sin. Nathan declared it by a parable. It came upon him like a thunderbolt. Out of his own mouth was he condemned. And, upon conviction, he manifested, as every child of God will, a spirit of holiness. He did not, like a proud man, resent the charge. He did not, even as a self-righteous man, plead his meritorious services for a balance to his evil deeds; but he cast himself, in deep repentance, upon the mercy of God for pardon and life. The fifty-first Psalm, written on that occasion, exhibits the deepest penitential feelings.

With this eminent saint, did God solemnly renew the covenant of grace;—that covenant which had been established with Adam, with Noah, with the patriarchs, and with the church in the wilderness: and in his zeal for God, David subdued the holy city, Zion—Jerusalem; brought into it, with joyful acclamation, the Tabernacle; perfected the national worship, especially its sacred music, and gathered materials for a Temple, which should fill the earth with its glory.

His character can never be contemplated but with admiration and love. His writings have been a most precious inheritance to the church. Here saints have, in all ages, read their own experience. Here, they have found their joys and sorrows accurately portrayed; and, as the delineation has passed before their eyes, their soul has been melted and comforted within them. Here, in multitudes of songs, the character and offices of Christ, his glorious work on earth and in heaven, the blessedness of the church, and its future enlargement and perfection are sweetly sung;—and the pious have been furnished from that day to this, and will be furnished from this to the latest period of time, with the language and sentiments of devout praise. Forty years did David reign. He was a man of war, and he subdued all the nations around him; but he lived solely for the glory of God, and he advanced that glory beyond any monarch that ever sat on a throne. Having made the most magnificent preparations for the national Temple, and appointed his son Solomon his successor, he died, A. M. 2985, "full of days, and riches, and honor."

Soon after Solomon's advancement to the throne, God appeared to him in a dream, and promised him wisdom and knowledge, and riches, and wealth, and honor, granted to none of the kings that had been before, or should come after him. He was accordingly a prince of great wisdom, splendor, and glory. He reigned forty years; and, while he walked in the steps of David, his father, he in like manner promoted the divine glory; but in the latter part of his life, he was led by his strange wives into idolatry, and brought upon himself the wrath of Jehovah. There is reason, however, to believe that he became a penitent before his death, as the book of Ecclesiastes appears to be the production of a mind which had tasted the bitterness of sin, and been reclaimed to duty.

His reign was chiefly distinguished for the erection of the Temple on which David had "set his affection."

The Tabernacle had remained the place of sacrifice. For about forty-six years it was kept at Shiloh. During the reign of Saul, it was removed to Nob. In the time of Eli, the ark was taken from it and carried into the army; was captured by the Philistines, and afterward sent back to the city of Kirjathjearim. About seventy years after, it was carried to Mount Zion, by David. His object in building the Temple, was to provide for it a permanent and noble abode. This building was probably the most magnificent and costly Temple the world had ever seen. It was not so remarkable for its size, being but about one hundred and fifty feet in length, and one hundred and five in breadth,* nor would it probably compare with modern architecture. But the costliness of its

---

* Prideaux. Some say 90 feet by 30, and 45 in height.

materials, and the splendor of its furniture, almost exceed belief. David and his princes consecrated to it 108,000 talents of gold, and 1,017,000 talents of silver.* About 180,000 men were employed in its formation. It was erected on Mount Moriah, the place where Abraham offered up Isaac, and was seven years in building: every thing was prepared at a distance, so that the sound of the hammer was not heard upon it. It looked toward the east; and had a porch in front, twenty cubits wide, ten deep, and one hundred and twenty in height. On each side of its entrance was a pillar eighteen cubits high and twelve in circumference, adorned with chapiters and two hundred pomegranates. Beyond this porch was the sanctuary or Holy place; which was forty cubits in length, twenty in breadth, and thirty in height, containing ten golden candlesticks, ten tables, with twelve loaves of showbread on each, the golden altar of incense, the silver trumpets, the standards of weight and measure, and the sacred treasures. Beyond this, in the west end of the Temple, and separated from the Holy place by a fine veil, and a two-leaved door of olive tree, was the Oracle, or Holy of Holies, into which only the High Priest might enter on the day of atonement. This was twenty cubits square, and contained the ark with its furniture. Solomon made two new cherubims of olive tree, which overshadowed the mercy seat, and reached to the sides of the house. This Holy of Holies had no windows, and was always dark. The walls of the Temple were of fine cedar and polished marble. On the inside were carved figures of palm trees and cherubims, and every part within and without was overlaid with pure gold.

In front of the Temple was the court for the Priests and Levites. It was surrounded by a low wall of about four feet in height, and contained the brazen altar, twenty cubits long, twenty broad, and ten high; and the brazen sea and lavers. Beyond this was the outer court, surrounding the whole, and enclosed by a high wall, into which every clean Hebrew and proselyte of the covenant might enter, and see, over the low wall, the operations of the priests on the altar.

When the building was finished, the ark and golden utensils were placed in it; and the Shechinah or cloud of glory entered it, to take up its abode between the cherubims. I

---

* A talent of gold is computed at £5475, and a talent of silver at £342 3s. 9d. If this be a correct computation, it was indeed an immense sum.

was then dedicated by Solomon, in presence of all the tribes of Israel, to Almighty God, in a prayer, which, for comprehensiveness, solemnity, and true devotion, has rarely been surpassed:—by seven days feasting, and by a peace offering of 20,000 oxen, and 120,000 sheep, which were consumed by fire from heaven. It then became the regular place for the worship of God; which consisted of sacrifices, songs, and prayer.

The dedication of the Temple took place 3000 years from the foundation of the world, and 1004 years before the birth of Christ.

This building was a beautiful type of the body of Christ, in which dwelt the fullness of the Godhead;—of the Gospel church, reared up with lively stones, and the residence of the Holy Spirit;—of the heavenly world, the literal Holy of Holies, where our great High Priest appears for us before the Eternal Majesty, and where God is worshipped by an innumerable company of angels and the spirits of just men made perfect. John saw no temple in heaven, for the Lord God and the Lamb are the temple thereof.

The promises of earthly prosperity made by God to Abraham, were all in this period fulfilled. His seed possessed in quietness and peace, the promised land. They had multiplied as the stars of heaven. They enjoyed great plenty. Every man sat down under his own vine and fig tree. Their fame went abroad among all nations; God was their God; a wall of fire round about them, and a glory in the midst of them; and they, in regular observance of his statutes and ordinances, were his people.

Their state was eminently typical of the blessed state of the church, when Christ shall reign from the river to the ends of the earth; yea, of that exalted state when the judgment being past, God shall bestow upon her the eternal blessings of his covenant in heaven.

It has already been remarked, that the book of Ruth, and part of the first book of Samuel, were probably written by that head of the school of the prophets. The remainder of the first, and the whole of the second of Samuel, are supposed by writers of considerable authority, to be the work of Nathan, the prophet, and of Gad, the seer. The next book which was added to the sacred canon, comprised the Psalms of David. This book was not originally as it now appears. Some hymns in this collection, particularly the ninetieth, are supposed to have been written by Moses. Some, particularly the 137th, by Ezra, during the captivity. And some by Asaph, Jeduthun, and Ethan. The name of David is prefixed to seventy-three. It is generally thought that Ezra collected the whole of these sacred songs, and placed them in their present order.

In this flourishing age of the church, the people of God also received for their guide and consolation, the book of Proverbs, of Ecclesiastes, and the Song of Solomon.

The first is written after the manner of the wise men of antiquity, who chose to compress their instructions into short sentences, which are easily circulated and long retained. It contains chiefly the maxims of Solomon;—a prince who was extensively acquainted with the vices and follies, and best interests of men; and who was divinely inspired to give us rules for conduct in every rank and condition of life. They are so beautiful, and so useful, that no man of taste can fail of receiving pleasure in their perusal; and every youth may be made wiser and better for them.

The second was also the production of Solomon; and is supposed to have been written in the decline of life, after he had been seduced to idolatry, and brought to repentance. It is viewed by many as a dialogue between an infidel and a man of piety, where the former advances the loosest Sadducean philosophy, to which the latter replies with the greatest keenness and severity. But if we choose not to adopt this opinion, we must consider the wise man as sometimes using the language of unbelief ironically, for the purpose of exposing its odious character.

The Song of Solomon is a dramatic poem of the pastoral kind. It was written in the days of his youth, and is the most figurative part of Scripture. In describing a ceremonial appointment, he presents to view a spiritual concern, which that very appointment is often used in the Scripture to symbolize; and if this spiritual allegory has been used by the irreverent with unbecoming levity, the pious mind will clearly discover through the types of Solomon and his bride, the union between Christ and his church portrayed in a very lovely and engaging manner.

These three books are all that the Holy Spirit was pleased to preserve for the edification of the church, of the works of the man who spake three thousand proverbs; whose "songs were a thousand and five; who spake of trees from the cedar that is in Lebanon, even to the hyssop that springeth out of the wall;" who "spake also of beasts and of fowls, and of creeping things, and of fishes;" and they are probably all that would be eminently useful in rearing this great moral edifice.

CHAPTER V.

Declension of religion in the Jewish nation. God's judgments for it. Precious seasons to the church of God in the days of Hezekiah and Josiah. History of the prophets.

GREAT outward prosperity has ever been destructive to the interests of religion. The power, wealth and splendor of the Hebrew monarchy in the days of Solomon, both corrupted him and his nation. Soon after his death, Jeroboam came among the people; a fit instrument in the hand of the prince of the power of the air, for demoralizing and destroying them. Ten tribes revolted under his treacherous dealings from God, 975 years before Christ, and all Israel and Judah went after the calves of Dan and Bethel, and the god Baal, and forgot the God of their fathers.

During the three hundred years which succeeded this revolt, scenes were transacted both in Israel and Judah, which scarce found a parallel among heathen nations. The house of God was converted into an idolatrous temple, altars were erected for Baal, the great idol of the Phenicians; children were made to pass through the fire to Moloch, witchcraft, enchantments, and other profanations were practiced, to the corruption of the true religion, and the promotion of all manner of wickedness; and prophets and righteous men "were stoned, were sawn asunder, were tempted, were slain with the sword; wandered about in sheep-skins and goat-skins; being destitute, afflicted, tormented."

In the fierceness of his anger, God inflicted upon them those judgments which Moses threatened, if they forsook him. In the year 722, B. C., Salmanezer, a king of Assyria, invaded Samaria, the capital of the ten tribes, and after three years siege, took it and destroyed the kingdom; carried the greater part of the inhabitants into captivity, and dispersed them throughout Assyria. And after the lapse of a little more than a century, in the year 588, Nebuchadnezzar, king of Babylon, invaded Jerusalem; destroyed the city and Temple;* took all the treasures of the house of the Lord, and of the king's house; the king, and princes, and chief men and artists, and carried them to Babylon. These tyrants were but the saw, the axe, the rod and the staff, in God's hands to punish his people. They did it in the pride of their hearts; not knowing that they executed the divine decree. The happy land, which four hundred years before was the seat of piety and great worldly prosperity, was now laid waste; stripped of its inhabitants, and reduced to iron bondage.

But in looking over that dark period, in which iniquity abounded in the Jewish nation, we find the spiritual church was not destroyed. God remembered his promise. A holy seed was preserved. Even in the days of Elijah the prophet, when the persecutions were so violent that scarce any were seen avowing themselves on the Lord's side, and Elijah thought he was alone, God had 7000 secret ones who had not bowed the knee in idol worship. Some peculiarly precious seasons the church was permitted to enjoy. Many of the kings of Judah were friendly to the true religion, upheld the Temple worship, and protected the prophets. Rich consolations had the church in the days of Hezekiah. His reign began about 731 B. C., and continued twenty-nine years. He made David his pattern, and trusted in God with all his heart. He destroyed idolatry throughout his dominions. He called together all the Priests and Levites, opened the house of God which his father had impiously shut up, and restored divine worship. He caused his people to keep the passover, and invited the ten tribes, who had for a very long period neglected it, to unite with them. He kept skilful scribes to write out copies of the Holy Scriptures. He was a man of prayer, and his fervent supplications availed to his recovery

---

* The Temple remained but a little period in its original glory. About 34 years after its dedication, Shishak carried off its golden treasures, 1 Kings xiv. 25. It went fast to decay under Jehoram, Ahaziah, and Athaliah. Soon after Joash robbed it to satisfy the demands of Hazael. And after him, Ahaz gave its treasures to Tiglath Pilesar; removed the brazen altar; took the brazen sea from off the oxen, and the brazen lavers from their pedestals, and placed them on the ground, and brake many of the sacred vessels, and shut up the Temple. Hezekiah repaired it, but he was obliged to rob it of much of its wealth for Sennacherib. Manasseh reared altars to the hosts of heaven in its courts. Josiah purged the Temple and replaced the ark of God; but before its final destruction it was much marred; yea, scarce bore any marks of its original magnificence.

from dangerous sickness. His reign was truly precious and joyful to the people of God.

Another season of rest and consolation the church enjoyed about a century after, in the days of Josiah. In the interim between these excellent monarchs, the throne of Judah had been filled by a monster in wickedness. Manasseh reigned fifty-five years, and bent the whole energy of his government to the restoration of idolatry, and destruction of the knowledge and worship of God. He was the most impious man that ever reigned in Israel or Judah. When, therefore, Josiah came to the throne, religion was in Judah at its lowest ebb. This is strikingly shown in the fact, that when he was repairing the Temple, the workmen accidentally found among the rubbish, the law of God which was lost; or rather had been thus providentially preserved from the hands of Manasseh. It was read to the king; and when he heard the curses which were denounced against the Jews for not keeping it, and which had already been executed on the ten tribes, he wept and rent his clothes.

This pious prince went through the land, and thoroughly rooted out idolatry. He assembled the whole nation together at Jerusalem, and caused them to hear the law of God, and entered with them into a solemn covenant with Jehovah. He also caused them to keep the passover with a degree of solemnity which had never been known from the days of Samuel to that time. He made the people acquainted with the law of God, and caused them to walk in his statutes. He was a precious man of God. His heart was tender, and he humbled himself before God and met the divine acceptance. He was truly a nursing father to the church.

During this dark period also, the church was supported by a succession of eminent prophets; who boldly reproved the nation for their vices; revealed the purposes of Jehovah, and continually pointed the righteous to their great Redeemer.

In the reigns of Ahab, Jehoram, and Jehosephat, lived Elijah and Elisha. They were successively heads of the schools of the prophets; were men of great holiness and boldness, and denounced terrible judgments against injustice and idolatry in Judah and Israel. The former gained a signal triumph over the prophets of Baal and the prophets of the grove. He assembled 450 of the one, and 400 of the other on Mount Carmel, that the people might have a fair trial whether Jehovah or Baal was God Sacrifices were then prepared, and the issue was to rest upon the descent of fire from heaven. In vain did the false prophets call upon their gods. But no sooner did Elijah invoke Jehovah, than fire came down from heaven and consumed his sacrifice. The people beholding the miracle, cried out, "The Lord he is the God;" and, at the command of Elijah, slew all the prophets of the grove and of Baal. His life was often exposed, but God miraculously preserved it, and enabled him to gain many triumphs over his enemies. The last miracle he performed was, dividing the waters of Jordon, that he and Elisha and fifty young prophets might pass over. Immediately there appeared a chariot of horses and fire; and Elijah entering the chariot, was carried in a whirlwind, into heaven. Elisha cried after him, "My Father, my Father, the chariot of Israel and the horsemen thereof," the strength and protection of my country. He was a type of John the Baptist. So distinguished and eminent was this man, that 750 years after, he with Moses, appeared and conversed with the Saviour in his transfiguration.

On Elisha fell the mantle of Elijah as he ascended. With this he divided the waters of Jordon, and returned to Jericho. He performed many miracles, and possessed a far larger share of spiritual influence than any other man of his time. By some young men of a certain city which was given to idolatry, he was mocked and reviled, and told to "go up," "go up" like Elijah if he could; toward whom God, in vindication of his servant, came forth in wrath, and by wild beasts destroyed them all. Some time after his death, a dead body being thrown into his sepulchre, revived as soon as it touched his bones. Neither of these men wrote any prophecy or history for the future instruction of the church. The distinguished prophets who succeeded, wrote under inspiration of God; and their prophecies form parts of the sacred canon.

Jonah, the first in the order of time, was commissioned to warn Ninevah, a heathen city, of destruction, and call its inhabitants to repentance. That he might be chastened for disobedience, and also be a symbol of Christ, who was to be entombed three days and three nights in the grave, he was swallowed up and retained for this period by a great fish. His warnings produced the desired effect. The Ninevites turned to the Lord with weeping, fasting, and mourning, and the judgment was averted.

Amos, the next, was a herdsman. He was not of the schools

of the prophets. He predicted the captivity and destruction of Israel; the restoration of the kingdom of David, and the blessed reign of the Prince of Peace. His images are drawn from the scenes of nature.

Hosea resided chiefly in Samaria. He prophesied sixty-six years. His book is a continued strain of invective against the sins of Israel. He foretold their captivity and distress; the reception of the Gentiles into the church; the present state of the Jews; their future restoration; the coming of the Saviour, and the final judgment. He also denounced some judgments against the Gentile nations. His style is beautiful and his writings are powerful.

Isaiah was of the seed royal. Tradition reports that he was sawn asunder in the reign of Manasseh. He was the brightest luminary of the Jewish church. So clearly does he describe the Messiah and his kingdom, that he is often emphatically styled the evangelical prophet. In early life he was blessed with a remarkable vision of Jehovah sitting in glory, and worshipped by the Seraphim. It was, we are told by John,* a vision of Christ, and is an incontrovertible proof of his real divinity. The view caused the prophet to lie low in the dust and bewail his own sinfulness; but a seraph touched his lips with a live coal from the altar, and intimated that his sin was purged. Immediately he received a commission to declare the judgments of the Lord. He prophesied about sixty years, commencing at the close of the reign of Uzziah, and was an eminent counselor of some of the kings. The first part of his book consists chiefly of declarations of sins and threatenings of judgment; then follows predictions of judgments on various nations; some plain history, and the most precious promises to the church—promises of the redemption and glorious kingdom of the Messiah, of the double restoration of the Jews, and the blessed millennium. His style is a perfect model of the sublime. He stands to this day, unrivalled in eloquence.

Micah was cotemporary with Isaiah, and has much of his style and spirit. He exclaims against the wickedness of the ten tribes; foretells the Assyrian invasion, and the destruction of Jerusalem; the return of the Jews from captivity; the birth of Christ at Bethlehem Ephratah, and the peace and prosperity of the Christian Church.

---

* John xii. 41.

Nahum appears to have prophesied just as Sennacherib was returning from Egypt, with the intention of destroying Jerusalem; and with great fire and spirit, he utters an illustrious prophecy against Ninevah, which was fulfilled in a little more than a century after its delivery.

Zepheniah was of royal extract, and lived in the time of king Josiah. In terms wonderfully descriptive, he denounces vengeance against the wicked Jews; the Philistines; the Moabites; Amonites; Ethiopians and Assyrians; and promises a restoration of the captive people of God.

Joel takes no notice of the ten tribes, but confines himself to Judah, and may therefore be supposed to have lived after the first captivity. He predicts a fearful famine, and directs to repentance, fasting, and prayer, as the means of deliverance. His most remarkable prophecy is of the general outpouring of the Spirit on the day of Pentecost.

Jeremiah was devoted to the prophetic office before his birth. When first commissioned, he prayed to be excused because of his youth. But God bade him go forward and fear nothing, for he would be with him and make him as a brazen wall against his enemies. He began to prophecy, in the thirteenth year of Josiah, and prophesied forty years. For his boldness in reproving vice and predicting judgments he suffered the most cruel persecutions, and is said, by Jerome, to have been stoned to death. His prophecies are of a very distinguished and illustrious character. They relate chiefly to the captivity, the precise time of its duration, and the downfall of the neighboring nations. Some of them extend through remote ages. His style is less lofty than that of Isaiah, but breathes a tenderness of spirit which deeply interests the affections of the reader.

Besides his prophecies, he wrote the book of Lamentations, in which he bewails the desolations of Jerusalem, with wonderful tenderness. " Every letter seems written with a tear, every word is the sound of a breaking heart." But whether it is a prophecy of future events, or a description of scenes then present, is not easily determined.

About the same period, Obadiah predicted the destruction of the enemies of Judah, and the restoration of the Jews. His work is short, but has much beauty.

Habakkuk was the last who began to prophecy before the captivity. His style is poetical and beautiful. His description of God's descent from Teman, far surpasses in sublimity

CHAPTER 5.] PROPHETS. 79

any description ever given of any heathen god. He predicts the downfall of the enemies of the church, and pleads with God for her deliverance.

These and other prophets who succeeded them, were instructed in future events by dreams and visions, by audible words, and immediate inspiration. The holiness of their doctrines, their miracles, and the accomplishment of their predictions, afforded indisputable proof that they were taught of God.

They published their predictions, by uttering them loud in public places; by posting them on the gates of the temple, where they might be read; and sometimes by highly expressive actions: Isaiah walked naked* and barefoot; Jeremiah broke the potter's vessel; and Ezekiel publicly removed his household goods from the city, to express correspondent calamities which were about to descend upon the enemies of Jehovah. Sometimes also, they taught by revealing transactions seen in visions, which could not have well been submitted to in reality; thus conveying instruction with great force.

Many of their predictions had a double meaning. They related first to some event which would shortly occur, but chiefly to one of which that was only the type, and which was far distant. Different predictions, therefore, such as those of the first and second dispersion, of the first and second restoration, of the first and second coming of Christ, were mingled in one; a vast period was often embraced in one prophecy, and what a cursory reader would suppose to belong to a particular people in a particular age, often embraced great portions of the human family, through many successive generations.

Their style was highly figurative, bold and magnificent. They drew their imagery from the luminaries of heaven, from the ocean, the mountain, the storm, from their native scenery, from their temple worship and the idolatrous rites of the heathen; and if sometimes it partook of an indelicate cast, it was because of the taste of the age, or because they would more indignantly express the divine abhorrence of the sins of the people.

Their predictions were necessarily obscure, that they might not control human freedom, and appear to produce their own accomplishment. But so numerous and express were they

---
* He laid aside his royal and priestly vestments, to show that the government and priesthood would be overthrown. This gives no warrant to those who appear in a state of perfect nudity as a sign.

6*

respecting the advent of Christ, as to occasion, about the time of his birth, both among Jews and Gentiles, a very general expectation of the appearance of some illustrious personage.

"The testimony of Jesus, is the spirit of prophecy; and he who can contemplate that spirit operating through four thousand years, and be an infidel, would not be persuaded though one rose from the dead."

TABLE *of the Prophets who prophesied before the Captivity.*

	BEFORE CHRIST.	KINGS OF JUDAH.	KINGS OF ISRAEL.
Elijah,	from 912 to 896	Jehosaphat.	Ahab.
Elisha,	906 to 839	Jehoram, Jehoash.	Jehoram. Jehu.
Jonah,	856 to 784	Jehoash.	Jehu and Jehoahaz.
Amos,	810 to 785	Azariah.	Jeroboam 2d.
Hosea,	810 to 725	Azariah.	Jeroboam 2d.
Isaiah,	760 to 698	Uzziah, Jotham, Ahaz, Hezekiah and Manasseh.	Pekah, Hoshea.
Micah,	750 to 710	Jotham, Ahaz and Hezekiah.	Hoshea.
Nahum,	720 to 700	Hezekiah.	
Zephaniah,	650 to 610	Josiah.	
Joel,	640 to 610	Josiah.	
Jeremiah,	629 to 588	Josiah, Jehoiakim	
Obadiah,	607 to 580	Jehoiakim.	
Habakkuk,	612 to 595	Zedekiah.	

CHAPTER VI.

Babylonish captivity. Ezekiel. Triumphs of faith. Prophecies of Daniel. Providence of God relating to Cyrus. Restoration of the Jews. Temple rebuilt. Preservation of the church through Esther. Favorable decrees of Artaxerxes to Ezra and Nehemiah. Their labors and success at Jerusalem. The last of the Prophets. Closing of the sacred canon. Zoroaster.

In the year 588 B. C. the destruction of Jerusalem, of the Temple, and the nation was rendered complete. The remnant of this once happy and flourishing people, was carried captive to Babylon, and scattered throughout the East. Their sufferings were without a parallel. Every curse and wo which had been denounced upon them by God through his prophets, if they forsook him, were strictly and literally fulfilled. But amid the treachery of friends, and persecution of enemies, the church lived. "The bush burned with fire, but the bush was not consumed." God had a seed to serve him; men of prayer, who sat down by the rivers of Babylon and wept when they remembered Zion—who, in recollection of their beloved homes, their Temple worship, and the God of their fathers, said, " If I forget thee, O Jerusalem, let my right hand forget her cunning. If I do not remember thee, let my tongue cleave to the roof of my mouth ; if I prefer not Jerusalem above my chief joy."

Among the children of the captivity was the prophet Ezekiel. He was a descendant of Aaron, of the tribe of Levi ; and was carried captive with Jehoiachin and placed on the banks of the river Chebar. He began to prophecy six years before the destruction of Jerusalem by Nebuchadnezzar, and continued to prophecy sixteen years after. In the fifth year of his captivity, and thirtieth of his age, the Lord appeared to him on a throne, supported by cherubims and wheels, signifying angels and changing providences ; and directed him to go and declare his mind and will to the captive Jews. They had made themselves miserable from supposing that the remnant at Jerusalem were in happy circumstances. He corrected their error, by showing them the melancholy state of Jerusalem, and the still greater calamities which awaited it, because of the total apostacy of the Jews. He occasionally adverted to the certain destruction of their enemies; predicted the advent of the Messiah, and the final restoration of the Jews. His style is bold and tragical. Many of his prophecies are obscure. The last nine chapters, furnish a description of a new temple and city, seen in vision, under which seems to be shadowed the glorious church universal

But the most eminent saint and the most exalted personage in the church at this time, was the prophet Daniel. He was descended from the kings of Judah, and was carried captive in the fourth year of Jehoiachin. He flourished during the reigns of several monarchs, and died in old age, after the capture of Babylon by Cyrus. Because of his birth, beauty and wisdom, he was selected among others to receive a princely education, and stand in the presence of Nebuchadnezzar. By his extraordinary qualities, he conciliated the favor of monarchs, and was elevated to great rank and power; but, sanctified by the Spirit, he maintained a close walk with God, professed his religion and continued steadfast in prayer, in defiance of the greatest dangers. Often were he and his companions tempted by the greatest possible allurements—by life itself, to renounce their religion and become idolaters, but nothing could move them. They feared God rather than man. And their heroism and fortitude spread the knowledge of God among all nations.

History presents no greater exhibition of moral sublimity, no greater triumphs of faith than are to be witnessed in Shadrach, Meshach, and Abednego. Throughout the east, idolatry was at its height, and God was unknown. Vast kingdoms were summoned by Nebuchadnezzar, the haughtiest of monarchs, to the plains of Dura, to bow down before an immense idol, which he had set up. These companions of Daniel* were accused and brought before the king as disobedient to his command. A tremendous fiery furnace was prepared for the disobedient, and they were threatened with being instantly cast into it. Had these pious youths yielded, Satan's triumph would have been complete. But the seed of the woman was to bruise the head of the serpent, and they stood firm. The mighty mass of idolaters gnashed on them with their teeth. But they stood firm. They were cast into the furnace. But God was with them. One like to the Son of Man was seen walking with them in the fire, and the fire was not permitted to singe their garments, or the hair of their head. The king, astonished, called them forth and cast their accusers into the furnace to their immediate and awful destruc-

---

* Where Daniel was at this time is uncertain; probably he was absent, or so much in favor at court, that the idolaters durst not touch him.

tion. And behold the result! " I make a decree," said this mightiest of human monarchs, " That every people, nation, and language which speak any thing amiss against the God of Shadrach, Meshach, and Abednego, shall be cut in pieces, and their houses shall be made a dunghill." It was a glorious triumph over the powers of darkness.

The prophecies of Daniel are the most magnificent and extensive of any which were ever delivered. They chiefly respect the rise and fall of the four great monarchies of the world, which were to be succeeded by that kingdom which should not be destroyed. They furnish a striking exhibition of the power and destruction of Antichrist, and distinctly assure men of a general resurrection to a life of everlasting shame, or everlasting blessedness. Before him was the map of divine providence; and with such accuracy did he delineate future events, that Porphyry, a bitter enemy of Christianity, could only maintain his cause by the assertion that his prophecies were written after the events had occurred.

His first prophecy was contained in his explanation of Nebuchadnezzar's dream. This mighty monarch beheld in vision, a great image, whose head was of fine gold; whose breast and arms were of silver; whose belly and thighs were of brass; whose legs were of iron, and whose feet were part of iron and part of clay. He saw, till a stone was cut out without hands, which smote and destroyed the image, and became a great mountain, and filled the whole earth. In his explanation, Daniel showed that the head of gold represented the Babylonian empire, which was renowned for its riches; the breast and arms of silver, the Persian empire; the belly and thighs of brass, the Macedonian empire, which, under Alexander, ruled the whole earth; and the legs of iron, and feet of iron and clay, the Roman empire, which was stronger than any that had gone before it, but which was composed of a mixture of all nations, and which, therefore, was partly strong and partly weak. Having thus clearly pointed out these four great empires, he uttered an illustrious prediction of the kingdom of Christ which the God of heaven should set up, and which, imagined by the stone, should break all these kingdoms to pieces, and stand forever.

Forty-eight years after, the same things were revealed to Daniel, and by him to the church, under the similitude of wild beasts. By a lion, who shadowed out to him the Babylonian empire; by a bear, the Medo-Persian; by a leopard, with four heads, the Macedonian, which after the death of Alexander, was divided into four kingdoms; and by a beast which was dreadful and terrible, and strong exceedingly, and which had great iron teeth, and ten horns, the Roman, which should be divided into ten kingdoms. While he was considering, a little horn arose, in which were eyes like the eyes of a man, and a mouth speaking great things, shadowing forth the Man of Sin, the papal hierarchy; which should speak great things against the Most High, and wear out the saints. To this succeeded a most sublime view of the universal reign of Christ, and of the coming of the ancient days to judgment. "Thousand thousands ministering unto him, and ten thousand times ten thousand stood before him; the judgment was set, and the books were opened."

Besides these, Daniel had other visions of the events of nations, which have long since been realized, and of some, probably, which are yet to come to pass; but there is one class of his prophecies peculiarly interesting to the church. By Gabriel was revealed to him with great exactness, the time when Messiah, the Prince, should appear. "Seventy weeks," said he, "are determined upon thy people, and upon thy holy city, to finish the transgression, and to make an end of sins, and to make reconciliation for iniquity, and to bring in everlasting righteousness, and to seal up the vision of prophecy, and to anoint the Most Holy. Know therefore and understand, that, from the going forth of the commandment to restore and to build Jerusalem, unto the Messiah the Prince, shall be seven weeks and three score and two weeks. And after three score and two weeks shall Messiah be cut off, but not for himself." A day, in prophetic language, is a year. The period predicted therefore, was 490 years from the commission given to Ezra by Artaxerxes, to the crucifixion of Christ; or 434 years from the completion of the second temple, which was exactly fulfilled. With the like accuracy, also, did this prophet predict the duration of the Man of Sin and the reign of the prince of darkness; which will be fully seen when the kingdom and the dominion, and the greatness of the kingdom, shall be given to the saints of the Most High.

What a view had this prophet of events in the womb of time! How clearly manifest it is that "known unto God are all his works, from the foundation of the world;" that he works by a fixed plan, that he determines the end from the beginning; and that while man is perfectly free and pursues his own pleasure. God sits on the throne, accomplishing, in his own time and way, and through the instrumentality of man, his glorious purposes. Well might Daniel exclaim in prospect, and we, in the fulfillment of these purposes, "Blessed be the name of God forever and ever, for wisdom and might are his. And he changeth the times and the seasons; he removeth kings, and setteth up kings; he giveth wisdom unto the wise, and knowledge to them that know understanding. He revealeth the deep and secret things; he knoweth what is in the darkness, and light dwelleth with him."

In the land of bondage the church might have been left to perish, but God was with her; and when the time for her deliverance had come, so clearly and fully predicted by his prophets, he provided means for its accomplishment. One hundred and fifty years before, he had declared by Isaiah, that he would raise up Cyrus, who should deliver this people.* In the ordinary course of human events, this distinguished man came to the height of power. He was the son of Cambyses, the king of Persia; and as he advanced in life, became an eminent warrior. In conjunction with his uncle Darius the Mede, he besieged Babylon. But it was a city of amazing strength, and its conquest appeared beyond the power of man. Under its walls and through the centre of the city, ran the Euphrates. This had once been turned into a vast lake excavated for its reception, while a passage could be made under its bed to unite two palaces, which stood on its opposite banks. Cyrus resolved to break down the embankment which had been formed, turn the water into the old excavation, and march into the city in the dry bed of the river.

Having fixed his plan, he determined to prosecute it on a night when Belshazzar and all his court were engaged in rioting. This Belshazzar was one of the most impious princes who had filled the throne. That night he drank from the gold and silver vessels which were taken out of the temple at Jerusalem, he, and his lords, and his concubines, making a mock of the God of heaven. For such impiety, Jehovah awfully chastised him. For he caused a hand to appear and write on the wall. At beholding it, fear and astonishment seized the king, he called his magicians, and diviners, and astrologers, but none could read the writing. Daniel, the prophet, was instantly summoned, and he read, "MENE,

---

* Isaiah, xlv. 1.

MENE, TEKEL, UPHARSIN," giving the interpretation, "God hath numbered thy kingdom and finished it. Thou art weighed in the balance and found wanting. Thy kingdom is divided and given to the Medes and Persians." No sooner was the warning given, than Darius and Cyrus entered the city, and Belshazzar was slain. Thus ended the Babylonian empire. Thus was destroyed the golden head of Nebuchadnezzar's image, 539 years B. C., and thus were fulfilled the many prophecies which Isaiah, Jeremiah, Habakkuk, and Daniel, had delivered against it.

Of the new kingdom of the Medes and Persians, the arms and breast of the great image, Daniel was made prime minister. His exaltation excited the envy of the presidents, and princes; and when they could find nothing against him, they artfully laid a plan to destroy him for his religion. To the great grief of Darius, he was cast into the den of lions because he would go to his chamber and three times a day pray to the God of heaven. But God shut the mouths of the lions, and he was brought out in safety. His enemies were destroyed, and his influence at court was greater than ever.

In a few years, Cyrus succeeded to the throne. Daniel had carefully computed the seventy years of Judah's captivity, predicted by Jeremiah, and had made earnest supplication unto the Lord that he would remember his people. He showed the king, we have reason to suppose, the predictions of Isaiah respecting him, and the purpose for which God had raised him up, and earnestly interceded with him to affect the deliverance on which his heart was placed. The king's heart was in the hands of the Lord, and he excited that heathen prince to make this wonderful proclamation : "The Lord God of heaven hath given me all the kingdoms of the earth, and he hath charged me to build him an house at Jerusalem, which is in Judah. Who is there among you of all his people, his God be with him, and let him go up to Jerusalem."

Atheists ascribe all things to chance, and earthly politicians glory in developing the secret springs of action ; but the Bible shows us an Almighty Governor sitting on the throne of the universe, and wielding the destinies of nations at his pleasure Nothing is of so much consequence in the eyes of men, as a vast, splendid, and powerful empire. But the mightiest kingdoms are raised up and destroyed in entire subserviency to the good of the church. The whole history of the world is but a history of the divine decrees. Babylon, the glory of kingdoms, was raised up to be a furnace for the church; and when she was sufficiently purified, Babylon was destroyed that the church might not perish in bondage. Her deliverer was predicted ages before his birth, and was conducted to princely power by the hand of God. His acquaintance with the Israelites and the divine purposes was through the eminent prophet who had been miraculously preserved from death. How awful and glorious is the sovereignty of God! He called the ravenous bird from the east to execute vengeance upon Babylon, and deliver his people. How weak and contemptible are they who fancy they control the affairs of nations! "Surely the princes of Zoan are fools." The balance of power is in his hands who weigheth kings and nations.

Forty-two thousand people, chiefly of the tribes of Judah and Benjamin, with seven thousand servants, returned the first year, under Zerubbabel, to the Holy Land, 535 B. C. Though of two tribes, they were blended together under the name of Jews—an appellation which they have from that day to this sustained. They carried with them all the golden vessels belonging to the Temple, which Nebuchadnezzar had pillaged. After providing themselves suitable habitations, they assembled at Jerusalem; celebrated the feast of trumpets; restored the altar of the Lord for burnt offerings, and commenced rebuilding the Temple. But they soon met with a powerful opposition from the Samaritans.

The Samaritans were a people who were brought by Shalmaneser when he carried the ten tribes out of their own land, from Babylon, from Cuthah, from Ava, from Hameth, and from Sepharvim, and made to dwell in the desolate cities of Samaria. These foreigners intermingled with the lower classes of the Israelites, who remained in the land, and formed a mongrel race, claiming connexion with the Jews and heathen. Being harassed by lions, they sought protection from Jehovah, the God of the country, and obtained from an exiled Hebrew priest, a copy of the five books of Moses.*

---

* This being the most ancient copy of the Pentateuch, has been considered of great importance in relation to biblical criticism. It differs in about two thousand instances from the Jewish copy. But it has been shown in a late learned work of Gesenius, that the Jewish is the original copy, and that all the variations of the Samaritan may be easily accounted for. The Samaritans are now reduced to less than 200 persons. They reside at Neplos, the ancient Sychar, or Sychem. The Samaritan is the original Hebrew character.

Hearing of the return and undertaking of the Jews, this people came and offered to unite with them; but as they were not of the children of Israel, would not put away their idols, and cared but little about the true religion, the Hebrews would have no connexion with them; which so enraged the Samaritans that they opposed them with bitterness, bribed some of the counselors of Cyrus to act against them, and for many years greatly retarded their work. And when Cyrus and Daniel were dead, and a new monarch was upon the throne, they made such representations to him of the former rebellious character of the Jews, that he issued a decree against the rebuilding of the Temple, and the work ceased. In opposition to the Jewish Temple, they built one on Mount Gerizim, where they said men ought to worship. Between them and the Jews has ever subsisted the most bitter animosity.

Under a succeeding reign, the prophets Haggai and Zechariah exhorted the Jews to go on with their work. And when the governor asked for their warrant in undertaking it again, they appealed to the decree of Cyrus. This appeal was sent to Darius, the king, who caused search to be made. The decree was found; liberty was granted them to finish the Temple, and means were furnished from the king's treasury. In twenty years from their return, the building was completed and dedicated to God with great solemnity and joy, B. C. 415.

This second Temple, however, had but little of the magnificence of the first. The aged men who beheld it, wept at the contrast. Besides its inferior workmanship and covering, it was destitute of the Shechinah, or cloud of glory, over the mercy seat; of the holy oracle, or approach to God by Urim and Thummim; of the perpetual fire which came down from heaven in the wilderness; and of the two tables of the testimony, on which God wrote with his finger the ten commandments. But yet the glory of this latter house was to be greater than that of the former; for into it the Desire of all nations was to come, who would fill it with his praise.

Two eminent prophets, Haggai and Zechariah, returned with the children of the captivity. They were raised up to reprove the people for their sins; to call them to repentance, and encourage them in building the second Temple. The most eminent prediction of Haggai was of the Messiah's coming into his Temple, when God should shake the nations. Zechariah predicted with wonderful minuteness, his riding into Jerusalem on an ass, and a colt the foal of an ass; his being valued at thirty pieces of silver; and his death, by the avenging sword of Jehovah. He also described the destruction of Jerusalem by the Romans; the conversion and bitter grief of the Jews for having pierced the Messiah, and their final admission by baptism into the privileges of the Gospel covenant. His style is much like that of Jeremiah, whose spirit the Jews said had descended upon him.

This dreadful captivity cured the nation of idolatry. They never more went after the gods of the heathen.

It was but a remnant that was restored to their native land, and this was from the tribes of Judah and Benjamin. The ten tribes were doomed to a long dispersion among the eastern nations. Their descendants, it is supposed, are still distinctly visible.

In a subsequent period, in the reign of Ahasuerus, called also Artaxerxes, this whole people, embracing the Church of God, came near an utter extermination. For Haman, the prime minister of his court, unable to brook the contumely shown him by Mordecai, who probably only refused to render him certain honors because he viewed them as due to God alone, procured a royal decree for their entire destruction throughout the whole world. But Esther, a Jewess, had been exalted to royalty; and through her intercession, the plot was defeated and the Jews were saved. This great event happened 452, B. C. In commemoration of it, the Jews instituted the feast of Purim, or lot, because Haman ascertained by lot the day on which the Jews were to be destroyed.

In no part of the sacred writings, do we more clearly behold the wonderful steps of divine providence for the preservation of the church. The most trivial circumstances paved the way for the accomplishment of the most important events. A Jewess orphan became the queen of the greatest empire on earth, through the whim of a monarch in a drunken revel. A restless night of the king brought to the highest honors the object of Haman's implacable rage, and the man on whom the salvation of the church rested. The uncertain humor of a despot was overruled to regard favorably the petition of his queen, who approached him at the hazard of her life, for the safety of her people. And when the church was actually consigned to ruin, it was only saved by a counter decree which gave the Jews liberty to defend themselves against their enemies. In all this concatenation of circumstances, there was nothing miraculous. All happened according to the ordinary course of human affairs, and yet all was directed by the finger of God. God brought Esther to the kingdom "for such a time as this." She saved her people, and made this mighty Ahasuerus favorable to the church during the whole of his reign. By whom the book of Esther was written, is unknown. It has been ascribed to Mordecai, to Ezra, and to Nehemiah.

Seventy-eight years after the decree of Cyrus, 457 B. C. Ezra was commissioned by Artaxerxes (the Ahasuerus of the book of Esther,) governor of Judea.* He went up to Jerusalem with about 1700 persons, bearing a munificent present of silver and gold from the king and his counselor, to the Lord God of Israel, and a proclamation to all the treasurers beyond the river, requiring them to furnish whatsoever should be commanded by the God of heaven, for his house; all, probably, obtained through the intercession of queen Esther. Like a truly pious man, who placed his dependence on the God of heaven, Ezra observed at the river Ahava, a day of fasting and prayer; and God was with him, and made all his way prosperous before him. He found the people in a low state. They had intermarried with the Gentiles in the land. Ezra convened them, severely rebuked them, compelled them all to put away their strange wives, and publicly read to them from a pulpit of wood, the law of God. The Holy Spirit was poured out, and the people turned to the Lord with weeping, fasting, and mourning; entered into solemn covenant with God, and became greatly reformed.

Ezra was of the sacerdotal family, and was an eminent scribe. He not only wrote the book which bears his name, but compiled from ancient records, the books of Chronicles, collected all the books of which the sacred Scriptures did then consist, made such additions to them as were necessary for their completion, and placed them in their proper order. In transcribing he put the Hebrew writings into the square character of the Chaldeans, after which the ancient Hebrew character fell into disuse excepting with the Samaritans, who have retained it to this day. Ten years after, Nehemiah went to Jerusalem with a commission from the same king to

---

* From the decree granting this commission, are to be dated the seventy weeks of Daniel.

repair the walls and set up the gates of Jerusalem. He was a Jew, of exalted heroism and piety, who had obtained the place of cup-bearer to the king; not improbably through the influence of queen Esther. Under him the people fortified the city, though they were so opposed by the Samaritans, as to be obliged to carry arms to their work. Nehemiah returned to the Persian court, but he soon came back with a new commission, and entered with great zeal upon the business of re-peopleing Jerusalem and of reforming the nation; especially in their abuses of the daily worship and of the holy Sabbath. His government continued near forty years. His last act of reformation was in the year 409 B. C. He died, probably, soon after this, about seventy years of age.

Under the administration of these excellent men the custom was introduced of reading publicly the law and the prophets in the synagogues, every Sabbath day. Before the captivity, there were but very few copies of the sacred Scriptures. In the time of Joshua, only one copy of the law was in existence. The people, therefore, were very ignorant of it. But by this new regulation, copies were greatly multiplied. Synagogues, or churches were built in every town, and every synagogue had one copy.

Cotemporary with Ezra and Nehemiah, was the prophet Malachi. He was raised up to censure the people for the same offences that had excited the indignation of the governors, and to declare that God would punish and reject them and would make his name great among the Gentiles. He predicted the coming of John the Baptist, and the sudden appearance of the Lord in his temple, to take vengeance on his enemies, and be glorified in them that fear him. His style is inferior, as he lived in the decline of the Hebrew poetry. He was the last of the prophets. By him the canon of the Old Testament was completed about 400 years before Christ.

Table of the Prophets who prophesied after the Captivity.	
Daniel,	between 606 and 534 B. C.
Ezekiel,	between 595 and 536.
Haggai,	about 520.
Zechariah,	about 519.
Malachi,	between 436 and 400.

For many ages, the false religions of the east had remained

stationary; but in this period, Magianism received considerable strength from the writings of Zoroaster. He was a native of Media. He pretended to a visit to heaven, where God spake to him out of a fire. This fire he pretended to bring with him on his return. It was considered holy, the dwelling of God. The priests were forever to keep it, and the people were to worship before it. He caused fire-temples every where to be erected, that storms and tempests might not extinguish it. As he considered God as dwelling in the fire, he made the sun to be his chief residence, and therefore the primary object of worship. He abandoned the old system of two gods, one good, and the other evil, and taught the existence of one Supreme, who had under him a good and evil angel; the immediate authors of good and evil. To gain reputation, he retired into a cave and there lived a long time a recluse, and composed a book called the Zendavesta, which contains the liturgy to be used in the fire-temples and the chief doctrines of his religion. His success in propagating his system was astonishingly great. Almost all the eastern world, for a season, bowed before him. He is said to have been slain, with eighty of his priests, by a Scythian prince whom he attempted to convert to his religion. It is manifest that he was well acquainted with the Jewish Scriptures, and that he derived his whole system of God dwelling in the fire, from the burning bush, out of which God spake to Moses. He gave the same history of the creation and deluge that Moses had given, and inserted a great part of the Psalms of David into his writings. The Mehestani, his followers, believed in the immortality of the soul, in future rewards and punishments, and in the purification of the bad by fire; after which they would be united to the good.

CHAPTER VII.

Civil government of the Jews. Sanhedrim. Religious order. Degeneracy in piety Conflicts for the High Priesthood. Joshua slain in the Temple. Destruction of the Persian and erection of the Grecian monarchy. Daniel's vision of the ram and the he goat. Fulfillment of prophecies against Tyre. The Jews favored by Alexander. Course and end of the he goat. Of the four horns which stood up in its place. Death of Simon the just. Septuagint version of the Scriptures. Ptolemy's violation of the Holy of Holies. The Jews favored by Antiochus the Great.

From the completion of the Scriptures of the Old Testament to the birth of Christ, was a period of about 400 years. It was a period of which indeed we have no inspired history: but as the great Edwards well remarks, it was a period whose events are much the subject of Scripture prophecy: so that, if we have no later writer than Malachi, still we have, in the Bible, a complete history of the church; "the account is carried on, the chain is not broken till we come to the very last link of it in the consummation of all things." God also has provided profane historians, who, from the cessation of scriptural history, have given us authentic and full accounts of his providential dealings with his church and the nations of the earth, and enabled us to behold the exact fulfillment of his prophetic revelations.

After the return of the Jews from captivity, they remained in a feeble state, under the Persian monarchs. The last of their governors from among themselves, was Nehemiah. At his death they were transferred to the prefecture of Syria, by which they were subjected to an easy tribute. They lived, however, under their own laws, governed by the High Priest, and might have been a happy people, had it not been for long continued and violent contests by brothers and others nearly related, for the sacerdotal dignity, and the tyrannical conduct of some who were raised to it. An office so holy, should ever have been filled by holy men of God; but, like the pontificate in after ages, it was sought for by men of ambition and avarice, as a place in which the vilest passions might be gratified. As its civil authority came from the Syrian governor, it was purchased and retained by money, and the worst political artifices. The nation was thrown by contending candidates, into violent conflicts, and was burdened with heavy taxes to satisfy the demands of the prefect.

At a subsequent period, we find associated with the High

Priest, in the government of the nation, a grand council called the Sanhedrim, consisting of seventy-two judges, which possessed the power of life and death. The Jews called it "a hedge to the laws;" and maintained that it was instituted by God in the days of Moses, when he appointed seventy-two elders to aid him in the government. But as we find no account of it in the Old Testament, it is evident that it was an institution of modern date. Basnage and others have fixed its first institution in the time of the Maccabees. Its authority extended over all the synagogues in the world, and no appeal could be made from its sentence.

The religious services of the Jews continued much upon the plan established by Ezra and Nehemiah. A synagogue or church was built in every city. At the east end was a chest or ark, bearing a resemblance to the ark of the covenant in the Temple; in which was placed the Pentateuch, written upon vellum. The people assembled for prayer, three times every day; in the morning, afternoon, and evening. On the Sabbath day and on festival days, the law and the prophets were read and expounded. Their form of worship was much the same as in Christian assemblies, and is retained to this day.

As has been remarked, the Jews were cured by the captivity, of their idolatry. They ever looked upon that sin as the cause of their curse. In the great revival under Ezra, they consecrated themselves anew to God, and would have been happy, had they continued a holy people unto the Lord, looking, with lively faith, to the coming of the Desire of all nations. But alas! they soon degenerated into a cold formality and debasing superstition; and, instead of purity of morals and true devotion, offered little to God but a fiery zeal for the rights and ceremonies of the church. Could we look among the mountains and valleys of Judea, we should, no doubt, in every age find many a devout Simeon and praying Anna, " waiting for the consolation of Israel." God has ever had a people to serve him.

This nation he had owned in his gracious covenant. Here, under his word and ordinances, lived the true church. Here many souls were trained up for glory. But history chiefly presents us the painful conflicts of violent men, contending for the priesthood, and not less violent doctors, corrupting the law of Moses, and introducing the tenets and customs which made void the commandments of God. These, with their results, must be recorded, that a full view may be presented of the state of the church, and the providences of God in relation to it.

So early as the year 366 B. C. we find a conflict for the High Priesthood, terminating in blood, and bringing great oppression upon the Jewish nation. Johanan, the son of Jehoida, had succeeded his father in the High Priesthood, but Joshua, his brother, having insinuated himself into the favor of Bagoses, governor of Syria, obtained of him a grant of the office. A dispute ensued; and Joshua was slain by Johanan in the inner court of the Temple. This act of violence so enraged Bagoses, that he imposed an enormous fine upon the pontiff and Temple annually, for seven years.

A few years after this unhappy event, the Jews imprudently engaged with the Phenicians in a war against Ochus, the Persian monarch; in consequence of which he entered Judea, took Jericho, and carried captive many of the Jews into Egypt, and sent others to the borders of the Caspian sea.

The Persian monarchy, (the breast and arms of silver, of the great image of Nebuchadnezzar,) had now continued about 200 years; but according to the sure word of prophecy, it was drawing to its close to be succeeded by the Grecian; represented by the belly and thighs of brass. For the accomplishment of this purpose, God raised up Alexander, the son of Philip, king of Macedonia, and endowed him with talents for the accomplishment of vast and glorious undertakings. Actuated by an ambition to conquer the world, this prince went forth furiously with a small but powerful army, against Darius, king of Persia, and became a triumphant conqueror of armies and dominions, which had been considered invincible, and established on the ruins of the Persians, the third great empire of the earth. These events took place 334—0 B. C.

Besides the general representations of it in the image of Nebuchadnezzar, and in Daniel's vision of four beasts, that distinguished prophet had another more particular and striking view of it in his vision of the ram and the he goat. "Then I lifted up mine eyes" said Daniel, "and saw, and behold there stood before the river a ram, which had two horns, and the two horns were high up, but one was higher than the other, and the higher came up last." This ram, according to the interpretation of Gabriel, was the empire of the Medes and Persians. "I saw," says the Prophet, "the ram pushing westward and northward and southward so that no beast might stand before him." Under Cyrus and his successors, the Persians pushed their conquests on every side. " And as I was considering, behold an he goat came from the west, on the face of the whole earth and touched not the ground ; and the he goat had a notable horn between his eyes." By the angel Gabriel the prophet was told that this rough goat was the king of Greece, and the great horn that was between his eyes, was the first king. " And he came," said Daniel, " to the ram that had two horns which I had seen standing before the river, and ran unto him in the fury of his power. And I saw him come close unto the ram, and he was moved with choler against him, and smote the ram and break his two horns, and there was no power in the ram, to stand before him, but he cast him down to the ground and stamped upon him and there was none that could deliver the ram out of his hand."

This wonderful prophecy thus delivered 230 years before, received a most exact fulfillment in the rapid and irresistible movements of the Grecian conqueror. Alexander, the leopard in a former vision, and the he goat from the west in this, flew with incredible swiftness, and came upon his enemies before they were aware of him or could place themselves in a posture of defence. At the river Granicus he met Darius with all his army. He commanded 35,000 men, while Darius had five times that number. But he regarded him not. He ran unto him in the fury of his power, and he smote the ram and break his two horns. Media and Persia were no more. He routed all the armies, took all the cities and castles, and subverted forever the Persian empire. Thus did this mad and ferocious heathen prince become the instrument of effecting, in part, the divine purpose declared by Ezekiel,* "I will overturn, overturn, overturn it and it shall be no more, until he come whose right it is, and I will give it him."

Having overthrown the Persian empire, Alexander pushed his conquest into Phenicia. Every place opened its gates until he came to the ancient city Tyre, where he met a serious check. Tyre belonged to the tribe of Asher, but wes never taken from the Canaanites. Situated upon the sea, it became a place of great trade, opulence and splendor. But it abounded also in pride and wickedness, and gloried over Jerusalem, the city of God, when she was chastened ot heaven. God therefore determined to display over it his

---

* xxi. xxvii.

righteous indignation, and by his prophets, he declared that he would destroy it utterly.* He first brought against it Nebuchadnezzar. It was a city of amazing strength; and for thirteen years this mighty potentate besieged it, until "every head was made bald and every shoulder was peeled." At length it was taken 572 B. C., and the predictions of the prophets were, in part fulfilled. But the inhabitants removed themselves and their effects to an island, and it was not utterly destroyed. It was for Alexander to complete the divine purpose. He found it again populous and strong; but after a costly and terrible siege he took the city by force, put 8000 of the inhabitants to the sword, crucified 2000, and sold 30,000 for slaves. After this it never recovered its glory. It is now, in fulfillment of the divine decree, a place for fishermen to spread their nets. So true is it that God reigneth in the earth, and will do all his pleasure. " The Lord of hosts hath purposed, and who can disannul."

The next movement of this weapon of the Lord, was against Jerusalem. The Jews pleading their oath to Darius, refused to furnish Alexander with supplies for his army while encamped against Tyre. This exceedingly enraged that successful monarch, and he determined to wreak his vengeance upon Jerusalem. At his approach the Jews were thrown into the greatest consternation. They immediately offered to God sacrifices, prayers and supplications; and, being directed, as it is said, in a vision by night, Jaddua, the High Priest went out to meet the conqueror, dressed in his pontifical robes, with all the priests in their sacerdotal vestments, and the people in white garments. Struck with awe at the solemn spectacle, Alexander hastened forward, and bowed himself to the earth before the High Priest, and worshipped Jehovah, whose name was inscribed on the mitre. Parmenias, his favorite, astonished at his behavior, inquired why he did thus? Alexander who well knew how to improve every occurrence in his own favor, assured him that when he was at Dio, in Macedonia, and deliberating with himself what he should do, this very pontiff, in this habit, appeared to him in a dream, and encouraged him to pursue the war against the Persians, assuring him of complete success in all his undertakings. The king embraced the High Priest, entered Jerusalem in a friendly manner with the procession, and

---

* Isaiah xxiii. Ezekiel xxvi. xxvii. xxviii.

offered sacrifices to God in the Temple. Jaddua then showed him the prophecies of Daniel, which predicted the overthrow of the Persian empire by a Grecian king. This produced a feeling of great exultation in the king, and made him favor the Jewish nation. He suffered them to remain unmolested under their own laws, and in the enjoyment of their own religion; exempted them from the usual tribute on the seventh or Sabbatical year, and gave many of them a place with important privileges, in a new city which he built in Egypt, and which he called Alexandria, after his own name. No power was yet to destroy a place where God had recorded his name.

Beholding the attention which the conqueror paid to the Temple and city of Jerusalem, the Samaritans immediately advanced to meet him, and asked the like favors; but as they were not Jews, they plead in vain; and when, a short time after, some of them mutinied against his Syrian governor, he drove them all from Samaria, and planted there a small colony of Greeks. The Samaritans retired to Shechem under Mount Gerizim, the place of their temple, and there they have remained to the present time.

It will not be uninteresting to trace the further course and end of this distinguished man, so plainly pointed out in prophecy, and raised up for the execution of such important purposes. From Jerusalem, Alexander went into Egypt; founded the city of Alexandria, and visited the heathen temple of Jupiter Ammon, situated about 200 miles in the deserts of Lybia. Having caused himself to be declared the son of that heathen god, he returned to Syria and Persia; overcame again the Persians who had gathered against him; pushed his conquests beyond the Indus, and would gladly have gone beyond the Ganges; but his soldiers refused to follow him farther, and he returned to Babylon. There he suddenly died of a fever, produced by a drunken revel, 323 B. C. in the thirteenth year of his reign, and thirty-third year of his age. Thus, when the "he goat had waxed very great and when he was strong, the great horn was broken." He had subjected to himself all the countries from the Adriatic sea to the Ganges, embracing all the habitable world then known. God had raised him up for this purpose. He had marked out, hundreds of years before, his victorious path. He gave him his talents and his success, and carried him through all his difficulties. Alexander was unquestionably a great military commander, but he knew not God. He formed himself on the model of Homer's heroes, and was destroyed by vain glory. His ambition was to conquer the world; and to effect this object, he could wade through seas of blood; totally regardless of human happiness. His triumph led him to the grossest sensuality, and he died as a fool dieth, in bacchanalian revelries. Thus we see that God, who is higher than the highest, can employ the wicked to accomplish his purposes, though they mean not so; and when they have fulfilled his designs, then he casts them out of his hand as no longer useful, except it be in their everlasting destruction for their own vices and follies.

"The great horn was broken, and for it came up four notable ones from toward the four winds of heaven." This termination of the distinguished prophecy, Gabriel thus interpreted: "Now, that being broken, whereas four stood up for it, four kingdoms shall stand up out of the nation, but not in his power." It was now literally fulfilled. Alexander's brother and sons took the throne, but they were all soon murdered, and the horn or kingdom was entirely broken. The governors of provinces usurped dominion, and being reduced to four, they divided Alexander's empire into four kingdoms, which are the four horns which stood up for the one which was great and terrible. Cassander held Macedon and Greece, and the west parts. Lysimachus had Thrace, Bithynia and the northern regions; Ptolemy took Egypt and the southern countries; and Seleucus, Syria and the provinces of the East.

Lying between these various kingdoms, Judea was often greatly distracted with their wars. At first it was held by Laomedon, one of Alexander's captains. He was soon subdued by Ptolemy. The Jews however would not violate their engagements to him. They therefore drew upon them the wrath of Ptolemy, who not being able easily to subdue so strong a place as Jerusalem, took advantage of their regard for the Sabbath, entered the city unresisted on that holy day, and carried one hundred thousand of the inhabitants with him into Egypt. Their firm character and sacred regard to their oath attracted his favor, and he placed many of them in stations of power and trust. Some he settled in Lybia and Cyrene. From these descended the Cyrenian Jews, of whom mention is made in the Acts of the Apostles.

In the year 292 B. C. died Simon, called the just, High Priest of the Jews. He was a man of distinguished uprightness and purity of character. He was an ardent patriot, who repaired and fortified the city and Temple. By him, it is supposed, the canon of the Scriptures of the Old Testament was perfected and settled in the Jewish Church. The genealogy in the book of Chronicles is evidently carried down to about this period, and some books, especially Malachi, were written after Ezra had copied out the sacred writings. No one, it is certain, later than Simon, ventured to perfect the holy oracles; for he was the last of the grand synagogue—a council of 120 elders, who, in regular succession, from the time of Ezra, labored to restore the Jewish state and extend a correct knowledge of the Scriptures.

The whole of the sacred books thus collected and arranged, is called the Old Testament, simply because it contains the former covenant, or the Mosaic dispensation; though that in reality occupies but a very small part of it—the historical books, the book of Job, the Psalms, and the prophets, having no particular connexion with it. In the arrangement which was made, a strict order of time was not observed. A division of the books into chapters and verses, was not made until the thirteenth century of the Christian era. Even a division of letters into words was then unknown. A whole line was written as though it was one word.

Ptolemy Philadelphus, who succeeded Soter, 285 B. C. was very favorable to the Jews. He ransomed many of those who had been brought captive into Egypt, and established others on favorable foundations in his own dominions. He was a great pattern of learning, and collected a library of seven hundred thousand volumes or manuscripts. During his reign the Jewish Scriptures were translated from the Hebrew into the Greek language—forming the Septuagint version. It was formerly the popular belief, from the tradition of one Aristeas, that, desirous of forming a perfect library, and hearing of the books of Moses, Ptolemy sent to Jerusalem for seventy elders, who came to Alexandria, where they were shut up in the island of Pharos, in separate cells, until each one had translated a particular portion; that these translations all being compared and found to agree, were approved; when the elders were sent back with magnificent presents. But this opinion is now exploded, and it is commonly supposed that this Greek version was made privately at Alexandria, by learned Jews, who had been carried thither by Ptolemy Soter, and who retained the Hebrew, and had become conversant with the Greek language. But in whatever way the Septuagint was formed, the translation was a great event. The Scriptures had hitherto been locked up in a language, known only to a small, obscure, and despised people. And not only so, but even among the Jews, the Hebrew ceased to be spoken as a living language, soon after the Babylonish captivity. The sacred books are now put into the popular language of the age, the language of courts, of armies, and of literature. The Jews who were scattered over the earth, and who were fast changing their language for the Greek, found the Scriptures following them, and legible by them. This version was soon brought into universal and common use. Christ and his Evangelists and Apostles quoted from it, though they lived in Judea. From this all the early versions were made—the Illyrian, the Gothic, the Arabic, the Ethiopic, the Armenian, and the Syriac. It was in common use in the churches for several centuries after Christ, and is to this day, in the Greek and most of the oriental churches. It generally expresses the same sentiments with the Hebrew, though often in very different terms.

Such Jews as mingled with the Greeks after the conquests of Alexander, spoke their language, and used the Septuagint version, were called Hellenist Jews.

Though the Jews remained subject to the Egyptians, yet other nations, beholding their diligence and fidelity, were very favorable to them, and granted them many privileges. This was particularly the case with Seleucus Nicator, king of Macedon, who allowed them the same privileges with his own subjects.

About the year 217 B. C. Antiochus the Great, king of Syria, resolved to conquer Jerusalem. But Ptolemy Philopater, king of Egypt, resisted him and drove him back to his own territories. The Jews, in consequence of this, paid him great homage, and cordially welcomed him to their city. Coming into the Temple, Ptolemy offered sacrifices to the God of heaven, and made many gifts to the people. But he would not leave the place until he had seen the Holy of Holies. Against this the priests and people solemnly remonstrated as an awful profanation, which would bring upon him and them the Divine vengeance. But the more he was opposed, the more determined he became; and pressing into the most holy place, he was smitten with inexpressible terror, and carried out by his attendants.

He returned to Egypt in great wrath with the Jews, and bit

terly persecuted all who were in his dominions. He first forbade every man access to him who did not sacrifice to his gods. He next directed that the Jews, who, by the favor of Alexander, had held the first rank, should be enrolled in the third, or lowest, and that when enrolled they should be stamped with a hot iron, with the mark of his god Bacchus; and that if any refused enrollment they should be put to death. He then ordained that as many as would renounce their religion and become heathen, should be restored to their former privileges; but only three hundred out of the many thousands in Alexandria, were seduced to apostacy. He finally resolved upon the destruction of the whole nation. And first gathering together the Jews in Egypt, and binding them in chains, he let loose upon them his elephants; but these, having been made drunk with wine and frankincense, turned upon the spectators and made dreadful havoc among them. Ptolemy, fearing the vengeance of heaven, turned from all his wicked purposes, and restored the Jews to their former privileges.

The Samaritans improved every opportunity which was afforded, to show their enmity to the Jews. They often plundered and ravaged parts of their country, and carried many of the inhabitants into captivity, selling them for slaves. This was particularly the case during the reign of Ptolemy Philopater. .

This oppressed people saw again, at the death of Ptolemy, (B. C. 204,) days of prosperity; for wearied with allegiance to Egypt, they placed themselves under the protection of Antiochus the Great, king of Syria, and offered him their assistance. Antiochus rewarded them by a restoration of Jerusalem to its ancient privileges. He also liberated all who were slaves in captivity; exempted all the Jews who should return to their capital from taxes, for three years; presented a large sum from his own private purse, for repairing the Temple. Antiochus was assassinated 187 B. C. for robbing the temple of Belus of its treasures. He was called the Great, because of his valor, prudence, industry, and success. The transactions of his life, and the wars in which he was engaged with Ptolemy, were accurately delineated in the eleventh chapter of the prophecy of Daniel, from the tenth to the nineteenth verse.

Under his son and successor Seleucus, the Jews enjoyed the privileges and immunities which had been granted them by Antiochus; and might have enjoyed many years of peace and quietness, had it not been for a bitter contention between Simon, the governor of the Temple, and Onias, the High Priest. The former, proving unsuccessful, fled to Appollonius, governor of Palestine, and gave him an exaggerated account of the treasures in the Temple. When Seleucus heard it, he resolved to possess them, and sent his treasurer to bring them away. But, while in the act of robbery, Heliodorus, the treasurer, was suddenly struck with awful terror, by a vision, which caused him instantly to quit the city, fearing the power and wrath of God. The whole of the reign of Seleucus is expressed in the twentieth verse of the eleventh chapter of Daniel. He was little besides "a raiser of taxes."

CHAPTER VIII.

Desolations of Jerusalem under Antiochus Epiphanes. Jason erects a gymnasium Temple shut up for three years. Bold and artful plot of Antiochus to extirpate the church. The Temple consecrated to Jupiter Olympus. Jewish martyrdom. General revolt under Mattathias. Wars of the Maccabees. Death of Antiochus. Prophecies fulfilled in him. Destruction of the Grecian, and establishment of the Roman empire, the legs and feet of Nebuchadnezzar's image. Prosperous state of the Jews under Jonathan and Simon. Apochryphal books.

WE have hitherto contemplated the Jews in favorable circumstances. They had had some internal conflicts and outward oppressions, but they had also enjoyed the protection of mighty monarchs, and had become a populous and wealthy nation. Vital piety had exceedingly declined, especially after the death of Simon the Just; but the Temple stood in its glory, and its service was strictly observed. But we are now to contemplate an awful and melancholy reverse. We are to behold the whole nation nearly destroyed; their religion almost extirpated, and the Temple of Jehovah dedicated to Jupiter Olympus.

The successor of Seleucus in the Syrian monarchy, was Antiochus Epiphanes. He took the throne 175 B. C. The prophet Daniel predicted that he should be a "vile person."*
Such he proved himself, by all his private and public conduct. The first of his acts which seriously affected the Jews, was his selling the High Priesthood to Jason, brother to Onias,

---
* Daniel xi. 1.

the reigning High Priest, for 360 talents, about 90,000 pounds sterling; and issuing an order for the removal of Onias, a person worthy of this sacred trust, to Antioch; there to be confined for life. Jason, despising the religion of his ancestors, and resolved to make himself popular with the unprincipled youth of his nation, procured also a royal decree for the erection of a gymnasium, or place for games and amusements, similar to those established in Grecian cities; and by example and rewards, encouraged the people to attend upon it, and conform to the manners and customs of the heathen. The flood gates of vice being set open, all respect for the law of Moses and the Temple, was soon swept away; the very priests mingled in the amusements of the gymnasium; the altar of God was forsaken, and vice, immorality, and infidelity stalked forth triumphant.

Jason, however, enjoyed his power but a short period. After a reign of three years, he was supplanted by Menelaus, his brother, a greater monster in wickedness than himself, B. C. 174. Such men sought the office, first because it was hereditary in their family; but chiefly, because it now embraced the temporal government of Jerusalem. Menelaus publicly apostatized to the religion of the Greeks, and drew as many as possible in his train. He sold the sacred vessels from the sanctuary, to pay the enormous sum of three hundred talents, by which he had supplanted his brother; and caused Onias, who had reproved him for his sacrilege, to be put to death. But some virtue remained with the people, for they resented this sacrilege, put to death the instrument by which it was effected, and sent messengers to Antiochus, complaining of its vile author.

In strict fulfillment of the divine prediction in Daniel xi. 25, this vile king advanced with his armies, and conquered Egypt. Ptolemy Philometer fell into his hands, but he was not destroyed. On the contrary, he had his liberty, and sat at the table of Antiochus as Daniel predicted he would, v. 27. "And both these kings' hearts shall be to do mischief, and they shall speak lies at one table." The Jews had a false report of his death, and Jason immediately marched into the city with a thousand men, to avenge himself on Menelaus. Antiochus hearing of this, and of the rejoicings in Jerusalem, supposed that the whole city and nation had revolted from him, and hastily marched into Jerusalem, put to death 40,000 persons, and sold an equal number for slaves. He broke into the Holy of Holies, robbed the Temple of the altar of incense, the show-bread table, and the candlestick of seven branches, which were all of gold; the recent gifts of friendly monarchs, and to show his contempt and hatred of the Jewish religion, he sacrificed a hog upon the altar of burnt offering. He made Philip, a man of ferocious spirit, governor of Judea, and restored Menelaus to the High Priesthood. Jason died a miserable vagabond. In about two years, the Egyptians revolted from Antiochus, and he again fell furiously on them. But the Romans interposed, and demanded a cessation of hostilities. Antiochus having read the decree of the senate, said he would consult with his friends about it. But the Roman Ambassador drew around him a circle in the sand, and required his answer before he passed its bounds. Afraid of this bold and rising power, he acquiesced; but he turned and wreaked his vengeance on the unoffending Jews. He sent twenty-two thousand men under Appollonius, to sack Jerusalem. The inhabitants were unaware of his horrid intentions, until the Sabbath after his arrival; when all being assembled for worship, he let loose upon them his troops, who butchered all the men within their reach, took the women and children to sell for slaves; set fire to the houses; demolished the walls, and carried away all the treasure. The Temple was suffered to stand, but a fortress was built near it, for the molestation of all who should approach it, so that no one dared to come near, and the daily sacrifice ceased. Such as escaped the carnage, fled to the mountains, and lived in great distress and hardships.

Antiochus gloried in the greatest barbarities. In the language of Daniel, he had "peculiar indignation against the holy covenant," and he determined to destroy the Jewish religion, or extirpate the nation. He issued, therefore, a decree, that all nations within his dominions should forsake their former rites and usages, and should conform to the religion of the king, and worship as he worshipped, under the severest penalties. To insure success, he placed inspectors in every province, and directed them to treat the disobedient, (and these he knew would be Jews only,) with the greatest severity. An old and cruel minister, one Atheneas, was sent to Jerusalem with a commission to destroy any one who offered sacrifices to the God of Israel, or observed the Sabbath, or practiced circumcision. He consecrated the temple of Jehovah to Jupiter Olympus, and set up his statue upon the altar of burnt offering. He also set up altars, groves, and statues in all parts of his dominion, and required an absolute uniformity of worship, or the forfeiture of life. It was one of the boldest attempts to extirpate the religion of a nation ever made.

But God was in the midst of his church, and the gates of hell could not prevail against her. The land might be desolate; the Temple might be shut up or polluted; the daily sacrifice might cease, but there were many temples of the Holy Ghost in which the fire of devotion burned with unwonted brightness. It was, however, an awful season for the Jews. They were hid in the caves of the rocks, where they worshipped God, and subsisted on roots and herbs. Hypocrites threw off their disguises and proclaimed themselves heathen; and the Samaritans, who had said to the Jews in their prosperity, we will go with you, for we are bone of your bone, now ran to Antiochus and declared themselves not to be Jews, and requested that their temple might be dedicated to the Grecian Jupiter. When the saints were brought to martyrdom, their intrepid firmness filled the tyrant with rage and madness. Among others who were put to a violent death, were the venerable Eleazer, and an aged woman, with her seven sons.* Their triumphant deaths strengthened their brethren, and the tyrant found it was not in his power to destroy the worship of Jehovah.

To violence, Antiochus added the most seducing arts to bring the Jews to a compliance with his orders. Among his chief officers was one Apelles, whom he sent to the city of Modin, there to establish the heathen worship. Apelles assembled the people, and addressing Mattathias, a venerable priest, of the Asmonean family, endeavored by compliment and promises, to induce him to lead the way in apostatizing from God and sacrificing to the idol. But Mattathias feared God; and, with a loud voice, declared in hearing of all the people, that "no consideration whatever, should induce him or any of his family, ever to forsake the law of their God; but that they would still walk in the covenant which he had made with their forefathers, and observe all its ordinances, and that no commands of the king should make any of them depart from it." Of such a man the world was not worthy. He stood for God in defiance of the greatest dangers. Looking

---

* See Plate 1.

round, he beheld an apostate already bowing before the idol which Apelles had set up. Immediately, with the zeal and spirit of Phinehas, and in obedience to the law of Moses, he ran upon him and slew him. By the assistance of his sons, he slew also Apelles, and those who attended him, destroyed the idol, and then fled to the mountains.

It was the signal for revolt. It was the commencement of a defensive war, which terminated in the deliverance of Judah. Large numbers of Jews flocked immediately to his standard, and made a bold and vigorous defence of their civil and religious privileges. Finding that the royal army took great advantage of the Sabbath, Mattathias and his party agreed to defend themselves on that holy day. Their adversaries, therefore, had no opportunity to gain advantages over them as before; but were struck with terror at their boldness and fortitude, and every where yielded before them. The graven images were destroyed; the Jewish synagogues were opened; the law and the prophets* were read; the practice of circumcision was revived; and, in the short space of a year, there was a general restoration of religious order.

Mattathias was permitted to enjoy but a little season his holy triumphs. The close of the year 166 B. C., saw him resting from his labors. With his dying breath he exhorted his sons to constancy and courage in defence of their liberties and the religion of their fathers. His son Judas was appointed his successor. He raised a small but resolute army, and erected his standard, on which was inscribed a motto from Exodus xv.—" Who is like unto thee among the gods, O Jehovah." This was written by an abbreviation, formed by putting the initial letters of the Hebrew words together, which made the word MACCABEES. Hence all who fought under this standard were called Maccabees or Maccabeans.

Judas was an illustrious warrior. He soon made the Syrians, the Samaritans, and apostate Jews tremble before him. Powerful armies were sent against him, but were obliged to retire in ignominy. In his last battle he gained a signal victory with about 3,000 men, over Lysias, the Syrian governor,

---

* Antiochus forbade the reading of the law in the synagogues, and the Jews substituted the prophets. From this time both the law and the prophets were read every Sabbath day.

with an army of 65,000. The latter, abandoning all attempts to subdue the victorious Maccabees, they marched to Jerusalem, destroyed the idols which Antiochus had set up; pulled down the altar which the heathens had erected; purified the Temple, made a new altar, candlestick, and table of pure gold; hung a new veil before the Holy of Holies, and caused the worship of God, which had been interrupted for three years and a half, to be resumed in its primitive splendor. In commemoration of this event, an annual festival was appointed, called the *feast of dedication*, which was continued until the days of our Saviour, and honored by his presence. The Jews, however, were unable to take the tower, which overlooked the Temple. This, and the continual incursions of the surrounding nations, who were exasperated at the re-establishment of the Jewish nation and religion, marred exceedingly the happiness of the people, kept them humble, and tried their confidence in God, amid the most astonishing victories.

While the Maccabees had been regaining their liberties, Antiochus was engaged in wars in the east; but no sooner had intelligence reached him of their boldness and success, than he was filled with violent rage, and he resolved upon the entire extirpation of the whole house of Israel. But no sooner had he made his vow and set out upon his march towards the devoted nation, than he was seized with an incurable and horrid disease, which soon put an end to his life, 164 B. C. With his dying breath, he acknowledged that his sufferings were justly inflicted by the God of Israel, for his bitter persecutions of that people. This vile prince, and great oppressor of the church, was more particularly pointed out by Daniel, in his eleventh chapter, from the twentieth verse, than any other ruler whom he noticed. Porphyry, one of the most bitter enemies to Christianity, acknowledged that no prophecies were ever delivered more clearly, or fulfilled more exactly, but said they were written after the events foretold had taken place, and were no other than historical narratives. But Daniel's prophecies were written in Chaldee, and had actually been translated into Greek before any of these events transpired.

About this time, the Grecian Empire, denoted by the belly and thighs of brass of Nebuchadnezzar's image, was overthrown, and the Roman, marked out by the legs of iron, and the feet part of iron and part of clay, established. The Romans founded their city, 753 B. C.; yet they were but little known in the east until about 274 B. C., when hearing of their victories over the nations around them, Ptolemy Philadelphus, king of Egypt, sent ambassadors to make an alliance with them. This led them to interfere in the contentions of the eastern monarchs, until, finally, they brought them all under their dominion, and established the most extensive and powerful empire the world had seen. But the feet were part of iron and part of clay. As the Romans extended their dominion, they embraced in their empire vast hordes of barbarous nations, which so weakened it, that it was ultimately divided into ten lesser kingdoms, denoted by the ten toes of the image. The efforts of Judas, after the death of Antiochus, to defend himself against the heathen nations around Jerusalem, who had confederated to destroy all who worshipped Jehovah, were uniformly successful. This exceedingly enraged Lysias, the guardian of the young monarch, Antiochus Upator, who immediately brought against Jerusalem an army of 80,000 men, with all the horse of the kingdom, and eighty elephants, determining to make Jerusalem an habitation for the Gentiles, set the High Priesthood for sale, and make gain of the Temple. But Judas and his army, having, as usual, implored aid from heaven, fell upon him, slew eleven thousand foot and sixteen hundred horsemen, and put all the rest to flight. Peace ensued. Through the influence of the Romans, the Jews were no longer obliged to conform to the religion of the Greeks, but were permitted every where to live according to their own laws. This was the first time the Church of God ever felt the power of Rome, B. C. 163.

But this peace was of short duration. The war was first renewed by the men of Joppa. Judas was again successful, and laid siege to the tower of Acra, which overlooked the Temple. This brought from Antioch the young king, with an hundred thousand foot, twenty thousand horse, thirty-two elephants and three hundred chariots of war. The watchword of Judas was "VICTORY IS OF GOD." Having given this, he attacked the enemy, and made a great slaughter, but was unable to resist such a mighty force, and retreated into Jerusalem. The monarch pursued and laid siege to the sanctuary. The Jews defended themselves with bravery, and were reduced to the lowest extremities, when the royal army was called away to quell a rebellion in Syria. A truce was granted, and the king was admitted within the walls. These he promised to leave untouched; but beholding their strength, he disregarded his oath and leveled them with the dust.

The apostate High Priest Menelaus, now hoped for a restoration to his office, but his character was well understood by the Syrian government, and they condemned him to a horrid death, and appointed Alcimus, a man of equal baseness, to the office. The people, however, refused to admit him to the altar. It had been predicted by the prophet Isaiah, that there should " be an altar to the Lord in the midst of the land of Egypt," and Onias, the proper heir to the priesthood, indignant at this appointment, went thither, and on the ground of this prophecy, petitioned Ptolemy to grant him liberty to erect a temple in his dominions. The Egyptian king assigned him a place in Heliopolis, the city of the sun. A temple was erected after the model of the temple of Jerusalem, and divine worship was instituted. This temple stood 224 years, when it was destroyed by Vespasian.

Alcimus, rejected of the people, sought protection of Demetrius, the monarch of Syria. Powerful armies were sent to his support. For protection, Judas sought an alliance with the Romans. A league of mutual defence was made. But before the embassy had returned, the royal armies were but too successful; the small army of Judas was surrounded, and he fell, covered with wounds, a martyr to his country, 160 B. C.

The death of this illustrious warrior was a severe stroke to the Jewish nation. They were at once scattered and devoured as sheep before ravenous wolves. Their calamities had never been greater than they now were, since the captivity. Still, however, hoping in God, the Jews flocked around Jonathan, the brother of Judas, and made him their leader.

Jonathan appears not to have possessed the military prowess of his brother; but he was a man of courage and prudence. He continued at the head of the nation seventeen years, when he and his children, and about a thousand of his guards were treacherously assassinated by Tryphon, a Syrian usurper, in the city of Ptolemais, 144 B. C. But two years was he troubled by the Syrians, with whom his brother had had such errible conflicts. For finding so able a commander at the nead of the Jewish forces, and being disturbed by their own internal divisions, they made peace, and solemnly engaged never to renew the war.

Jonathan improved the season of peace for the restoration of civil and ecclesiastical order. He repaired the wall of Jerusalem, and formed alliances with the Romans. The wicked Alcimus, having the presumption to break down the wall which he had built round the sanctuary, by order of the prophets Haggai and Zechariah, to separate the Gentiles from the Jews, was, it is said, smitten of God, and perished in agony. The priesthood remained vacant for seven years, when the people pressed it upon Jonathan, and the appointment was confirmed by the Syrian monarch.

Tryphon, the base murderer of Jonathan, aiming at the throne of Syria, immediately besieged Jerusalem; but the people elevated Simon, the surviving brother of Judas and Jonathan, to the head of the army, and he was afraid to make any attack. Simon continued both general and High Priest, for the term of eight years; when he was treacherously murdered by his son-in-law, B. C. 135. His reign was one of much prosperity to the Jewish nation. They had friendly alliances with the Romans and Lacedemonians; enjoyed the civil and religious institutions of their fathers, and were victorious over the petty marauders who troubled them. Simon erected at Modin, a very costly monument of white marble, over the sepulchre of his father and brothers, which was for centuries a famous sea-mark, and which was standing so late as the days of Eusebius, 200 years after Christ.

With the death of Simon terminates what is usually called the history of the Maccabees. This history is chiefly contained in the first book of the Maccabees, which was probably written by some cotemporary author, who had been an actor in the scenes which he so minutely and feelingly describes. It was never admitted into the sacred canon, but approaches nearer the style of sacred history than any work extant, and is generally received as an accurate account of the events of that period. From it Josephus chiefly copied the history of that period. The second book of Maccabees consists of several pieces compiled together. It is written with much less accuracy than the first, and contains much that is extravagant and fabulous.

The Apocryphal books, which are often printed and bound with the sacred volume, were all probably written in these latter days of the Jewish Church. They are, therefore, venerable for their antiquity; and some of them, as the first book of Maccabees, impart valuable historical information; others, as the books of Wisdom and Ecclesiasticus, afford much useful instruction; but none of them have any title to inspiration. They were never admitted into the canon of the Jews, to whom alone were committed the oracles of God. They formed no part of the Septuagint version. They were never quoted, either as prophetic or doctrinal, by our Saviour or his apostles. Some of their authors disclaim all pretensions to inspiration; and some of them contain things which are weak and low; utterly inconsistent with probability and chronology, and at variance with the general character of divine truth. They are considered as canonical, and as of equal authority with the writings of Moses and the prophets by the church of Rome; but they certainly ought never to be connected or circulated with the sacred volume.

CHAPTER IX.

Prosperous state of the Jews under Hyrcanus. Royalty re-established. Jerusalem taken by the Romans. End of the Asmonean princes. Herod the Great. The Temple repaired and enlarged. Family of Herod. Sceptre departed from Judah. Religious sects among the Jews—Pharisees, Sadducees, Essenes, Herodians, Galileans, Karaites. Different orders of men—Scribes, Rabbis, Nazarites. Wickedness of the Jews, and of the heathen. State of the civil world. Reflections on the providence of God.

SIMON was succeeded in the Jewish government and priesthood, by his son, John Hyrcanus, 135 B. C. Antiochus Sidetes king of Syria, hearing of the death of Simon, marched against Jerusalem, determined to subdue it. A tremendous siege ensued, and the inhabitants almost perished by famine. They sued at length for peace. Antiochus granted it, requiring the Jews to deliver up their arms, demolish their fortifications, and pay him an annual tribute. The sudden death of this monarch enabled the Jews soon after to cast off the foreign yoke, and they were never again subjected to the Syrian power. Hyrcanus maintained his authority twenty-nine years, and died in peace, greatly lamented. Under him the Jews enjoyed greater prosperity, and were raised to greater heights of glory, than they had ever attained since the Babylonish captivity. By him the capital of the Samaritans, and the Temple which was erected on Mount Gerizim, were destroyed. The Samaritans, however, continued to have an altar on that Mount, and to worship there.

Under his reign, the Edomites joined themselves to the Jews, and both Jacob and Esau became consolidated in one nation. The Jews recognized two kinds of proselytes—proselytes of the gate and of justice. The former renounced idolatry, but did not conform strictly to the law of Moses; such were Naaman, the Syrian, and Cornelius, the centurion. They were admitted into the Temple to worship God, but came no further than into the outer court, which was hence called the court of the Gentiles. The others observed the whole Jewish law. They were initiated by baptism, sacrifice and circumcision, and were admitted to all the privileges of the Jews. Such did the Edomites become.

Hyrcanus was succeeded by his son Aristobulus. He assumed the title of king. He was the first Jewish ruler, who, after the Babylonian captivity, wore a crown. He was a prince and High Priest of great cruelty. He put to death his own mother and brother, and at the close of one year died in great horror of conscience, for his crimes. During his reign, the Itureans were vanquished, and compelled, as was the custom towards all captives, to receive circumcision, and be engrafted into the Jewish state.

Alexander Jannæus, his brother, ascended the throne upon the death of Aristobulus. He was a martial prince, and fought many successive battles with the surrounding nations. But he had a more terrible enemy at home than abroad. This was the sect of the Pharisees, which had occasioned much trouble to John Hyrcanus, but which now came out in open war against this sovereign, and endeavored to drive him from the throne. They hired foreign troops, and compelled him once to flee to the mountains alone. At length, however, he gained a decisive victory over them, took 800 of them captive and caused them all to be crucified in one day. This rebellion lasted six years, and cost the lives of about 50,000 of the faction. He reigned twenty-six years, and left the throne to his wife, 79 B. C.

This woman committed the government entirely to the Pharisees, by which she acquired great popularity. But having the power in their hands, they immediately commenced a violent persecution of the Sadducees, a rival sect, who had been the supporters of Alexander. This was followed with much shedding of blood until they were placed for security, at their own request, in the several garrisons. Alexandra died in the ninth year of her reign.

Her son Hyrcanus had been made High Priest and immediately ascended the throne on the death of his mother. But he was driven from it in a short time by Aristobulus, a younger brother. Antipater, governor of Idumea, and father of Herod, took the part of Hyrcanus. The two contending parties appealed to Pompey, the Roman general, and made him arbitrator between them. The shrewd Roman heard them with apparent impartiality, but deferred a decision of the controversy. Aristobulus, jealous of his rival, prepared for war. The Roman general immediately caused him to be imprisoned, and marched his army against Jerusalem. The party of Hyrcanus received him with open arms, and the faction of Aristobulus, who had thrown themselves into the Temple, were but for about three months able to hold out against so powerful an enemy. Twelve thousand Jews were killed by the Romans, and many destroyed themselves. When the Temple was finally taken, the priests moved not from the altars, but suffered themselves to be butchered without resistance, by the soldiery, to the astonishment of Pompey.

Thus did the holy city and Temple fall into the hands of the Romans, 63 B. C. and on the very day which the Jews kept as a solemn fast, for the capture of Jerusalem and the Temple by Nebuchadnezzar, king of Babylon. Pompey wished to see the interior of the Temple. But the Jews protested against it as an awful profanation. With his superior officers, however, he pressed in, lifted the veil, and looked within the Holy of Holies. The whole he treated with great respect. All the treasures he left untouched; and he ordered the priests to offer sacrifice as directed by the law of Moses.

But, according to the prediction of Jacob, the sceptre was not to depart from Judah, nor a law-giver from between his feet, until Shiloh should come. We therefore find the Romans leaving the Jews still to govern themselves. Hyrcanus was continued in the High Priesthood with the appellation of prince, but the walls of Jerusalem were demolished, the Jewish territory was reduced, and the nation was compelled to pay a disgraceful tribute. Aristobulus and his sons were carried to Rome to adorn Pompey's triumph. It was, however, but a short period before this disturber of the public peace obtained his liberty, and Judea was again thrown into desolating dissensions.

CHAPTER 9.] REIGN OF HEROD THE GREAT. 115

Pompey was overpowered by the partizans of Julius Cæsar; who, at the death of that renowned warrior, usurped the supreme authority at Rome. Antipater had assisted him in his wars in Egypt, and was rewarded by the office of lieutenant of Judea, 48 B. C. He soon obtained important posts for his two sons,—the government of Jerusalem for Phasael, and of Galilee for Herod. Cæsar confirmed Hyrcanus in the Priesthood, and conferred such favors upon the Jewish nation, that it could hardly be perceived that they were in bondage to any people.

There was nothing stable, however, among this people, nor even in the thrones of the mighty. Julius Cæsar, one of the most splendid men that adorns the page of civil history, was assassinated in the senate-house; and Hyrcanus was ejected from his rank and station, by Antigonus, the son of his great rival. His vengeance fell also upon the governors of Jerusalem and Galilee. But Herod fled into Egypt, and from thence to Rome; where he put himself under the protection of Mark Antony, who was then in power. Antony gave him the kingdom of Judea. He collected an army; and after a long and distressing war, took the holy city, 37 B. C. Antigonus, the son of Aristobulus, was put to death. He was the last of the Asmonean family. They had reigned in Judea for one hundred and twenty-nine years.

The sceptre now passed for the first time, into the hands of a foreign prince, but still the Jews continued to be governed by their own laws, and their Sanhedrim was the general court of Judicature. We feel, however, when we behold so great an event as this, that the coming of Shiloh is near.

Herod was a monster of cruelty. He was ever filled with jealousy, and all his real and supposed enemies he put, as far as lay in his power, to most cruel deaths. The adherents of Antigonus first felt his rage; their blood flowed freely, and their estates filled his empty coffers. Only two were spared from the Sanhedrim. Disqualified himself for the priesthood, he made Ananel, an inferior and obscure priest, High Priest; but he soon displaced him, and gave the office to Aristobulus, the brother of his wife Mariamne; but him however, he in a short period caused to be drowned in a bath. To give himself authority and power with the Jewish nation, he married Mariamne, a beautiful and accomplished woman of the Asmonean family, the grand-daughter of Hyrcanus; but though he

9*

oved her passionately, she, for his murder of her brother, as bitterly hated him; and in his fury for it, he put her to death. He condemned also her mother and three of his own sons to the loss of life, and exhausted the treasure and spirit of the nation, by his cruel oppressions.

As might naturally be expected, this monster in wickedness despised the Jewish religion and laws. The High Priest he set up and removed, without any regard to hereditary right. He made it continually the great object of his reign, to introduce Roman luxury, and the worship of heathen gods. He built Grecian Temples, and set up idols for worship, and established theatres and games in honor of Augustus the Roman Emperor.

Having reigned in this manner fourteen years, and amassed great treasures, the people became exceedingly disgusted with him; wherefore, to gain their favor, he resolved, 17 B C., to rebuild the Temple. For about nine years, he employed upon it 18,000 men. He made it considerably larger than the Temple which was built by Solomon. Its length and breadth were now one hundred cubits. It was built of immense stones of white marble, which were covered with large plates of pure gold.

Its inclosure was about a furlong square. This was surrounded by a high wall, on the inside of which were erected three galleries, the narrowest about thirty feet wide, and fifty high, but the largest was forty-five feet wide, one hundred high. These galleries were supported by 162 pillars of marble, each about twenty-seven feet in circumference. The wall of this inclosure had four gates towards the west, and one on each of the other sides. The Temple was encompassed with beautiful porches, which were paved with marble. Solomon's porch was at the east gate of the Temple, called beautiful. The women had their separate court, and entered by the east gate, which was overlaid with Corinthian brass. A golden eagle, the arms of the Roman empire, was placed over each gate. And when the Temple was finished, it was with great solemnity dedicated to God. As the whole was executed as a repair of the Temple built by Zerubbabel, it was called the second Temple, into which "the Desire of all nations should come." And as it was continually receiving additions for many years after, the Jews might say in the time of our Saviour, with propriety, " Forty and six years was the **Temple in building.**"

Finding that the sceptre had now about departed from Judah, the pious in Jerusalem were earnestly looking for the coming of Shiloh. They accurately computed also the seventy weeks in Daniel's prophecy, of the coming of Christ, and found that they were about completed. Devout people waited day and night in the Temple for the consolation of Israel; and they who had no special wish for the Messiah in his true character, were looking forward to him as a deliverer from the Roman yoke. So much expectation of the promised king, could not but be viewed by such a man as Herod with the deepest jealousy. And when the long looked for moment arrived, when the promised seed was born, when the glorious Saviour of men entered our world, to set up that kingdom which should break and destroy all kingdoms, immediately this worst of tyrants resolved to destroy him. But by the overruling providence of God he was delivered out of his hands, and in the following year this inhuman tyrant died of a most loathsome disease and in great tortures, having reigned thirty-seven years.

He carried his brutality to the last. For, to prevent the nation from rejoicing at his death, he convened all the distinguished men, shut them up in a castle, and ordered their instant death the moment he should expire. But the order was not executed. Such was the man into whose hands the church had fallen, when her promised deliverer arose. He was called great, but he was chiefly great in crime, and was detestable as he was wicked and base. He left his dominion to three sons;—his kingdom to Archelaus; Gaulonites, Trachonites, and Batanea, to Philip; Galilee and Perea to Herod Antipas.

As this family were intimately connected with the rising Christian Church, some account of them will be both interesting and instructive.

Archelaus interred his father with great pomp. At the commencement of his reign, the Jews, indignant at the profanation of the Temple, pulled down the Roman eagle, which Herod had placed over each of the gates. This occasioned great contentions, and much shedding of blood. His brother Herod contended with him at the Roman court for the crown, but he held it about seven years. His reign was one of such violence and tyranny, that the people brought against him accusations to the emperor, and he was banished to Vienne in France, where he died. Such was the cruelty of his temper, that when Joseph and Mary heard that he reigned in the room of his father Herod, they were afraid to return into Judea with the holy child Jesus. He was succeeded by Roman governors, one of whom was Pontius Pilate. Of Philip, tetrarch of Iturea and Trachonites, little mention is made in the evangelical history.

Herod Antipater, tetrarch of Galilee, was early engaged in war with the Arabs, because he divorced his wife, the daughter of Aretas, their king, that he might marry Herodias, the wife of his brother Philip, who was still living. For this connexion John Baptist reproved him, and lost his life. Soon after John's death, Herod was sent into exile, and he and his wife and Salama all came to a miserable end.

There was another Herod, called Herod Agrippa, who reigned in Judea during the life of the Apostles. He was grandson of Herod the great. He murdered James, and apprehended Peter. While at Cesarea, celebrating some games in honor of Claudius, the inhabitants of Tyre and Sidon sent deputies to him to solicit his favor. Splendidly dressed, he made an oration, and the people shouted, "It is the voice of a god." He was gratified by the impious flattery, and was smitten of heaven with a most tormenting disease, and eaten up of worms, having reigned about ten years. He was the father of Agrippa, Berenice, Drusilla and Mariamne.

The sceptre was now wholly departed from Judah, and the lawgiver from between his feet, for Shiloh had come. The Jews were no longer governed by their own rulers and laws, but by the Roman power. Herod the Great had broken down the power of the Sanhedrim, though it still existed in form, so that Christ and his apostles, and Stephen the deacon, were brought before it. But it possessed not the power over life and death. "It is not lawful," said the Jews to Pilate, "for us to put any man to death." Such was the wonderful fulfillment of the ancient prophecy of Jacob. Other vast nations had long since lost their power, and been buried in oblivion, but Judah had retained her sceptre, because she was protected of heaven.

In the latter age of the Jewish nation, and at the time of our Saviour's appearance, the Jews were divided into a great variety of religious sects. All these acknowledged the authority of the law of Moses, and united in their forms of worship, but they were so far separated by their peculiarities, as to be continually involved in the most bitter hostilities.

The largest and most popular was the sect of the Pharisees. Their rise is uncertain. They probably rose from some small beginning to their great power and consequence. As early as the days of Hyrcanus and Janneus, they threw the nation into great commotion. They believed in the existence of angels, both good and bad, in the immortality of the soul, the resurrection of the body, and future rewards and punishments; but they considered the tradition of the elders, as of equal authority with the written law; and in many places they explained the latter by the former, and explained it in a way directly contrary to its true meaning. Thus they made the commandment of God of none effect, by their traditions. These traditions, they contended, were delivered by God to Moses on Mount Sinai, and preserved through succeeding generations. By these they were instructed that thoughts and desires were not sinful, unless they resulted in evil actions; that fasting, ablution, and almsgiving, made atonement for sin, and that men could even perform works of supererogation. They expected justification through the merits of Abraham.

They derived their name from a Hebrew word which signifies to separate, because they pretended to an uncommon separation from the world, and devotedness to God. They valued themselves upon their frequent washings, fastings, and long prayers; their gravity of dress and gesture; their mortified looks; their scrupulous tithings; their building tombs for the prophets, that they might appear more righteous than their fathers who slew them; their care to avoid every kind of ritual impurity; enlarging their philacteries,* and the borders of their garments; and on their diligence and zeal in making proselytes. But under this specious exterior, they neglected justice, mercy, and truth, and practiced the most abominable vices. They were a race of most demure hypocrites, properly compared by our Saviour to whited sepulchres. They hated the Lord of life and glory, and persecuted him to death.

Of the Pharisees there were several distinct classes—as the truncated Pharisees, who scarcely lifted their feet from the ground, that they might appear in deep meditation; the

---

* These philacteries were pieces of parchment, &c.

striking Pharisees, who walked with their eyes shut that they might avoid the sight of women, and therefore struck continually against the wall as they walked; and the mortar Pharisees, who wore a cap resembling a mortar, which would only permit them to look upon the ground. They ruled entirely the common people, and had all their votes for every civil and religious office.

The next most powerful sect was that of the Sadducees. They were the infidels of the nation. They derived their name from Sadoc, a disciple of Antigonus, who was president of the Sanhedrim, 260 B. C. His master had taught that our service of God should be wholly disinterested, without any regard to a future state. Sadoc from hence reasoned that there was no future state, no heaven nor hell, no resurrection, angel, or spirit. His followers looked upon death, therefore, as the final extinction of soul and body, and maintained that the providence and retributions of God were limited to this world. On this ground only, they pretended to worship and serve God. They rejected the traditions of the Pharisees.

This sect was comparatively small, and was composed chiefly of men of high rank and affluence. Such men gladly embraced this system, because it permitted them to live in sinful indulgence, without any fear of future punishment. Their system was the child of depravity, and it was awfully hardening. We never hear of a Sadducee converted to the Gospel of Christ. The whole sect ever remained bitter opposers of the humble, self-denying doctrines of the Cross. Caiphas and Ananias, the murderers of James the less, were Sadducees.

A third sect were the Essenes. They took their rise about 200 years B. C., and were really an order of monks. They lived in solitary places, and objecting to sacrifices, came seldom to the Temple. They are not therefore mentioned in the New Testament. They were perfect fatalists. They agreed with the Pharisees, except in the resurrection of the body, which they denied. They considered the laws of Moses as an allegorical system of spiritual and mysterious truth; and while they pretended respect to the moral, totally neglected the ceremonial law. They lived in great abstemiousness; renounced marriage; adopted proselytes and children; held riches in contempt; maintained a perfect community of goods; never bought or sold any thing among themselves; wore white garments; rejected every bodily ornament; and triumphed over pain and suffering. They exceeded all other Jews in the strict observance of the Sabbath, and lived quietly, and without noise; engaged much, as they pretended, in heavenly contemplation. They took their name from the Syriac verb *asa*, to heal, because they inquired much into the cures of diseases, especially the moral diseases of the mind. They had their origin in Egypt; 4000 of them resided on the western shore of the Dead Sea. The Therapeute, was a rigid sect of them, and resided chiefly in Egypt.

The Herodians, a fourth sect, derived their name from Herod the Great. They coincided with that monarch in his views of subjecting the Jews to the Romans. It was therefore a fundamental principle with them, that it was right for the Jews to comply with idolatry and heathen customs, if required by their superiors; and also, that it was a duty to submit and pay taxes to him whom conquest had made their master. They were therefore opposed to the Pharisees, and being also opposed to Christ, they unitedly engaged to catch him in his speech. Had he replied to the question, "Is it lawful to give tribute to Cæsar?" in the negative, the Herodians would have accused him to the Emperor; or in the affirmative, the Pharisees, who would acknowledge no foreign prince, would have accused him to the people. Christ, by his wisdom, avoided the snares of both. When he charged his disciples to beware of the leaven of Herod, he no doubt had particular reference to their compliance with the idolatrous rites of the heathen. The Sadducees were generally Herodians.

The Galileans were a few inhabitants of Galilee, who were instigated by one Judas to resist the Roman tax. By this resistance they began the war with the Romans, which terminated in the destruction of the nation. They held the religious sentiments of the Pharisees. Some of them, while worshipping at Jerusalem, were barbarously murdered by Pilate, in the court of the Temple, and their blood was mingled with their sacrifices. Our Saviour was accused as a Galilean, who went about stirring up the nation to revolt, and refusing to give tribute to Cæsar.

The Karaites were the protestants of the Jewish nation. The name denotes a scripturalist, and was given them about twenty years before the birth of Christ. They boldly protested against all the traditions of the elders, as having no divine authority, and strictly adhered to the written law. They have been, from that day to this, the most pious and orthodox of all the sects.

Besides these religious sects, there were three orders of men which claim particular notice—the Scribes, Rabbis, and Nazarites.

The Scribes were originally men who registered the affairs of the king. At a subsequent period they transcribed the books of Scripture, and thus became more conversant with it than other men. In our Saviour's time, they were an important order of men, who expounded the law and tradition of the elders; taught them in the schools and synagogues, and reasoned concerning them before the Sanhedrim. They are variously called scribes, lawyers, doctors of the law, elders, counselors, and rulers, and those who sat in Moses' seat. They were a most wicked class, who abominably perverted the Scriptures.

The title Rabbi, was given to men of rank in the state, but especially to Jewish doctors, who were eminent for learning. It was given to John by his disciples; to Christ, by Nicodemus and the wondering populace. Those who received it among the doctors, claimed an absolute dominion over the faith of the people. But it was a title wholly disapproved of by our Saviour. He said to his disciples, " be not ye called Rabbi ;" i. e. covet no such distinctions in the Church of God ; aspire to no honor but that of faithfully serving your Lord and Master.

The Nazarites were a class of men separated from the world for some limited period, or for life, by a vow. During their vow, they were never to cut their hair, or drink any wine or strong drink. They were to attend no funeral, nor enter a house defiled by the dead. When the days of their offering were fulfilled, all their hair was shaved off at the door of the tabernacle, and burnt under the altar. Every seventh day they were called to offer peculiar offerings. Those who, like Sampson, Samuel, and John Baptist, were dedicated for life, had no occasion for these offerings. Such as lived far from Jerusalem, cut their hair in the places where their vow was finished, but deferred their offerings until they came to the Temple. Paul once, on some special occasion, became a Nazarite of Corinth, shaved his head at Cenchrea, and made his offering at Jerusalem.

CHAPTER 9.] GENERAL CORRUPTION OF THE JEWS. 123

Christ was styled a Nazarite or Nazarene, from the circumstance of his spending much of his life at Nazareth. No particular prophecy which is preserved to us was thus fulfilled, but the general spirit of prophetic writings respecting him clearly was; for these indicated that he should be a true Nazarite, a person uncommonly separated from his birth, to the service of God. Well, therefore, might the evangelist say, " it was fulfilled which was spoken by the prophets, he shall be called a Nazarene."

Amid the clashing of various sects, the formality and hypocrisy of the Pharisees, the monkish austerity of the Essenes, and the freethinking of the Sadducees, vital piety had almost expired with the nation. The Jews indeed adhered to the worship of the one true God, and venerated the Mosaic law, but they fully believed that they could atone for the vilest transgressions.

They looked for the Messiah, but they expected him only as a temporal prince, who would deliver them from Roman bondage, by a zealous performance of external rites; they so gave themselves up to the grossest wickedness, that Josephus, their eminent historian, remarks, "Had the Romans delayed calling these abandoned wretches to account, their city would either have been deluged by water, or swallowed by an earthquake, or destroyed like Sodom, by thunder and lightning."

As was remarked in the history of idolatry, the rest of the world was now sunk in the most deplorable state of heathen superstition. All nations imagined the upper world to be filled with superior beings, whom they called gods; one or more of which, they supposed, to preside over every province, people, family, element, production and passion. These deities were diverse from each other in nature, sex, rank, and power, and were all appeased and honored by peculiar gifts, rites and ceremonies. Over all, a supreme divinity was generally supposed to preside, who, though more excellent than the rest, was controlled by the fates.

Through a national ambition, the Greeks and Romans gave the names of their own deities to those of other nations whom they subdued; but religious wars were unknown; for every nation suffered their neighbors to enjoy their own gods, rites, and ceremonies, considering them as their peculiar province. Some of these gods were furnished from the natural world, as the sun, moon, and stars; but the most of them were deified heroes. Statues and other representations of them were placed in their temples. These temples were exceedingly magnificent. An amazing priesthood was richly supported; but their prayers and ceremonies were of the most foolish and debasing character. There were certain institutions called *mysteries*, to which only a few were initiated, and which were very imposing upon the common people.

But in the whole system of paganism there was no tendency to virtue. Indeed, morality seems never to have had a place in the religion of a pagan. In the high *mysteries*, things were transacted which outraged common decency. Almost every god was a patron of some vice. The gods themselves were supposed to be guilty often of the basest crimes. The Greeks and Romans, therefore, the most refined nations of antiquity, were sunk in the lowest sensualities. Their own best writers, such as Horace, Tacitus, Juvenal, confirm the account given of the low moral character of the people, in the second chapter of the Epistle to the Romans. Philosophy has done all that it ever can do, unassisted by revelation, in the discovery of truth, and reformation of mankind; and it finally debased the human mind by the most perplexing subtleties, and spread abroad the most demoralizing sentiments. The most popular sect was that of Epicurus, who maintained that pleasure was the chief end of man's existence, and that it was no matter in what way it was obtained, though it was through the lowest sensual indulgence. These powerful nations had no knowledge of the true God, of human accountableness, and the future state of the soul. Satan every where reigned tri umphant, and no ray of hope appeared to the eye of reason, of any release from his iron bondage.

At the same time, the state of the world was admirably adapted to the rapid diffusion of the Gospel of Christ. The Roman empire was in its greatest glory. All the nations of the known world were subjected to it; dominion and peace were every where established. Vast nations, therefore, were united in friendly intercourse; many and barbarous tribes were reduced to civilized life. Literature had risen to a height never before obtained. The Grecian tongue was almost every where read or spoken. Free access was had to all nations, and the Gospel could easily be preached to every creature under the whole heaven.

In concluding the second great period in the history of the church, let us pause and reflect on the wonderful providence of God. He had now protected and preserved her during a period of 4000 years, while nation after nation had risen and sunk like the waves of the ocean. All the prophecies respecting her and the nations of the earth, which were due, had hitherto been strictly fulfilled. The four great empires had risen in succession, and had been the rod of God's anger, or instruments to her good. All the sacrifices and offerings of the law had fully shadowed forth the one great sacrifice which was now to make reconciliation for iniquity, and bring in everlasting righteousness. "Her walls had been continually before him." The past was a pledge for the fulfillment of promises of future good. He who raised up the four vast monarchies of the earth, would now set up a kingdom which should never be destroyed, and which should break in pieces and consume all kingdoms. Well might all people exclaim with an heathen prince, "How great are his signs, and how mighty are his wonders! His kingdom is an everlasting kingdom, and his dominion is from generation to generation."

PERIOD III.

FROM THE BIRTH OF CHRIST TO THE PRESENT TIME.

CHAPTER I.

Birth of Jesus Christ. Jesus circumcised. Welcomed by saints and angels. Worshipped by the wise men. Sought for by Herod. Carried into Egypt. Conversant at twelve years with the Doctors. Lives in retirement until thirty years of age. Birth, character, and work of John the Baptist. Jesus baptized by him, and consecrated to the Priesthood. Christ's ministry. Abolition of the Jewish, and establishment of the Christian Church. Christ's Priesthood. His death, resurrection, and ascension. Jesus, King in Zion. Evidences of his divine mission.

JESUS CHRIST, the Saviour of men, was born of the Virgin Mary, at Bethlehem in Judea, in the year of the world four thousand; four years before the vulgar era. His miraculous birth was foretold with astonishing precision, by the prophet Isaiah.* To Mary it was revealed before conception, by the angel Gabriel. Like other wonderful works of God, it has been the scoff of the wicked; but the pure in heart behold in it a striking correspondence with the purity and dignity of the Redeemer's person and office.

Mary was a direct descendant from David, through Nathan. Christ was therefore of the seed of David, according with the language of prophecy, though not of the royal line. Her genealogy is given by Luke. Before his birth she was espoused to Joseph, a direct descendant from David in the royal line. He became his reputed father. His genealogy is given by Matthew. Hence Jesus might be called, KING OF THE JEWS.†

The place of his birth was predicted by Micah. "But thou, Bethlehem Ephratah, though thou be but little among the thousands of Judah, yet out of thee, shall he come forth unto me that is to be ruler of Israel, whose goings forth have been from of old, from everlasting." Thither his parents, who were inhabitants of Galilee, were brought in the fullness of time, by an imperial edict, to be enrolled for taxation.‡

---

*Isaiah vii. 14. †Isaiah v. 2.
‡ An objection has been raised against this part of inspired history from a well authenticated fact, that Cyrenius, in whose days this taxing is said

Obscurity and lowliness marked his birth. He was laid in a manger.

On the eighth day from his birth, the holy child was circumcised, from a sacred regard to divine institution, and called Jesus, because he should save his people. As sent and anointed of God, to perform the work of Mediator, he was the Christ or Messiah ; and hence he has sustained the double appellation, JESUS CHRIST.

The birth of the Saviour filled the hearts of the people of God, who had been looking for his advent, with exceeding joy. Simeon and Anna, aged saints, paid him, as he was presented in the Temple, their joyful gratulations. An innumerable company of angels were heard, by shepherds in the field, praising God and saying, "Glory to God in the highest, and on earth peace, good will toward men." An extraordinary star or meteor appeared in the heavens, and conducted certain wise men to worship him;—going before them, as did the pillar of fire before the Israelites in the wilderness until they came to Jerusalem. No earthly prince ever entered the world in such majesty and glory. The question of the wise men, "Where is he that is born King of the Jews?" troubled Herod and all Jerusalem. The bloody monarch, without delay, sought his death. And when baffled in his scheme by an overruling providence, he made havoc of all the children of Bethlehem under two years; bringing on a scene of wo, like that on which the prophet Jeremiah, ages before, had fixed his eye. "Rachel weeping for her children, and would not be comforted." The holy child was carried into Egypt, where he remained, until, directed by heaven, his parents returned and dwelt in Nazareth.

Such a concurrence of circumstances must have made the infant Messiah the object of general attention, to an extent of which, we, at this distance of time, can have but faint conceptions.

At twelve years of age, his parents took him with them on their annual visit to Jerusalem, at the feast of the passover. There he conversed with the Jewish doctors, and the divinity

---

to have been, was not governor of Syria until ten or twelve years after the birth of Jesus. But the difficulty is solved, by distinguishing between the enrollment of the citizens, and the actual collection of taxes, which was not until the time of Cyrenius. The avidity with which infidels seize such apparent contradictions, shows the weakness of their cause.

shone forth in him. "All were astonished at his understanding and answers." When sought by his parents, from whom he had wandered, he said, Wist ye not that I must be about my father's business? a proof that he did not remain till manhood ignorant of the great purpose for which he came into the world. He submissively returned with them to Nazareth where he remained until he was about thirty years of age, probably in the employment of his father, who was a carpenter.

"Great is the mystery of godliness, God manifest in the flesh." Not only the person of the Redeemer, but the lateness of his appearance, and his obscurity after the great excitement at his birth, and conversation with the doctors in the Temple, are unaccountable to many.

The occurrence of events is resolvable only into the divine sovereignty. God brings every thing to pass according to his own pleasure. Yet to the inquiry, Why did not the Saviour appear hundreds and thousands of years before? it may be replied, that by delay time was given for a full exhibition of the evil nature and power of sin, and of the utter insufficiency of all ordinary means to reform the world; while his character and offices, life and death, were marked out by a great variety of typical and verbal predictions, by which the world were at once qualified to judge of his character and work, whenever he should appear. On the subject of his retirement, it may be remarked, that he came to be an HIGH PRIEST in the Church of God, and that he refrained from becoming a preacher of righteousness, until he had attained his thirtieth year, and might strictly conform to the Jewish law. It is manifest, from the astonishment produced by his conversation with the doctors, that he might at any period have called to himself the attention of the world. The rulers were alarmed at his birth, but they soon died, and the power passed into the hands of others, who knew him not. The mass of the people were ignorant and vicious. They looked only for some great temporal prince, who should deliver them from Roman bondage. If their attention had once been excited by a wonderful child, who appeared amid many signs, it would soon subside, as he passed from their notice. Especially as it was an age of general expectation, when others were probably held up to view as the long expected deliverer. But he was not unknown and forgotten by the pious. His mother treasured up every thing in her heart, which developed his greatness. And had we a more minute history of his course, we should doubtless find many of the people of God looking anxiously toward him as a wonderful messenger from Heaven. "He increased in wisdom and stature, and was in favor with God and man."

Malachi the last of the ancient prophets, closed his writings and the canon of the Old Testament, with a prediction of John the Baptist, under the character of Elijah the prophet.

That holy man was born six months before the Saviour, of Zecharias, an aged priest, and Elizabeth. He was to be the forerunner of Christ. In apparel, temper, austerity, boldness in reproving vice, and zeal for God, he strongly resembled that eminent prophet whose name he bore. In about the twenty-eighth year of Christ, he began to proclaim to men the approach of the gospel kingdom, to call sinners to repentance, and to baptize such as confessed their sins and turned to God.

His baptism was not Christian baptism. It was not administered in the name of the Father, of the Son, and of the Holy Ghost. It was not an initiation into the Christian Church, for the gospel dispensation was yet to come. It was one of those divers washings which belong to the Jewish economy. He disclaimed a baptism like to that of Christ. Some, therefore, who had been baptized with the baptism of John, afterward received Christian baptism from the hands of Paul. They had not so much as heard of the Holy Ghost.*

While John was baptizing at the river Jordan, Jesus came to be baptized of him. He came not as a sinner confessing his sins, to be baptized unto repentance, for he was perfectly holy; not to receive any emblem of regeneration, for he needed no change of heart; not to be admitted into the Christian Church, for this was not yet established; but to be legally and solemnly consecrated as High Priest to his people. Under the law, the priests were consecrated to their office by baptism and anointing with oil.† John, evidently not fully understanding the purpose of Jesus, hesitated at a compliance with the request, thinking that he, as a sinner, had need to be baptized of him; but Christ told him to suffer it, for he must fulfil all righteousness. He had been circum-

---

* Acts xix. † Exodus xxix.

cised in infancy, and had shown respect in all his conduct, to those divine institutions which were still binding upon the people, and he would not force himself into the priesthood in a way which would be illegal. He was therefore baptized by John and anointed, not with oil, but by the Holy Ghost. For "lo! the heavens were opened, and the Spirit of God descended like a dove and lighted upon him." Immediately he retired into the wilderness, where he spent forty days in fasting and prayer, and was tempted by Satan. With detestation and abhorrence, he baffled, by scripture, all the enticements of this arch seducer, who, in his malignancy, had destroyed the first Adam, but who was now to be bruised in the head by the seed of the woman, the second Adam, the Saviour of the world.

Fully qualified for his arduous work, Jesus went forth in the power of the spirit, to set up the gospel kingdom, and to unfold that salvation to a dying world, which he would soon effect through his own death.

For three years and a half he went about through all the cities and villages of Palestine, preaching doctrines which the world had never before heard, and giving in works of benevolence, the most amazing manifestations of Almighty power. As no nation had ever been visited by such an exalted personage, so none was ever thus engrossed, astonished and gratified. Vast crowds thronged him, so that they trod one upon another; and had the common people been heard and gratified, he would have received the adoration of the nation. But the rulers and heads of contending sects, jealous of their rights, and envious, perpetually persecuted him; and ultimately, though according to the determinate counsel and foreknowledge of God,* put him to the excruciating death of the cross.

Jesus Christ was, in all respects, a man. He had a human body, and a reasonable and immortal soul. He had all the human appetites and affections; and all our emotions of joy and sorrow. He hungered and thirsted. He slept. He suffered, bled, and died. At the same time, he knew all things; could do all things; had all power in heaven and on earth, and was IMMANUEL, God with us. Sometimes the actings only of the human nature were seen in him; he was found eating, drinking, sleeping, praying, dying. Again, he was

---

* Acts ii. 23.

seen putting forth the powers of the divine nature; raising the dead; casting out devils; forgiving sin; rising from the grave; ascending to heaven, and sitting on the right hand of the majesty on high—angels, principalities, and powers being made subject to him.

As the PROPHET predicted by Moses, he improved every opportunity to instruct men in divine truth. Sometimes on account of the peculiar prejudices of the Jewish nation, he spake in parables; but these he explained to his disciples, so that his instructions are all plain and intelligible to the unlearned. On the great truths of natural religion, the being and perfections of God, with which the Jews, who had the law and the prophets, were well acquainted, he said but little. He came chiefly to show the ruined state of man as a sinner, and the way of salvation. He fully and clearly taught the total depravity of the human heart; (a) the moral blindness (b) and inability (c) or disinclination of men to submit to God; the absolute necessity of regeneration by the Holy Spirit; (d) divine sovereignty in the dispensations of grace; (e) his own divinity (f) and atonement by his blood; (g) justification by faith; (h) the great duties of repentance, (i) faith, (j) self-denial, (k) disinterested love, (l) universal and perfect obedience; (m) the certain perseverance of all saints in faith and holiness to eternal life; (n) the resurrection of the dead; (o) general judgment; (p) the eternal happiness of the righteous, and eternal misery of the wicked. (q)

"Never man spake like this man." Never man spake such truths;—spake with such plainness, simplicity, authority and power. Astonishment seized all who heard him. The common people gave him the most profound attention, and many were his friends and followers. But the great, the Sadducees and the Pharisees, finding their hollow-heartedness and abominations, exposed, said he was mad, a disturber of the peace, and a blasphemer.

In execution of his prophetic office, Christ abolished the Jewish, and established the Christian Church.

Properly speaking, there has, from the beginning, existed

(a) John v. 42. Mat. xv. 19. (b) John iii. 19. (c) John v. 40, and vi. 44. (d) John iii. 5. (e) Mat. xi. 25. (f) John x. 30. (g) Mat. xx. 28. (h) John iii. 18. (i) Luke xiii. 3. (j) John vi. 29. (k) Mat. xvi. 24 (l) Mat. v. 44. (m) Mat. v. 48. (n) John x. 27. (o) John v. 28. (p) Mat. xxv. 31. (q) Mat. xxv. 46

one Church, and but one. This is the Church of Christ, which he purchased with his own blood. But it has existed under different dispensations. For a long period it was in an unembodied state, without a testimony, a priesthood, or an altar. Under Moses it was brought out of Egypt; had a visible standing among the nations, and became subject to a great variety of ordinances. Christ, the great antitype of these, being now incarnate proceeded to their abolition; placed the Church upon a new establishment, and erected his spiritual kingdom, which should embrace both Jews and Gentiles, and fill the earth with its glory.

His work he gradually accomplished by referring his hearers to ancient Scriptures, and proving from them that he was the great end to which all the former rites and sacrifices did tend, and that these were no longer of use when he should appear; by opening wide the door of the church and declaring that he would draw all men, Gentiles as well as Jews, unto him;—by disregarding totally the Jewish priesthood, and introducing a new ministry into the church;—by passing all the Jewish feasts, and instituting the Lord's supper;—by instituting in place of circumcision, a new seal to the covenant, which God made with his people,—baptism, the washing with water in the name of the sacred Trinity, and commanding its imposition not only upon Jews, but on all nations;— and by prescribing in place of the ceremonial worship of the Jews, a new, simple, and spiritual worship which should be offered by the people of God, not only in Jerusalem, but in all parts of the world.

In these various ways did Christ, according to the prediction of Daniel, cause the oblation and the sacrifice to cease. He knew this would be the result. He predicted the destruction of Jerusalem, the temple and its services;—that not one stone of the temple should be left upon another, that Jerusalem should be trodden down of the Gentiles, and that all this should come to pass during the continuance of that generation.

The history of Christ's priesthood is written in tears and in blood. To the office of priest he was called of God and anointed by the Spirit of grace, which was poured upon him without measure. For it he was eminently fitted; for he was holy, harmless, undefiled, and separate from sinners, made higher than the heavens.

In his priesthood he interceded for his people. Whole nights he spent in prayer. Often did he kneel with his disciples at the throne of grace. The pardon of their sins, their sanctification and final salvation were blessings for which he often wrestled. The seventeenth chapter of John is a most solemn and melting intercession with his Father for all his followers to the end of the world. But his intercession on earth was but the commencement of that great work which he ever lives to perfect in heaven. There stands the Lamb before the throne as it had been slain, presenting the memorials of suffering, and pleading with the God of grace, and opening the holy, heavenly places to all his ransomed ones.

Without shedding of blood, there is no remission of sin. There is a fundamental principle in the moral government of God. And God extended mercy to the first parents of the human race, only in view of a great propitiatory sacrifice in a future age. To regulate the faith and fix the hopes of his people, the priests, under the law, were called continually to offer sacrifices and oblations. But these could not take away sin. Christ alone was mighty to save, and he came to take away sin by the sacrifice of himself. This may emphatically be called the great work for which he came into the world—to make " his soul an offering for sin," to " give his life a ransom for many," to " bear our sins in his own body on the tree," to " redeem us from the curse of the law, being made a curse for us."

How he could offer himself a sacrifice for sin without being guilty of suicide, might appear inexplicable to us, but he was to be slain by the hands of wicked men, who hated him without cause ; while he voluntarily came into the world to die for sinners ; predicted his death, and could at any moment have resisted all human power.

With calmness and solemnity he advanced to the hour of his deep humiliation, his excruciating sufferings. He knew what was in man. He saw clearly all the bitterness and malice that was kindled in the breasts of the Scribes and Pharisees against him, and he knew it would bring him to the most awful sufferings and death. But he did not avoid them. He did not resist them. He resigned himself up to their malignity that his work might be accomplished. Against a character so pure and spotless they found it difficult to proceed. They often endeavored to catch him in his speech, but they were confounded and driven away in shame. They would have rushed upon him and destroyed him without the forms of law ; but they feared the people.

Among his disciples was Judas, a vile hypocrite; who went to the Sanhedrim and agreed to betray him for the price of a slave. Jesus knew his treachery; and prepared for the events which awaited him. Eleven others had followed him who were very dear to him, and with them he purposed to keep the Passover before he should suffer. While at table with the whole, he distinctly pointed out Judas as his betrayer, and said ·to him, "What thou doest, do quickly." Judas, confounded and vexed, went immediately out. The Passover being finished, Jesus consecrated bread and wine, and instituted the sacrament of the supper, which he told them to observe till the end of time. He then made them that long and consolatory address which is recorded in the 14th, 15th, and 16th chapters of John; sang an hymn; offered up that excellent prayer which forms the 17th chapter, and then went out, about midnight, over the brook Cedron to the garden Gethsemane. There he thrice retired from his disciples for prayer, wrestling with God that if it were possible and consistent with the divine will, his sufferings might be prevented. An impression and fear of the divine wrath seemed for a time to overwhelm him; and in the agony of his soul, he sweat as it were great drops of blood. But his piety rose superior to his fears, and he said with holy submission, "Not my will, but thine be done."

Before the day dawned, Judas came with a band of ruffians, and took him and brought him before a convention of priests and elders. As they could find nothing of which to accuse him, they employed false witnesses, who declared that he had spoken against the Temple. But Jesus continued silent. At length the High Priest adjured him by God to tell him whether he was the Messiah. Jesus said he was; and would hereafter in great power and glory, judge the world. Caiaphas immediately rent his clothes; accused him of blasphemy; and the whole court declared him worthy of death. The next day they tried and condemned him again, and hurried him away to the judgment hall of Pilate, the Roman governor; they having lost the power of life and death. Pilate could find no fault in him, and sent him to Herod, then in Jerusalem, because he was a Galilean. But Herod made a mock of him, and sent him back to Pilate, who was afraid to condemn him. But the Jews demanded his crucifixion, and wished that his blood might be upon them and their children. Afraid of the mob, the Roman governor shamefully yielded to their entreaties, and condemned him to the death of the cross.*

Immediately an unbridled populace dragged him amid the grossest insults and abuse, to Golgotha, the place of execution, compelling him to bear his cross. Here they offered him vinegar and myrrh mingled with gall; stripped off his raiment, and nailed him through the hands and feet, to the accursed instrument of death. Two thieves were crucified with him, one on the right hand, the other on the left. On the top of the cross was written in Hebrew, Greek, and Latin, "THIS IS JESUS OF NAZARETH, THE KING OF THE JEWS."

By both rulers and people, he was ridiculed, as he hung suspended in the air; but with his dying breath, he prayed for his murderers, saying, " Father, forgive them, they know not what they do." At first, both the thieves joined in upbraiding him, but one became convinced of his guilt, and was the object of saving mercy. His weeping mother, who now realized the declaration of Simeon, " Yea, a sword shall pierce through thine own soul also," he commended to the care of John, the son of Zebedee. About noon, when he had hung perhaps three hours on the cross, the sun was supernaturally darkened three hours; and under the hidings of God's face, Jesus cried out, " My God, my God, why hast thou forsaken me ?" Some derided him, and said that he called for Elias. Shortly after, he said, " I thirst," and they gave him vinegar to drink. He tasted it; said " It is finished," commended his soul to God; bowed his head and gave up the ghost. Thus did Christ expiate the sins of men. Thus did he bear our griefs and carry our sorrows. " He was wounded for our transgressions, bruised for our iniquities, the chastisement of our peace was upon him, and by his stripes we are healed."

When he expired, the veil of the temple was rent from the top to the bottom, to signify that the ceremonial distinction between Jews and Gentiles was abolished; the earth shook; the rocks burst; graves were opened; and many saints which slept, arose and appeared in Jerusalem. The spectators were filled with terror. The centurion exclaimed, "this was a

---

* The Cross consisted of an upright post of about twelve feet, with a cross piece over the top. On this the unhappy sufferer was first laid. His arms were stretched upon the cross piece, and spikes were driven through the palms of his hands, and through his feet, fastening him to the instrument of death. The whole was then raised in the air, and suddenly

righteous man, was the son of God." "And all the people that came together to that sight, beholding the things that were done, smote their breasts, and returned." "It was the greatest and most solemn event that ever did, or will occur to the end of time."

The crucified body of our Lord was committed to Joseph of Arimathea, and decently laid in a new grave which he had hewn out of a rock in a garden. Christ had foretold his resurrection, and the rulers, apprehensive that his followers might steal the body, and say he had risen, sealed the sepulchre, and placed a guard to watch it, until the third day had passed. But all the prudence and power of men, could not frustrate the designs of heaven. God had determined that his holy One should not see corruption. It was necessary that Christ should rise from the dead, that he might gain a signal victory over him that had the power of death, and become the resurrection and life to all his followers. On the morning of the third day from his crucifixion, was a terrible earthquake. An angel appeared in a glorious form, causing the soldiers to flee in amazement, and rolled the stone from the door of the sepulchre. The Prince of life resumed his breath and active being, and went forth to the world a triumphant conqueror. If his death was the most solemn and awful event, his resurrection was the most joyful which ever occurred. Christ came forth to eternal life. "Death hath no more dominion over him." "I am he that liveth and was dead, and behold, I am alive forevermore, Amen." He came forth the first fruits of them that slept, to give new evidence of his divinity, and of the resurrection of the saints, and to enter in presence of the world into his glory. He mingled not much again with the people. He was seen repeatedly by his disciples, and once by more than 500 followers. He remained on earth forty days instructing in the things of his kingdom. At the end of this period, he met his disciples at Jerusalem; directed them to remain there until they should be endued with miraculous powers by the Holy Ghost, and then go and preach the gospel to every creature. He told them of his Almighty power, and assured them of his presence with them and their successors to the end of time. He

---

thrust into a hole for its support, and the wretched victim was there left to hang, until, through loss of blood, or hunger, he, in intense agony, expired; yea, until his dead body was borne off by carnivorous birds.

HIS EXALTATION.

then led them to the mount of Olives, and there blessed them, and was parted from them and carried up into heaven; there to intercede for his church; to prepare mansions for his followers, and to sit on his throne as KING in Zion, who, through all ages, takes care of his church, controls and punishes his enemies, and will be glorified in them that believe.

Thus terminated the amazing incarnation of the Son of God. Infidelity has seldom had the effrontery to deny the existence of this illustrious founder of the Christian religion. The difficulty of accounting for the existence of Christianity in the world on any other supposition than that of his real being, has probably restrained from this. But Jesus Christ has ever been a stumbling block to the Jew, and foolishness to the Greek. "He came unto his own, but his own received him not." The Jews looked for a great temporal prince, and they would not endure any man who should pretend to be the Messiah in a poor and low condition. The Greek, the refined, the philosophical, the voluptuous, in every age, have been disgusted with the humble and spiritual nature of his kingdom and the self-denying precepts he has placed before them. But whoever looks carefully at the birth, life, death, resurrection, and ascension of Jesus of Nazareth; at all the ancient types and prophecies* which were fulfilled in him; at the sublimity of his doctrine; the purity of his precepts; the holiness and beneficence of his life; the number and character of the miracles he wrought; (for he healed the sick,

---

* To lead the reader to reflect on the wonderful minuteness of the predictions relating to Christ in the Old Testament, the following are subjoined as referred to in the single Evangelist of Matthew.

		Matthew					Matthew	
Isaiah	vii.	14.	i.	23.	Jer.	vii.	11.	xxi. 13.
Micah	v.	2.	ii.	6.	Psalm	viii.	2.	xxi. 16.
Hosea	xi.	1.	ii.	15.	———	cxviii.	22.	xxi. 42.
Jeremiah	xxxi.	15.	ii.	18.	———	cx.	1.	xxii. 44.
Judges	xiii.	15.	ii.	23.	Is.	viii.	14.	xxi. 44
Is.	xl.	3.	iii.	2.	Ps.	xli.	9	xxvi. 33
Is.	ix	1.	iv.	15.	Zech.	xiii	7.	xxvi. 31.
Is.	liii.	4.	viii.	17.	Is.	l.	6	xxvi. 57.
Is.	xlii.	1.	xii.	17.	Zech.	xi.	13	xxvii. 9.
Jonah	i.	17.	xii.	40.	Psalm	xxii.	18.	xxvii. 35.
Is.	vi.	9.	xiii.	14.	———	xxii.	2.	xxvii 46.
Psalm	lxxvii.	2.	xiii.	35.	———	lxix.	21.	xxvii. 48.
Isaiah	xxxv. 5.	6.	xv.	30.	Isaiah	liii.	9.	xxvii. 60
Zech.	ix.	9.	xxi.	5.				

cleansed lepers, restored sight to the blind, caused the lame to walk, cast out devils, fed thousands from food sufficient only for a few, stilled the tempestuous sea, raised the dead to life,—all glorious acts of benevolence, and acts of infinite power only,) whoever considers what the state of this world would be, did all mankind receive the doctrines and truths, and obey the precepts and imitate the example of Christ ;— must exclaim, as did the centurion at the crucifixion, TRULY THIS WAS THE SON GOD.

CHAPTER II.

Number and character of Christ's disciples. Death of John the Baptist. The twelve Apostles chosen. The Seventy sent. History and character of the Twelve. Descent upon them of the Holy Ghost. Outpouring of the Spirit on the day of Pentecost. Three thousand added to the Church. Boldness and success of Peter and John. Holiness and harmony of the Church. Detection of hypocrisy. Institution of the office of Deacon. Martyrdom of Stephen. Persecution and dispersion of the Church. The gospel carried to the Samaritans and dispersed Jews. Conversion of Saul.

The astonishment excited by the appearance, preaching, and miracles of Christ, was such as we might naturally look for from their novel and divine character. But the ill success of his ministry could never be satisfactorily accounted for by those who deny that man is alienated from his Maker, and that salvation is "not of him that willeth, nor of him that runneth, but of God that showeth mercy." Immense multitudes constantly pressed upon him wherever he went, either to hear his doctrines, or witness his miracles ; but very few became sincerely attached to his person ; very few were even convinced that he was the Messiah, and entered his spiritual kingdom. Those who were assembled at Jerusalem after his ascension, are said to have been but about an hundred and twenty ; and at that great meeting in Galilee, where all who were attached to his cause that could conveniently assemble, were probably gathered together, there were but about five hundred. Well might the prophet Isaiah commence his fifty-third chapter, containing a remarkable exhibition of the humiliation and sufferings of Christ, with the exclamation, "Who hath heard our report, and to whom is the arm of the Lord revealed ?" But Christ knew it to be for the best, and he rejoiced in spirit at the dispensations of grace.

But few of his followers were among the rich or the noble. We indeed read of Zaccheus, a man of wealth ; Nicodemus a ruler; Joseph an honorable counselor; and a certain nobleman, who believed with all his house—evincing that divine grace can triumph over the most exalted condition of life; but the mass of his friends were from the lower ranks, and his special favorites were Galileans, a despised people, and chiefly fishermen or publicans. His own life was one of great poverty and reproach; and his doctrines marred the pride of the noble, and condemned the luxurious habits of the wealthy.

John the Baptist, who united in himself the two dispensations, the old and the new, was perhaps the first who received Jesus. He pointed him out to others as the Lamb of God. He had become the head of a religious sect, and had many followers, whom he had baptized. But when informed that Jesus had begun to preach and to baptize by his disciples, and that the whole country was going after him, he showed the greatest humility and submission to him, as his exalted Redeemer. He declared that he had no honor but that which came from God, and that he could have no greater joy than in seeing Christ increase, while he should decrease. He recommended Jesus as endowed with an unmeasurable fullness of the Holy Ghost; and assured all who heard him, that the wrath of God would abide on unbelievers in his gospel.

John was for a time revered by Herod; but he had the faithfulness to reprove that vile man for marrying his brother's wife, and was imprisoned. Laid aside from his work, his faith seems in some degree to have failed; he therefore sent two of his disciples to ask Jesus if he was the Messiah. Perhaps he designed also to turn their attention from himself to the great Redeemer. Jesus told them to declare to John what miracles he performed, and the great fact which distinguished him as a teacher from all the philosophers which had ever undertaken to instruct mankind, "That to the poor the gospel was preached." Soon after, he was beheaded to gratify the malice of Herodias,—excited by his bold reproof of Herod. His disciples took his body and buried it, and went and told Jesus. The Pharisees said he had a devil, but Christ bore witness of him as one of the greatest and best of men.

From among his followers, Jesus selected twelve to be his daily companions and intimate associates, whom he commissioned as Apostles, or preachers of his gospel. This number was probably chosen, in correspondence to the twelve patriarchs, or twelve tribes of Israel. It signified that he was head, or High Priest of the Jewish nation. The

11*

persons chosen, were Simon Peter, and Andrew his brother; James, the son of Zebedee, and John his brother; Philip and Bartholomew; Thomas and Matthew; James, the son of Alpheus, and Simon, called Zelotes; Judas, the brother of James, and Judas Iscariot. Their mission was confined at first, to the land of Israel. They were directed to declare to the lost sheep of the house of Israel, that the kingdom of heaven, the kingdom which was the subject of prophecy, which they and their fathers had looked for with the greatest anxiety, and which the Messiah was to set up, was at hand; and, as a confirmation of their doctrine, they were empowered to work miracles, to heal diseases, cast out devils, and, in many other ways, suspend or counteract the laws of nature. They were cast upon the charity of the people for support, and were directed to shake off the dust of their feet, against any family or city which should reject them.

At a subsequent period he commissioned and sent forth seventy other disciples, (answering evidently in number to the Sanhedrim, and showing thereby, that their power had passed into his hands,) on the same errand, two by two; giving them similar authority, and commending them in like manner, to the charity of the public. They were holy men; but it was a new and wonderful employment, and they were put in possession of powers which made them appear as gods upon earth. No wonder, therefore, that they should soon return, as they actually did, not a little elated with the fact, that even the devils were subject to them through his name. But Christ solemnly admonished them to beware of pride which had hurled Satan from heaven; and told them, that he indeed enabled them to tread on serpents and scorpions, and over all the power of the enemy; but that they must not rejoice in this, that they held the spirits in subjection, but rather that their names were written in heaven.

But the twelve constituted his family. They were his intimate friends, his chosen companions. He therefore sent them forth but once during his life to preach the gospel. When he traveled, they accompanied him. What he spake in parables to the multitude, he privately expounded to them. When he fed the multitude, they distributed the provision. They were with him in his retirement, and partook of the supper at its first institution. He often talked to them about his sufferings, and committed to them the keys of his kingdom.

With the exception of Judas, the traitor, they were sincere men. Their hearts had been changed by the Spirit of God. They admired, loved, and trusted their Saviour, shared with him his privations and sorrows; and devoted themselves entirely to his service. When they were first called to follow Christ, they were very ignorant. Matthew had been a publican or tax-gatherer; the others, were all, probably, fishermen of Galilee. But under the instruction and guidance of Christ, they made rapid advancement in the knowledge of divine things; and with his holy example daily before them, they soon learned to set lightly by the world, to treat one another with condescension, kindness, and love, and to live as expectants of a better country.

While the grace of God had enlightened their understandings and purified their affections, it left unchanged their natural constitution or animal temperament, so that as great a diversity of character is observable among them, as among any others of the same number, in the various conditions of life; and so distinctly are the good and bad qualities of each marked and preserved throughout their course, as to furnish a striking evidence of the authenticity and truth of the sacred history.

With great fidelity they had followed Jesus through good report and ill report, and they thought they could follow him to death. Christ knew that they would fail in the moment of trial, and assured them of it; but Peter, always ardent, bold, and warmly attached to his master, declared, that though all men should deny him, he would not. But when the band of soldiers bound Christ, betrayed by Judas, all forsook him and fled; and, though Peter followed and mingled with the crowd, at the trial, yet, when charged with being one of his followers, he declared, with an oath, I know not the man. Jesus beheld him at the moment. Peter's heart melted, and he went out and wept bitterly.

The season of Christ's suffering and burial, was to the Apostles one of thick darkness and awful perplexity. Their master they beheld hanging upon a cross. He, to whom they had looked for crowns and sceptres, was laid low in the sepulchre of Joseph. For three days, they were borne down by sorrow; agitated with fear, and enveloped in gloom. But, like the sun emerging from the shade of some heavenly body, and suddenly giving light and joy to millions from whom it had been obscured; Jesus came forth from the shades of death to the view of his despondent disciples, and gave them new vigor and life. By this event, more wonderful and astonishing than any thing they had as yet witnessed, their confidence in Christ was greatly animated and strengthened. It was both a fulfillment of his promise, and a most triumphant conquest over death and hell.

But their views of the nature of his kingdom were as yet imperfect. With the nation in general, they were impressed with the idea, that Messiah's kingdom was of this world. When, therefore, he appeared after his resurrection, they asked him, " Lord, wilt thou at this time restore the kingdom to Israel?" But this error was soon erased from their minds by his conversation, and by his ascension to heaven. That great event put a final period to every expectation they had cherished of an earthly kingdom. And it was a most illustrious confirmation of the truth of his pretensions. For had he now descended to the grave, and perished like the world around him, all his wonderful works, even his resurrection, might not have been sufficient to dissuade some from the belief that he was an impostor, who never expired, though he hung upon the cross, and that he would never enable them to realize his promises. But now, after accompanying him through the whole of his ministry, and hearing him speak words which never man spake; and seeing him perform works which never man did; after beholding him hanging on the cross, laid in the tomb, and according to his own express prediction, bursting the bands of death, and rising to their view; after this, to behold him ascend on high, to see him go to that heaven, where he had promised to prepare for them mansions of bliss, they were all ready to exclaim with one mind and one voice, Surely the Lord HE IS GOD. They saw Jesus go where no impostor can go. They saw him ascend, not like Elijah by means of a chariot of fire, but in a manner far more sublime and wonderful, by his own Almighty power; and while wrapt in astonishment, were informed by two angels that he had gone to heaven, and would come in like manner, as they had seen him go to heaven. By this event, therefore, their views were greatly changed, and their faith was established too firmly to be shaken. From the Mount Olivet they returned to Jerusalem, where they continued with one accord in prayer and supplication, until the fulfillment of the promise of the Father to baptize them with the Holy Ghost. By this they were to be still more enlightened in the nature of the Gospel kingdom; to receive the gift of tongues; and to be endued with new fortitude and zeal in their master's service.

CHAPTER 2.] PENTECOST DAY. 143

Their number had been diminished by the villanous perfidy of Judas. When he saw that he had betrayed innocent blood, smitten by remorse of conscience, he returned the thirty pieces of silver, and went and hanged himself—an awful warning to all apostates. The disciples were desirous of filling his place, and while they waited in prayer for the descent of the Spirit, they appointed Barnabas and Matthias as candidates for the Apostolic office : looked up for divine direction, and cast lots. The lot fell upon Matthias, and he was numbered with the Apostles. In this act, however, they perhaps were premature. It was for Christ to choose his own Apostles ; and, in due time, he selected Saul and called him to the Apostleship.

Having their number, as they supposed, complete, and being all united in love, and engaged in fervent prayer, they soon received the promised blessing. It came on the day of Pentecost ; an era of the divine mercy. Suddenly the place in which they were, was shaken as by a rushing mighty wind— an emblem, as Nicodemus had been taught, of the Spirit; and they beheld in the room cloven tongues like as of fire, which sat upon each of them. Instantly their minds were more enlightened, their hearts were filled with more love and zeal for Christ, they were strengthened, animated, and joyful; and, to their own utter amazement, were enabled to speak the various languages of mankind.

This descent of the Holy Spirit formed a new era in the lives of the Apostles, and of the church of God. We no longer find the twelve, the ignorant, timid, worldly-minded men they had been. The nature of Christ's kingdom; the benevolence of his errand; the perishing condition of the world; their high and holy office ; were all full before them, and took an amazing hold of their minds and hearts. They now cheerfully sacrificed the world, were ready to go forth and stand before kings and Gentiles and Jews, preaching the unsearchable riches of Christ, and to lay down their lives, if Christ might be glorified in them.

They instantly commenced their ministry, by preaching the Gospel according to Christ's express command, first to the Jews, that, if possible, they might bring that deluded people to the saving knowledge of the truth. Astonishment filled the minds of all who heard them. Jerusalem was at that time crowded with Jews from every country. In consequence of the numerous wars in which they had for centuries been engaged, with the heathen nations, the people were scattered in all parts of the Roman empire. Multitudes had, from time to time, been carried away captive, and not a few had gone from their own land for security and peace. These generally adopted the language of the people among whom they resided; but strictly adhered to the religion of their fathers; and as much as possible, the pious among them went annually to Jerusalem, to the feast of Pentecost At the very moment, therefore, that the Apostles were endued with the wonderful powers of speaking in divers tongues, there were devout men out of every nation, in Jerusalem;—Parthians, and Medes, and Elamites, and the dwellers in Mesopotamia, and in Judea and Cappadocia, in Pontus and Asia, Phrygia and Pamphylia, in Egypt, and in the parts of Lybia about Cyrene, and strangers of Rome, Jews and Proselytes, Cretes and Arabians; all these heard the Apostles speak, every man in the tongue in which he was born. The native Jews who understood not these languages, and were disposed to ridicule the Apostles, said, " These men are full of new wine." The charge roused the spirit of Peter, and, in an ever memorable sermon, he showed them the utter improbability of the thing, from its being only the third hour of the day, when no Jew was ever found in that situation; that this was an accomplishment of a prophecy of Joel, by the power of that Jesus whom they had rejected before Pilate, and with wicked hands crucified and slain; but who, according to the prediction of David, God had raised up to sit on his throne. A close application of truth to their consciences, a bold charge upon them as murderers of the Lord of life and glory, was not made in vain. The multitude were pricked in the heart. Curiosity at the wonderful miracle, was turned into distress for themselves. They felt that they were exposed to the wrath and curse of God for their vile treatment of his Son; and exclaimed, in the anguish of their souls, Men and brethren what must we do? Peter opened to them the treasures of the gospel, and directed them to that same Jesus whom they had crucified, for eternal life. He called them to immediate repentance, and submission to God in the ordinances of the gospel; assuring them of the remission of their sins, and the gift of the Holy Ghost. The effect was glorious. Three thousand were converted to the Lord, and on a profession of faith and repentance, were baptized in the name of the Father, the Son, and the Holy Ghost.

This was the first administration of christian baptism and the commencement of the CHRISTIAN CHURCH.

And as it was begun through the instrumentality of Peter, in this event was fulfilled the declaration of Christ, "Thou art Peter, and on this rock will I build my church."

To us, it may appear surprising that so much should have been effected in one day. It was nine in the morning when Peter began his sermon, and with many other words besides those which are recorded, did he exhort the people to salvation. It could have been therefore only in the after part of the day that their confession was received, and they were baptized and admitted into a covenant relation with God. But the Apostles were full of the Holy Ghost, and able, probably, to discern spirits; and if some were received who were not sincere converts, it was only in accordance with the well known fact that there must be tares with the wheat. The conduct of the Apostles, however, cannot be viewed as a warrant for ministers in succeeding outpourings of the Spirit, to receive a multitude upon their first expression of penitence and faith, into the church; for, by their fruits we must know them.

The glorious work of grace resulted not only in the submission of multitudes to christian ordinances, but in much holiness of heart and life. The enmity of the heart to divine truth was subdued, and the doctrine of the Apostles was received in love. A spiritual union and fellowship was formed, to which the world were strangers. The selfish heart was laid aside, and a new and unheard of benevolence was substituted in its place. The most of these converts were poor. Such of them as were rich, sold their possessions, and threw all they had into a common fund for the benefit of the whole. The fear of the Lord came upon every soul, and a spirit of prayer was excited in every breast. Common food was received with a gladness before unknown; and in the Lord's supper, and the worship of the Temple, a joy was felt unspeakable and full of glory. So powerful and happy were the results of that great revival of religion.

In one sense it was miraculous; but in no other, than is every revival. It was not effected by the miracles the Apostles wrought. Had they spoken in divers tongues with the same fluency, on any other subject, no such effects would have been produced. It was effected by the power of the Holy Ghost, through the instrumentality of truth,—by presenting plainly to men, their sin and danger, and calling them to repentance and holiness. Joel had, ages before predicted this outpouring of the Spirit, and the sacred historian says, it was the Lord that added daily to the church of such as should be saved. Here, therefore, as in all revivals, we see God effecting his great purposes of sanctifying mercy, while men are awakened and turned to the Lord by the truth.

Soon after the day of Pentecost, Peter and John cured a well known beggar of lameness. This miracle brought together a great concourse of people; and Peter embraced the opportunity to charge upon them the sin of crucifying Christ, and to call them to repentance. The multitude listened with the most profound attention. But the magistrates, who were Sadducees and enemies to the doctrine of the resurrection, were grieved and vexed, and rushed upon the Apostles and put them in prison until the next day. They then brought them before the High Priest and council, and asked by what authority or power they did this? Peter, who once trembled at the voice of a maid, answered with astonishing boldness, "In the name of Jesus of Nazareth, whom they had crucified, but whom God had raised up, and in whom alone salvation was to be found." The magistrates were afraid to touch them. The boldness of Peter was unexpected, and the miracle none could deny. They dismissed them, charging them no more to speak in the name of Christ. The Apostles departed, protesting against the charge, and held a meeting for prayer, in which they enjoyed much of the divine presence and blessing, and were animated to go forth with new boldness in the cause of Christ.

The number of disciples was now increased to above five thousand, and they lived in great harmony and love;—were followers of God as dear children.

But as it had been in the Jewish, so was it in the Christian Church. All were not Israel who were of Israel. There had been a Judas among the twelve; and now among the converts to Christianity, were brought to light two gross hypocrites. Ananias and Sapphira pretended to give unto the Lord all their possessions, while they gave only a part. Peter exposed their deceit, and the Lord struck them dead. It was an awful judgment; but it showed the church the sin of hypocrisy; the impossibility of concealing any thing from God; and must have led every professor to a serious and careful examination of his own state.

The influences of the Spirit were long continued. Converts were multiplied. The Apostles were endued with astonishing powers of healing. The sick were brought from all the cities round about Jerusalem, and cured of their diseases; and while the attention of the multitude was thus excited by such wonderful works of mercy, their hearts were melted by the power of the Gospel.

The continued success of the Apostles again aroused the indignation of the rulers, who hated every thing which called the attention of men to a future world. They seized them once more and cast them into the common prison. But what could bars and bolts do against the power of the Almighty? God sent his angel at midnight and opened the prison doors, and bade them go preach in the Temple. What a miracle! How must it have confounded those hardened rulers! It ought to have subdued them. But they once more summoned the Apostles to appear before them and inquired how they dared fill Jerusalem with their doctrine, and bring Christ's blood upon them. Peter soberly but boldly told them they must obey God, rather than man, and again charged them with the crucifixion of Christ, whom God had exalted to be a Prince and a Saviour. Instant death would probably have been their portion, had it not been for the timely counsel of Gamaliel, an eminent doctor of the law. He told the rulers to let them alone, for if their work was of men, it would come to nought, but if it was of God, they could not overthrow it, and it behooved them to be careful not to fight against God. His advice was followed. The Apostles were only beaten and charged to keep silence. But they were not moved They departed, rejoicing that they were counted worthy to suffer shame for Christ.

A circumstance about this time occurred, which occasioned the creation of a new office in the church. The church embraced both native and foreign Jews. The latter were called Hellenists, or Grecians, because they spoke the Greek tongue. These supposed that, in the daily supply of the poor, the Apostles had shown a partiality for the widows of the Hebrews; and murmured against them. The Apostles immediately called together the disciples and informed them that seven men of eminent piety must be appointed to superintend that business; while they would confine themselves to prayer and preaching. Their advice was followed, and Stephen, Philip, Procorus, Nicanor, Timon, Parmenas, and Nicolas, were appointed and ordained to the office of Deacon, by prayer and the imposition of hands.

These men were bold and strong in the faith of Christ.

Stephen especially, was empowered to work miracles, and to resist and overcome all opposition which was made by disputers against the Gospel. His ability and success excited the malice of the wicked; and they suborned men to accuse him of blasphemy. Upon being called to answer the charge, he boldly rebuked the Jews, by giving a history of their nation, and showing that, in betraying and murdering Christ, they had but imitated the conduct of their fathers, who treated Moses and the Prophets with contempt. "They were cut to the heart and gnashed on him with their teeth." But he, "full of the Holy Ghost, looked up stedfastly to heaven, and saw the glory of God, and Jesus standing at the right hand of God." Of this, he made full confession. It filled his enemies with madness, and they cast him out of the city and stoned him to death. With his expiring breath, he commended his soul to God; like his divine master, prayed for his murderers, and FELL ASLEEP. Thus died the first Christian Martyr, full of faith and hope; and favored with clear views of his Redeemer. He was buried by the church with great lamentation; but his spirit had ascended to glory.

Blood had now been shed; and it was the signal of a tremendous persecution of the followers of Jesus. They were unable to stand before it, and fled from Jerusalem to the surrounding country. But they were not deterred from preaching the Gospel. On the contrary, they were excited to greater boldness; and, wherever they went, they proclaimed Christ and the resurrection. Philip, the next to Stephen in faith and zeal, and who was also a preacher, carried the Gospel to the Samaritans, and instructed and baptized an Eunuch of the queen of Ethiopia, whom he met in the way, returning from Jerusalem, where he had been to worship. Others traveled as far as Phenice, Cyprus, and Antioch, preaching to Jews only; but by their labors, many converts were made, and many churches were established. Thus was the blood of the martyrs the seed of the church. The disciples were driven from Jerusalem, that they might diffuse the Gospel through the earth.

Among the bitter persecutors of the followers of the Redeemer, was one, whose life and actions form a most interesting portion of the history of the church. This was Saul of Tarsus. His parents were Jews, who resided in that city. According to the custom of the Jews, with whom it was a leading maxim, " He who teaches not his son a trade, teaches him to be a thief," he was early taught a particular trade,—tent-making. He was next sent to Jerusalem and placed under the instruction of Gamaliel, the most eminent doctor of the age, that he might become thoroughly acquainted with the Jewish law. He was a youth of noble endowments, of commanding eloquence; in religion, of the straitest sect of the Pharisees; in temper, proud, active, fiery, not able to brook opposition, and feeling it to be doing God service to crush every new, and what appeared to him, heretical sentiment. He was one. therefore, in whom meek-eyed Christianity, as she advanced with her claims to the homage of men, might expect to find a most malignant foe. As a signal of this, we first behold him at the bitter persecution of the martyr, Stephen, consenting unto his death.

With a furious zeal, he soon raged, searching out the Christians, beating them in the synagogues, and either compelling them to disown Christ, or causing them to be put to death. Having done all that infuriate malice could do in Jerusalem, he obtained a warrant from the High Priest to go to Damascus, whither some Christians had retired, and bring all whom he found there to Jerusalem. How terrible is the native enmity of the human heart to the gospel of Christ! How insatiable is an unhallowed and misguided zeal! Had the violent persecutor been suffered to proceed, what awful ravages would he have made of Christ's little flock! But the wolf was to be changed into the lamb. God had separated him, not to die by a thunderbolt of his wrath, but to preach that very Gospel which he had persecuted. And this was the moment which divine wisdom chose for the exhibition of grace. As he was on his way, suddenly a beam of light, far outshining the splendor of the sun, darted upon him from heaven, and a voice addressed him, Saul, Saul, why persecutest thou me? The raging persecutor fell to the earth, crying, Who art thou, Lord? With a majesty which will make all sinners tremble in the judgment, the Lord said, "I am Jesus whom thou persecutest. It is hard for thee to kick against the pricks." At a sight of the terribleness and compassion of the Saviour, his heart relented, and he inquired with earnestness, and a readiness to serve him forever, Lord, what wilt thou have me to do?

Thus, not through the power of a miracle, for the bare witness of a miracle will never change the heart, but through the power of the Holy Ghost, the miraculous appearance and address of the Saviour became instrumental of effecting a complete change in bitter Saul. And a change, how great! In his self righteousness he had thought himself one of the best of men, but now, he saw that he was the chief of sinners. The law of God was brought home to his conscience, and he died. All hope of salvation from his own merit, was entirely at an end; and he fled to Christ, seeking pardon through his blood, and consecrating himself wholly to his service.

By his terrified companions he was led into Damascus, for he was struck with blindness. In that city dwelt Ananias, a devout Christian, and probably one of the seventy, whom the Lord directed, that the ministry might be honored, to go and instruct Saul in the great business to which he was called. Amazement filled his breast as the commission sounded in his ears. He well knew the character of the man. He dreaded the wolf in sheep's clothing. Could the Lord be deceived? Momentary expostulation, he would venture. "Lord, I have heard by many of this man, how much evil he hath done to thy saints at Jerusalem, and here he hath authority from the chief priests to bind all that call upon thy name." But one word from the Saviour silenced his fears, and commanded his confidence, and he went straightway to the anxious inquirer, with the friendly salutation, Brother Saul! assuring him that the Lord had sent him, that, by him, he might receive his sight and be filled with the Holy Ghost. At the touch of Ananias, scales fell from his eyes; his mind was calm and joyful; he professed his confidence in his Saviour: was baptized, and immediately preached Christ in the synagogues.

What emotions must have been excited by this man's preaching! Here were the saints, who, but a week before, were trembling at his approach, as lambs before the hungry wolf. There were the Jews, who had anticipated the hour of his coming, as the hour of triumph over men whom, of all others, they most hated. What an assembly! Were a company of infidels collected to hear Christianity reviled by some Hume, or Voltaire, or Paine, and a number of the followers of Christ doomed to sit and hear their ribaldry and abuse, when suddenly the oracle of infidelity should become the advocate of truth, and address himself with awful solemnity to the hearts and consciences of his former companions, and warn them to flee from the wrath to come; what shame! what confusion! what gnashing of teeth would there be among them! And what holy triumph would sit on the countenances of the wondering saints! It would give but a faint idea of this assembly. Here was slaughter and death expected by some, and a gratification of the most malignant passions by others: all suddenly checked and turned away. The result was such as might be expected. The triumph of the saints could not be borne. Such a man could not be suffered to live. Enraged at Saul, for so suddenly quitting their ranks and becoming the advocate of Christianity; confounded by the weight of his arguments; and dreading the effects of his conversion; the Jews determined to kill him, and closed against him the gates of the city. But his friends let him down in a basket from the window of a house built on the wall, and he escaped into Arabia. How long he continued in that region is unknown, but from thence he returned to Damascus, and it was three years before he went up to Jerusalem to visit the disciples. When he did go there, they were afraid of him, and believed not that he was a disciple, (an evidence either of very little intercourse among the early Christians, or of great seclusion on the part of Saul.) But Barnabas related unto them the circumstances of his conversion, and how he had preached boldly at Damascus, so that they gave him the hand of fellowship. At Jerusalem he became an active and bold minister of the Lord Jesus. Here, while praying in the Temple, he went into a trance, was caught up into the third heaven, and heard things which might not be uttered. Here again the Jews attempted to kill him. But he was preserved through the vigilance of his friends, who sent him to Tarsus.

The conversion of Saul took place in the second year after the death of Christ. It was a very instructive event. It showed to the world that a man may be greatly engaged in the concerns of religion; be the strictest formalist; think that he does God service, and have an undoubting assurance of his own salvation, and be a total stranger to vital piety. It was an illustrious exhibition of the sovereignty of God, who has mercy on whom he will have mercy, and who employs, if he please, those who have been his greatest adversaries, in the most honorable post in his kingdom. And it was an incontestible evidence of the truth of Christianity.* Let the unawakened sinner and the formal Pharisee, contemplate the state of Saul before his conversion, and remember it is their own.

---

* See Lyttleton's Conversion of Paul.

CHAPTER III.

The Gospel preached to the Gentiles. Cornelius and his family baptized. Martyrdom of James. Revival at Antioch. Saul and Barnabas ordained Missionaries to the heathen. Ministry of Paul. Constitution of the Christian Church. Its early moral and religious state. Character of the Apostles' preaching. Writers of the New Testament. Firm establishment of the kingdom of Christ. Opposition of the Jews. God's judgment upon them. Destruction of Jerusalem. Dispersion of the Jews. Opposition of the Roman Emperors Nero and Domitian. Martyrdom of Paul and Peter. Early heresies.

THE conversion and early labors of Saul, formed another era in the Christian Church. The enemies of Christianity, forsaken by their leader, and convinced or silenced by his powerful preaching, retired from the field of persecution; great numbers were added to the Lord; the churches every where had rest, and were edified; "walking in the fear of the Lord, and the comforts of the Holy Ghost."

For a period of about six years after the ascension of Christ, the Apostles continued to preach the Gospel to the Jews only, wherever they could find them throughout the Roman empire. But in general they rejected it, and bitterly opposed and persecuted all who proclaimed it. The Lord therefore directed the Apostles to turn their attention to the Gentiles.

The Gentiles were abhorred by the Jews. They were viewed by them as hated of God and devoted to destruction. The Apostles were possessed of this common prejudice. They would never, therefore, of themselves, have offered so great a blessing as salvation to the heathen, and if some, from any motive should have done it, they would at once have been viewed guilty of sacrilege. But the Great Shepherd, who had other sheep besides the Jews to gather in, knew how to prepare the minds of his ministers for so rich a work.

In Cesarea, the residence of the Roman governor, lived Cornelius, a centurion, a devout man who had been reclaimed from idolatry, and who, according to the light which had been afforded him, worshipped God; was just, exemplary, and eminently charitable. This man was warned of God to send for Peter, and hear from him the words of eternal life. At the same time, Peter was instructed by a vision from heaven, not to call any man common or unclean. When, therefore, the messengers of Cornelius came to him at Joppa, he went with them without delay, and declared to the centurion and his household, the glorious Gospel of the grace of God While he was preaching, the Holy Ghost fell on all his hearers, and they were converted to the Lord, and by the ordinance of baptism, admitted to the Christian Church. Such were the first fruits of the Spirit among the Gentiles. Thus was the wall of partition, which had stood for ages between Jews and heathen, broken down. How valuable was the Gospel to one of the best men the heathen world could boast! Before he heard it, he was highly esteemed among men, but he had no peace in his own breast. He had been daily an anxious inquirer at the throne of grace for peace and life. He now found in them the doctrine of forgiveness, through the blood of Christ. The best men in heathen lands deserve our compassion, for they know nothing of pardoning mercy, or the consolations of the Holy Ghost. Let the pride of narrow-minded, selfish men, who have long considered themselves the sole favorites of heaven, be rebuked. Among those whom such hate and view as outcasts, may be some of the brightest jewels in the Redeemer's crown.

The christian temper was happily exhibited by the brethren at Jerusalem, when they heard of this unexpected enlargement of the Church. They viewed it at first indeed as irregular, and were disposed to censure Peter; but no sooner had he declared his divine commission and related to them the operation of the Spirit, than they glorified God for his mercy. Some measures may often be accounted inconsistent with long established principles and customs; and men may be brought into the kingdom of Christ, who, for various reasons, we might have supposed would never have a place there; but when satisfactory evidence is given that such, even through these means, are truly converted to the Lord, all prejudices are, by the correct mind, sacrificed; the hand of fellowship is extended, and God is glorified.

Herod sat at this time on the throne of Judah. He was a vile prince; and was surrounded by no less vile Sadducees and Herodians, whom he found it for his interest continually to gratify. They hated the Christians, and he therefore commenced against them a violent persecution. He first seized James, the son of Zebedee, and condemned him to death. Eusebius relates that his accuser, beholding his faith, was struck with remorse, and by the power of the Spirit, was suddenly brought to repentance and confessed Christ, and that both were carried to execution and beheaded together. The tyrant next seized Peter, and confined him in chains. But God had further need of him in the church below, and while the brethren were engaged in prayer for him, the angel of the Lord delivered him from his chains, set open the prison doors, and restored him to the disciples. The miserable monarch was soon after brought for his pride and cruelty to a most horrid death. His intended victim lived to old age, and preached the Gospel throughout Pontus, Galatia, Cappadocia, Asia, and Bithynia.

For five years, Saul of Tarsus remained in his native city and province, preaching the gospel; with what success is not known. But he was not forgotten by the brethren. Some of the disciples had fled from Jerusalem, in the persecution to Antioch, the metropolis of Syria, where they preached the Lord Jesus. Their labors were crowned with great success. Tidings of this were received with joy by the church at Jerusalem, and they sent Barnabas, "a good man, full of the Holy Ghost and of faith," to assist them. No sooner had he reached the city, than he saw the need of more laborers, and he went to Tarsus for this powerful advocate of the cause of Christ, and brought him to Antioch; where they labored together with much success for a whole year. The church was enlarged and prosperous; and as many of its members were wealthy, and actuated by holy love, they made liberal contributions for the poor saints at Jerusalem—distressed by a famine. Here, as an epithet of opprobrium, the followers of Jesus were first called CHRISTIANS; an epithet which is, in truth, the most honorable and blessed a man can sustain.

To remain there, where many teachers of reputation had assembled, and where seasons of refreshment were afforded, would have been pleasant. But the Head of the church had a great work for these disciples to perform; and the prophets and teachers at Antioch were directed by the Holy Ghost to set apart Saul and Barnabas to the great work of evangelizing the heathen. Accordingly, they were separated as missionaries of the cross, and ministers of salvation to the Gentiles, with fasting and prayer, and imposition of hands, and sent forth to their field, which was the world.

Here properly commences the mighty Apostolic work of him who was the most distinguished instrument ever employed of bringing this fallen world to the knowledge of Christ.*

His course may be divided into three parts. The first, reaching from this appointment, to the Council at Jerusalem. The second, from this Council, to the close of his labors in Greece. The third, from his last visit at Jerusalem, to his death.

In the first, Paul and Barnabas went to Cyprus, where Sergius Paulus, the Roman governor, was converted, and Bar-jesus, for his opposition, was struck blind; then to Perga in Pamphylia; then to Antioch in Pisidia, where Paul preached a long and powerful sermon, by which multitudes were converted to the Lord, but which so exasperated the Jews, that they expelled him out of their coasts. Driven thence, they went to Iconium; but being in danger of stoning, they retired to Lystra and Derbe. There they healed a man who had been lame from his birth, and were taken by the people for gods in the likeness of men. But no sooner had they quieted the adoring populace, than that same populace, stirred up by the envious and base Jews, turned against them and stoned them, so that Paul was supposed to be dead. But God had designed him for great purposes; and he rose up, by divine power, and returned to Antioch. Such was the first mission of the Apostle. In it he made many converts, organized many churches, and ordained ministers to break to them the bread of life.

But these churches, especially the church at Antioch, were infested with men who would compel the Gentile converts to observe circumcision and the ceremonial law. It was a bold and wicked attempt, which, however, has been often repeated from that day to this, to substitute external righteousness for faith in Christ, as the ground of justification. Discerning saints saw that the evil must be withstood, and Paul and Barnabas were deputized to go to Jerusalem and ask advice of the Apostles and elders. A Council was called, the first known in the Christian Church, in which it was determined: That such observances should not be required, only that Gentile converts should abstain from blood, from idols, from fornication, and from things strangled. With this decision, they returned to Antioch, and the churches had rest.

---

* He who had been called Saul is now, in the Scriptures called Paul, some think from Paulus Sergius, who was converted under his preaching; but it is most probable Paul was his Roman, and Saul his Grecian name.

The second period of Paul's ministry was upon a new and unexpected theatre. A vision appeared to him in the night, inviting him over into Macedonia to preach the Gospel. With Silas and Timothy for his companions, he passed without delay into Greece—renowned for science and learning, and subject to a most splendid and fascinating idolatry. There he preached with such irresistible energy, that soon important churches were collected at Philippi, Thessalonica, Berea, and Corinth. It is delightful to contemplate this great Apostle crossing the Hellespont, bearing a treasure to that land of science and arts, infinitely more valuable than all that human wisdom had ever discovered; and pressing forward through mockings, imprisonment, and stonings, until his feet stood on Mars Hill, where, amid temples, altars, and statues, he declared to the Athenians, the most philosophical and refined people, and to the Areopagus, the most able court on earth, the UNKNOWN GOD.

In the polished city, he had but little success. Dyonysius, a member of the Areopagus, and a woman named Damaris, believed. But the mass of the Athenians were ruined by luxury and a deceitful philosophy. From Greece he went to Jerusalem, and having saluted the church, he went over all the country of Galatia and Phrygia, strengthening the disciples. At Ephesus, where was the great temple of the goddess Diana, the most splendid heathen temple existing, he abode two years, working miracles, and preaching the Gospel with great power. Having finished his work there, he visited all the churches in Greece, and then set his face, for the last time, to go up to Jerusalem. In this period of his Apostleship he performed his greatest labor and gave the most glorious extension to the Gospel of Christ.

In the last period, he was chiefly a prisoner. He was brought before governors and kings; but he feared not their faces. He boldly vindicated his conduct and cause, and put his enemies to silence. As he reasoned of righteousness, temperance, and judgment to come, Felix trembled. As he related the wondrous story of his conversion, King Agrippa was almost persuaded to be a Christian. Appealing to Cæsar, he was carried to Rome; but his Lord did not desert him. He preserved him amid dangers, and so overruled events at Rome that he had no trial; but lived two years in his own hired house, teaching with much success the things pertaining to the kingdom of God. A large Church was there instructed and nourished by him. Some of the imperial household a concubine and cupbearer of Nero, belonged to it. He even stood before Nero himself, and testified the Gospel with the same boldness as he had done before Felix and Agrippa. It is probable that he once more had his liberty and visited the eastern churches. If he did, he again returned to Rome, for there it is reported he suffered martyrdom in the year 65—just thirty years after his conversion.

Such were the labors of Paul—a man of a noble and capacious mind, of extensive learning, profound reasoning, consummate fortitude, and wonderful patience and benevolence. He viewed himself as the least of all saints, and was entirely devoted to his Lord and Master.

Through his exertions and those of the other Apostles and disciples, the civilized world was, in thirty years after the ascension of Christ, filled with a knowledge of the Gospel. We have no means of ascertaining the number of churches which they planted; but it was great. Their Master had given them the power of speaking all the languages of the earth; working miracles; of foretelling future events; an unheard of zeal and heroism in his service; an elevation above the frowns and flatteries of the world, and death itself; and a wisdom which all their adversaries were not able to resist. The Apostles and teachers were few in number; all felt themselves engaged in the most important of all causes. To these is to be attributed, under God, the vast extension of the Gospel at so early a period; an extension, which when we consider the state of the world and the instruments employed, furnishes the highest evidence of its divine origin.

CONSTITUTION OF THE CHRISTIAN CHURCH.

A church consisted of an assembly of Christians in one place who had professed Christ; been baptized in the name of the Father, Son, and Holy Ghost, and who united in worship, and in the celebration of the Lord's Supper. It was called the body of Christ, and those that composed it, members in particular.

To each church was attached a Pastor and Deacons.

When Christ ascended up on high he instituted various teachers in the church, called apostles, prophets, evangelists, pastors, and teachers, for the work of the ministry.

The Apostolic office was personal and temporary. To it belonged extraordinary privileges and miraculous powers; and it was eminently useful in propagating Christianity and founding churches. It ceased with the men whom Christ himself appointed to it.

The Prophets were designated to explain the Old Testament prophecies, and foretell things which should come to pass through inspiration of the Holy Ghost. Their office also was confined to the first days of Christianity.

The Evangelists were appointed to labor wherever they could be useful in Christian and heathen countries, without being attached to any particular charge. They were like missionaries and evangelists at the present period.

Pastors and Teachers were synonymous; though some have supposed that the appropriate business of the Teacher was, to defend the doctrines of Christianity; while the Pastor took a general care of the flock, and attended to the minor pastoral duties. These were attached to a particular church, and ministered to it, as Bishops or overseers, being set apart by prayer and fasting, and imposition of hands, and the right hand of fellowship originally by the Apostles, and successively by such as had by them been introduced into the ministry.

Christ placed all his ministering servants upon an equality of rank. He told them that they were brethren, and forbade their receiving any title of distinction which should give one a pre-eminence over another,—condemning the various grades of Christian ministers which have since been established, and the various titles which have since been conferred, elevating a few above their brethren around them.

In the primitive churches, reigned great simplicity of form and worship. Equality existed among the members. They chose their own Pastors. They spent much time in prayer and praise. Letters from the Apostles and other churches were publicly read, and the word of God was publicly expounded. Their assemblies were generally held in private houses, as they had no public edifices.

The Jewish Christians continued for a time strictly to regard the synagogue worship, but they and all Gentile converts convened too, on the first day of the week, the day on which Christ rose, the day which, doubtless through the Lord's appointment, now became the Christian Sabbath, and which was called the Lord's day. The Lord's Supper was administered at the close of worship; and, as many of the disciples were poor, opulent brethren brought food of which all partook in what were called *agapae*, or feasts of love.

They received in great simplicity and purity, as the foundation which they built, the doctrines which had been taught by Christ and the Apostles. They banished forever all idolatry, and worshipped the one living and true God—the Father, the Son, and the Holy Ghost; viewed man as totally depraved, dead in trespasses and sins, under the curse of the law; received in love, the great doctrines of atonement by the blood of Christ; of election; regeneration by the Holy Spirit; justification by faith; adoption; the resurrection of the dead to eternal happiness or eternal misery, according to moral character.

They practiced a purer morality than the Gentile world had ever known. Their former companions looked on them with amazement, because they did not run with them to the same excess of riot. But they had come to the knowledge of God and his law; of the way of duty and safety; their hearts had been filled with holy love; and they now lived like rational, immortal beings, whose great business was to honor God and do good to their fellow men.

Such was the moral state and character of the primitive churches. But they kept not their glory. The gold soon became dim. Some deceivers were among them, who corrupted the mass. False teachers early introduced errors in doctrine. Believers grew cold and lukewarm; and through the power of indwelling corruption and the temptations of the world, fell into very reprehensible sins. A vain and deceitful philosophy came near destroying the church at Corinth. That church also was thrown into dissensions about their leading ministers. One was for Paul and another for Apollos. They abused the Lord's Supper; and even an incestuous person was among them. The Galatians were drawn almost away from Christ to a dependence for justification on a strict observance of the ceremonial law. Among the Philippians were those who walked as enemies of the cross of Christ, whose god was their belly. Peter and Jude describe to us some horrible enormities of nominal Christians, who looked for justification by faith without works. Among the seven promising and excellent churches of Asia, there was scarce one that retained, at the end of forty years, her original purity of doctrine or practice.

And yet it was the golden age of the church. Who would not have lived in that period and heard the Apostles preach and witnessed their miraculous operations; and beheld the astonishing outpourings of the Spirit; and seen the heathen casting their gods to the moles and the bats; and mingled in joyful worship with those who had seen our Lord?

The Apostles were fishermen, unlearned men, and for this reason have been despised by the world; but no class of men so command our admiration and love. He who made them, enlarged their native powers; gave them astonishing wisdom and fortitude; and shed abroad in their hearts a spirit of love and compassion for their fellow men, second only to that of him who died for us. They published to man the pure Gospel. Christ had directly or indirectly declared all the great doctrines of the Gospel. What he taught would have been lost to the world had they not committed it to writing, for future generations. This they did through inspiration of the Spirit. What Christ taught needed to be taught again and more fully and explicitly; for he spake in a region of darkness, and the darkness comprehended him not. Even his own disciples had but a very imperfect understanding of what is now plain to us. It was in vain for him therefore to labor much with them, until after he had finished his work. "I have many things," said he, "to say to you, but ye cannot bear them now, nevertheless when the Spirit of all truth is come, he will reveal them to you." Christ's promise was fulfilled. They were taught more perfectly the great scheme of redemption; all the doctrines and precepts of Christianity; the offices, ordinances and affairs of the church through every age of the christian dispensation and its final glorification in heaven. Whatever they spoke or wrote, they spoke or wrote as taught of God, and is to be received as precisely of the same authority as the words of Christ himself. Of the places where nine of them labored and died, scarce any thing is recorded. Probably they labored and died near Jerusalem.

The Biographers of our Lord were Matthew, Mark, Luke, and John.

Matthew was a publican or tax-gatherer, living at Capernaum. He wrote his Gospel soon after the ascension, A. D. 37 or 38, first, it is supposed, in Hebrew and then in Greek.

Mark was the son of a pious woman in Jerusalem. He was not one of the twelve Apostles; but was a companion of Paul, Peter and Barnabas in their travels. He wrote his Gospel in Greek about the year 63, at Rome, at the request of the church there.

Luke was not an Apostle; but a physician of Antioch, who

early attached himself to the Apostles and was a close companion of Paul in his travels. He was a man of learning and wrote very pure Greek. When he wrote his history of Christ is uncertain.

John was the youngest of the twelve, was the beloved disciple, and one of the best men that ever lived. He was a witness of the transfiguration; sat next to Jesus, on his couch, at the passover, and saw his agony in the garden. To him Christ committed his mother from the cross. He was at the Council in Jerusalem about the year 50. Soon after that, he took the pastoral care of the church at Ephesus, where he probably remained many years. He outlived all the Apostles.* He wrote his Gospel at Ephesus about A. D. 97, or 98, evidently to declare our Saviour's divinity, which many were disposed to deny. He inserted in it but a few things recorded by the other Evangelists; probably considering it unnecessary. He wrote what they had omitted; particularly, that last conversation which Christ had with his disciples at the institution of the supper and his intercessory prayer.

The question has been asked why more and fuller accounts of Christ were not given? More and fuller might have been. John says, if all were written which Jesus did, the world would not contain the books. More actually were written, as

---

* A few fragments have been collected of this beloved disciple, though their authenticity is doubted. Such it is said was his regard for the truth, that once, while in the public bath at Ephesus, he perceived there Cerinthus, an open heretic, and came out hastily, exclaiming, " Let us flee, lest the bath should fall while Cerinthus, an enemy of the truth, is in it." It was like him who charged a Christian lady not to receive him into her house, nor bid him God speed who preached another Gospel.

Hearing, in his old age, of a lovely youth who had apostatized from the Christian faith, and become the head of a band of robbers, he went to the mountains and demanded of the robbers the sight of their captain. Beholding the venerable Apostle, the youth fled. John followed and cried, My son, why fliest thou from thy father, unarmed and old. Christ hath sent me. The youth stopped, trembled and wept bitterly. John prayed, exhorted and brought him back a penitent to the company of the Christians.

When very old he constantly repeated in his exhortations, "Children, love one another."

In his old age he wrote his three Epistles. By Domitian he was, says Tertullian, cast into a cauldron of boiling oil, from which he came out unhurt, and then was banished to the Isle of Patmos, where he wrote his Revelations. He again returned to Asia, where he lived three or four years, a pattern of charity and goodness. He died in the beginning of the second century, being about an hundred years of age.

Luke informs Theophilus. But these alone have been transmitted to us by the Holy Ghost, doubtless because, in the divine mind, they were sufficient. He that rejects these books would reject more. The discovery of a fifth Gospel, would have no more effect than would the discovery of one of the four, had the world have been possessed of but three. No man was ever, it is presumed, converted by the consideration that there were four histories of Christ rather than three. No man would be converted by five, who is unconvinced by the four.

The Acts of the Apostles, the great history of the early spread of the Gospel, was written by Luke, A. D. 63, but it is evidently far from being a full account. The Apostles felt a deep solicitude for the spiritual welfare of the churches which they had planted. They had taught them the fundamental doctrines of Christianity. But these were, in many cases, supplanted by gross errors, introduced by false teachers The standard of morals in that age was low; and corrupt practices were witnessed among the professed followers of Christ. These circumstances induced the Apostles, Paul, Peter, James, Jude, and John, to address letters to these churches, for their instruction, correction, and edification. These letters, written under inspiration of the Holy Ghost, form an exceedingly valuable part of the sacred volume. They unfold the great principles of Christianity, and exhibit all the distinguishing traits of Christian character.*

The last book of the sacred canon, the Revelation of John. was formed in the isle of Patmos, whither he was banished near the close of life and of the first century, and published

---

* *Order, time, and place, in which the Epistles were written.*

	A. D.	Place.		A. D.	Place.
1 Thessalonians,	52,	Corinth.	Hebrews,	63,	Rome.
2 Thessalonians,	52,	do.	1 Timothy,	64,	Nicopolis.
Galatians,	52,	do.	Titus,	64,	Macedonia
1 Corinthians,	57.	Ephesus.	2 Timothy,	65,	Rome.
Romans,	57.	Corinth.	James,	61,	Jerusalem.
2 Corinthians,	58.	Philippi.	1 Peter,	64,	Rome.
Ephesians,	61.	Rome.	2 Peter,	65,	do.
Philippians,	62,	do.	1, 2, 3, John,	80—90,	Ephesus.
Colossians,	62,	do.	Jude,	64,	do
Philemon,	62,	do.	Revelations,	96 or 97,	do.

The subscriptions to the Epistles are spurious, for they are contradicted often by the books themselves.

soon after his release at Ephesus. Excepting an introduction and a description of a vision of Jesus Christ, and an address of commendation and reproof to the seven churches of Asia, it is a most sublime and wonderful prophetic exhibition of the great events which should occur in the providence of God, especially those which relate to his church, of the millennium, and the judgment; of the eternal happiness of the righteous, and the endless misery of the finally impenitent. The Evangelical History, the Epistles, and Revelation, are called the New Testament, because they fully unfold God's gracious covenant with his people. It is supposed they were first collected together by John.

That glorious kingdom spoken of by Daniel in his explanation of Nebuchadnezzar's dream; which God was to set up in the most splendid period of the Roman empire; which was to break in pieces and consume all earthly kingdoms and stand forever, was now firmly established. God has set his King on the holy hill of Zion, and before the close of the first century, subjects were gathered out of almost every people and nation in the known world. Churches were planted from Hindostan to Gaul; stated means of grace were established and brought into operation; an army of missionaries was wageing an exterminating war against idolatry, and the lusts and passions of men; and the Spirit of God in its resistless energy, was making the word, in their hands, effectual to the conviction and conversion of a multitude whom no man could number.

Such triumphs over sin and hell were not obtained without exciting in the prince of this world, the most artful, malignant, and deadly hostility.

The first opposition which arose against the church of Christ, was from those to whom the gospel was first preached;—the Jews, the ancient covenant people of God. A degenerate race, holding only the forms of religion; proud, hypocritical, and ambitious in the extreme, had crucified the Lord of glory; and now, when they saw the church arise, in spite of all their efforts to suppress it, and the blood of Christ come upon them and their children, and their Temple worship forsaken and priesthood despised, they persecuted the followers of Christ with relentless rage in Jerusalem and throughout Judea and Galilee, and every country wherever they were in their dispersions. Some, in fulfillment of Christ's prediction, they crucified; others they scourged in their synagogues, and all, they persecuted from city to city.

Such ingratitude, perverseness and rebellion; such treatment of his Son, his messages of mercy, his Apostles and servants called aloud for the vengeance of God. The divine patience was exhausted. Dear as their fathers had been, God now gave them up to the blindness of mind, and hardness of heart, to fill up the measure of their iniquity. He rejected them and cast them off from being his people, and suffered their enemies to make an utter extermination of their city and nation.

Under Vespasian, the Romans invaded the country, and took the cities of Galilee, Chorazin, Bethsaida, and Capernaum, where Christ had been rejected; destroyed the inhabitants and left nothing but ruin and desolation.

Jerusalem was destroyed A. D. 70. Its destruction was distinctly foretold by Christ; but no tongue can tell the sufferings of its devoted inhabitants. Josephus, who was an eye-witness of them, remarks, " that all the calamities that ever befel any nation since the beginning of the world, were inferior to the miseries of his countrymen at that awful period.

After the death of Herod, the Jews were subject to Roman jurisdiction, but they were divided into violent factions, led by profligate wretches, and soon openly revolted from the imperial dominion. Warned by Christ before his crucifixion,* of the storm that was about to burst upon the devoted city; the Christians all fled to Pella, a city beyond Jordan. On the day of the passover, the anniversary of the crucifixion of Christ, Titus, the Roman general, encamped before Jerusalem with a formidable army. A tremendous siege ensued. The Jews defended themselves with astonishing valor; but they were unable long to resist the power of the Roman engines. To accelerate the ruin, Titus inclosed the city by a circumvallation, strengthened by thirteen towers, by which the prophecy of Christ was fulfilled, " the days shall come upon thee, when thine enemies shall cast a trench about thee, and compass thee around on every side."† Then ensued a famine, the like to which the world has never witnessed. An eminent Jewess, frantic with her sufferings, devoured her infant. Moses had long before predicted this very thing.‡ " The tender and delicate woman among you, who would not venture to set the sole of her foot upon the ground for delicateness, her eye shall be evil towards her young one, and towards her

---

* Matt. xxiv. 15.   † Luke xix. 43.   ‡ Deut xxviii. 56.

children which she shall bear, for she shall eat them for want of all things, secretly in the siege and straitness wherewith thine enemy shall distress thee in thy gates." Hearing of the inhuman deed, Titus swore the eternal extirpation of the accursed city and people.

On the 17th of July, the daily sacrifice ceased, according to the prediction of Daniel,* no proper person being left to minister at the altar.

The Roman commander had determined to save the Temple, as an honor to himself, but the Lord of Hosts had purposed its destruction. On the 10th of August, a Roman soldier seized a brand of fire, and threw it into one of the windows. The whole Temple was soon in flames. The frantic Jews, and Titus himself, labored to extinguish it, but in vain. Titus entered into the sanctuary, and bore away the golden candlestick, the table of show-bread, and the volume of the law, wrapped up in a rich golden tissue. The complete conquest of Jerusalem ensued. Christ had foretold that "there should be great tribulation, such as was not since the beginning of the world." During the siege, which lasted five months, eleven hundred thousand Jews perished, ninety-seven thousand were taken prisoners. The number destroyed during the war, which lasted seven years, is computed at one million four hundred and sixty-two thousand. This city was amazingly strong. Upon viewing the ruins, Titus exclaimed, "we have fought with the assistance of God." The city was completely leveled, and Tarentius Rufus ploughed up the foundations of the Temple. Thus literally were the predictions of Christ fulfilled, "thine enemies shall lay thee even with the ground, and there shall not be left one stone upon another."†

The state of the Jews after the destruction of Jerusalem, was indescribably wretched. Indeed, in consequence of the number slain and carried captive, and the vast multitude of fugitives to other lands, the country was almost depopulated. Only a few women and old men remained about Jerusalem. All the land of Judea was sold by an imperial edict, and the tribute was confiscated which had been annually paid to the Temple. They no longer existed as a nation, but were scattered through the earth, and have continued to this day, a wonder, a reproach, and a by-word among all nations.

---

* Daniel ix. 27.   † Luke xix. 44

Such were the judgments of heaven upon the first opposers of the gospel of Christ.

But the most terrible opposition with which the Gospel met, because supported by the greatest worldly power, was from the Roman Emperors. Every system of religion had been tolerated among Pagan nations, because it tolerated, in turn, every other system. But Christianity was an exclusive system. It utterly condemned and discarded all the gods of the heathen as vanity and a lie, and turned into derision all the absurdities of pagan superstition. It waged an exterminating war against all the sacrifices, temples, images, oracles, and sacerdotal orders of Greece and Rome; cut off an immense multitude of priests, of augurs, attendants, and artists, from their ordinary means of subsistency; and was so simple in its form of worship, having no visible symbol of Diety, as to appear to the common people, little better than Atheism. By the heathen, therefore, the Christians were accounted a detestable race; and the ingenuity of the priests was employed in increasing the public prejudice against them, by representing them as the cause of all the judgments of Heaven which descended upon mankind.

Ten general persecutions they are said to have suffered in the early ages of the church; besides many that were limited to particular provinces. This exact number, however, it is difficult for us to verify; but we can specify two before the close of the first century, and others at the commencement of the second, in which the number of martyrdoms was prodigiously great and the sufferings of Christians were beyond description.

The first persecution commenced under Nero, about the year of our Lord 64, and continued about four years. This inhuman monster set fire to the city of Rome, that he might have the pleasure of seeing the conflagration. The odium he incurred nearly cost him his head. To clear himself, he charged it upon the Christians, and inflicted upon them the most awful sufferings. The following account, given by Tacitus, an heathen historian, is entitled to the fullest credit, and gives us many interesting and valuable particulars. " But neither the emperor's donations, nor the atonements offered to the gods, could remove the scandal of this report, but it was still believed that the city had been burnt by his instigation. Nero, therefore, to put a stop to the rumor, charged the fact, and inflicted the severest punishments for it, upon the Chris-

CHAPTER 3.] MARTYRDOM OF PAUL AND PETER. 167

tians, as they were commonly called, a people detestable for their crimes. The author of this sect was Christ, who was put to death by Pontius Pilate. The destructive superstition which was by this means suppressed for the present, soon broke out again, and not only overspread Judea, where it first arose, but reached even to Rome, where all abominations from every quarter are sure to meet and find acceptance. Some who confessed themselves Christians, were first apprehended, and a vast multitude afterward upon their impeachment, who were condemned, not so much for burning the city, as for being the objects of universal hatred. Their sufferings and torments were heightened by mockery and derision. Some were inclosed in the skins of wild beasts, that they might be torn in pieces by dogs; others were crucified; and others, being covered with inflammable matter, were lighted up as torches at the close of the day. These spectacles were exhibited in Nero's gardens, where he held a kind of Circensian show, either mixing with the populace in the habit of a charioteer, or himself contending in the race. Hence it came to pass, that criminal and undeserving of mercy as they were, yet they were pitied as being destroyed merely to gratify his savage and cruel disposition, and not with any view to the public good."

Tacitus had the common feeling about Christianity as a destructive superstition, and about Christians as undeserving of mercy; but his testimony shows the extent and horror of the persecution, and the pity excited in the minds of the people. This persecution ceased at the death of Nero, who destroyed himself; he having been condemned by a decree of the senate, to be whipped to death.

In this persecution, Paul and Peter suffered martyrdom. The former, after his two years imprisonment at Rome, once more visited and confirmed the churches; but, returning to Rome, about the year 65, he found no mercy from Nero. He had converted to the faith the tyrant's concubine and cup-bearer, and had displayed before him the terrors of the judgment. Such a man was not to be tolerated. He was slain with the sword, by Nero's order.

Peter probably* came to Rome, about the year 63. Here he wrote his two espistles. During the violence of persecu-

---

* It is thought by many that Peter never came to Rome, but spent his life in the east. 7*

tion, the brethren begged him to retreat. But he chose to remain, warned of his end, it is reported, in a vision by Christ. He was crucified with his head downward—a kind of death which he requested, because he had denied his Lord and Master.

A second general persecution broke out about 94, under Domitian; a prince greatly resembling Nero, in his temper and conduct. He almost extirpated the church by his cruelties. Forty thousand Christians were put to death. By him the Apostle John was banished to the isle of Patmos, where he had his revelations. By him also, Flavius Clemens, a man of consular dignity, and Flavila Domitilla, his niece or wife, who had become distinguished Christians, were put to death.

Opposition of a deadly character also arose against the church, from another quarter, in the early stage of its existence. Pretended friends rested in her bosom, who propagated doctrines utterly subversive of the Gospel of Christ. Tertullian and Theodoret reduce them to two classes, the Docetæ and the Ebionites. The former denied the supreme divinity of Christ, and also that the Son of God had any proper humanity, and asserted that he died on the cross in appearance only. The latter asserted that Jesus Christ was a mere man, though of a most excellent character. They both denied atonement by his blood, and expected justification by their own works. Among the former were the Nicolatians, whom Christ himself mentions to John with utter abhorrence. They had many disgusting peculiarities; allowed a community of wives, and indulged themselves without restraint in sensual pleasures. Against these heresies, John wrote his epistle, in which he fully asserts the real proper divinity of the Saviour. The Ebionites considered the law of Moses as obligatory upon all men, and as bringing salvation. They by their activity and zeal in propagating error, and perplexing the early Christians, drew from Paul some of his best epistles. The watchfulness and power of the Apostles, and the care shown by the friends of truth and godliness, to keep themselves distinct from all who perverted the Gospel, preserved the churches from destruction

CHAPTER IV.

General state of the church from the first century to Constantine. Extension of the Gospel. Change of means. Persecution in Bithynia. Pliny's letter to Trajan. Writings of Clement. Death of Simeon. Martyrdom of Ignatius. Favorable decree of Antoninus Pius. Persecutions under Marcus. Justin Martyr. Polycarp. Persecutions in France. Rest to the churches under Commodus. Corruptions of the second century. Increase of rites and ceremonies. Easter.

THE history of the Church of Christ, from the close of the first century to the commencement of the fourth, is one of continual enlargement, but of gradual and deep declension in doctrine and holy practice; and of awful suffering from the fires of persecution. It was not, as it had been under the ancient dispensation, a distinct nation, governed by its own rulers and laws, appointed by God; but it was composed of a vast multitude, who lived in all parts of the Roman empire, who had been persuaded to renounce idolatry, and enlist under the banner of the Lord Jesus Christ; and who were united in small associations or churches—each enjoying the ministration of the Gospel and Christian ordinances from a stated Pastor.

Every year, converts to Christianity were prodigiously multiplied, until one of the Fathers could say, " We have filled all your towns, cities, islands, castles, boroughs, councils, camps, courts, palaces, senate, forum;" but we have no means of correctly ascertaining the exact time when the Gospel was carried to various distant nations, or who were, in all cases, the favored instruments of disseminating the truth. We have already seen with what amazing rapidity it spread during the ministry of the Apostles. But it is not like an art or a science, which mankind find useful to themselves, and which is no sooner known by one nation, than it is carefully sought for and possessed by every other. It must be carried to the world, and pressed upon their notice by those who possess it; and it will be carried by those only who are constrained by the love of Christ. Had the church retained her first zeal and love, not a nation or family would long have remained without the Gospel. But her love and zeal subsided, until few efforts were made to bring men to the acknowledgment of Christ, except for purposes of worldly ambition. It is certain, however, that Christ was known and worshipped as God, among the Franks, Germans, Spaniards, Celts, Britons, and throughout the East, before the close of the second century; and that, at the end of the period we are considering, Christianity became the acknowledged religion of the whole Roman empire.

As the church advanced in age, and became widely extended, the means of increase and strength were in some respects changed. The Apostolic office had ceased. The sacred canon being closed, prophets were no more. As the Gospel was received by different nations, among whom preachers were raised up, there was no farther use for the miraculous gift of tongues. And as it was essential that the world should be convinced by miracles that Christ and the first promulgators of truth only, were inspired from Heaven, the power of healing diseases and interrupting the established laws of nature, was soon withheld; at what exac period, has been the subject of much dispute, but is of little moment. One thing is certain, that men are converted by the Gospel, by evangelical truth, and not by miracles; and that, as far as true religion was spread, and men were gathered into the kingdom of God, it was by the preaching of Christ and him crucified. This remained the standing means of salvation.

Copies of the sacred Scriptures were multiplied and circulated to as great an extent as they could be, in an age when the art of printing was unknown, and the mass of Christians were neither learned nor wealthy. The Latin versions were chiefly used, because that language was generally spoken throughout the Roman empire.

Most of the emperors who reigned in the second century, were of a mild and lenient character; and, under their administration, the churches enjoyed many seasons of tranquillity, though occasionally they were called to pass through the fire. Before the close of the first century, Nerva had granted toleration to the church, and restored the Christian exiles. But his successor, Trajan, renowned for his philosophic virtues, if he did not issue edicts against the Christians, suffered the populace to wreak their vengeance on them, and destroy them at their pleasure.

A violent persecution raged in Bithynia. Not knowing what course to pursue, Pliny, governor of the province, addressed a letter to the emperor, which, as it gives such an account of the Christians, as a heathen of intelligence and candor would form, and an official relation of the persecutions of the age, deserves, together with the answer of Trajan, a place in every ecclesiastical history. It was probably written in the year 106 or 107, soon after the death of the Apostle John.

C. PLINY TO TRAJAN, EMPEROR.

"Health. It is my usual custom, Sir, to refer all things of which I harbor any doubt, to you. For who can better direct my judgment in its hesitation, or instruct my understanding in its ignorance? I never had the fortune to be present at any examination of Christians, before I came into this province. I am therefore at a loss to determine what is the usual object of inquiry or of punishment, and to what length either of them is to be carried. It has also been with me a question very problematical: whether any distinction should be made between the young and the old, the tender and the robust; whether any room should be given for repentance, or the guilt of Christianity once incurred, is not to be expiated by the most unequivocal retraction; whether the name itself, abstracted from any flagitiousness of conduct, or the crimes connected with the name, be the object of punishment. In the mean time, this has been my method, with respect to those who were brought before me as Christians. I asked them whether they were Christians. If they plead guilty, I interrogated them twice afresh, with a menace of capital punishment. In case of obstinate perseverance, I ordered them to be executed. For of this I had no doubt, whatever was the nature of their religion, that a sullen and obstinate inflexibility called for the vengeance of the magistrate. Some were infected with the same madness, whom on account of their citizenship, I reserved to be sent to Rome, to your tribunal. In the course of this business, informations pouring in as is usual when they are encouraged, more cases occurred. An anonymous libel was exhibited, with a catalogue of names of persons, who yet declared that they were not Christians then, nor ever had been; and they repeated after me an invocation of the gods and of your image, which, for this purpose, I had ordered to be brought with the images of the deities. They performed sacred rites with wine and frankincense, and execrated Christ, which, I am told, no Christian can ever be compelled to do. On this account, I dismissed them. Others named by an informer, first affirmed, and then denied the charge of Christianity; declaring that they had been Christians, but had ceased to be so, some three years ago; others, still longer; some even twenty years ago. All of them worshipped your image, and the statues of the gods, and also execrated Christ. And this was the account which they gave of the nature of the religion they once had professed, whether it deserves the name of crime or error, namely—that they were accustomed on a stated day to meet before daylight, and to repeat among themselves a hymn to Christ, as to a god, and to bind themselves by an oath, with an obligation of not committing any wickedness; but, on the contrary, of abstaining from thefts, robberies and adulteries; also, of not violating their promise, or denying a pledge; after which it was their custom to separate, and to meet again at a promiscuous, harmless meal, from which last practice, however, they desisted, after the publication of my edict, in which, agreeably to your orders, I forbade any societies of that sort. On which account I judged it the more necessary to inquire, by torture, from two females, who were said to be deaconesses, what is the real truth. But nothing could I collect, except a depraved and excessive superstition. Deferring therefore any farther investigation, I determined to consult you. For the number of culprits is so great, as to call for serious consultation.

"Many persons are informed against, of every age and of both sexes; and more still will be in the same situation. The contagion of the superstition hath spread, not only through cities, but even villages in the country. Not that I think it impossible to check and to correct it. The success of my endeavors hitherto forbids such desponding thoughts; for the temples, once almost desolate, begin to be frequented, and the sacred solemnities, which had long been intermitted, are now attended afresh, and the sacrificial victims are now sold every where, which once could scarcely find a purchaser. Whence, I conclude that many might be reclaimed, were the hope of impunity on repentance absolutely confirmed."

TRAJAN TO PLINY.

"You have done perfectly right, my dear Pliny, in the inquiry which you have made concerning Christians. For truly, no one general rule can be laid down, which will apply itself to all cases. These people must not be sought after. If they are brought before you and convicted, let them be capitally punished; yet with this restriction, that if any one renounce Christianity, and evidence his sincerity by supplicating our gods, however suspected he may be for the past, he shall obtain pardon for the future on his repentance. But anonymous libels ought, in no case, to be attended to; for the precedent would be of the worst sort, and perfectly incongruous to the maxims of my government."

From this important correspondence, we learn that Christians were then very numerous:—that they every where worshipped Christ as God; that their morals were not only unimpeachable, but of an high character, and that, because of the spirit of Christianity, the heathen temples were almost desolate, and the sacrificial victims could scarce find a purchaser. This is the testimony, not of a Christian, but of a heathen governor. Strange that such men as Trajan and Pliny should not have been allured by a religion which made such good men and peaceable citizens; or, at least, should not have withheld from them entirely the arm of persecution. But there is no coincidence between the religion of a virtuous pagan, and the Gospel of Christ. The one fosters human pride; the other, humbles man in the dust; so that often the bitterest enemies of the cross, are those who have made the greatest attainments, as they themselves think, in the moral virtues.

The order of Trajan, however, was favorable to the Christians, as it forbade all search to be made after them, and prohibited all anonymous libels and accusations, though it still left the door open for persecution and death.

From this correspondence also, and from the other historical records of the age, we learn that the Christians were looked upon with the utmost contempt. Pliny calls their religion "a depraved and excessive superstition," and views their attachment to the Gospel, as a sullen and obstinate inflexibility, demanding the vengeance of the magistrate. No epithets could be too debased to be heaped upon them. They were called atheists, magicians, haters of the light, self-murderers, eaters of human flesh; and were accused of unnatural crimes, which are not to be mentioned. But their accusers could bring nothing against them, excepting that they would not invoke the gods and execrate Christ; and when any apostates would do this, they were at once forgiven and admitted into favor, notwithstanding these charges of gross immorality.

Had we correct biographical notices of those who conversed with them, and survived the Apostles, we should, no doubt, find many among them who illustriously adorned the doctrine of God their Saviour. The writings only of Clement, who presided nine years over the Church of Rome, and whom Paul calls his fellow laborer, whose "name is in the book of life," have come down to us. He wrote an epistle to the Corinthians, at the close of the first century; which presents him as strongly attached to the fundamental doctrines of the Gospel, and animated by a truly apostolic spirit; and the Corinthians, as still possessing the faith, and hope, and charity of the Gospel, though tarnished, as in the days of Paul, with pride and a schismatical spirit.

The successor of James, in the pastoral office at Jerusalem, was Simeon. The church had fled to Pella, when the city was encompassed with the Roman armies; but it returned to Judea, about the beginning of Trajan's reign, after quiet was restored, and the city in some measure rebuilt. There Adrian found them worshipping in a small building upon Mount Zion, when he came to repair Jerusalem. Simeon lived to a great age. Being accused before Atticus, the Roman governor, he was scourged many days and then crucified, A. D. 107.

In the same year, Ignatius, who presided in the church of Antioch, suffered martyrdom for the faith of Jesus. He had in his youth been a disciple of John, and had been intimately acquainted with Peter and Paul. Peter, it is said, laid hands on him when he was ordained to the pastoral office. Having continued in the pastoral charge about forty years, he presented himself before Trajan on his way to the Parthian war, hoping to avert a storm which was then ready to burst on the Christians. "What an impious spirit art thou," said Trajan, "both to transgress our commands, and to inveigle others into the same folly to their ruin!" "Theophorus ought not to be called so," answered Ignatius, "forasmuch as all wicked spirits are departed from the servants of God. But if you call me impious because I am hostile to evil spirits, I own the charge in that respect. For I dissolve all their snares through Christ, the heavenly king." Traj. "Pray, who is Theophorus?" Ign. "He who has Christ in his breast." Traj. "And thinkest thou not that gods reside in us also, who fight for us against our enemies?" Ign. "You mistake in calling the demons of the nations by the name of gods. For there is only one God, who made heaven and earth, the sea and all that is in them; and one Jesus Christ, his only begotten Son, whose kingdom be my portion.' Traj. "His kingdom, do you say, who was crucified under Pilate?" Ign. "His, who crucified my sin with its author, and has put all the fraud and malice of Satan under the feet of those who carry him in their hearts." Traj. "Dost thou then carry him who was crucified with thee?" Ign. "I do; for it is written, 'I dwell in them, and walk in them.'" Then Trajan pronounced this sentence against him. "Since Ignatius confesses that he carries within himself him that was crucified, we command that he be carried, bound by soldiers, to great Rome, there to be thrown to the wild beasts for the entertainment of the people."

This excellent man, "full of faith and of the Holy Ghost," was hurried off to the place of suffering. On his way to Rome, he stopped at Smyrna to visit Polycarp. They had been fellow disciples of John. Their meeting was joyful. Seven epistles were written by him to as many churches before he reached the end of his journey. From these, which are still extant, though perhaps corrupted, we learn that the churches of Asia retained much evangelical purity, though they were often greatly perplexed by heresies, and borne down by persecution; that the deity, manhood, and atonement of Christ, were doctrines unspeakably precious: and that an entire separation from all who deny the fundamental doctrines of Christianity, was the foundation of their long continued prosperity. When he came to Rome he was anxious for a speedy martyrdom, and had his wish granted, for he was immediately led into the amphitheatre and thrown to the wild beasts. His bones were carefully collected by his friends and carried to Antioch.

Trajan was succeeded by Adrian, A. D. 117. This emperor was respectfully addressed by Quadratus and Aristides, two excellent Athenian Christians, in behalf of the churches; and by them he seems to have been induced to direct that the calumniators of Christians should not only not be heard, but should be punished; and that, if any were presented before the magistrates, they should be condemned only as it should appear that they had broken the laws. This was the most favorable decree that had ever been made relating to the followers of Christ.

During Adrian's reign, appeared a great impostor among the Jews, called Barchobebas, because he pretended to be the Star prophesied of by Balaam. Defeated in every way and reduced to the greatest extremities, the Jews received him with open arms. He came out in rebellion against the emperor, but was soon defeated and slain. In the conflict, however, the Christians were great sufferers; for the Jews, looking upon them as the authors of their calamities, every where inflicted upon them the greatest cruelties.

The next emperor, Antoninus Pius, was still more favorable to the Christians. In the third year of his reign, A. D. 140, Justin Martyr, a very able defender of the truth, presented him an apology for Christianity, which had no small influence on his mind. An edict issued by him, in consequence of complaints made from Asia of the Christians, as the cause of the earthquakes, speaks volumes in his praise, and in praise too, of the persecuted.

"THE EMPEROR TO THE COMMON COUNCIL OF ASIA."

" I am quite of opinion that the gods will take care to discover such persons. For it much more concerns them to punish those who refuse to worship them, than you, if they be able. But you harass and vex the Christians and accuse them of atheism and other crimes, which you can by no means prove. To them it appears an advantage to die for their religion; and they will gain their point, while they throw away their lives rather than comply with your injunctions. As to the earthquakes which have happened in past times, or lately, is it not proper to remind you of your own despondency, when they happen, and to desire you to compare your spirit with theirs and observe how serenely they confide in God! In such seasons you seem to be ignorant of the gods, and to neglect their worship. You live in the practical ignorance of the supreme God himself, and you harass and persecute to death those who do worship him. Concerning these same men, some others of the provincial governors wrote to our divine father Adrian, to whom he returned answer, 'That they should not be molested, unless they appeared to attempt something against the Roman government.' Many, also, have signified to me concerning these men, to whom I have returned an answer agreeable to the maxims of my father. But if any person will still persist in accusing the Christians merely as such—let the accused be acquitted, though he appear to be a Christian, and let the accuser be punished."

This was certainly no ordinary, and we are assured by Eusebius, it was no empty edict; for it was fully put in execution, and gave the church about twenty-three years of peace and prosperity. But such seasons she was liable to abuse; provoking against her the anger of heaven. From worldly mindedness and stupidity, however, she was again soon roused by the fires of persecution.

In the year 161, Pius was succeeded by Marcus Antoninus, a man of eminence in the schools of philosophy; whose meditations, humanity, and beneficence, have gained him the plaudits of succeeding generations, but whose pride and self importance made him scorn the doctrines of the cross; made him, for nineteen years, a bitter persecutor of the followers of the meek and lowly Jesus. Very able apologies were made for the Christians by Justin, Tatian, Athenagoras, Apollinaris, Theophilus, and Melito; but they were regarded by Marcus as a vain, obstinate, and evil-minded race, and left without relief, to the most cruel tortures. So much, however, were former edicts regarded, that none could be condemned unless some crime was brought against them; but the enraged heathen priests and corrupt judges, found no difficulty in suborning false witnesses, and procuring the death of all who were brought before them.

In the year 163, the able apologist, Justin, slept in Jesus. He was educated a philosopher, and was, probably, the most learned man, who, from the days of the Apostles, had embraced Christianity. In early life he wandered through all the systems of philosophy in pursuit of God and happiness, but found no satisfaction. At length he examined the Gospel, and found peace for his soul. To the cause of the Redeemer he consecrated his habits of study, and became its able supporter. His views of Christian doctrine were once, in the main, evangelical; but he was nearly ruined by a philosophizing spirit. Of those who denied the deity of Christ, he thus expressed himself: "There are some who call themselves Christians, who confess him to be the Christ, but still maintain that he is a mere man only, with whom I agree not; neither do most of those who bear that name agree with them; because we are commanded by Christ himself not to obey the precepts of men, but his own injunctions, and those of the holy prophets. As for myself, I am too mean to say any thing becoming his infinite deity." His apologies for Christianity are still extant, and are very valuable.

This learned and excellent man was imprisoned, whipped, and beheaded for the crime of being a Christian. We have his testimony to the interesting and important fact, that the churches in his time examined those they received, not only concerning their creed, but concerning a work of grace in their hearts.

But the most distinguished martyr of the age, was Polycarp. This venerable man was the disciple of John,—was intimate with the apostles, and was ordained by them over the church of Smyrna. The learned Usher says, it is beyond all question, that he was the angel of the church of Smyrna, to whom the apocalyptical epistle was sent. If so, his martyrdom was there particularly predicted. For seventy years he had been a firm pillar in the church. Against the heretics of the age, especially the Docetae, who denied the humanity of Christ, rejected the Old Testament, and mutilated the New, he opposed himself with the greatest firmness. To Marcion, their chief, who one day called out to him, " Polycarp, own us ;" " I do own thee," said he, "to be the first born of Satan." Ireneus informs us, that he often heard from his lips an account of his conversations with John, and others who had seen our Lord, whose sayings he rehearsed.

This venerable man was brought to the tribunal in the hundredth year of his age. The proconsul told him to reproach Christ and he would release him. " Eighty and six years," said Polycarp, " have I served him, and he hath never wronged me, and how can I blaspheme my King who hath saved me ?" " I have wild beasts," said the proconsul. " Call them," said the martyr. " I will tame your spirit by fire." " You threaten me with fire which burns for a moment and will be soon extinct; but you are ignorant of the future judgment, and of the fire of eternal punishment reserved for the ungodly. But why do you delay ? Do what you please." The fire being prepared, and he being bound, a distinguished sacrifice, clasped his hands, which were tied behind him, and said, " O Father of thy beloved and blessed Son, Jesus Christ, through whom we have attained a knowledge of thee, O God of angels and principalities, and of all creation, and of all the just who live in thy sight, I bless thee that thou hast counted me worthy of this day, and this hour, to receive my portion in the number of martyrs, in the cup of Christ, for the resurrection to eternal life, both of soul and body, in the incorruption of the Holy Ghost, among whom may I be received before thee this day as a sacrifice well savored and acceptable, which thou the faithful and true God has prepared, promised beforehand, and fulfilled accordingly. Wherefore I praise thee for all these things, I glorify thee by the Eternal High Priest, thy well beloved Son, through whom, with him in the Holy Spirit, be glory to thee, both now and forever. Amen,"

Eleven brethren from Philadelphia suffered with him, A. D. 167. If the Lord Jesus Christ died as a mere martyr to the truth, how inferior was he in fortitude, to his servant Polycarp. " O my Father," said he, " If it be possible, let this cup pass from me." But he was an atoning sacrifice, called to bear his Father's wrath, for our sins.

By the persecutions of Antoninus, our attention is here directed to a country hitherto unknown in ecclesiastical history. Flourishing churches had been planted in Vienne, and Lyons in France, then called Galia; probably by the churches of Asia. The account given by themselves of their sufferings, under Severus, the Roman governor, will be read with great interest by all who love to trace the children of God in their Christian warfare. It affords a very full account of the humility, meekness, patience, magnanimity and heavenly-mindedness of the martyrs; of the influences of the Holy Spirit; of the supports of religion, under the most excruciating sufferings, and must excite in every reader, a spirit of gratitude to God, for the inestimable blessings which we, in this age of light and liberty, are permitted to enjoy.

The epistle of the Churches of Vienne and Lyons, to the Brethren in Asia and Phrygia.

ABRIDGED.

" The servants of Christ, sojourning in Vienne, and Lyons in France, to the brethren in Asia, Propria, and Phrygia, who have the same faith and hope of redemption with us; peace and grace and glory from God the Father, and Christ Jesus our Lord.

" We are not competent to describe with accuracy, nor is it

in our power to express the greatness of the affliction sustained here by the saints; the intense animosity of the heathen against them, and the complicated sufferings of the blessed martyrs. The grand enemy assaulted us with all his might; and by his first essays, exhibited intentions of exercising malice without limits and without control. He left no method untried to habituate his slaves to his bloody work and to prepare them by previous exercises against the servants of God. Christians were absolutely prohibited from appearing in any houses, excepting their own; in baths; in the market; or in any public place whatever. The grace of God, however, fought for us, preserving the weak and exposing the strong; who, like pillars, were able to withstand them in patience, and to draw the whole fury of the wicked against themselves. These entered into the contest, and sustained every species of pain and reproach. What was heavy to others, to them was light while they were hastening to Christ, evincing, indeed, that *the sufferings of this present time are not worthy to be compared with the glory that shall be revealed in us.*

"'The first trial was from the people at large; shouts, blows, the dragging of their bodies, the plundering of their goods, casting of stones, and the confining of them within their own houses, and all the indignities which may be expected from a fierce and outrageous multitude; these were magnanimously sustained. Being led into the Forum by the tribune and the magistrates, they were examined before all the people, whether they were Christians; and, on pleading guilty, were shut up in prison till the arrival of the governor. Before him they were at length brought, and he treated us with the greatest savageness of manners. The capital martyrs discharged their part with all alacrity of mind. Others seemed not so ready—as yet weak, unable to sustain the shock of so great a contest. Ten lapsed, whose cases filled us with great and unmeasurable sorrow. Persons were now apprehended daily, of such as were counted worthy to fill up the number of the lapsed; so that the most excellent were selected from the two churches, even those by whose labor they had been founded and established. They seized at the same time, some of our heathen servants, who, by the impulse of Satan, fearing the torments which they saw inflicted on the saints, at the suggestion of the soldiers, accused us of eating human flesh, and of various unnatural crimes, and of things not fit even to be mentioned or imagined, and such as ought not to be believed of mankind. These things being divulged, all were incensed to madness against us, so that if some were formerly more moderate on account of any connexions of blood, affinity or friendship, they were then transported beyond all bounds with indignation.

"Now it was that our Lord's word was fulfilled—'The time will come, when whosoever killeth you will think that he doeth God service.'—The holy martyrs now sustained tortures which exceed the powers of description; Satan laboring by means of these tortures, to extort something slanderous against Christianity. The whole fury of the multitude, the governor and the soldiers, were spent in a particular manner on Sanctus of Vienne, the deacon; and on Maturus, a late convert indeed, but a magnanimous wrestler in spiritual things; and on Attalus of Pergamus, a man who had ever been a pillar and support of our church; and lastly, on Blandina, through whom Christ showed that those things that appear unsightly and contemptible among men, are most honorable in the presence of God, on account of love to his name, exhibited in real energy, and not in boasting and pompous pretences. To every interrogatory, Sanctus answered, I am a Christian. Having exhausted all the usual methods of torture, they at last fixed red hot plates of brass to the most tender parts of his body. But he remained inflexible. Some young persons whose bodies had been unexercised with sufferings, unequal to the severity of the confinement, expired. Pothinus, bishop of Lyons, upwards of ninety years of age, and very infirm and asthmatic, yet strong in spirit, and panting after martyrdom, was dragged before the tribunal, treated with the greatest indignity, thrown into prison, where, after two days, he expired.

"The martyrs were put to death in various ways. Maturus, Sanctus, Blandina, and Attalus, were led to the wild beasts in the amphitheatre, to be the common spectacle of Gentile inhumanity.

"Cæsar sent orders that the confessors of Christ should be put to death, and that the apostates from their divine master should be dismissed. These were interrogated separate from the rest, as persons soon to be dismissed, and made a confession to the surprise of the Gentiles, and were added to the list of martyrs. A small number still remained in apostacy; but they were those who possessed not the least spark of divine faith, had not the least acquaintance with the riches of Christ in their souls, and had no fear of God before their eyes; whose life had brought reproach on Christianity, and had evidenced them to be the children of perdition.

" On the last day of the spectacles, Blandina was again introduced with Ponticus, a youth of fifteen. They were ordered to swear by the idols ; and the mob perceiving them to persevere immovably, were incensed, and no pity was shown. Ponticus, animated by his sister, who was observed by the heathen to strengthen and confirm him, after a magnanimous exertion of patience, yielded up the ghost. After Blandina had endured stripes, the tearing of the beasts, and the hot iron chair, she was inclosed in a net and thrown to a bull ; and having been tossed some time by the animal, and proving quite superior to her pains, through the influence of hope and the realizing view of the objects of her faith and her fellowship with Christ, she at length breathed out her soul. Even her enemies confessed that no woman among them had ever suffered such and so great things.

"'The bodies of the martyrs having been contumeliously treated and exposed for six days, were burnt and reduced to ashes, and scattered by the wicked into the Rhone, that not the least particle of them might appear on the earth any more. And they did these things as if they could prevail against God, and prevent their resurrection—and that they might deter others, as they said, ' from the hope of a future life ;—on which relying, they introduce a strange and new religion, and despise the most excruciating tortures, and die with joy. Now let us see if they will rise again, and if their God can help them, and deliver them out of our hands.'"

Antoninus was succeeded, towards the close of the second century, by Commodus; under whom, though he himself was a most profligate prince, the church enjoyed about twelve years of peace and rest. During this period, many of the nobility of Rome, with their whole families, embraced Christianity, and the Gospel was widely extended.

The second century was not favorable to the rise of new and powerful heresies. The great line of distinction was yet between pagans and Christians. The question was,—Will you bow to the idols, or are you a follower of the Lord Jesus Christ ? The Christians were too much oppressed to be contending with each other, and had too much of the simple faith of Jesus to give heed to seducing spirits. Opposers theie were, as in the first century, to the deity and humanity of Christ, and to the doctrines of grace, who ran into a thousand unmeaning subtleties and fancies, according with the philosophy of the age; and one Montanus pretended that he was the *Paraclete*, or Comforter, whom the divine Saviour, at his departure, promised to send to his disciples, to lead them into all truth, and who was to perfect the Gospel by adding new precepts, requiring holiness and more abstraction from the world than Christ had demanded. He had many followers in Asia and Africa. But no new doctrine was able in this period to create any extensive and permanent interest.

Owing, however, to a co-operation of a number of powerful causes, there was in this century a vast increase of useless rites and ceremonies. The Christians innocently desired a spread of Christianity. Instead of depending on the power of truth and holy example, under the operation of the Spirit, they attempted to please both Jews and heathens, by an adoption of forms and ceremonies from their religions. They were called atheists, because of the simplicity and spirituality of their religion; and, to avoid this reproach, they were induced to have a more visible and splendid worship, to multiply temples, altars, days of fasting, peculiarites of dress, and splendid ceremonies. To give importance to Christian doctrine, the symbolical manner of teaching, popular in that age, was introduced; and, to express their new and solemn engagements to Christ, military rites and phrases were brought into the peaceful kingdom of the Redeemer. Having once, from these and other causes, departed from the simplicity of Christian worship, the multiplication of rites and ceremonies ceased not for centuries.

Christ had instituted the Supper as a memorial of his death; but, not content with this, his followers soon began to commemorate, annually, almost every remarkable event which occurred in the first establishment of Christianity. The great anniversary festivals, which had in this century gained footing, were in commemoration of the death and resurrection of Christ, and of the outpouring of the Spirit upon the Apostles. The first, which was called Easter, or the paschal feast, because the day of Christ's death was considered as the same as that on which the Jews celebrated the passover, was soon the occasion of a disgraceful schism, which rent asunder the Christian world. The Asiatic Christians observed this festival on the fourteenth day of the first Jewish month; and, three days after, commemorated the resurrection of Christ. The Western Christians celebrated it the night before his resurrection, that they might connect his death and resurrection in one festival. Frequent conferences were held among distinguished men in the East and the West. Towards the close of the second century, Victor, bishop of Rome, endeavored to compel the Asiatic churches to submit to the Western custom, and failing in his attempt, broke all communion with them. Each party retained its own custom until the fourth century, when the council of Nice abolished that of the Asiatics, and reduced all the churches to uniformity.

CHAPTER V.

Conduct of the Roman Emperors in the third century. Extension of the Gospel. Decline of piety. Increase of useless rites. Genuine fruits of the Spirit. Tertullian's account of the conduct of the Christians. His character. Ireneus. Origen. Cyprian. Question concerning Infant Baptism. Novatians. Sabellians. Manicheans. Attacks of Heathen Philosophers. Porphyry. First great declension of Christianity. Tremendous Persecution under Dioclesian. Elevation of Constantine to the Roman Empire. Abolition of the Ancient Religion of Rome. Establishment of Christianity throughout the Empire.

THE remainder of the period, referred to in the beginning of the last chapter, was, excepting in its close, similar to that which has just been described; presenting a constant succession of persecutions from pagans, frequently relieved by Emperors who were friendly to the Christian cause. In the year 203, the Emperor Severus made a law, forbidding any subject of his empire to change his religion. This law was designed to retard the spread of the Gospel; and, being severely enforced, brought many, of both sexes, to the most cruel deaths. A few years after, the fires of persecution raged under Maximin. But the most dreadful persecution of the third century, was under Decius, who ascended the imperial throne, A. D. 249. He ordered the prætors, on pain of death, to extirpate the whole race of Christians without exception; or force them by torments, to bow to the heathen gods. This persecution raged about two years; vast multitudes were destroyed. But other emperors were extremely clement, and some, especially Philip and his son, so favorable to the Christians, as to produce a general impression that they were in heart with them. There was, therefore, a great advancement of the church in the third century; the persecution doing but little to retard, and much to purify her. The immunities of Christians, were, also, considerably increased, and, under most of the emperors, they were advanced to places of power and trust.

The limits of the church were considerably extended. Origen carried the Gospel into Arabia. Pantænus into India. And some zealous missionaries planted churches at Paris, Tours, and Arles, in France; also at Cologn, Treves, and Mentz, in Germany, and passed into Scotland.

Almost proportionate with the extension of Christianity, was the decrease in the church of vital piety. A philosophizing spirit among the higher, and a wild monkish superstition among the lower orders, fast took the place, in the third century, of the faith and humility of the first Christians. Many of the clergy became very corrupt, and excessively ambitious. In consequence of this, there was an awful defection of Christians under the persecution of Decius. Some wholly renounced Christianity, while others saved themselves either by offering sacrifice, or by burning incense before the heathen gods, or purchasing certificates from the heathen priests.

Amid the decline of piety and under the influence of the course already mentioned; useless rites and ceremonies continued to increase. The minds of men were filled with the oriental superstition concerning demons and apparitions, and with the business of exorcism and spells. Those who were not baptized or excommunicated, were carefully avoided as possessed of some evil spirit. And when any were baptized, the evil demon, with much form and ceremony, and loud shouting, was driven out, and the baptized were crowned and clothed with white garments as conquerors over sin and the world. The sign of the cross was, in this early period, supposed to possess power to avert calamities, and to drive off demons, and was carried by Christians wherever they went. Fasting was in high repute. Prayers were offered three times a day, and forms began to be introduced. Sermons were long, full of trope and figure, in affectation of Grecian eloquence. And saints began to feel that there could be no piety out of the bounds of a particular church government.

But notwithstanding these degeneracies, many and precious were the fruits of the Spirit. The church existed in an empire the most corrupt and abominable that the world had ever seen. But amid the grossest sensuality, practised without remorse, or loss of character, by men in the highest ranks, many of her fruits were holiness to the Lord. If she had not the purity of the first century, she had still a self-denial and elevation above the world, a fortitude under suffering, and a spirit of subordination, which no where else existed, and an attachment which made the wondering heathen exclaim, " Behold how these Christians love one another." Such was the strictness of her discipline, that a clergyman, once deposed for immorality, was never restored to his order; and a communicant once cast out for his vices, might be restored, but on a second ejection, could never be admitted to the church; though he might not be beyond the mercy of God and final salvation. Men spared no pains or expense, to obtain multiplied copies of the Word of God.

The Sabbath was strictly regarded, and the sacrament was weekly administered. This ordinance, however, began to be misused—being considered essential to salvation, and administered with pomp, even to infants.

To the powers that were, they submitted for conscience sake. The fires of persecution raged, the most odious calumnies were invented, men, vile and contemptible, exercised the most wanton barbarities under the ensigns of office. The Christians were amazingly numerous, and were possessed of learning, wealth, and talents; many of them were officers and soldiers in the Roman armies, and had they been disposed, might have given the government the greatest trouble, and perhaps overturned it completely; yet, no instance of insurrection, or resistance to civil authority, was known among them, for they remembered God had said, " Vengeance is mine." Their bitterest enemies could bring no other charge of treason but this, that they refused to worship the gods of Rome.

Their benevolence was such as the world had not before, and has scarce since seen. They not only gave their treasures to their own poor, but they exerted themselves to relieve distress and suffering, wherever they could find it. The Jew passed by the wounded Samaritan, and the Greek harangued about virtue, but never erected an hospital or an alms-house. But the church in Rome supported, at one time, a thousand and fifty widows. Christians felt that they did not deserve the appellation they bore, unless they spent their lives in doing good. Whole and immense estates were consecrated to public charity Having renounced the luxuries of the world, they did not need great wealth, and they viewed their poor brethren as on a level with themselves, as sinners, ransomed by the blood of the Son of God.

But their number and character is best shown by a writer of their own time:

"We pray," says Tertullian, in his apology for the Christians, "for the safety of the emperors to the eternal God. We look up to heaven with out-stretched hands, because they are harmless; with naked head because we are not ashamed; without a prompter, because we pray from the heart; constantly pray for all emperors, that they may have a long life, a secure empire, a safe palace, strong armies, a faithful senate, a well-moralized people, a quiet state of the world; whatever Cæsar would wish for himself in his public or private capacity. Were we disposed to act the part, I will not say of secret assassins, but of open enemies, should we want forces and numbers? Are there not multitudes of us in every part of the world? It is true, we are but of yesterday, and yet we have filled all your towns, cities, islands, burroughs, councils, camps, courts, palaces, senate, forum :—*We leave you only your temples.* For what war should we not be ready and well prepared, even though unequal in numbers; we—who die with so much pleasure, were it not that our religion requires us rather to suffer death than inflict it? If we were to make a general secession from your dominions, you would be astonished at your solitude. We are dead to all ideas of worldly honor and dignity; nothing is more foreign to us than political concerns. The whole world is our republic. We are a body united in one bond of religion, discipline and hope. We meet in our assemblies for prayer. Every one pays something into the public chest once a month, or when he pleases, and according to his ability and inclination, for there is no compulsion. These gifts are, as it were, the deposits of piety. Hence we relieve and bury the needy, support orphans and decrepit persons, those who have suffered shipwreck, and those who, for the word of God, are condemned to the mines for imprisonment. This very charity of ours has caused us to be noticed by some :—' See,' say they, ' how these Christians love one another.' "

Tertullian lived at Carthage in the latter part of the second, and beginning of the third century. In early life he was a lawyer, but became a presbyter of the church. He was a man of profound learning, of warm and vigorous piety; but of a temperament melancholy and austere; and unhappily adopted, in the close of life, the visions of Montanus. He is the first Latin writer of the church, whose works have been transmitted to us.

About the same period flourished Ireneus, bishop of Lyons. He was a Greek by birth, and a disciple of Polycarp. " I can describe," says he, in a letter to a friend, " the very spot in which Polycarp sat and expounded, and his coming in and going out, and the very manner of his life, and the figure of his body, and the sermons which he preached to the multitude, and how he related to us his converse with John and with the rest of those who had seen the Lord; how he mentioned the particular expressions, and what things he had heard from them of the Lord and of his miracles, and of his doctrine. As Polycarp had received from the eye-witnesses of the Word of life, he told us all things agreeably to the Scriptures. These things, then, through the mercy of God inviting me, I heard with seriousness: I wrote them, not on paper, but on my heart; and ever since, through the grace of God, I have a genuine remembrance of them; and I can witness before God, that if that blessed Apostolical Presbyter had heard some of the doctrines which are now maintained, he would have cried out, and stopped his ears, and in the usual manner, have said, O good God, to what times hast thou reserved me, that I should endure such things? And he would immediately have fled from the place in which he heard such doctrines."

Ireneus was ordained successor to Pothinus, A. D. 169, and suffered martyrdom under the persecution of Severus, in the beginning of the third century. He was a man of much meekness, humility, dexterity and resolution. He had a true missionary spirit. He was a superior Greek scholar, and doubtless might have obtained the luxuries and pleasures of Asia, but these he renounced from the love of souls. He went among the Gauls, learned their barbarous dialect, and conformed to their plain and homely fare. He wrote five books against the heresies of the age, which have been transmitted to us;—precious relics of antiquity.

About the middle of this century, two men shone with distinguished brightness;—Origen a presbyter and catechist of Alexandria, and Cyprian, bishop of Carthage.

In his youth, Origen saw his father beheaded for professing Christianity, and all the family estate confiscated. But Providence provided for him. A rich lady in Alexandria became his friend and patron. He applied himself to study, and soon acquired prodigious stores of learning. While pursuing his studies, he distinguished himself by his attachment to the martyrs, and was often in peril of his life. He early became a catechist in the school at Alexandria. Multitudes crowded to hear him, and were impressed by his instructions. His daily habit was one of excessive austerity. Hearing of the power of his doctrine, Mammea, the mother of the emperor, sent for him to hear him. At the age of forty-five, he was ordained a priest, and delivered theological lectures in Palestine. In diligence and learning, he surpassed all men. Of this the remains of his Hexapla is the memorial. To confront the Jews, who always objected against those passages of scripture which were quoted against them, as not agreeing with the Hebrew version, he undertook to reduce all the Latin and Greek versions then in use, into a body with the Hebrew text, that they might be at once compared. He made six columns. In the first, he placed the Hebrew as the standard, and in the next, the Septuagint, and then the other versions according to their dates—passage after passage. The whole filled fifty large volumes. It was found fifty years after his death, in an obscure place in the city of Tyre, and deposited in a public library. The most of it was destroyed in the capture of the city, A. D. 653. It was called the Hexapla, a work of six columns.

As a theologian, he was ruined by the Platonic philosophy; and unhappily introduced a mode of explaining scripture which was of incalculable injury to the church. He supposed it was not to be explained in a literal, but in an allegorical manner; and that the meaning of the sacred writers was to be sought in a hidden sense, arising from the things themselves. This hidden sense he endeavored to give, and always did it at the expense of truth. This hidden sense he farther divided into the moral and mystical. The latter was of his own creation and very wild. He seems to have been but little acquainted with the plain, evangelical doctrines of the Gospel; to have adopted most fatal errors; to have given no offence in his preaching to men of the world; but, on the contrary, to have been very popular with philosophers and philologists, and men of wild fancies and visionary notions; and was much honored by courts. He introduced the practice of selecting a single text as the subject of discourse. He suffered martyrdom, but no man did more to corrupt the simplicity of the Gospel, and his vast popularity gives us a low idea of the state of religion at that day.

Cyprian was no less great, but a very different character. He came late in life into the vineyard of Christ, without the learning of Origen, but with great abilities, and a heart devoted to the service of God. He was slain by the law; made to feel himself poor and wretched in the bond of paganism, and to inquire with earnestness for light and salvation. His conversion was sudden, but effectual, and he entered deeply into all the doctrines of grace. For twelve years he was bishop of Carthage,—strong in Episcopacy,—and, on the subject of miracles, unhappily wild. Thinking it his duty to save life, he once went into retirement during the persecution of Decius; but was as active when hidden from the view of his enemies, as when in public. He gave the Scriptures a literal interpretation. He maintained strict discipline in the churches, and, by his firmness and perseverance, gained the victory over a most powerful party who would open wide the door of pardon and reconciliation to all the lapsed. He effectually resisted many heresies; recovered many apostates; and, through his example and influence, the north of Africa, now covered with gross Mahommedan darkness, was, for many years, as the garden of God. He fell a glorious martyr to the cause of truth, A. D. 257, under the persecution of Valerian. .He bound the napkin over his own eyes. A presbyter and a deacon tied his hands, and the Christians placed before him handkerchiefs and napkins to receive his blood. His head was then severed from his body by a sword. His writings cannot fail to be read with pleasure and profit.

A letter of his, claims a place in ecclesiastical history, as throwing some light on a much disputed subject. A council of sixty-six bishops was held in Attica, over which Cyprian presided, for regulating the internal affairs of the churches. A question came before them whether infants should be baptized immediately after their birth, or on the eighth day. In a letter to Fidus, Cyprian says, " As to the case of infants, of whom you said that they ought not to be baptized within the second or third day of their birth, and that the ancient law of circumcision should be so far adhered to, that they ought not to be baptized till the eighth day, we were all of a very different opinion. We all judged that the mercy and grace of God should be denied to none Our sentence, therefore, dearest

CHAPTER 5.] NOVATIANS. MANICHEANS.

brother, in the council, was, that none, by us, should be prohibited from baptism and the grace of God, who is merciful and kind to all." While it was melancholy to see Christians so early connecting the grace of God with baptism, it is worthy of remark, that in the year 253, it was a question before sixty-six faithful ministers, not whether infants were the proper subjects of baptism, but whether they should be baptized immediately after their birth, or, according to the custom of circumcision, on the eighth day.

Two other men, Gregory Thaumaturgus, bishop of Neo-cesarea, and Firmilian, bishop of Cappadocia, pupils of the famous Origen, were distinguished lights of that period, though they were much injured by the eclectic philosophy. The miracles ascribed to Gregory by subsequent historians, deserve no credit. Many others have left able controversial writings. Indeed the defenders of Christianity were a mighty host.

In this century, a large body of Christians dissented from the main church, under Novatian, a priest of Rome; and a man of genius, learning, and eloquence; and of unimpeachable moral character; maintaining that the ·Church of Christ ought to be pure, and that a member, who had fallen into any offence, should never be re-admitted to communion. They obliged such as came to their party to be re-baptized. They were called Novatians, and seem to have walked closely with God.

In this century, also, a number of new sects, the Sabellians, Noetians, and others arose, denying the proper doctrine of the Trinity, and each having some peculiarities, relating to the character of Christ. Paul of Samosata advocated the same cause with the modern Socinians.

A most odious and violent sect was that of the Manicheans. It can hardly be called Christian. It was a motley mixture of Christianity with the old Magianism of Persia. Its founder, Manes, pretended that he was the Paraclete or Comforter who came to perfect the Gospel. His fundamental principle was that there were two original independent principles, one immaterial and supremely good; the other material, and the source of all evil, but actuated by an intelligence. He rejected as false the Old Testament and most of the New; and imposed great severities upon his followers. The Manicheans were headed by a President, who represented Jesus Christ. They were a monstrous sect, and show to what excesses the religious world were tending.

The heathen philosophers relaxed in this age none of their former zeal against Christianity, and lost none of their bitterness. They were headed by one Porphyry, a Syrian; a writer of much genius and cunning;—but more virulent than formidable. His captious reasonings against the book of Daniel have been mentioned in a former part of this work. These philosophers wrought much mischief by drawing comparisons between Christ and the sages of antiquity. Thus persuading many that there was no essential difference between philosophy and Christianity, and that Jesus was only one of the same order with Socrates and Plato, they brought them to feel that they could esteem both, and that it was not inconsistent with Christianity to remain in the religion of their ancestors. But while they and their cause have passed away, and the Lord has had them in derision, their attacks furnish strong evidence of the virtues and graces of the Christians.

The Church of Christ sustained its high and holy character but a little period after the age of the Apostles. It however remained very reputable until after the middle of the third century. From that period it was not the spiritual edifice it had been.

Cyprian says, that even before the Decian persecution, "long peace had corrupted the discipline. Each had been bent on improving his patrimony, and had forgotten what believers had done under the Apostles, and what they ought always to do. They were brooding over the arts of amassing wealth. The pastors and deacons each forgot their duty. Works of mercy were neglected, and discipline was at its lowest ebb. Luxury and effeminacy prevailed. Meretricious arts in dress were cultivated. Fraud and deceit were practiced among brethren. Christians could unite themselves in matrimony with unbelievers; could swear not only without reverence, but without veracity. Even bishops deserted their places of residence and their flocks. They traveled through distant provinces in quest of pleasure and gain, gave no assistance to the needy brethren at home, but were insatiable in their thirst for money. They possessed estates by fraud and multiplied usury. What have we not deserved to suffer for such conduct?"

One cause of the early declension of knowledge and piety in the church, doubtless was the neglect of education for the sacred ministry. Theological seminaries were unknown and what knowledge candidates for the pastoral office gained, was acquired from intercourse with learned bishops and pastors. At Alexandria, indeed, was a famous school under Pantænus, Origen, and Cyril, where theology to some extent, but of a very imperfect character, was taught; but we search the records of the first eight centuries in vain for any proper theological seminaries.

In the latter part of the third century the church had a long period of rest, and then indeed a great and general declension took place in doctrine and practice; and it is with difficulty that we can find for centuries, many of the genuine fruits of the Spirit. Still she had become embodied, and from many causes operating powerfully on the hopes and fears, the lusts and passions of men, she became a gigantic power in the earth. But forsaking God, she was given once more to the spoiler.

In the beginning of the fourth century, she passed through a furnace seven times heated. For eight years, a persecution raged, which spared neither age nor sex, in any part of the Roman world; which was unparalleled for its tortures and horrors; and which, to all human appearance, would root Christianity from the earth. Satan came down in great wrath. It seemed his last and most vigorous effort to save his cause. The church, lukewarm, engrossed with the world and distracted with divisions and heresies, was not prepared to meet it, yet she stood the shock with amazing heroism. Some suppose that it was in the days of this persecution that John "saw under the altar the souls of them that were slain for the word of God, and for the testimony which they held. And they cried with a loud voice, saying, how long, O Lord, holy and true, dost thou not judge and revenge our blood on them that dwell on the earth."

Dioclesian was at this time clothed with the imperial purple. He had an associate, Maximian, and under him two Cæsars, Galerius and Constantius. Of these, Galerius was the most savage, and did the most to instigate Dioclesian, who was himself averse to bloodshed, to the most cruel extremities. The persecution began at the feast of the Terminalia, in Nicodemia, A. D. 302, by pulling down all the churches of the Christians; burning their sacred books and writings, taking from them their civil rights and privileges, and rendering them incapable of any civil promotion. Soon after, a fire broke out in the royal palace. The Christians were accused as the incendiaries, and numbers were put to torture. Some tumults also arose in Armenia and Syria, which were by the heathen priests charged upon them. The clergy were cast into prison, and given up to the most insupportable punishments, the rulers hoping that if the pastors renounced Christianity, the people would follow them. Vast numbers of learned and excellent men fell a prey to this stratagem. In the year 304 a new edict was published, in which the magistrates, throughout the Roman Empire, were directed to compel all Christians, without distinction of rank or sex, to renounce Christianity and sacrifice to the gods, and were authorized to employ the most cruel torments in their work. The church was now reduced to the last extremity; for the magistrates were like so many hungry tigers, let loose upon defenceless lambs. In France less ferocity was exhibited than in other places, from the influence of Constantius, who was favorably inclined to the Christians.

A recital of their sufferings may appear to many almost incredible, but it is delivered to us by faithful eye-witnesses, and confirmed by pagan historians. It should make us grateful to God for the blessings we enjoy.

Some were thrown to wild beasts, inclosed in vast amphitheatres, for the entertainment of the people on great festal days, and instantly torn to pieces and devoured. Others, with their wives and children, were burned to death in their own houses. Some were beaten with clubs, rods, thongs of leather, and ropes. Nails were driven into their sides, bellies, legs, and cheeks. Some were suspended by one hand from a portico, suffering the most severe distension of all their joints, others were bound to pillars face to face, their feet being raised above ground. They were hung about wooden engines, having every limb of their bodies distended by certain machines. Plates of heated brass were applied to their bodies. They were seated in red hot iron chairs. They were slain by the axe and the sword. They were suspended by their feet, with their head downward, over a slow fire. Sharp reeds were thrust under the nails into the fingers. Melted lead was poured down their backs, and into the bowels. Tongues were cut out. Multitudes were deprived of one eye, and cauterized and debilitated in one leg by a hot iron, and sent to the mines. Seventeen thousand, it is said, were slain during one month.

In Egypt alone, 150,000 suffered martyrdom by the hands of their persecutors, besides 700,000 who came to their end in banishment or the public works.

> "From torturing pains to endless joys,
> On fiery wheels they rode."

The pagans at length thought they had accomplished their object. A medal was struck for Dioclesian, with this inscription, "Nomine Christianorum deleto." "The name of Christians being extinguished." The pagan worship was every where set up in great splendor. It was the darkest period which the Christian Church had seen. But He who had established her, had promised that the gates of hell should never prevail against her. A remnant remained who wrestled with the angel of the covenant, and prevailed. The time of their deliverance was at hand. The arm of Jehovah was uplifted, and Satan fell as lightning from heaven.

In the year 312, the emperor Dioclesian died. His successor, Maximin Galerius, who had been the author of the heaviest persecutions, also soon came to his end. He was horrid in death. In frantic agony he cried out, "It was not I, but others who did it." In the West, Constantius Clorus died in Britain, A. D. 306. He had renounced idolatry, was a man of strict morals, and had favored the Christians. The army forced Constantine, his son, to accept the purple. At the same time, Maxentius, son-in-law to Galerius, assumed the imperial dignity at Rome. A civil war ensued. In marching to battle, Constantine felt the need of some divine assistance. He had seen his father reject Polytheism, and treat with kindness the Christians. He felt anxious to know their God. Historians report that he prayed for light, and that, while marching with his forces, a miraculous cross appeared to him in the air, with the inscription, "Conquer by this;" that the same night Christ appeared to him in his sleep, with the same sign of the cross, and directed him to make it his military ensign. Such a report must have had a great effect upon his enemies. True, it might have been. Greater miracles have been wrought. But the age of miracles had passed away. The chief design of miracles, which was to support revelation, had long before been accomplished. Nor was Constantine a favorite of heaven. A dream he probably had; and from that time, the Emperor became the open advocate of Christianity, and the banner of the cross was displayed in his armies. Over all his enemies he was conqueror, and for many years, was sole master of Rome. In the year 324 he published edicts and laws, by which the ancient religion of the Romans was abolished, and Christianity was established as the religion of the empire.

This great and astonishing revolution in the religious world, great as it was unexpected, to those who, a few years before, saw Christianity almost extinct amid the flames of persecution, appears to have been clearly predicted by John in the opening of the sixth seal. Then, indeed, the idolatrous heaven, filled with Jupiter, and a thousand deities, " departed as a scroll when it is rolled together, and every mountain and island were moved out of their places."

That gigantic power which had hitherto been employed to crush Christianity, and which would, ages before, have driven every vestige of it from among men, had not God been its helper, was now engaged to demolish the kingdom of darkness, and to exalt Christ in the earth. The heathen temples were pulled down; images of gold and silver were melted and coined into money; great idols, curiously wrought, were brought to Constantinople and drawn with ropes through the principal streets, for the scorn of the people. The heathen priests were cast out, dispersed and banished. Every place of power and trust in the state and army, which had before been filled by heathen, was now occupied by professed followers of the Lord Jesus Christ. Immense and splendid Christian temples were every where erected and richly endowed; and the greatest honor was put upon all preachers of the Gospel. Constantine put an end to pagan rites; to sorcery and divination, those great supports of false religion; publicly exposed the mysteries which had been kept secret; stopped the savage fights of gladiators; ordered the strict observance of the Lord's day; furnished the churches with copies of the sacred Scriptures; stood up with respectful silence, to hear the Gospel from Eusebius, of Cesarea; dedicated Christian temples himself with great solemnity; yea, made Christian orations, one of which, of considerable length, is preserved to us; and taught all the soldiers in his army to pray to the God of the Christians.

The sincerity of the man, who, in a short period, effected such amazing changes in the religious world, is best known to Him who searches the heart. Certain it is, that his subsequent life furnished no evidence of conversion to God. He waded without remorse through seas of blood, and was a most tyrannical prince. If it be asked, Why he so patronized Christians? The answer may be found in the state of the world. Paganism had nearly expired. Christianity had gained deep root in the earth, and how could he with the least worldly policy do otherwise than he did, especially as all his opposers were the supporters of paganism.

But with him, we have but little concern. The work was the Lord's. He was indeed the distinguished instrument of effecting it. Happy for him, if he had a saving interest in that Redeemer, whose cause he so illustriously upheld. But every circumstance shows the mighty power of God. That little sect which three centuries before sprang up in Judea, and seemed in the eyes of the world too contemptible for notice, now filled the earth with its glories. That little seed which was then planted, had sprang up and became a great tree, under whose branches the nations reposed for comfort. The success was in strict accordance with prophecy, and proved to the nations that it was the Lord God that had set up his kingdom on the ruins of the kingdom of Satan, and would ultimately triumph from the river to the ends of the earth.

The joy felt by Christians throughout the Roman empire at this unexpected revolution, was beyond the power of language to express. They had hitherto been only suffered to live. Few privileges were theirs. Few enjoyments but those which sprang from communion with God;—while they were often obliged to hide in the rocks and caves of the earth, from whence they were dragged forth to suffer the most cruel deaths. Could the truly pious among them have looked forward to the issue, and seen all this worldly magnificence operating as poison to the very vitals of the church, they would have lamented the change, and preferred the endurance of further trials; but all were impressed with the belief that now Christ was coming to take to himself the kingdom and the dominion, and the greatness of the kingdom under the whole heaven. The worldly minded among them saw every thing in the change to gratify their pride and ambition; rushed with avidity into all places of power and dominion, and hailed Constantine as the greatest of human benefactors.

At the change, Satan gnawed his tongue for pain. The heathen priests and vast crowds of subordinate officers, who had gained their subsistence in the idol worship, saw their darling gods trampled in the dust; their own consequence at an end, and their means of support entirely cut off. Great multitudes, indeed, were mere warriors and courtiers who were attached to the heathen superstition because it was the religion of the state, and were zealous in it because zeal gained them promotion. Such readily renounced it and became Christians when they saw their emperor fighting successfully under the banner of the cross. Others more intelligent and reflecting, had long in their hearts despised the whole system of idol worship, while they had prostrated themselves with apparently the profoundest reverence. Such rejoiced to see the establishment of ages overturned, though they knew not what would arise in its stead. But others, some from interest, and some from sincere attachment, struggled vehemently for the expiring cause. They beheld with indignation and grief the destruction of their temples and gods. They aspersed the emperor in the foulest language, and predicted the greatest calamities to his family and kingdom. They were never again able to persecute the Christians as they had done, but they occasionally rallied, and grew terrible for a season, until at length, through the excellency of Christianity and the power of the state, and the contempt into which their own gods and rites had sunk, they dwindled away and were found no more.

CHAPTER VI.

Results of the revolution under Constantine. Rise of Arianism. Council of Nice. Death of Constantine. Succeeding emperors. Julian's attempt to restore paganism. His defeat in rebuilding the Temple at Jerusalem. Persecutions in Persia. Eusebius. Basil. Chrysostom. Jerome. Augustine. Pelagianism. Civil revolution in Europe. Daniel's vision of the ten horns. Conversion of the barbarous nations. Franks. Irish. Britons. Progress of error and superstition in the fifth and sixth centuries.

THE revolution under Constantine, was one from which almost every thing which the Christian values, might be hoped; but alas! such is the depravity of human nature, it was one in which almost every thing of evangelical worth was lost. Constantine brought the world into the church, and the church was paralyzed. The number of nominal Christians was indeed increased a thousand fold. A new spring was given to missionary effort; and in this century a number of barbarous tribes among the Armenians, the Ethiopians, the Georgians, the Goths, and the Gauls, were partially enlightened by the Gospel of Christ. The work of translating and circulating the Holy Scriptures, also, received great encouragement; though, for the former, few had learning and industry sufficient. The Latin version of Jerome, though far from being correct, stands pre-eminent over all others that were made. Schools were established, and libraries were formed for Christian youth; and the study of philosophy and the liberal arts were encouraged, that Christianity might not suffer by a comparison of her advocates with the erudition and skill of the sages of paganism. Immense and splendid temples were erected and richly endowed; and a great priesthood was regularly organized and liberally supported. The body existed, but the spirit had fled. Constantine set up an immense national church; but the humility, faith, and the spirituality of the age of Polycarp had passed away. Constantine did not find it in the church which he thus raised to worldly glory; and how could he create it there by those means which always destroy vital piety?

Among the more retired, in the humble walks of life, there was, no doubt, much true religion. There must have been much to support the sufferers through the Dioclesian persecution. Many of these sufferers, with their children, were humble followers of Christ for many years. Some of the ministers were worthy of a better age. But the most of those who were exalted to places of power and trust, were engaged in pompous rites and ceremonies, and knew but little of the humiliating and sanctifying doctrines of Christianity. Indeed, their elevation to wealth and power was followed by an amazing increase of luxury and vice. Bishops contended with bishops about the extent of their jurisdictions; vied with princes in their style of living, and showed that they placed their heaven upon earth. Having such spiritual guides, the mass of the people soon became exceedingly corrupt. Shoals of profligate men, allured by gain, or driven by fear, pressed into the church; discipline ceased, and superstition reigned without control. The Gentile converts to nominal Christianity, brought into the church a taste for the public processions and prayers, by which they had been accustomed to appease their gods; hastily transferred the virtues which had been supposed to belong to their temples and their ablutions to Christian temples and Christian ordinances; and were at once disposed to deify the Apostles and early Christians, as they had been accustomed to do the heroes of antiquity. The old Christians found themselves associated with a new world of admirers, who knew nothing about their religion, and who were easily subjected to the most abominable impositions. Prodigies and miracles, therefore, beyond number, were multiplied. The bones and relics of dead saints performed wonders. Dust and earth brought from Palestine, was viewed as a certain and powerful remedy against the violence of wicked spirits. And, before the close of the century, the great business of the lower order of priests was to impose in ten thousand ways, in the vilest manner, upon the credulity of the ignorant multitude.

The erection of splendid temples, and introduction of a splendid worship, gave rise also to a vast variety of additional rites and ceremonies. These, in general, were copied from the heathen worship, and such was the amalgamation of the two religions, as to differ very little in their external appearance. Gorgeous robes, mitres, tiaras, wax tapers, crosiers, processions, lustrations, images, gold and silver vases, are mentioned as common to both Christian and heathen churches. What deplorable degeneracy from the simple worship of the Apostles!

The great festivals were five in number;—commemorating the birth, death, resurrection, and ascension of Christ, and the day of Pentecost, but were rather days of public licentiousness than of pious exercises. Fasts were greatly multiplied, under the idea that they repelled evil spirits.

From being the outpourings of a broken heart and a contrite spirit, the public prayers degenerated into vain bombast; and in consequence of an intimate connexion with the Grecian schools, the sermons of the divines partook of the nature of an oration, and were clapped and applauded, as were orators in the forum by the Christian assemblies.

Two principles were introduced into the church, which propelled her in her downward course, and led brother to imbrue his hands in his brother's blood; and this too, thinking that he did God service. The first was, "That it is an act of virtue to deceive and lie, when by that means, the interests of the church may be promoted;"—the other, that "Errors in religion, when maintained and adhered to, after proper admonition, are punishable with civil penalties and corporeal tortures." Strange that men who professed to serve an holy master, and to be looking toward an holy heaven, should so soon set at defiance the solemn denunciation of Christ against the fearful and unbelieving, the abominable, and all liars; and, that, with scorched flesh and broken limbs, they should kindle the fires of persecution against their own companions!

In such a degenerate period, it could not be expected that the fundamental doctrines of the Gospel should remain uncorrupt. They had before lost much of their influence over the minds of men; but until this time they had remained entire in most of the churches. A number of violent dissensions had arisen on account of discipline; and sentiments extremely erroneous had been formed and advocated by a few powerful minds; but hitherto, no large churches had been seen to deny the fundamental doctrines; and to build their hopes of salvation on a different faith from that which had been generally received as the faith of the primitive Christians.

Two parties, the Donatists and the Meletians, were formed in Africa, about the commencement of the fourth century, by contentions about power and place, which for a long time, were persecuted and oppressed as dangerous schismatics; but it does not appear that they adopted any corrupt sentiments. Among them, probably was much true piety.

But there was at this time a great departure from the ancient faith relating to the divinity of the Saviour.

As early as the days of John, there were those who denied the divinity of Christ; and in every succeeding period, there were ingenious minds, fond of giving some new explanation of the doctrine of the Trinity which should free it from its inherent mystery; but none had made much impression on the churches.

In the church of Alexandria, was a presbyter named Arius; a man venerable in his appearance, severe in his habits, monastic in his dress; a subtle logician and a commanding orator. This man openly maintained that the Son was essentially and totally distinct from the Father; that there was a time when he was not; that he was the first and noblest of all created beings; was a mutable creature, and capable, as men are, both of sin and holiness. He preached continually to a crowded audience, and presented his doctrine to every one with whom he associated in private.

He soon gained many proselytes, both among the common people and men of rank and influence. Alexander, his bishop, assembled two councils, the last contained an hundred ministers, which condemned his opinions, and excluded him from the fellowship of the church.

Spiritual war was then proclaimed, which soon terribly raged throughout the Christian world. Arius retired into Palestine, and opened a correspondence with many eminent men, whom he endeavored to bring over to his faith. Among his warmest admirers, and greatest supperters, was Eusebius of Nicomedia, the metropolis where the emperor usually resided. Constantine beheld the breach with grief. He wished to have one great, harmonious, splendid, religious empire. He wrote to the two parties and exhorted them to peace. But it was in vain. He then called an immense council of 318 bishops, from all parts of Christendom, to meet at Nice, in Bithynia. They were convened in the year 325, and supported solely at his expense. Such a council had never before been witnessed. It was the first general council. The emperor himself came to it, threw their mutual accusations into the fire, and exhorted them to peace. This being in vain, the doctrine of Arius was canvassed and condemned. He was deposed, excommunicated, and forbidden to enter Alexandria.

In this council a creed was adopted, called the Nicene creed. The dispute concerning Easter was finally adjusted. The ordination of new converts was forbidden; also, the translation of bishops, priests and deacons, from one city to another. The Meletian controversy, for a time was settled. The Novatians were invited to return to the bosom of the church, as they held nothing at variance with the fundamental doctrines. Attempts were made to put upon the clergy the yoke of perpetual celibacy, but did not succeed.

Something of the fear of God, and a spirit of discipline, was therefore existing. And how could it be otherwise? It was a council of martyrs. Many of them had passed through the fires of persecution, and bore on their bodies the marks of the Lord Jesus. One appeared debilitated by the application of hot irons to both his hands. Others appeared deprived of their right eyes. Others of a leg.

Arius was deposed, but not silenced. He and his friends made the most vigorous efforts to persuade the Christian world that they had been unjustly condemned, and to gain a restoration to their former rank and privileges. The sister of the emperor favored their cause. In her last moments, she prevailed on Constantine to recall Arius from banishment, to repeal the laws which had been made against him and his party, and even to permit them, in various ways, to oppress the leading members of the Nicene council. This was done in the year 330. But Athanasius, the successor of Alexander in the bishopric of Alexandria, refused to receive Arius as a presbyter under him. For his firmness, he was, in turn, deposed and banished into Gaul. The church in Alexandria, however, was true to its principles, and, though Arius had been reinstated with great solemnity, they would have no connection with him. Constantine then ordered him to Constantinople. He had supposed that all would be peace, for he had been made to believe that Arius was unjustly condemned; that there was no essential difference between him and his accusers. He now required his opinion of the Nicene creed. Arius, without hesitation, subscribed it, and swore to his sincerity in doing it. The emperor could never conceive of men's subscribing to the same words, who had entirely different views. This was the case in that period. The church said that Christ was God. The Arians allowed it, but in the same sense that rulers and angels are styled gods in scripture. Deluded by the apparent frankness of Arius, Constantine ordered Alexander, bishop of Constantinople, to receive him to communion; Alexander could not resist, but gave himself to fasting and prayer. The Arians were flushed with success; but while parading in triumph through the streets of the city, Arius was seized with an anguish in his bowels, retired by himself and suddenly expired, A. D. 336.

Soon after, Constantine, who had been the instrument in the hand of God, of amazing changes in the religious world, went to his eternal reward, having first received baptism, which had now superstitiously attached to it saving efficacy, from the hands of Eusebius, bishop of Nicomedia.

His successor, Constantius, favored the cause of the Arians He entered heartily into their views, and from the year 337 to 361, violently persecuted their opposers. Athanasius, who, after a banishment of more than two years, had returned, was obliged to flee to Rome. A number of his friends were scourged and imprisoned. The greatest severities were inflicted upon many ministers who held the Nicene creed. Some were banished, others loaded with irons, and scourged to death. The Arians multiplied creeds upon creeds, laboring so to express themselves, that no essential difference might appear between them and others; and multitudes might be able to subscribe, without disturbing their consciences. Among those who were induced to do this, was Liberius, bishop of Rome. The Arians filled all the high places in the church, and were exceedingly ambitious of wealth and power. Eusebius of Nicomedia, the zealous friend of Arius, was made patriarch of Constantinople.

In the year 349, Constantius was constrained, by the popular voice, to reinstate Athanasius in his see. It was a moment of triumph to his friends. But his enemies determined his utter destruction, and accused him of the foulest crimes. Athanasius retired to the deserts, and secreted himself among some monks, who refused to betray him to his persecuting adversaries. For nearly forty years, Arianism reigned, especially in the East, almost without a check, and it became a proverb, "All the world against Athanasius, and Athanasius against all the world."

No sooner had the Arians attained to the high places than they split into various parties. They could not agree among themselves in their views of the character of Christ. A multitude of new sects sprang up among them, under the names of Semi-Arians, Eusebians, Aetians, Eunomians, Acasians, Psathyrians, &c., &c., who were as hostile to each other, as they were to the Nicene party.

The Arian controversy also produced a multitude of other sects, which, for a time, distracted the Christian world; but which have long since passed away, and been lost like the tumultuous waves in the ocean.

Constantius died in the year 361. His successor, Julian, was no friend to Christianity in any shape, and all parties were obliged, for a season, to hide themselves in the dust. Jovian, the next emperor, was a Trinitarian, and in his reign almost the whole world renounced the Arian system. Valentinian, and Valens, two brothers, succeeded Jovian. The former was the patron of the Trinitarians; the latter, of the Arians. Valens renewed in the East the spirit of persecution, and many were banished.

Gratian and Honorius, the next emperors, were active in suppressing paganism, and extending Christianity. But their successor, Theodosius, who came to the empire in 379, entered on the boldest measures both for destroying idolatry and establishing an uniform religious faith. He drove the Arians with terrible violence from their churches, and exposed them

CHAPTER 6.] ATTEMPT TO REBUILD THE TEMPLE.

to the greatest calamities throughout his dominions. Unquestionably it was a most criminal abuse of authority; but he seemed to have no idea that religion is to be established in the minds of men by reason and not by force, and but little experimental acquaintance with that system he was so zealous to establish.

As the secular arm had now, for many years, been turned against different portions of the professed followers of Christ, the pagans came out of their dens and took courage. They rejoiced in the contentions among Christians; and when they saw the Arians depose those who had deposed them, they said, "The Arians have come over to our party." One bold and daring effort more, therefore, Satan determined to make, to drive Christianity from the earth, and regain the seat of empire.

Julian had been educated a Christian, was a public reader in the church of Nicomedia, and zealous for Christianity, though he probably was never acquainted with the true spirit of the Gospel. But, through his enmity to the Constantine family, and the artifices of the philosophers, he apostatized from his professed faith and bent the whole force of his empire to the reinstitution of pagan idolatry. He was a man of great talents, dissimulation and cunning, and he pursued those measures which must have ended in the extermination of Christianity had it not been the cause of God. For he not only repealed the laws made against idolatry, opened the heathen temples, raised up an immense priesthood, and set the whole machinery of paganism in motion throughout his vast empire; but he labored, in a thousand ways, to undermine Christianity, by destroying its moral influence. He made the Christians continually the object of ridicule, calling them Galileans; shut up their schools; took from them their civil and religious privileges; broke up the clergy by depriving them of their incomes, and burdening them with taxes and civil duties; befriended the Jews; reformed the morality of paganism to make it acceptable to the pious, and used every insnaring artifice to draw over the unwary. He abstained from open persecution, because he saw that the blood of the martyrs had been the seed of the church. But if he did not take away life, he deprived it of peace and comfort.

But Julian found that there was a power above him. In defiance of heaven, he undertook to build the Temple of Jerusalem. "He committed the conduct of the affair," says Amianus Marcellinus, a writer of that period, and an enemy to Christianity, "to Alypius of Antioch, who set himself to the vigorous execution of his charge, and was assisted by the governor of the province; but horrible balls of fire breaking out near the foundations with repeated attacks, rendered the place inaccessible to the scorched workmen from time to time, and the element resolutely driving them to a distance, the enterprise was dropped." Gregory, Nazianzen, Ambrose, and Chrysostom, who lived at the same time, and the ecclesiastical historians of the next age, all attest the same facts.

To what depression the church would have been reduced by so formidable an enemy had he lived to old age, none can tell. A merciful providence removed him after a reign of one year and eight months, in the 32d year of his age. He had attempted the conquest of the Persians, and was killed by a Persian lance. Conscious of his fate, he filled his hand with his blood, and casting it into the air, said, "*O Galilean, thou hast conquered.*"

This was the last persecution of Christianity by pagan Rome. Pagans, however, beyond the bounds of the empire, continued to defend their ancient superstitions by arms, and massacred multitudes who bore the Christian name. This was particularly the case in Persia, where, from the year 330 to 370, a most destructive persecution raged, and an incredible number of Christians were put to death—the Magi and the Jews persuading Sapor the monarch, that the Christians were friendly to the Roman emperor.

The fourth century produced some men of eminent learning and piety. Among them were, in the east, Eusebius, bishop of Cæsarea, to whom we are indebted for the best history of the church; Athanasius, patriarch of Alexandria, the firm and powerful opponent of Arianism; Basil, surnamed the great, bishop of Cæsarea, an eminent controversialist; Ephraim, the Syrian, a man of much sanctity of life and conversation, whose moral writings were an honor to the age; and John Chrysostom, bishop of Constantinople, one of the most able preachers that has adorned the Christian Church. To strong powers of mind and a lively imagination, Chrysostom added fine powers of oratory, and commanded immense audiences. He was an able commentator on Paul's epistles. In opposition to Origen, he adhered to the literal sense of Scripture, maintaining it to be the true. He was the firm supporter of the doctrines of grace, and a bold reprover of vice, and fell a victim to the persecution of his foes. He was banished from the See of

Constantinople and died at Pityus on the Euxine sea, A D. 407, aged 53.

In the west, was Ambrose, bishop of Milan, a man of eminent piety and learning, and Jerome, a monk of Palestine, whose writings are very voluminous. He translated the Bible into Latin. His translation was called the Latin Vulgate, and was afterwards exclusively adopted by the Roman church. But it contained many errors. By his own writings he contributed much to the growth of superstition. Still, he was the most able commentator of all the Latin Fathers. Hilary of Poictiers, a man of singular attachment to the Gospel in its simplicity, and a firm defender of the doctrine of the Trinity; and Lactantius, who, in his divine institutions, exposed the absurdity of the pagan rites, lived about the same period. Ulpilas also deserves notice. He was zealous in civilizing and converting the Goths. He translated the four Gospels into their language.

But by far the most distinguished and valuable man of the second age of the church, was Augustine, bishop of Hippo, in Africa, who flourished in the latter part of the fourth and beginning of the fifth century. He was born in Numidia, and converted about the year 354, when near thirty years of age, in an evident outpouring of the Spirit upon the churches, by which vital godliness was much revived from its low state, especially in the East. His confessions, in which he gives an account of his conversion, may be read with profit by Christians in every age. He was early raised to the bishopric of Hippo, and by his humble piety and powerful defence of the fundamental truths of the Gospel, soon became the admiration of the Christian world. His best commentary was on the Psalms. He died in the year 430, at the age of seventy-six. He was a star of the first magnitude, and was a guide for centuries after to Christians, who, amid the darkness of Popery, desired to walk in the truth.

But the theological writers of that age are not to be compared with modern divines. Their folios will not repay the trouble of a perusal.

Augustine was raised up to defend the doctrines of grace These doctrines had remained fundamental from the apostolic age, though they had been much corrupted by Justin, Origen, and others, who were led astray by a deceitful philosophy But when, in the days of Constantine, the world came into the church, they were a dead letter. All were viewed as

Christians, who professed Christianity, though they knew not in their own experience that there was a Holy Ghost. A great part of the Christian world, therefore, were ready to subscribe to a system which rejected the necessity of the grace of God; should a man arise with the talent and boldness to promulge one.

Such a man was Pelagius. He was born in Britain; but made Rome his residence. There in company with Cælestius, an Irish monk, he avowed about the year 410, a denial of the total corruption of human nature, and of the necessity of the enlightening, renewing, and sanctifying operations of the Holy Spirit. Cælestius was at first the most open. At Carthage he labored much to propagate his sentiments. He was pressed with the custom of the church in baptizing infants, as a proof of her belief in all ages, that infants were depraved; but he persisted in his sentiments, and was condemned as a heretic, in the year 412.

Pelagius went to Jerusalem, where he found patronage and formed disciples. His opinions were warmly opposed by Augustine, who firmly maintained entire depravity; the necessity of divine grace; that there is an eternal purpose of God or predestination with regard to those who shall be saved, and that they, and they only, will finally obtain it. The Christian world was distracted. Council after council was held, and decree after decree was passed, condemning or approving the opposite parties; but in 420, the secular arm was raised, and Pelagianism was suppressed throughout the empire. A new sect, however, soon arose, favored by Cassian, a monk at Marseilles, called the Semi-Pelagians, who allowed the necessity of divine grace to preserve in holiness, though not to commence it, and who were long engaged, especially in France, in controversy with the followers of Augustine.

In the remainder of the fifth, and whole of the sixth century, the reader of ecclesiastical history finds but little that engages his attention. The church, washed, sanctified, and justified in the name of the Lord Jesus, and by the Spirit of God, is scarcely visible. Immense changes took place in the civil world which could not fail to affect the visible kingdom of the Redeemer.

In the year 476, the western part of the Roman empire was dissolved by the incursions of a fierce and warlike people from the northern part of Europe, who had for more than half a century been overspreading Italy, Gaul, and Spain, and

CHAPTER 6.] THE TEN HORNS OF THE BEAST.   209

erecting new kingdoms in these beautiful countries. This great event was depicted in the vision of Daniel, ages before, in which he beheld a beast, dreadful and terrible, which had ten horns. This beast was the Roman empire, and these horns were ten kingdoms, into which it is now divided by the barbarous nations. How wonderful the providence of God! "He seeth the end from the beginning."

These barbarians, the Goths, Huns, Franks, Herulians, and Vandals, were idolaters and strangers to Christianity, but they concerned themselves but little about religion of any description, being chiefly intent upon wealth and power, and were for the most part, induced to renounce their idolatry and become nominal, but wretched Christians. Some, however, of the old pagans, who remained in the empire, hoped to revive their ancient worship, and, in a few instances, instigated the heathen to acts of cruelty and oppression towards those who would not bow to their idols.

Had these idolaters been of the character of the old opposers of Christianity, they might, in this degenerate age of the church, have easily exterminated it from the earth. But they came down from the cold regions of the north for comfort and improvement; and finding Christianity in all respects a better religion than their own, they embraced it; and it had in time, the happiest effects in softening their manners and refining their morals. They adopted the Arian system, and the Nicene believers received from them the bitterest persecutions.

One of the ten kingdoms was that of the Franks. Clovis, their king, had married Clotilda, niece of Gondebaud, king of the Burgundians. Her own nation had already embraced Christianity, because they thought the God of the Romans most able to protect them against their enemies. Such low ideas had these barbarians of the Gospel of Christ. But they, as well as the Vandals, Suevi and Goths, had sided with the Arian party. Clotilda, however, was attached to the Nicene faith. She labored much for the conversion of her husband to the Christian faith; but he was obstinate, and when her child, which had been baptized, died, he attributed its death to its baptism. At length, fearing destruction in a battle with the Alemans, he prayed to Jesus Christ for victory; promising that if he would grant it, he would become a Christian. Victory ensued, and he was baptized at Rheims, and received into the general church, A. D. 496; but he was never an honor to any religion. Three thousand of his army were baptized with him. This was an important event. All the other rulers of the world were either bowing to pagan deities, or avowing the Arian opinions. Clovis and his people embraced and revived the faith of the primitive churches.

In this century, also, the Irish were led to renounce idolatry, and embrace Christianity; partly by the exertions of Palladius, but chiefly through the zeal of Patrick, a Scot, who has usually been styled the Apostle of the Irish. He died A. D. 413, at the great age of one hundred and twenty.

The ancient Britons were idolaters. Their priests, the Druids, had some notions of a supreme divinity, and of immortality, but they worshipped subordinate deities, as Taranus, the thunderer, Hesus, the god of battles, Andrasse, the goddess of victory; and their immortality was little more than the Indian notion of the transmigration of souls. They built great temples of massy stone, in which they performed bloody rites. One of these, STONEHENGE, is still in part remaining. They secured a great revenue by compelling all the inhabitants to extinguish their fires on a certain day in the winter, and come and kindle them again from the sacred fire of the Druids. This they withheld from such as had not paid their revenues.

They held sacred the Mistletoe. They were notorious, above all other heathen priests, for the practice of pretended magic. When a chief was afflicted with sickness, they sacrificed a human victim. Naked women assisted at the bloody rite.

Such were the abominations of the ancient inhabitants of England.

When and by whom the knowledge of Christianity was first introduced there, is unknown. It is certain there were Christians there soon after the days of the Apostles, and they probably came from Rome. They were persecuted; and Christianity, as well as the Druidical religion, was exterminated by the Saxons, Angles, and other tribes who conquered the country. These practiced their idolatries for about one hundred and fifty years. They worshipped the Sun, Moon, Thuth, Odin, Thor, Frigga and Surtur. From these are derived the English names of the seven days of the week. They had idols in wood, stone and metals, temples and a regular priesthood. Their rites were bloody.

One day, in the sixth century, Gregory, an eminent man

at Rome, was walking in the market place, and beholding a number of fine youth, with clear skins, flaxen hair, and beautiful countenances, for sale, he inquired from whence they came, and whether they were Christians. On being told that they were pagans from Britain, his compassion was excited On asking further by what name they were called, he was told they were Angli. "Well," said he, "may they be so called, for they have angelic countenances, and ought to be made co-heirs with the angels in heaven." And when farther informed that they came from the province of Deira, (now Durham,) he exclaimed, " De Dei ira! from the wrath of God they must be delivered." And it being added that Ella was their king, he replied, " Hallelujah ought to be sung in his dominions." Gregory soon offered his services as a missionary to England, but they were not accepted. When, however, in a few years, he was raised to the popedom, he sent forty monks under Augustine, to convert the English nation. They entered Britain in 597, and were kindly received by Bertha, a pious descendant of Clovis, who had married Ethelbert, king of Kent; permitted to preach the Gospel, and had a residence assigned them in the city of Canterbury. The king soon declared himself a convert, and his subjects followed his example. Other kings in the Saxon heptarchy, were soon persuaded, with their people, to renounce idolatry, and in a short period, the whole island became nominally Christians.

Of the religion of the English converted to Christianity, we have very imperfect accounts. One fact speaks highly in its praise. Missionaries issued forth, who spread the light of truth through Bavaria, Friesland, Cimbria and Denmark, delivering the North and West of Europe from pagan darkness and idolatry. The venerable Bede, who died in 735, was an ornament to the age in which he lived. He translated the Psalter and the Gospels into the Anglo Saxon, and wrote a valuable church history. Alcuinus, one of his pupils, and who became the instructor of Charlemagne, deserves mention for his learning and piety. But a great and general degeneracy soon took place. The Danes broke up every thing good in the nation. When Alfred came to the throne in the ninth century, there was scarce a priest who understood Latin enough to construe his daily prayers. His efforts to restore learning and religion were princely. The whole Bible was translated by his order. He began to translate the Psalms himself. But when he had passed away, monachism reared its head, and the light which had been permitted to shine in Britain was extinguished, and gross darkness brooded over the land. As the papacy arose, the monarchs found that a convenient engine in the despotic exercise of civil power, and soon the whole country was subjected to its tremendous dominion.

In the east, some Indians on the Malabar coast were converted to Christianity, by the Syrian Mar Thomas, as early as the fifth century. Their churches still remain. The principal propagators of Christianity, subsequent to this, were the Nestorians, who gained a firm footing in Persia, established their patriarch at Seleucia, passed over Tartary and India, and penetrated even into China. A prodigious number of people through all these countries, which are now overrun by Mahometanism and idolatry, were induced to embrace Christianity.

We cannot, however, form a very exalted opinion of the conversions of this period, either in the east or west. They were little more than nominal,—a change of religion; and, in many cases, the converted retained many of their heathen customs, and all their vices. Yet they paved the way for the establishment of the kingdom of the Redeemer in the hearts of men.

Two men of eminent piety adorned the sixth century; Fulgentius, bishop of the Ruspæ, in Africa; and Gregory first, bishop of Rome. The one lived near the beginning, the other near the close, and were both authors of much celebrity and merit. Gregory introduced Christianity into England.

The Emperor Justinian, who succeeded to the Roman empire, A. D. 527, was an eminent champion for Christianity, though he seems himself to have been unacquainted with vital piety. He endeavored to bring all nations to nominal subjection to Christ; built sumptuous temples, and suppressed every where what remained of idolatry. In his time, Chosroes, king of Persia, waged a most cruel and desolating war against the Christians and the God of Christians.

The disputes in which the churches had been involved concerning the nature and person of Christ; the depravity of man, and the necessity of divine grace in order to salvation, had elicited much truth, so that these great subjects were now much better understood by many throughout Christendom in the fifth and sixth centuries, than they were for a considerable period before the reign of Constantine. But unhappily, almost every part of the Christian world were fiercely engaged for the peculiarities of some distinguished leader of a sect or party, who had the boldness to advance some new opinion, overlooking, as of no value, the great essentials of Christianity. The numerous sects into which the Arians split, maintained with vehemence their peculiar views.

In the East, the Nestorians, a powerful body, had broken off from the general church. Their leader, Nestorious, a bishop of Constantinople, in the fifth century, had affirmed, that in Christ there were two persons, or two natures united by one operation and will, and that, as only the human nature could proceed from Mary, it was improper to call her the mother of God. In this he was opposed by Eutyches, an abbot of monks, who declared that in Christ there was but one nature, that of the incarnate Word, which proceeded from Mary, who ought, therefore, to be called the mother of God. His adherents were called Eutycheans. Both were successively condemned by general councils. The Theopaschites were furious in maintaining that all the three persons in the Godhead suffered on the cross. The Monophasites, that the divine nature absorbed the human. The Corrupticolæ, looked upon the body of Christ as corruptible; and the Agnoetæ, upon the human nature of Christ as knowing all things. The Donatists increased and became powerful amid violent persecutions in Africa. The Manicheans also continued to disperse in the East, their wild opinions of two original principles, good and evil.

Before the close of the sixth century, the world was at ease, and superstition had made most rapid strides. The great mass of ministers were excessively ignorant, and led away themselves by the strangest phantasies, did little but delude and destroy the people. A thousand rites were performed; each one of which was supposed to have some wonderful power. A thousand relics were produced, whose touch, it was said, could heal the body and the mind. The most marvellous feats, called miracles, were performed. The most superstitious services were rendered to departed souls. Images of saints were worshipped, under the belief, that such worship drew down their propitious presence. Tombs and grave yards were viewed as the places most frequented by departed spirits, and were the general rendezvous of the ignorant. The doctrine of purgatory, or the purification of souls by fire, beyond the grave, had gained strong hold of the minds of the multitude. Some starved themselves with a frantic obstinacy. Some, possessed of a superstitious phrensy, erected high pillars, and stood on them for many years. The leader of this debased class of men, was one Simeon, a Syrian, who, to climb as near to heaven as he could, passed thirty-seven years of his life upon five pillars, of six, twelve, twenty-two, thirty-six, and forty cubits high; attracting the admiration of the world around him. Such things are disgusting to the rational and pious mind. It is a subject of gratitude that religion is not answerable for them. Religion is the love of God and men, holiness of heart and life; not the superstitious veneration of a bone, or standing upon stilts a spectacle of folly. These things belong properly to the history of the age, to the history of the kingdom of darkness, and not of the church of Christ. Let those who will, stumble over them, and fall into a like fatal whirlpool, the whirlpool of infidelity. "Wisdom is justified of her children." Such reflections will be more needed as we advance; for a period of Egyptian darkness is before us.

CHAPTER VII.

Monachism. Its rise and progress. Reflections on its odious character. Mahometanism Appearance of Mahomet in Arabia. His religion. Extension of the Saracen empire Destruction of the eastern churches. Present extent of Mahometanism.

In the seventh century, two immense powers, the Mahometan and the Papal, arose, which laid the East and West in melancholy desolation.

Before we enter upon their history, we will take a view of Monachism, which had already, for two centuries, prevailed in the earth.

At an early period, the simplicity of the Gospel was, in various ways, materially injured by an amalgamation with the philosophy of the age. It was one principle of that philosophy, that "for the attainment of true felicity, and communion with God, it was necessary that the soul should be abstracted from the body here below, and that the body should be macerated and mortified for this purpose." This was a principle which many, especially who had once been heathen, were ready to engraft on the Gospel; and a considerable number of both sexes were to be found, even in the third century, giving themselves up to austerities and solitude, and a perpetual contemplation of spiritual objects. A practice which thus probably commenced with pious people, who were actuated by good motives, was soon perverted to the most abominable superstition and wickedness.

One Antony, a youth of Alexandria, on entering a church, and hearing our Lord's words to a young ruler, "Sell all that thou hast and give to the poor," resolved, literally, to observe the direction, and to set an example of self-denial, such as the world had never before seen. He parted with all he had, retired into the desert, and practiced through a long life, the greatest possible austerities. His fame spread throughout the world. Great numbers resorted to see him, and hear his conversation. Multitudes followed his example, and if the "wilderness, and the solitary place," were not glad for them, they were, at least, to a surprising extent, filled with them. Many of those who thus secluded themselves from the world, Antony formed into a regular community; inducing them to live together, and prescribing rules for their observance. Thus originated the first regular monastic order. Antony died A. D. 356, at the extreme age of 105. During his life he manifested much zeal for the truths of the Gospel, and was particularly honored with the friendship of Athanasius, who wrote his life. His property at his death consisted of one old garment, given him by Athanasius, two sheep skins, and a sackcloth.

His chief disciple, Hilarion, introduced his monastic regulations into Palestine and Syria. Others, actuated with a zeal, which, had it been properly directed, might have given salvation to the world, carried them into other countries, so that, in a little time, Europe, Africa and Asia, were "filled with a lazy set of mortals, who, abandoning all human connexions, advantages, pleasures and concerns, wore out a languishing and miserable life, amidst the hardships of want, and various kinds of suffering, in order, as they pretended, to arrive at a more close and rapturous communion with God and angels."

As some followed the instructions, and others the example of Antony, the monks were at first of two kinds, called the Cænobites and the Eremites. The former associated together in one building, under a spiritual father. The latter lived like Antony, alone, in the wildest deserts, often without habitation or clothing, or much sustenance, besides the roots and herbs which nature afforded.

In no part of the world was monachism carried to such extravagant length as in the burning regions of the east. In Europe, the monks were at first laymen of respectable standing, who only united themselves to some order bearing the name, rather than the thing; many of them were the most learned and respectable men in society; but in the east, multitudes gave themselves up to the wildest phrensy, living more like savage animals than rational men.

The increase of the monks in succeeding centuries, their austerities, superstitions, and frauds, almost exceed rational belief. In the east, whole armies might have been raised from among them, without apparently diminishing their number. St. Martin, who founded the first monasteries in Gaul, was followed to his grave by no less than 2,000 monks. Parents early devoted their sons and daughters to perpetual celibacy in the gloomy recesses of a cloister, thinking it the highest possible felicity to which they could raise them. Multitudes who did not join them, consecrated to them their wealth, that they might have the prayers and intercessions of these holy men; dying tyrants and debauchees gave them princely fortunes to quiet their own consciences, by which means the monastic orders became possessed of immense treasures.

Every age teemed with new orders formed by some adventurous leader, who had the boldness and ingenuity to devise some new regulations. In England, where monasteries had been introduced by Augustine and his companions, an abbot named Congall, induced an incredible number of people to abandon all the duties and pleasures of social life, and live in entire solitude, under rules of his devising. His disciples spread over Ireland, Gaul and Germany, and covered the land with swarms of the most lazy drones.

The vices and extravagancies of the monks, which began to be past all endurance, led Benedict of Nursia, a man of piety and intelligence, to institute in the year 529, a rule of discipline, by which monks should be more orderly and regular, subject to few austerities, and more useful to society, especially in educating youth. This discipline was exceedingly popular, and the Benedictine order soon swallowed up all others. It was patronized by the Roman pontiffs, and was endowed with immense riches by the opulent; but luxury, intemperance, and sloth, soon reigned in the convents of Benedict, and his humble saints were the prime leaders in all the political factions which distracted Europe

By the rules of their founders, every order was devoted to reading. Hence, libraries were formed in every monastery, and in these, fortunately, the ancient authors, sacred and profane, were carefully preserved through that awful period, when the interests of literature were laid waste throughout Europe by the barbarous incursions of the northern nations.

In the eighth and ninth centuries, the monks were held in the most astonishing veneration. Immense sums of money were devoted to building convents throughout Christendom. Kings and dukes and nobles descended from their high stations in society, and shut themselves up in these convents, for communion with God. And in return, monks and abbots were taken from cloisters and placed at the head of states and armies; under the pretence that none were so fit to govern men as those, who, having subdued their own appetites and passions, were the peculiar favorites of heaven. But as they increased in power, they sunk in ignorance, licentiousness and debauchery, and were torn by dissensions, jealousies, and most bitter animosities.

In the tenth century arose in France a set of reformers called the order or congregation of Clugni; who were, for a season, renowned throughout Europe for their sanctity and virtue. Their discipline was received by almost all monasteries, new and old, which gave them a vast spiritual dominion; but no sooner had they reached the summit of worldly prosperity, than they sunk under their own licentiousness, which had become equal to that of any preceding order. In the eleventh century arose in Burgundy, the congregation of Cistertians; which, for a time, gave rule to all the monastic orders. The famous order of the Carthusians also commenced their existence about this period. Their institution was melancholy, and especially in relation to female devotees savage in the extreme.

In the twelfth century flourished Bernard, an abbot of much learning and eloquence. He died 1153, leaving 160 monasteries of his order. Abelard was his opponent; a man, too, of much learning. He died 1143.

The thirteenth century formed a new era in the history of Monachism. The monastic institutions were rolling in wealth. They were uncontrollable by any power. They had lost sight of all religious obligation, and were sunk in luxurious indolence. To break up these immense establishments, Innocent III. the Roman pontiff, instituted an order, which should look down with contempt upon wealth, hold no possessions, and subsist wholly on charity. This was called the Mendicant order or begging friars; and, patronized by him, it immediately grew to such an enormous size that Europe could scarce sustain the burden.

About 1260, arose the Flagellants, or whippers, a fanatical multitude of both sexes, and all ranks and ages, who, encouraged by these mendicant orders, ran through cities and villages, with whips in their hands, lashing their naked bodies, to appease the Deity, and strange as it may appear to us, were greatly revered.

In the year 1272, Gregory reduced the extravagant multitude of mendicants to four societies, viz: the Dominicans, and Franciscans, the Carmelites, or followers of the prophet Elijah, and the hermits of St. Augustine. The head of the first was Dominic, a Spaniard, austere, violent, overbearing, unfeeling, who greatly distinguished himself by an impetuous attack upon the opposers of papacy in France. With him originated the inquisition. The head of the second was Francis, a man who had led a most dissolute life, but became suddenly very devout, and instituted an order which should, if possible, exceed all others in absolute poverty. The other two were old establishments, and were never of much note compared with the Dominicans and Franciscans.

These orders of mendicants were suffered to travel wherever they pleased, and live upon the charity of the public. They assumed marks of gravity and holiness which no other order had ever shown. Their popularity was unrivaled. Large cities were cantoned out for their accommodation. The treasures of the world were laid at their feet. From no other hands would the people receive the sacraments; and with them they were zealous to deposit their dead. Vast multitudes thought it their highest happiness to be admitted into the mendicant orders. Many made it an article in their last wills that their bodies should be wrapped in old Dominican or Franciscan rags, and be interred among the mendicants. For three centuries, these two orders governed Europe. They filled every important post in church and state; taught in all the universities and schools; and though they quarreled most violently with each other, they were the very soul of the Papal power, and through that, gave law to empires, states and nations. But their monkish cowl concealed the most scandalous immoralities and vices.

The Dominicans first came into England, A. D. 1221. The mayor of London permitted them to erect a convent by the Thames, on a street which is still called Black Friars, from the color of their dress. The Franciscans came into England soon after. Their establishment was at Canterbury.

To give a full account of all the operations, corruptions, superstitions, frauds and enormities of the monks; their bitter animosities and contentions, would require volumes. Their history sickens the heart. To see men, under pretence of great devotedness to God; leading the most loathsome, filthy life; sometimes casting off all clothing and going on all fours like beasts; secreting themselves in dens and holes; or wandering about in the extremes of wretchedness, with their hair and beard of an enormous length, and their bodies covered with vermin; eating of choice the most nauseous food; wearing heavy chains; fastening grates upon their breasts and back; girding themselves with bandages of bristles and sharp pointed wires; flogging themselves with thorn sticks; mutilating their bodies, until they often expired under their self-tortures; and these men commanding the reverence and homage of the world as saints, holy ones. What can be more revolting and distressing to a rational mind? And is this indeed Christianity? Is this the church which Christ redeemed to himself and renewed by his Spirit, that he might present it a glorious church, not having spot or wrinkle, or any such thing? Oh, no! We have turned away from her to contemplate this abominable excrescence, which grew upon her side, and which weighed her down even to the dust. But we shall see worse things than these.

MAHOMETANISM.

In the Revelations of John, the degenerate church was taught to expect the most desolating judgments from terrific adversaries. Already we have seen pagan Rome going forth, and hell following, with power to kill with the sword and with hunger, and with death and with the beasts of the earth. Ten fiery persecutions have blazed around the church. Her martyrs are before the throne of God. These woes are past. But under the figure of a star fallen from heaven to earth, to whom was given the key of the bottomless pit, and who should open that pit and let forth out of the smoke of the pit, swarms of locusts, to whom was given power as the scorpions of the earth, was depicted another adversary, who should now arise, and in whose days men should seek death and not find it, and desire to die, and death would flee from them.

Arabia had known but little of the power of the Gospel. Her people were ingenious and powerful, but groped in darkness. Here appeared the fallen star. Here Mahomet, the wicked impostor opened the bottomless pit, i. e. set up a false religion, which should darken the nations and send forth a host of scorpions, which should desolate some of the fairest portions of Christendom.

Mahomet was originally a tradesman. About the year 608, he formed the bold scheme of setting up a new religion in the earth, and becoming the head of empires. He retired to a cave in Mecca, where, as he pretended, with the assistance of an angel, but really of a Jew and a renegade Christian, he wrote the Koran, the only sacred book of the Mahometans.

He declared that there was one God, and that Mahomet was his prophet. To captivate Jews and Christians, he allowed both Moses and Christ to be true prophets; but represented himself as superior to both, in light and power, and sent of God to reform the systems they had established. He compiled his book from oriental tales and fables, from legendary trash of rabbis, and from the Jewish and Christian Scriptures, and made it a stange compound of blasphemy and folly. His ideas of providence were those of the fatalist. He forbade the use of swine's flesh and spiritous liquors, and required occasional fasts; but his morality was of the loosest character, allowing to men the free indulgence of their passions; and he promised to his followers a carnal heaven, where they should eternally indulge in the grossest sensualities.

When he announced himself as the prophet of God, a storm arose against him and he fled from Mecca to Medina. This flight occurred A. D. 622, and is called by the Mahometans, the Hegira; and is regarded as their grand epoch.

An immense multitude soon adhered to the impostor. He waged an exterminating war against all who refused to receive him. His proselytes were made by fire and the sword. No force or power could withstand him, and before his death, which happened A. D. 631, he was complete master of all Arabia.

With him did not end his religion. He had opened the

CHAPTER 7.]   MAHOMETANISM.   221

bottomless pit, and forth had issued deadly scorpions. With a zeal equal to their master, his followers every where spread his licentious and bloody system. Syria, Persia, Egypt, and other countries fell under its dominion. Their once flourishing churches now all found a grave. Jerusalem, where David had sung, and Isaiah had prophesied, and our Lord was crucified, and the Spirit had triumphed, fell in 637 before their ravages, and was given up to a long night of dreadful darkness.

In the year 713, the Saracens, as his followers were called, passed from Africa to Spain, reduced to slavery those Christians who had a name to live, but were dead, put an end to the kingdom of the Goths, which had continued for 300 years, and advanced into France, intending to overturn Europe and blot out the Christian name. But to them was given, only " The third part of men." An opposing power met them in France between Tours and Poictiers, A. D. 734, under Charles Martel, and defeated them with a tremendous slaughter, killing 370,000 in one day.

In a subsequent period, they made themselves masters of the fertile island of Sicily, and spread terror to the very walls of Rome.

In the East, they pushed their conquests to the extremities of India, compelling every people and nation to bow to the crescent. The sufferings of the church were exceedingly great. They were beheld by the Saracens with the utmost abhorrence, and treated rather like dogs than men. Immense numbers were induced to embrace their religion. Those who refused, were either slain or reduced to such extremities, that the light of Christianity, which once shone bright in Africa and Asia, was soon nearly extinguished.

In the beginning of the 13th century, a new and terrible power appeared in Asia, called the Ottomans, from Othman their leader, but now the Turks. They inhabited the northern coast of the Caspian sea. The Saracens persuaded them to embrace the religion of Mahomet. Oh! had some Christian missionaries but spread among them the light of the Gospel— but they were deceived by the terrible impostor. They soon contended with their teachers, overthrew the whole Saracen dominion, and became masters of all that fair portion of Asia and Africa, which Mahomet claimed. Composed of four sultanies, they were the four angels which were bound in the river Euphrates, and let loose to kill and destroy. Bajazet, the third sovereign from Othman, matured a plan for extinguishing the great empire, and with it the religion of Christ. But when he was just ready to fall upon Constantinople, Tamerlane, one of the mightiest of monarchs and warriors, who reigned over all the north and east of Asia, fell upon him at the head of a million of men; destroyed his army; took him captive, put him in an iron cage and carried him for a show through all his dominions. But Tamerlane, with his vast armies, embraced the religion of tho false prophet, and treated the Christians in the East with the greatest severities.

The Turks were checked, but not destroyed. They gradually became formidable to the Christians, and about a century after this defeat, A. D. 1453, Mahomet the Great took Constantinople, and with it all Greece, where Christianity had for a long period reigned so triumphant.

Such is a brief history of that terrific dominion which was let loose in the seventh century, from the bottomless pit. It was early rent by violent factions; there are now two principal sects of Mahometans, who differ concerning the right of succession to Mahomet; the Sheichs or Shiites, who are chiefly Persians, and the Sonnites, inhabiting East Persia, Arabia, Turkey, and Independent Tartary. There are about fifteen millions of Mahometans in Hindostan. A new and powerful sect has recently sprung up in Arabia, called Wahabees, who profess to be reformers. But all the different sects and factions have ever united in opposition to Christianity, and given it a blow in the Eastern world, and in beautiful Greece, from which it has never yet recovered. Mahometanism now extends over Turkey, Tartary, Arabia, Africa, Persia, and the dominions of the Grand Mogul, embracing about 100 millions of devoted subjects. It is an awful mystery in the providence of God. Oh, why is it permitted? When will all these vast nations bow at the feet of Jesus? The time is assuredly and rapidly approaching. "He that will come, shall come, and will not tarry." Mahomet shall be destroyed, and Asia, Africa, and Greece be free.

CHAPTER VIII.

Prophecies relating to the papacy. Its gradual rise. Grant of Phocas. Causes of the vast increase of papal dominion. Ignorance, superstition, and corruption of the age. Tradition substituted for the Bible. Subjection of heathen nations. Subserviency of the monks. Papal Rome idolatrous, and a temporal power, the little horn. Supposed time of her continuance. Election of Popes. Efforts at supreme dominion. Hildebrand's treatment of Henry. Thomas à Becket. Interdiction. The power given to the beast.

ABOUT the same time that Mahometanism appeared in the East, the papal power arose in the West; a power, which, while it pretended to support Christianity, was scarcely less destructive to vital godliness.

This power, also, was described with wonderful accuracy, ages before, by the spirit of prophecy. It is the little horn spoken of by Daniel, which should rise after the ten horns, and speak great words against the Most High, wear out the saints of the Most High, and think to change times and laws. It is the Man of Sin, who Paul told the Thessalonians, should be revealed; the Son of perdition, who opposeth and exalteth himself above all that is called God, or that is worshipped, so that he as God, sitteth in the temple of God, showing himself that he is God. It is the Antichrist, described by John; the terrible Beast in the Revelation which opened his mouth in blasphemy against God, and to whom it was given to make war with the saints, and to overcome them, and to have power over all kindreds and tongues and nations,—the Woman arrayed in purple and scarlet color, upon whose forehead was a name written—MYSTERY, BABYLON THE GREAT, THE MOTHER OF HARLOTS, AND ABOMINATIONS OF THE EARTH.

The Mahometan power rose suddenly, and, by the sword, spread rapidly over the earth; but the papal was, for more than five centuries, coming to its full growth.

In the third century, we find the bishops of Rome, Antioch, and Alexandria, commanding great respect and reverence, as bishops of primitive and apostolic churches, and assuming a place above all other bishops; and the bishop of Rome exercising a pre-eminence of order, though not as yet, of power over the other two.

When Constantine made Christianity the religion of the state, he effected but little alteration in the government of

18*

the church. The chief that he did, was to place himself at its head and make its government in some measure like that of the empire. The four bishops of Rome, Antioch, Alexandria and Constantinople, answered to his four pretorian prefects; under these were the exarchs, or patriarchs, who govern several provinces; then came the archbishops, who ruled over certain districts; then the bishops of dioceses and pastors of churches.

As Rome was the emporium of the world, its bishopric increased perpetually in grandeur, opulence and power. Its revenues became princely. Its dependents, like those of a monarchy. All the splendid trappings of royalty surrounded the incumbent. He sat on his throne, covered with sumptuous garments, attracting the admiration of the ignorant multitude. It became, therefore, a most seducing object of ambition. When a new bishop was to be elected, the whole city was agitated. Dissensions, tumults and cabals were witnessed, which would have disgraced the election of a worldly chieftain.

But the bishop of Rome met with a sudden and serious check in his progress toward spiritual dominion. Constantine had removed the seat of empire from Rome to Constantinople, and given the bishop of his capital a rank equal to that of any other spiritual power. Rome, however, did not surrender the ground it had taken. These two prelates at once became rivals. A contest was carried on for ages, which resulted in sundering entirely the Greek and Latin churches.

The former continued to acknowledge the dominion of the bishop of Constantinople, but from various causes his dominion rather decreased, while that of Rome soon gained amazing strength and power. The bishops of Rome were, many of them, men of talents and vast ambition. Leo I., called the Great, who flourished in the fifth century, was a man of uncommon genius and eloquence, indefatigable in his efforts for spiritual dominion. Gregory the Great, also, in the next age, distinguished himself in a violent contest with the bishop of Constantinople, and in extending the bounds of the See of Rome.

At length in the commencement of the seventh century, the emperor Phocas conferred upon Boniface III., bishop of Rome, the title of œcumenical, or universal bishop. This title had been usurped by the bishop of Constantinople, but it was now in this public manner taken from him and conferred upon the bishop of Rome; and this, too, by one of the most odious tyrants that ever lived. What they had thus obtained, the Roman pontiffs used every effort to hold; and they did hold it—a power which no other earthly potentate ever possessed. It is from this grant of Phocas that many date the establishment of the papal power, though the most decisive marks cf Antichrist, idolatry and false doctrine, did not appear until a later age. But the period of her establishment was not the period of her full growth. On the contrary, she was as many centuries gaining her astonishing dominion, as she had been rising to the point at which we can now view her. An account of some of the great causes which contributed to her enlargement, and of the various steps by which she marched on to the summit of power, will give a general view of the ecclesiastical world from the seventh to the fourteenth century.

The period before us was one of extreme ignorance, superstition, and corruption.

The world was sunk in Egyptian darkness. The cultivation of the human intellect was abandoned. The incursions of the barbarous nations from the North, had driven every thing like literature into the cells of the monasteries. Books were unknown among the common people; and had they been known, they would have been useless, for few were acquainted with the art of reading. The great mass of the clergy were incapable of reading the Apostle's creed. Even the bishops in general were unable to compose any thing like a sermon, and delivered to the people insipid homilies, which they had taken from the writings of Augustine and Gregory. Such an age was exceedingly favorable to artful and daring men, who continually made pretensions to authority, which few had the ability to question.

It was also an age of deep superstition. Men had scarce any rational views of religion. They had almost wholly lost sight of the character of God, and the state of the heart, of the Gospel of Christ, and of the duty which God requires of man. The doctrine of salvation by faith in Christ, was almost as unknown as at Athens, in the days of Paul. The minds of men were wholly turned to an attendance on a multitude of rites and ceremonies as the sure way of gaining heaven. These, issuing from the papal throne, gave the Popes an immense control over the heart and conscience. The multitude easily learned to look up to them as standing in the place of God, and to be honored as God. And it was a circumstance extremely favorable to the ambitious designs of the Popes, that those vast barbarous nations, which had overspread the fair fields of Europe, had been accustomed to regard their priests with an awful superstition; and to attribute to their arch-druid little less than godlike power Easily were such men made to transfer all this reverence to those who officiate at Christian altars, and to give to the Roman pontiff the authority and power of the arch-druid.

Above all, it was an age of awful corruption. In the East, the Holy Spirit had, to human appearance, ceased to operate. In the West, there was indeed to be found some piety. God, in every age, it is believed, has had a people to serve him. The gates of hell have never been suffered entirely to prevail against the Church of Christ. What piety there was, however, was chiefly in nations remote from Rome, and newly converted; though here and there was one to be found in the seat of the beast who had not his mark in their forehead, and who made vigorous opposition to him, and excited much trouble. The spirit of prophecy had declared, that through the long night of popery, there should be two witnesses who should prophecy in sackcloth. But, in general, the civilized world, from the seventh to the fourteenth century, was sunk in the lowest depths of moral corruption. No law of God, requiring holiness and forbidding sin, was placed before men. Morality did not enter into the religion of the age. He who would practice some rite, or possess some relic, or pay a sum of money, was assured of heaven, though he were a thief and a murderer. Mankind, therefore, were left to go fearless into eternity, amid the grossest vices; while no cultivation of mind or manners existed to keep them above the sensualities of brutes.

The priests and bishops were a most worthless, stupid, and corrupt race. They often passed their lives in the splendor of courts, or at the head of soldiers, and aspired to the honors and authority of Dukes, Marquises, and Counts. Even the Roman pontiffs, with a few exceptions, were monsters of iniquity, who sought the chair as a place of dominion, and who were perpetually guilty of the most flagitious wickedness. In such an age of corruption, what could be expected, but that every law, human and divine, would be trampled upon, and the minds of men become enslaved by the most tremendous tyranny. Not more certain is it that the river runs into the ocean, than that licentiousness generates tyranny, while holiness results in civil and religious liberty.

The Bible had, through a cunning device of Satan, been supplanted. The Popes, who were continually seeking control of the spiritual world, gave the preference to human compositions above the Scriptures. The opinion of some renowned doctor, handed down by tradition, the decision of some council of former days, was regarded more than the word of God. Hence the Bible grew into disuse. It was really a dead letter, while the opinions of doctors, and results of councils were submitted to, as the voice of God; a circumstance which was employed to the establishment of the most terrible dominion, for the Popes were always able to forge such opinions and decrees, and impose them upon the people, as would subserve their purpose. Among such forged papers, were the famous *decretal epistles;* which were said to have been written by the early Roman pontiffs, and which were now brought forward with great triumph. By these, the people were made to believe that the extravagant pretensions of the Pope were no new things; but had been common, and had been submitted to in the first ages of Christianity.

The efforts made to convert the heathen, were also subservient to the enlargement of the dominion of the Roman pontiffs. These efforts commonly originated with them, and the converts from paganism early learned to look to them as the source of power and goodness. Some of those who went to preach among the heathen, were, indeed, excellent men; of an entirely different character from the Popes who sent them. Among these, may be mentioned, Willebrod, an Anglo-Saxon, who with eleven associates, " an excellent group," spread the Gospel in the seventh century through Bavaria, Friesland, Cimbria, and Denmark;—Boniface, who, in the next century, "an age of missionaries," erected the standard of truth in Germany;—Villehad, called the Apostle of Saxony;—Anscarius, who, in the ninth century, traveled among the Danes, Cimbrians, and Swedes, planting the Gospel with much success;—and Bernard, who, in the tenth, went to the Orkney islands. Some Greek missionaries, also, who, in the same century, carried the

Gospel from Greece into Russia, and prevailed on the Emperor and Empress to receive Christianity, and proclaim their country Christian—a daughter of the Greek church—were of an excellent character. But many, who went out under the patronage of the Roman pontiffs had no other motive but to extend the power of the Roman See ; and, to effect their purpose, they not unfrequently resorted to force. Christian princes also, in league with Rome, compelled conquered tribes to acknowledge the dominion of the Pope. The Pomeranians, Finlanders, Sclavonians, and Livonians, received baptism at the point of the spear.

But that which contributed more than any thing else to increase and strengthen the papal power, was the reigning spirit of Monachism. The Christian world was deluged with monks. Like the frogs of Egypt, they came up over all the land and entered into every dwelling. All these attached themselves to the Roman See. The Popes of Rome were careful to patronize them, that they might make them tools of their ambition. Every project of the Popes, whether right or wrong, was applauded by them, and whoever called the decisions of Rome in question, was denounced by them as enemies to God. Such a power there was no resisting.

These and other causes operated with a continually increasing force, through several successive centuries, to the enlargement of the dominion of the Man of Sin.

Early in the eighth century, the Roman church became idolatrous.

God, an infinitely pure Spirit, has justly required man to worship him in spirit and in truth, and has solemnly forbidden him to make any image or likeness of Him, or to worship and bow down before any picture or statue representing Him or any other object. But as we have seen in the history of idolatry, men soon changed the incorruptible God into an image made like to corruptible man ; worshipped the host of heaven, and unenlightened by divine truth, have been, in this way, the deluded votaries of Satan to the present period. The Gospel waged an exterminating war against idolatry in every form ; and we have seen it gaining the most astonishing victories throughout the vast Roman empire. It was the mightiest conquest that was ever achieved; and ought to be seriously contemplated by the Christian community, until they are roused by the view to go forth in their strength, and subdue the world to Christ. But the spirit of the Gospel had now nearly departed from the earth. Amid the gross ignorance and superstition of the age, men were fast loosing sight of the great object of spiritual worship. The world was preparing for a false fire of devotion. Satan knew his time. He cast in his seed. Men were not to be made to renounce Christianity and go back to the old idolatry. But the arts of sculpture and painting were to be introduced to aid in the worship of Christ, the Apostles and canonized saints; but really to drive the eternal Spirit and divine Saviour from the minds and hearts of men.

From small beginnings proceed the mightiest results. In Constantinople was an image of Christ on the cross. The Emperor Leo, seeing that it was an object of idolatry, sent an officer, in the year 730, to pull it down. Some women there remonstrated against it, as horrid sacrilege. The officer, disregarding their pleas, mounted a ladder and cut the face to pieces by three blows of a hatchet; when the women threw down his ladder and murdered the officer. Leo put the murderers to death; but to this day they are honored as martyrs in the Greek church.

In Rome, a passion for idolatry had already commenced and no sooner was this act of Leo's known there, than the whole city was thrown into confusion. The Emperor's statues were thrown down and trodden under foot. Gregory II. was then in the papal chair, who, for the zeal he showed in establishing image worship, and for exalting himself in the place of God, has, by many, been called the first Pope of Rome. He excommunicated Leo, and made an effort to have a new Emperor elected. The Italian provinces, which were subject to the Grecian empire, revolted, and massacred or banished the imperial officers. A civil war ensued. The emperor issued orders to have all paintings and statues destroyed; and the adherents of Rome were as active in multiplying and giving them reverence. Thus the Christian world were thrown into the most violent contentions, which resulted in horrid crimes and assassinations. Those who worshipped images, were called *Iconoduli*, or *Iconolatræ*, while those who opposed this worship, as gross idolatry, were called *Iconomachi* and *Iconoclastæ*.

But there was not virtue and piety enough, to insure a long

and effectual resistance. Image worship grew exceedingly popular in the Eastern churches, and it only needed the sanction of an Emperor to make it universal. Three Emperors had violently opposed it; but Irene, the widow of the last, openly favored it in the year 784. In the year 789, was held the second council of Nice, which confirmed the idolatrous worship, and rendered it equally prevalent in the East and in the West. Some, indeed, had the boldness to oppose it. A council of 300 bishops was held at Frankfort, which condemned the council of Nice, and the worship of images. Many of the British churches execrated the same. Charlemagne, the ruling potentate of Europe, barely tolerated so great a departure from the purity and simplicity of the Gospel. But the poison was deep. It had infected all orders of men. Rome was idolatrous;—was ANTICHRIST.

Many plead, in vindication of image worship, as others do of pagan idolatry, that the votaries are sincere worshippers of God, and only employ these intervening paintings, statues or idols, to help their devotions. But on the most favorable supposition, it is all a direct violation of the second commandment, and it will generally be found that there is an idea of sanctity connected with the painting, wood or stone. The worship of images in the papal church, was used as a direct and full substitute for faith in the atoning blood of the divine Saviour. The Scriptural way of salvation was entirely set aside, and he who would pay his daily devotions to some image or statue of Christ or a canonized saint, was viewed as an heir of life.*

Victorious in this contest, Rome entered with great violence into a contention with the Eastern churches, about the procession of the Holy Ghost; choosing to say that the Spirit proceeds from the Father and the Son, while the others contended that the Spirit proceeds from the Father by, or through the Son. About the same time, a new empire arose in the West, to which the Roman bishop adhered; and an irreparable breach was affected between the Greek and Latin churches.

---

* It is a striking fact, that in the catechism of the Roman church, the second commandment is omitted; and to make the ten, the tenth is divided into two.

In the year 755, the Pope became a temporal prince, "the little horn." For countenancing the dethronement of Childeric III., king of France, and crowning Pepin, Pepin gave to the Roman See the exarchate of Ravenna, Pentapolis, and twenty-one cities and castles. Charlemagne, his son and successor, aimed at the empire of the West. He accomplished his purpose, went to Rome and was crowned; and in return for services, ceded to the papal See several cities and provinces, and gave it a subordinate jurisdiction over Rome and the annexed territory—enabling it to become the seat of wealth and magnificence.

But the temporal power of the Roman pontiff was never to be compared with its spiritual. For a long time, bishops and councils endeavored to maintain some authority and influence, but they were ultimately all trodden in the dust. The Man of Sin came, as Paul said he would, " after the working of Satan with all power, and signs, and lying wonders, and with all deceivableness of unrighteousness in them that perish." He arrogated to himself god-like titles and attributes, King of kings, Universal Father, Master of the world; set himself above all laws, human and divine; by taxes and massacres, he oppressed and wore out the saints; he changed "times and laws," appointing innumerable fasts and feasts, new modes of worship and new articles of faith and supporting himself by the most infamous frauds and barefaced pretensions to miracles. The most powerful monarchs were powerless before him. Emperors led his horse and held his stirrup. Kings were stripped by him of their honor and power, and whole realms were deprived of every religious privilege.

For refusing to surrender to him the right of investiture, the right ever claimed by the princes of Europe, of conferring the most important places in the churches and monasteries upon whom they pleased, by the ceremony of presenting the ring and crozier, Hildebrand, Gregory VII., a Pope haughty and arrogant in the extreme, drove Henry, emperor of Germany, from his throne, and compelled him in the winter of 1077, to cross the Alps, and stand three days in the open air at the entrance of the pontiff's palace, with his feet bare, his head uncovered, and no other garment but a coarse woolen cloth thrown around his naked body, and implore forgiveness and a restoration to his dominions.

For sanctioning, as was supposed, the violent death of

Thomas à Becket,* archbishop of Canterbury, a man who had acquired, by his pretended sanctity, a most amazing power, Henry II., king of England, was compelled by Pope Alexander, to walk barefoot over three miles of flinty road, with only a coarse cloth over his shoulders, to the shrine of the murdered saint, where eighty monks, four bishops, abbots, and other clergy, who were present, whipped his bare back with a knotted cord, compelled him to drink water mingled with Becket's blood, and to give forty pounds a year for tapers to burn perpetually before the martyr's tomb.

For opposing him in the appointment of an archbishop of Canterbury, Pope Innocent III., in the commencement of the thirteenth century, excommunicated John, king of England—forbidding all persons to eat, drink, or converse with him, or do him service; absolving all his subjects from their allegiance; ordering the other monarchs of Europe to kill him, and laid the whole kingdom under an interdict, so that every religious privilege was taken away; every church was shut; no bell was heard; no taper lighted; no divine service performed; no sacrament administered; no priest was present, and no funeral solemnity was allowed in the burial of the dead; and no place of interment was permitted, but the highways.

Thus did the Popes take to themselves supreme dominion. The whole world they claimed as their property, which they gave to whomsoever they pleased. The inhabitants of heathen countries they treated as wild beasts; parceling out them and their lands at their pleasure. To the king of Portugal, the Pope granted all the countries east of Cape Non, in Africa, and to the Spaniards all to the west of it; showing himself as God. " The nations gave their power unto the beast, and they worshipped the beast, saying, Who is like unto the beast? Who is able to make war with him?"

---

* This murdered hypocrite was canonized as a saint. His brains were sent to Rome. A jubilee was appointed for every fifty years, when plenary indulgence was granted to all pilgrims who came to his tomb; 100,000 persons visited it at once. The most astonishing miracles were said to be performed, ages after, and a prayer was introduced into the service of his day, for salvation through the merits and blood of St. Thomas a Becket. Such was the deplorable superstition of the age!!

CHAPTER IX.

Measures adopted by the Roman pontiffs to secure their dominion. They fill all important stations. Increase their revenues. Send out Legates. Forbid marriage to the clergy. Hold over men the rod of excommunication. Establish the inquisition. Strengthen superstition. Canonize saints. Establish transubstantiation, purgatory, auricular confession. Worship in an unknown tongue. Make the Pope infallible. Institute the crusades, and military orders.

THE measures adopted by the Roman pontiffs to secure their dominion, were of a character with the unscriptural and odious tyranny which they exercised.

They assumed to themselves the power of filling all the important places in the church; of deposing and creating the bishops, abbots, and canons at their pleasure; so that in time there were scarce any in office to oppose them; for men were selected for these stations who would be tools of their ambition.

They reserved to themselves the revenues of the richest benefices; and, if any kings, or nobles, or bishops, had incurred their displeasure, the usual expiation was some large grant of land or money.

They sent Legates into the various provinces, with almost unlimited power to control their spiritual concerns. These were so many harpies; extorting money from the people by the vilest means; making impious sales of relics and indulgences, and also ecclesiastical benefices to the highest bidders.*

They commanded all priests to abstain from marriage, as inconsistent with the sanctity of their office. They held over all who in any manner opposed them, the threat of excommunication from the church; a judgment, which, in that age, was tenfold worse than death; for the whole community at once united in executing the sentence, some from thinking it the sentence of God, others fearing that if they, in the least, favored the excommunicated person, they should be subject to the like curse.

But a still more terrible scourge, by which the saints were worn out, and the dominion of the Pope was maintained, was the inquisition. This was established in the thirteenth century, and has continued a tremendous engine of power to this

---

*John XXII. is said to have left in his treasury, five and twenty millions of florins, of which eighteen millions were in specie, and the rest in plate and jewels, plundered from the subjected nations.

day. It was occasioned by the increase of heretics as they were called, i. e. of men who dared to think for themselves, call in question the power of the Pope, and view him as the Antichrist predicted by John. These were numerous in Gaul, and Innocent III. sent some Legates A. D. 1204, to extirpate them root and branch. Those bloodhounds, having Dominic at their head, were called inquisitors; and so servicable were they found to the papal cause, that the pontiffs established inquisitors in every city. A tremendous court was erected by them, first at Thoulouse, and afterwards in the various cities, embracing three inquisitors or judges, a fiscal proctor, two secretaries, a magistrate, a messenger, a reviewer, a gaoler, an agent of confiscated possessions, several assessors, counselors, executioners, physicians, surgeons, doorkeepers, familiars and visiters, all of whom were sworn to secrecy. By this court men were tried not only for heresy, or opposition to the court of Rome, but for magic, sorcery, Judaism and witchcraft, and either imprisoned for life, or put to the most lingering and tormenting death. To give it authority, the Emperor of Germany, and king of France were induced to grant it protection and maintenance, and to commit to the flames such as were pronounced by the inquisitors worthy of death. Thus was the inquisition established, the guardian of superstition, a most horrible tribunal, an engine of death, indescribably terrific, which has done more than any thing else to keep whole nations in subjection to the papal dominion, and has shed an ocean of innocent blood.

Holding emperors and kings in subjection, the Popes also frequently called out monarchs with their armies, to subdue the rebellious, and keep the world in bondage.

But men were bound by stronger chains than these. Fell superstition was increased by every art and device, until reason was lost, and the world raved in an awful mania. With the utmost hardihood, and a success which is altogether unaccountable, the pontiff and monks continually imposed upon the credulity of the multitude, by presenting to them pretended relics of ancient saints; a scull, a finger, a jaw, a bone, or a tooth. They even held up to the admiring crowd, the clothes in which Christ was wrapped in his infancy; pieces of the manger in which he was laid, of the cross on which he was hung, of the spear which pierced his side, of the bread which he broke at the last supper,—yea, portions of the **Virgin Mary's milk, and of the Saviour's blood.**

Having induced them to adore the relic, it was easy to lead them to adore the spirit of the saint: and hence proceeded the work of Canonization.

The deluded and the fanatical had long been accustomed to have a particular patron among the eminent saints who had departed from earth. The principle existed in the heathen idolatry. The gods of Greece and Rome were deified heroes. Papal Rome had become pagan, and she must have her tutelary divinities. Every man must have one for himself, from the degrading supposition that one was incapable of saving two persons. These saints virtually took the place of Christ as mediators between God and man. They were supposed to be able to avert dangers, heal maladies, keep off evil spirits, and fit the soul for heaven. The pontiffs profited by this new proneness to idolatry, and decreed that no deceased person should be considered a saint, unless canonized by them. This threw an immense power into their hands. They made the tutelary gods of the deluded people; and often made them, as in the case of Thomas à Becket, of those who had been their greatest minions. The first that was formally sainted by the bishop of Rome, was Udalric, bishop of Augsburg, in the tenth century.

At the head of the papal mythology, was placed the Virgin Mary. The world were led to look to her with an amazing reverence. She was represented as conceived in the eternal mind, before all creatures and ages; born without sin; her most holy body, then dead, as translated to heaven. Her image was in every temple. Christ could be approached only through her mediation. She was adored under numberless titles. In honor of her were instituted the rosary and the crown. The former consisted in fifteen repetitions of the Lord's prayer, and an hundred and fifty salutations of the blessed Virgin. The latter, in six or seven repetitions of the Lord's prayer, and six or seven times ten salutations, or *Ave Marias.* The house in which she lived at Nazareth, was said to be taken up by four angels and carried to Loretto, where it was visited by unnumbered pilgrims. The fraud was sanctioned by several successive Popes. In 1476, indulgences were granted to all who would celebrate an annual festival in honor of the immaculate conception of the blessed Virgin.

Church vied with church in pictures, images, statues of the canonized saints, especially of the Virgin Mary, and enormous prices were paid for supposed, and in most cases, false relics of them; the sight of which drew vast numbers, and no small gain, to the churches which held them.

Festival had been added to festival, until the people groaned under them; but in 1300, Boniface VIII. instituted the famous Jubilee. All who repaired to Rome every hundredth year confessing their sins, received absolution. This added so much to the power and wealth of Rome, that it was soon celebrated every fiftieth year, and is now every five and twentieth, with great pomp and magnificence.

The Popes strengthened themselves also, by an abuse of the sacrament. In the year 831, a monk named Pascasius Radbert, advanced the strange sentiment, that the bread and wine used in the Lord's supper, was, by consecration, converted into the body and blood of the Lord Jesus Christ, and was actually the same as was born of the Virgin Mary, as suffered on the cross, and was raised from the dead. The doctrine was too absurd and monstrous to be immediately received even in that gross age, and met with general disapprobation. It was however a monstrous doctrine, and that was sufficient to insure it a reception with some. Warm altercations ensued. The most odious tenets were charged upon each other by the contending parties. Some of the Popes saw it would exalt the priesthood: for if the meanest priest could convert bread and wine into the body and blood of Christ, what must be the power of the sovereign pontiff? and when it was brought before the fourth Lateran council in 1215, it was declared by Innocent III. to be a doctrine whose belief is necessary to salvation. Thus was the doctrine of TRANSUBSTANTIATION introduced, which has remained popular, and amazingly exalted the Roman clergy in the eyes of the people to this day.

From this proceeded the thin wafer, which the Catholics use in the sacrament, that no part of the precious body of Christ may be lost; and the prohibition of the wine to the laity— for if the bread is the real body of Christ, it contains his blood, and the wine is superfluous, and should not be wasted; only it might be used by the priests, who need a double portion. Communion in one kind, however, was never fully established until the meeting of the council of Constance. The procession of the Host followed. When the sacrament was to be administered to the sick, the priest was ordered to carry the host, or bread in procession, clothed with his proper garments, and lights borne before him. To complete the structure of superstition, the festival of the Holy Sacrament was instituted, 1264; as ordained by heaven, "to repair all the crimes of which men might be guilty in the other masses."

They laid hold, too, of the natural fears of men respecting the future state of the soul. They cunningly invented and imposed upon the world the belief, that as saints had some imperfections, they were not immediately to be admitted into heaven, but were located, for a time, in a place so near the abode of the wicked, that they should feel the heat of the flames of hell until they were sufficiently purified for heaven. Over this place, called Purgatory, the Popes pretended to have power. They declared, that an immense treasure of merit, consisting of the unnecessary blood of Christ, which had been shed, of the unnecessary good works of saints, which were called works of supererogation, had been committed to them to be dispensed for the release of such as were confined in that dreadful region, for any number of years they should see fit. To those who could not obtain release by any pilgrimage, or service, the Popes, in the plenitude of their benevolence, granted indulgences for certain sums of money, which should go into the papal treasury. The people were not only permitted to buy their own deliverance but the deliverance of their friends. And, to induce them to do this, pictures, representing the souls of individuals weltering in fire, were exposed in churches. Fraternities of monks were established, to wander through Europe, and beg and plead for them.

Yea, they went farther, and claimed, as the representative of St. Peter, the control of the keys of heaven and hell. Whosesoever sins were remitted, by the Pope and his clergy,· were remitted to them. The priests thus became confessors; and, if any failed to confess to them their sins, and receive absolution, they were to perish forever. This became a source of immense power and wealth; made men sin fearlessly; and, as the clergy lived in a state of celibacy, produced, throughout the Catholic countries, the most debased state of morals. Absolution from the future punishment of the most atrocious crimes, was fixed at a few shillings. A man might rob and murder his neighbor, go to his priest, receive pardon, and feel wholly at ease in his conscience and have no fear of a future punishment for his deeds.

Moreover, to hold the people in perpetual bondage, the Roman pontiffs forbade the worship of God in any language which the people could understand; requiring the use of the Latin tongue, which had become obsolete throughout all the churches. The Bible being supplanted by tradition, became a rare and neglected book, and the light of heaven was read and understood by few, and obeyed by none.

They finally declared the Roman church infallible. Its decisions, its decrees, were always right, how absurd and contradictory soever to plain common sense, to matter of fact, or to one another, they might be. Some ascribed this infallibility to the Pope, others to a general council; but the minds of the people at large, fully believed it was committed to the Catholic church, and, as this was governed by the Pope, it placed him in the seat of God.

Out of the superstition of the age, arose the crusades, or attempts to rescue Jerusalem from the hands of the Mahometans. The Roman pontiffs were not backward to improve these wild and mad undertakings, for the increase of their own power. Jerusalem was taken by the Saracens, A. D. 637. The Christians, who remained there, were treated with the greatest cruelties. These cruelties were witnessed by pilgrims, from Europe, who, on their return, excited by their relations, the indignation of all Christian nations. A general expectation prevailed throughout Europe in the tenth century, that, at the close of a thousand years, Christ would come to reign on earth, and would fix the seat of his empire at Jerusalem. It produced an unusual panic. As the period drew near, men left their employments, abandoned their connections, devoted themselves and their property to the churches and monasteries. Storms, earthquakes, and eclipses, were viewed as the immediate forerunners of the coming of Christ, and caused a complete abandonment of the cities. Private and public buildings, palaces and churches, were suffered to go to decay, as no longer useful. Multitudes were desirous of hastening to Jerusalem, and witnessing the descent of Christ, and it was thought the duty of all Christians to unite in chastising and expelling those barbarous infidels from the holy city, and relieving the persecuted and oppressed, and thus preparing the city for her King.

The first effort to rouse Christendom to the subject, was made by Pope Sylvester II., who in the tenth century, addressed an epistle to the church universal, as from the oppressed church in Jerusalem, calling for immediate relief. But little, however, was effected, until the close of the eleventh century. About that time, Peter, a hermit, who had been in military life, and had seen the miseries of the Christians in the East, wrapt in a coarse garment, his head bare, his feet naked; rode through Europe on an ass, bearing a weighty crucifix and a letter which he affirmed was written in heaven, and preaching to immense crowds in streets and churches, roused all the nations to an holy war. The Popes used every artifice to increase the excitement made by the hermit, and increase the number of spiritual soldiers. A plenary indulgence, a full absolution of their sins, was granted to all who should enlist. Amazing were the results. An immense multitude, computed at no less than 800,000, from the various nations of Europe, under illustrious commanders, set forth in the year 1096, to recover Jerusalem from the hands of the infidels. It was a motley assemblage of nobles, soldiers, monks, nuns, artists, laborers, boys, and girls, pressing forward; some from pious motives, some from the hope of gaining heaven, (for all who fell in battle, were assured of a high seat in the regions of bliss,) and many from the prospect of making their fortunes in the rich fields of Asia. Never was such enthusiasm felt on any subject. But a miserable fatality awaited the greater part of these adventurers; for acting more like an undisciplined band of robbers than Christians, they incensed against them the nations through which they marched, and were amazingly wasted away by famine, sword, and pestilence, before they reached the Saracen dominions. Such of the rabble as passed into Asia under Peter the hermit, were cut to pieces, by Solyman. The disciplined soldiers, however, were more successful, and in the year 1099, became masters of the holy city, under Godfrey of Bouillon, who immediately laid the foundations of a new kingdom. Such was the termination of the first crusade or *croisade*, as it was called in the French language, because its object was to extend the triumphs of the cross, and every soldier wore a consecrated cross of various colors upon his right shoulder.

No sooner, however, had the vast multitude returned to Europe, than the Saracens fell upon the new kingdom of Jerusalem, threatening it with an utter extermination. A new crusade was demanded to support the tottering empire; and in the year 1147, another torrent was seen pouring into the plains of Asia. This was headed by the two powerful monarchs, Conrad III. emperor of Germany, and Lewis VII. king of France; but it was wholly unsuccessful. By sword, by famine, by shipwreck, and the perfidy of the Greeks, they were wasted away, and the next year a miserable handful were seen retreating into Europe. The Saracens took courage, and, in the year 1187, recaptured Jerusalem, with horrible carnage and desolation.

The fanatical spirit, however, was not destroyed. It raged throughout two centuries. A third, a fourth, a fifth, and a sixth crusade were undertaken by the champions of the cross; and, as the final result, the Christians lost all footing in Judea, above two millions of lives and an incalculable treasure. Never were such wild and extravagant enterprises undertaken by any of the children of Adam. They were fit to proceed out from the age of deepest superstition and midnight darkness.

Some good and much evil resulted from them. No doubt their civil effects were extremely advantageous. They awoke the nations from the slumber of ages. They set mankind, bound down under a most terrible despotism, in motion. They made tribes and people, wholly unacquainted, known to each other, and gave the unpolished nations of the North and West, a knowledge of the refinement and arts of the East. They did much, therefore, indirectly to the production of a revolution in the religious world. They were among the earliest causes of the rise of civil and religious freedom. But their immediate effects upon the religious and moral state of the world were deplorable in the extreme. They augmented amazingly the power and authority of the Roman pontiffs. These became at once the military commanders of the European world. Emperors and kings were but subordinate officers in these tremendous armies. They enriched beyond all calculation the Roman See, churches and monasteries; for to them the pious crusaders bequeathed their lands, houses and money, and as few ever returned, they became their lawful possessors. Their demoralizing influence was such as no tongue can tell. The professedly pious world turned into a lawless banditti, and under pretence of extending the triumphs of the cross, abandoned themselves to the most flagitious and abominable crimes, without shame or remorse. If they went from home, a crowd of pretended saints, they came back desperate villains.

Such an opportunity the cunning pontiffs and monks did not lose to strengthen the superstition of the age. An army of dead men's bones, the pretended relics of all the saints from the martyr Stephen down to the latest age, was brought by the returning crusades from the tombs of Asia, and most carefully deposited in all the temples and monasteries of Europe. The Greeks and the Syrians knew how to impose upon the ignorance and superstition of the French, the English, and the Germans, and sold them these pretended relics at the highest prices. They were considered as the noblest spoils, compensating for all the toil, expense, and bloodshed of these wild enterprises.

The crusades, too, gave rise to three military orders in the Church of Christ. These were called the Knights of St. John, of Jerusalem, the Knights Templars, and the Teutonic order. Their general business was to support and extend Christianity, to protect the pious pilgrims of Jerusalem against the Mahometans and all foes, and to assist and relieve all wounded and needy soldiers. These orders indeed sustained for a while their great and good fathers, the Roman pontiffs, but they so increased in wealth, in vice, and savage barbarity, that the nations could not endure them. Some were suppressed by the arm of power, others were abandoned at the light of reformation.

Thus have we taken a view, not of the true Church of Christ, but of the " MAN OF SIN," of the terrible beast which opened his mouth in blasphemy against God, and to whom it was given to make war with the saints, and to overcome them, and to have power over all kindreds, and tongues, and nations. We have seen its rise, the extent of its power, and the artful means by which it strengthened itself in its terrible dominion. For near ten centuries it held all Europe, and has, for a much longer period, many of its countries, in the most horrid bondage.

For a long time the bishops of Rome were chosen by the suffrages of the whole Roman people ; but in consequence of the rage and violence of contending factions, the choice was taken out of their hands, and committed to a small number of men called Cardinals, and even the approbation of the emperor, once requisite, was soon rejected and despised. Some distinguished monk was commonly raised to the papacy. Sometimes opposing factions elected two Popes, when bitter contentions ensued. In 855, it is said, a woman disguised as a man, had the art to gain an election to the papal chair, and governed the church for two years. She is known by the title of Pope Joan. Many of the Popes reigned but a few months, and most of them but a few years. The number of bishops and Popes who have filled the See of Rome, is 250. John XII.

first introduced the practice in 956, followed by all his successors, of changing their name when chosen to the papacy.

The papists flatter themselves that their dominion will be forever. But the trump of prophecy, ages ago, proclaimed its end. Daniel says, it shall continue " a time and times, and the dividing of time." John gives its duration " forty and two months," and " a thousand two hundred and three score days." All these are the same period, 1260 years. For a time signifies a year. A time and times and the dividing of time, are three years and a half; which, according to the ancient Jewish year of 12 months, of 30 days each, is equal to 42 months, or 1260 days. If then the establishment of Popery was at the grant of Phocas, in A. D. 666, it will come to its end before the close of the nineteenth century. But if it was at the rise of image worship, and the little horn, it will not cease until 2000 years from the birth of Christ.

Thanks be to God, the power is already broken. Thanks be to God, the Bible was preserved through the long night of darkness, and has been brought forth pure and uncorrupt to bless mankind. Every step in the history of the reformation will call for the warmest expressions of gratitude and praise

CHAPTER X.

Two Witnesses, predicted by John. Their character. Why said to be two. Their history obscure. Traced out in an age of darkness. Leo and Constantine. Council of Constantinople and Frankfort. Alcuin. Council of Paris. Rabanus and Scotus. Claudius of Turin. Goteschalcus. Council at Trosly, Athelston, Afric, Arnulphus Witnesses in France, in England. Waldenses. Peter Waldo. John Wickliff and his followers. William Sautre. John Badby. Lord Cobham. John Huss and Jerome of Prague. Their adherents and followers. The Hussite war. Brethren and sisters of the Free Spirit.

IN the revelations to John, in which the papal power was so clearly predicted, we are presented with two Witnesses, who are to prophecy in sackcloth, during the continuance of the grand corruption. By these, it is supposed, are designated the true followers of Christ; who should, from age to age, bear witness to the truth. They are said to be two; a small, but competent number; the number required as suitable testimony by the law and the Gospel. " In the mouth of two witnesses shall every word be established." Their history, therefore, is that of the true church, while the history of

Popery is that of a monstrous corruption. But it is a history almost entirely hidden from us, in some periods; because the number of real Christians was exceedingly small, and because they were persecuted and trodden down, and without the means of giving their own history to a future age.

Amid the ravages of Mahometanism, Christianity nearly expired in Africa and the East. Constantinople remained a Christian city until the fifteenth century; but as early as the tenth, we find scarce any vestiges of piety among the Greeks. The witnesses to the truth, the men of piety, who abhorred the Man of Sin, and who formed the connecting link between the early Christians and the reformers, were chiefly to be found in the Western, or Latin church. The emperors Leo Isauricus and Constantine Copronymus, and the council of Constantinople, however, are not to be forgotten for the bold stand they took in the eighth century, against the worship of images, and the intercession of saints—the first great defection of the Roman church. With them may be connected Charlemagne, and the council of Frankfort, who, in 794, condemned in the West, the same abominations. Alcuin, an Englishman, and Paulinus, an Italian bishop, in the same age, raised their voice against the rising errors. The Paulicians, though they held some errors, bore witness against the errors of the seventh and eighth centuries.

In the ninth century, several princes warmly remonstrated against the increasing power of the Pope, and the worship of images. Lewis the pious, held a council at Paris, A. D. 824, which forbade that worship. Agobard, archbishop of Lyons, wrote against it. Rabanus, and Johannes Scotus, the two most learned men of the age, vigorously opposed the new doctrine of transubstantiation. But no man so powerfully stemmed the torrent of superstition as Claudius, bishop of Turin. He opposed the supremacy of the Pope, the doctrine of merit and transubstantiation, and the worship of images, preached the pure doctrines of the Gospel, and laid the foundations of those churches, which, long after, flourished in the vallies of Piedmont. He was a bright light, in an age of great darkness. In Germany, Goteschalcus bore witness to the doctrines of predestination and grace; defended them with great ability; was heard with deep attention, but was publicly condemned, whipped, and confined in a loathsome dungeon until he died, A. D. 869

The tenth century, was, as the papists acknowledge, an

iron, a *leaden*, an *obscure age*. "Then," says Baronius, their chief annalist, "Christ was in a very deep sleep, when the ship was covered with waves; and what seemed worse, when the Lord was thus asleep, there were wanting disciples, who by their cries might awaken him, being themselves all fast asleep." The church then sunk to its very lowest depression. Yet the witnesses lived. Some few pious men were carrying the Gospel to the heathen, and others were found declaiming against the abominations of Popery. A council at Trosly, in France, witnessed a good confession. Athelston caused the Scriptures to be translated into the Anglo-Saxon idiom, and Afric wrote against transubstantiation. Arnulphus, "a Luther in embryo," president of a council at Rheims, ventured even then, to call the Pope *Antichrist, sitting in the temple of God.*

The eleventh century differed a little from the tenth. It was almost equally sunk in wickedness and ignorance. The Pope reigned with absolute and awful sway. But there were some pious people in France, who ventured to deny the doctrine of transubstantiation, and the propriety of praying to martyrs and confessors. Thirteen of them were burnt alive, A. D. 1017. Others appeared in Flanders, who came from Italy, disciples of Gundulphus, who denied the papal doctrines. Berengarius of Tours, wrote against the doctrine of the real presence, and had many followers in France, Italy and England. A decree of the Pope, commanding celibacy among the clergy, met with great opposition throughout Germany, as unscriptural.

In the twelfth century, new light dawned upon the church. New and powerful witnesses appeared for the truth. In England, the constitution of Clarendon, forbidding all appeals to the Pope of Rome, without the king's license, were sworn to by the clergy and laity. Bernard inveighed loudly against the corruptions of Popery. Fluentius, bishop of Florence, publicly declared that Antichrist was come. Joachim, abbot of Calabria, in presence of Richard I. king of England, said, that Antichrist was born in the city of Rome, and would be advanced to the apostolic chair. Peter de Bruis, and Henry his disciple, exposed in France the corruptions of Popery, and were both martyrs. Arnold of Brescia did the same, and was burned at Rome, A. D. 1155; his ashes were thrown into the Tyber, that the people might not venerate his relics. Some faithful men sought refuge in England from the persecutions in Germany in 1160, who were condemned, whipped and tortured because they made the word of God the rule of their faith.

But the distinguishing witnesses of this, and the succeeding centuries, were the WALDENSES. They were a people scattered through the vallies of Piedmont. There, two centuries before, Claudius had sowed the seeds of truth, which had taken root. This people had long been poor and despised, but for their piety had been a spectacle to the world, and objects of enmity and malice. They had been called Vallenses, or dwellers in the valley; Cathari, or pure; Leonists, or poor men of Lyons; Sabbatati, for wearing wooden shoes and dressing with great simplicity, and Albigenses, from Albi, a town where many resided. In the year 1160, Peter Waldo, a merchant of Lyons, disgusted with the abominable practice in the papal church of falling down before the consecrated host and adoring it as God, sought for divine instruction from the Scriptures. Light shone upon his mind. He learned the doctrines of Christ, and had the four Gospels translated from the Latin into the French tongue and circulated among the people. It was an invaluable gift. As the Latin had become obsolete, a dead language, the Scriptures were inaccessible to all who could not read that. Waldo first put them into the hands of the multitude, and became himself an expounder of their doctrines. The effect was prodigious. Crowds flocked to hear him. Associations of men, adopting his sentiments, were formed. But the spirit of persecution arose. Waldo and his adherents were anathematized and obliged to disperse for safety. He retired first into Dauphiny, then into Picardy, and at last into Bohemia, where he died about 1170. He was a wonderful man. His piety, his labors, and the good he effected, have seldom been equalled. Wherever he went, the truth took deep root and spread wide. The word of God grew mightily, and converts were multiplied. From him the witnesses who testified to the truth against the errors of Popery, were called Waldenses. Neither his death nor the persecutions of the Pope, checked their growth. On the contrary, they increased amazingly throughout the south of France, Switzerland, Germany and the Low Countries. In Bohemia alone, it is computed there were not less in 1325 than 80,000.

Their religion was the religion of the Bible. By their adversaries they were charged with holding every monstrous heresy, and with the commission of every abomination. But it is evident, from the writings of their persecutors as well as their own, that their greatest crime consisted in denying the supremacy of the Pope, in affirming that the Scripture was the only rule of faith and practice, and ought to be read by all men; that masses were impious; that purgatory was an invention of man; that the invocation and worship of dead saints was idolatry; that the church of Rome was the whore of Babylon; that the marriage of priests was lawful and necessary; that monkery was a rotten carcass, and that so many commemorations of the dead, benedictions of creatures, pilgrimages, forced fastings, and the like, were diabolical inventions. Their moral character was that alone on earth which deserved at all the appellation of Christian.

The Waldensian churches looked for salvation by grace, through faith, the gift of God. They received the two sacraments, baptism, and the Lord's Supper, in their simplicity, rejecting the popish ceremonies. "About the year 1150," says Wall, "one sect among them declared against the baptism of infants, as being incapable of salvation, but the main body of the people rejected their opinion. And the sect that held to it quickly disappeared." Their discipline was severe. They gave a literal interpretation to the whole of Christ's sermon on the Mount, and allowed no wars, nor suits of law, nor increase of wealth, nor oaths, nor self-defence against unjust proceedings. They were poor and ignorant, and needed greatly the light of a future age. But it cannot be doubted, that among them existed truth and holiness. Luther rejoiced and gave thanks to God, that "he had enabled the reformed and the Waldenses to see and own each other as brethren."

On these faithful witnesses, fell the vengeance of papal Rome. For three centuries, an incessant persecution raged against them. All the horrors of the *Inquisition* were employed for their subjection. Armies were raised and sent to terrify them into submission or utterly extirpate them. By the axe, by fire, the sword, and other shocking barbarities, they were hurried into eternity. In France alone, above a million were slain for their adherence to the truth. In Germany and Flanders, too, they were persecuted with peculiar severity. The monks were urged by the Popes to treat them worse than they treated the Saracens. In the castle of Menerbe on the frontiers of Spain, 140 persons of both sexes were burned alive. Persecutions often drove the Waldenses to the top of the Alps in the dead of winter, where they perished. One hundred and eighty infants were at one time found dead there in their cradles. Four hundred little children were suffocated in a cave in the valley of Loyse, where they had been placed for safety. Often did this unhappy people change masters, and every new sovereign seemed anxious to commend himself to the Pope, by exterminating them with fire and sword. A reader of their sufferings feels himself to be among the ancient martyrs of Lyons and Vienne, and involuntarily exclaims with the poet,

"Avenge, O Lord, thy slaughtered saints, whose bones
Lie scattered upon the Alpine mountains cold."

But, *the blood of the martyrs was the seed of the church.* The Waldenses increased, so that in the fifteenth century, it is supposed there were not less than 800,000 in Europe. In Germany, they were called Lollards, from one Walter Lollard, who inveighed against the errors of Popery, and was burned alive, or from the dirges sung by them at funerals. But the witnesses prophesied in sackcloth. They were oppressed and kept in obscurity and silence by the power of the Pope. But God knew his secret ones. He saw the faith and patience of the saints. Their death was precious. Their eternity is glorious.

As in the persecution of Stephen, the saints were scattered abroad in the earth, so in that of the Waldenses and Lollards, they were driven through Europe. Some fled to England That country was completely subject to the papal dominion Its triumph was completed in the reign of John, when the whole kingdom was laid under an interdict. As many as twenty witnesses are mentioned by historians, who had raised their voice against it, but they were obliged to hide themselves. The mendicant orders were extremely numerous, and were so many harpies feeding on the vitals of the kingdom. The national universities had received great endowments, and were crowded with youth. The friars endeavored to recruit their number from among them; and such was their success, that parents were afraid to trust their sons there: so that the number of students at Oxford was reduced, in a short period, from thirty thousand to six thousand. This roused the indignation of John Wickliff, who had imbibed the sentiments of the

20*

Lollards. That distinguished man, the brightest light of the fourteenth century, was born in 1324, in Yorkshire. He ranked among the first scholars of that dark period, and was advanced to the mastership of Baliol college, and wardenship of Canterbury hall. But defending the university against the encroachments of mendicants, and writing against the tyranny of the Pope, and the superstitions of the age, he became the object of papal persecution, and was ejected from his office by Langham, archbishop of Canterbury. Wickliff appealed to the Pope, who deferred any decision upon his case for three years. In the mean time the reformer diligently studied the Scriptures, and made himself acquainted with the corruptions of Popery, and abominations of Monachism; and, by his writings and conversation, made the papal dominion in England tremble. The Pope in 1370, confirmed his ejectment; but he had made many friends, and king Edward III., bestowed upon him the rectory of Lutterworth. His activity and diligence were unremitted and unbounded. He clearly and boldly demonstrated the anti-christianity of Popery, of the mass, transubstantiation, purgatory, the seven sacraments; and exposed the idleness, debauchery, profligacy, and hypocrisy of the friars. Five bulls were issued against him from Rome, and twice was he summoned to appear before the papal authorities in London. Of the twenty-three opinions, for which he was persecuted, ten were condemned as heresies, and thirteen as errors. But he was saved from violent death. He died in peace at Lutterworth, of the palsy, A. D. 1387. He was an admirable man, learned, eloquent, bold, and truly devoted to the service of God. Before his death, he translated the whole Bible into the English tongue;*—a work of immense labor; but he was

---

* A specimen of Wickliff's New Testament, in the English of his time may be pleasing to some. Matt. xi. 25, 26. In thilke time Jhesus answeride and seid, I knowledge to thee, Fadir Lord of Hevene and earthe; for thou hast hid these thingis fro wise men and redy and hast schewid them to litil children : So, Fadir, for so it was plesynge to fore thee. Rom. ix. 17. And the Scripture seith to Farao, For to this thing have I styrred thee, that I schewe in thee my vertu and that my name be teled in al erthe. Therefore, of whom God wole, he hath mercy; and whom he wole he endurith. Thanne saith thou to me, what is sought ghit for who withstondeid his will ? Oo man, who art thou that answerist to God ! Wher a maad thing seith to him that maad it, What hast thou maad me so ? Wher a pottere or cley hath not power to make of the same gobet, oo vessel into onour, another into dispyt?
The pronunciation of the age, probably conformed to this spelling.

determined that men should have the Bible, that they migh. read it in their own language. Some partial versions had before been made in the Anglo-Saxon language, but they were obsolete. This, therefore, was a great gift to his countrymen. Together with his writings, so far as it could be circulated, when the art of printing was unknown, and the power of papacy was terrific, it produced great effects. Many were his followers in England and on the continent. They were known as Wickliflites and Lollards, and were terribly persecuted by the Inquisitors. His memory was precious. " All his conduct," says the University of Oxford, in a public testimonial given to his character, in 1406, " through life, was sincere and commendable ;" but the council of Constance in 1415, condemned his memory and opinions by a solemn decree; and about thirteen years after, his bones were dug up and publicly burnt.

As the Lollards increased, the clergy felt alarmed, for they saw plainly that the prostration of the monasteries and confiscation of church lands was endangered. Transubstantiation was denied by the new heretics, and their denial was made the test of heresy. Whoever was found guilty, was condemned to the stake. One William Sautre, a parish priest in London, and John Badby, a tailor, were tried, condemned, and burnt alive. But a more distinguished victim was Lord Cobham, a man of high birth, in favor of Henry V. He had searched the Scriptures, and become satisfied that transubstantiation, penance, pilgrimages, and image worship, were wrong, and he had the boldness to declare his sentiments. The monks eyed him with malice, and accused him to the king, Henry V. The king dreaded the sacrifice of so noble a subject, and endeavored to reclaim him. But Cobham had the spirit of a martyr. He had long been impressed with the errors of Popery, and the truth of the doctrines of Wickliff. He knew from experience, their worth. " Before God and men," said he to his accusers and judges, " I here solemnly profess, that till I knew Wickliff, whose judgment ye so highly disdain, I never abstained from sin ; but after I became acquainted with that virtuous man and his despised doctrines, it hath been otherwise with me ; so much grace could I never find in all your pompous instructions." The writings of the Reformer, he had carefully collected and scattered among the people, and he was now willing to die in their defence. When brought before the king, he said, " You, most worthy Prince, I am always prompt and willing to obey; unto you, (next my eternal God,) owe I my whole obedience. But as touching the Pope and his spirituality, I owe them neither suit nor service; for so much as I know him by the Scriptures to be the great Antichrist, the son of perdition, the open adversary of God, and the abomination standing in the holy place." The king turned angrily from him and delivered him over to the executioner. But the noble victim escaped from prison, and, being accused by his enemies of high treason, was outlawed, taken, and hanged as a traitor, and burnt hanging, as an heretic. Thus died Lord Cobham—a noble witness to the truth as it is in Jesus.

The Lollards increased; more than 100,000 were found in England. The government stood in great fear of them. The prisons in and about London were all filled. Thirty-nine persons were at one time suspended by chains from a gallows, and burnt alive for heresy and treason. In Scotland, James Retby was burnt alive in 1407. Whole families were obliged to quit their abodes for safety. Indeed for more than a century these persecutions raged with violence both in England and Scotland. No mercy was to be expected by men who read the Scriptures and spoke against the superstitions of Popery. Such as escaped the fire were branded on the cheek and compelled to wear a faggot on their sleeve to show that they were brands plucked out of the fire. But the burning of the witnesses was found to be no way to extinguish them.

On the continent, the writings of Wickliff produced similar effects as in England. They were carried by a student of Oxford into Bohemia, and there read by John Huss. This eminent man was born in 1373. For his learning and talents he was appointed Rector of the University of Prague. He was also a preacher of great celebrity in the chapel of Bethlehem. He never obtained sufficient light to renounce all the superstitious doctrines of the age, not even the monstrous doctrine of transubstantiation. His bitterest enemies, therefore, could never accuse him of heresy. But from reading the Scriptures and the writings of Wickliff, he acquired a spirit of holiness and an abhorrence of sin; and, having great decision and boldness of character, he declaimed vehemently against the monstrous vices and corruptions of all orders of clergy and monks, and drew upon him their wrath and indignation. For his holy boldness, he was summoned to appear before the council of Constance—an immense body, composed of all the dignitaries of church and state in Europe, convened to endeavor to satisfy the popular clamor which had already become loud, for a reformation in the church. Huss appeared there, A. D. 1414, having obtained a passport from the Emperor, assuring his safety in going and returning. He received only a mock trial. Many things were laid to his charge, but nothing criminal was proved against him. He persisted, however, in refusing to acknowledge himself in error, unless previously convicted of it from the Holy Scripture, even though he was declared to be so by the Catholic church; and this was enough to insure his condemnation. The Emperor shamefully delivered him into the hands of his enemies, and sentence of death was pronounced upon him. His books were condemned; he was degraded from his priestly office and burned alive. His blood-thirsty enemies had power to destroy his body, but could not subdue his noble spirit. At the place of execution he cried aloud; "Lord Jesus, I humbly suffer this cruel death for thy sake, and I pray thee to forgive all my enemies." When his neck was fastened to the stake and the wood was ready to be kindled, the elector Palatine offered him his life if he would retract. But, said he, "What I have written and taught was in order to rescue souls from the power of the devil and to deliver them from the tyranny of sin, and I do gladly seal what I have written and taught with my blood." The flame was kindled and he soon expired, calling upon God.

Thus fell before the power of the beast, one of the best of men; one of the greatest ornaments of the Christian Church. The world hated him, for he was holy. The Pope and his minions put him to death, not because he was in their view heretical in sentiment, for this he was not; he lived in a very dark age; the light of truth had not dawned upon his soul; but because, like John the Baptist, he openly condemned their licentiousness and hypocrisy.

His companion in life soon followed him to the stake. This was Jerome, of Prague. He had traveled into England for the enlargement of his mind, and had brought from thence the writings of Wickliff. These he faithfully studied, imbiding their spirit, and feeling it his duty to preach their doctrines. When Huss was imprisoned, he went to Constance to exhort him to steadfastness; but when seized himself and threatened with the most dreadful of all deaths, his heart failed him, and he had the weakness to deny all he had maintained as truth.

But his denial of the truth filled his soul with the deepest anguish, and he summoned fortitude to avow again the real sentiments of his heart and meet his fate. "I came," said he, "to Constance to defend John Huss, because I had advised him to go thither, and had promised to come to his assistance in case he should be oppressed. Nor am I ashamed here to make public confession of my own cowardice. I confess and tremble when I think of it, that, through fear of punishment by fire, I basely consented against my own conscience, to the condemnation of the doctrine of Wickliffe and Huss." Even Jerome, however, did not open his mind to all the light shed forth by the English reformer. He could not with him condemn the doctrine of transubstantiation. But he was a witness against many of the abominations of Popery, and went to the stake on the 30th of May, 1416. When bound for the slaughter, he raised his voice and sung,

"Hail! happy day and ever be adored,
When hell was conquer'd by great heaven's Lord."

When the flames had nearly done their awful work, he was heard to cry out, "O Lord, have mercy on me, have mercy on me. Thou knowest how I have loved thy truth."

The ashes of these early witnesses to the truth were scattered by the winds of heaven but their memory was precious. The inhabitants of Bohemia were shocked at the dreadful sacrifice which had been made of the best blood to the wickedness of the priests. The next year, about sixty of the principal persons of the country addressed a letter to the council, saying, "We can find no blame attached to the doctrine or life of John Huss, but, on the contrary, every thing pious, laudable and worthy of a true pastor. Ye have not only disgraced us by his condemnation, but have also unmercifully imprisoned, and perhaps already put to death, Jerome of Prague, a man of most profound learning and copious eloquence. Him, also, ye have condemned, unconvicted. Notwithstanding all that hath passed, we are resolved to sacrifice our lives for the defence of the Gospel of Christ, and of his faithful preachers."

These were men, ready to be led through all the perilous conflicts of a reformation, had they had enlightened guides. But alas! it was an age of awful darkness; and, though many saw the vices and abominations of Antichrist, yet none, as yet, saw the true way of reform. The best men had a poor understanding of the faith. The idea that the kingdom of

Christ was a spiritual kingdom, was embraced by but few if any. Errors of practice were distinctly visible, but errors of doctrine were not seen. The Romish church, in the council of Constance, passed a decree forbidding the use of the cup by the laity in the communion. This, added to the other enormities and corruptions of the age, roused the Bohemians to arms. About 40,000 assembled together on a mountain near Prague, which they called mount Tabor, where they raised a strong fortification, and put themselves under the direction of two chiefs, Nicolas and John Ziska, with the determination to revenge the deaths of John Huss and Jerome, and to obtain the liberty of worshipping God according to the dictates of their own consciences. Their numbers increased soon to an amazing extent; war was declared against Sigismund, the German emperor, and a deluge of blood was shed. Each party appeared to the other as enemies of the true religion, hated of God, and justly exposed to extirpation by fire and the sword. The most shocking and terrible acts of barbarity, therefore, were continually exhibited. At length, the papal party yielded; and, in 1443, a treaty of peace was concluded, in which the Bohemians were allowed the use of the cup in the sacrament, and the administration of the ordinance in their own language.

With these terms, the major part only were satisfied. These were called Calixtines. The remainder, who seem to have been the true Waldenses, wished for a more thorough reformaion from Popery and a restoration of Christianity to its primitive simplicity. They were called Taborites, and, through ignorance and fanaticism, went to many unwarranted excesses, and were the object of fiery persecution, especially from their brethren the Calixtines. In 1467, they formed a separate church and chose their own pastors. In 1480, their number was increased by an accession of some Waldenses, who escaped out of Austria, where they had been severely persecuted, and some of their pastors had been burned alive. But their enemies gave them no rest. The next year, the Hussites were all banished from Moravia, and were compelled to seek refuge in other countries for six years. Their number, however, did not much diminish. In the beginning of the sixteenth century they had in Bohemia and Moravia, two hundred congregations.

These poor, oppressed, and despised people appear to have formed the true Church of Christ in that age. They greatly needed the clear light of a future age, a clear view of the pure doctrines of the Gospel;* they were guilty of many acts of violence and rapine in defence of their religion, considered justifiable in that age; but among them, as among the early Waldenses, was a spirit of prayer, a spirit of holiness and abhorrence of the errors and corruptions of the Man of Sin, a strict discipline, a desire for the pure and simple worship of Jehovah, and a disposition to make the Scripture the only rule of faith and practice. Their covenant God, no doubt, beheld them in the thickets and clefts of the rocks, and heard their midnight songs of praise, and communicated to them his Holy Spirit. And if, as we have reason to believe was the case, they feared God, they are among the hundred forty and four thousand who now stand with the Lamb on Mount Zion.

The Taborites were those Bohemian brothers called Piccards and Beggards, who joined Luther in the reformation. Their descendants and followers are now to be found in the same countries.

The brethren and sisters of the Free Spirit, called in the Flemish, Beggards and Beguins, were a numerous people in Holland and Germany, who seemed to turn from the ceremonies and superstitions of Popery to something like inward piety and spiritual contemplation, and were most violently persecuted by the magistrates and Roman clergy in the fourteenth century.

---

* That the Hussites had many views, it is evident from the following articles of their creed, given by Æneas Sylvius, who was afterwards Pope Pius II.

The Pope of Rome is equal with other bishops.
Among priests there is no difference.
There is no purgatory fire.
It is in vain to pray for the dead, and an invention of priestly covetousness.
The images of God and the saints ought to be destroyed.
The blessing of water and palm branches is ridiculous.
The religion of the mendicants was invented by evil demons.
No capital sin ought to be tolerated, although for the sake of avoiding a greater evil.
Auricular confession is trifling; it is sufficient for every one in his chamber to confess his sins unto God.
The temple of the great God is the whole world.
The suffrages of saints, reigning with Christ in heaven, are implored in vain, forasmuch as they cannot help us.
The festivals of saints are altogether to be rejected
We should cease from work on no day, except that which is now called the Lord's day

Thus have we seen the *Witnesses* hitherto prophesying in sackcloth, from the first rise of the papal dominion. We shall now behold them indeed triumphant in the great reformation; though, wherever the Man of Sin rules, they will be subjected to oppression, and if possible, to death, until his dominion be taken away.

CHAPTER XI.

Circumstances in Europe favoring a reformation. Philip's triumph over Boniface. Removal of the Pope to Avignon. Great western schism. Mendicants unpopular. General demand for a reform. Council of Constance. Discouragements. Character of the Popes. Their power. Low state of religion and learning. Immediate causes. Avarice of the Popes. Sale of indulgences opposed by Martin Luther. Luther's birth and education. Retires into a monastery. Reads the Scriptures. Made professor at Wittemberg. Opposes Tetzel. Meets with applause. Circumstances favoring his cause. Summoned to Rome. Appears before Cajetan and Miltitz. Disputes with Eckins. Reformation commences in Switzerland. Erasmus. Melancthon. Frederick the Wise. Luther excommunicated. Burns the Pope's bull, and establishes the Lutheran church. Summoned to the diet at Worms. His defence and condemnation. Secreted at Wartburg. Reappears and publishes the New Testament in German. Preaches the Gospel with great success.

From what has passed before him, the reader will gain some general view of the deplorable state of the Christian world at the commencement of the sixteenth century. The papal power, was not, perhaps, so great as it had once been. Boniface VIII. may be viewed as having stood, in the fourteenth century, on that proud and guilty eminence of absolute spiritual and temporal dominion, which had been the desire of almost every pontiff through successive ages. Provoked by his haughty and overbearing demeanor, Philip, king of France, hurled him from his seat, and he died in disgrace and anguish. To prevent such almost uncontrollable dominion at Rome, Philip placed a Frenchman in the Papal See, and fixed his residence at Avignon in France. This remained the seat of the papacy for 70 years; a period called by the Catholics, the Babylonish captivity. But this removal from Rome greatly weakened the power of the pontiffs. It removed their personal influence, which had been immense, from the city. It gave their enemies in Rome an opportunity to cabal against them, and ravage with impunity *St. Peter's patrimony*. Many Italian cities revolted from the Pope. Decrees sent from Avignon were treated with contempt. Other parts of Europe caught the same feeling; and from this time, the thunders of the pontiffs were heard without much fear or dread.

Another circumstance arising out of this, which weakened the papal power, was the great western schism. The Romans, wishing to have the Pope reside at Rome, elected one in opposition to the Pope at Avignon. Europe became divided and distracted. For fifty years, the church had two and sometimes three Popes or heads, who did little but hurl anathemas at each other. The distress and scandal of the age baffle description.

The Mendicants also, throughout Europe, began to fall under a general odium. Their authority, rapaciousness, filth, and wickedness, provoked the rage of almost all classes. In England, the University made a resolute stand against them by her champion Wickliff; and in France many efforts were made to destroy their exorbitant power. Their internal conflicts were many and violent. These the pontiffs endeavored to subdue, and always with loss of power.

Besides the opposition of the true and faithful witnesses, the Romish communion found many in her own bosom, who, from time to time, exposed her vices and corruptions. Dante and Petrarch, in the fourteenth century, wrote against the corruptions of Rome; treating her as Babylon, and the Pope as Antichrist; and by their wit and raillery, did them incredible mischief. In the same age, Peter Fitz Cassiodor addressed a remonstrance to the Church of England against the tyranny and wickedness of Rome, urging a secession. Michael Cæsenus and William Occum exposed the various errors and heresies of John XXII. And Marsilius, a lawyer of Padua, wrote a treatise, entitled *The Defender of Peace*, in which he powerfully contested the papal claim to Divine authority, or pre-eminence over other bishops. In the year 1436, Thomas Rhedon, a Carmelite friar, saw the corruptions of the papacy, and so boldly exposed them, that he was burned alive. One Jerome Savanarola, an Italian monk, also inveighed against the corruption of the papacy, and preached the doctrine of free justification by faith in Christ. He, with two companions, were imprisoned and burned alive at Florence, A. D. 1499. Thomas à Kempis, the reputed author of the Imitation of Jesus Christ, who died in 1471, did much to enlighten the world in the nature of true piety. John Wesselus, of Groningen, shed much light on the surrounding darkness. Indeed, he has been denominated the light of the world, and the great forerunner of Luther; for he not only exposed the corruptions of popery, but preached many of those doctrines which Luther afterwards proclaimed, and which lay at the basis of the reformation.

These and other witnesses in the bosom of the papal church, had excited a general feeling throughout Europe in favor of a reformation. Loud and repeated calls were made upon the ruling powers for a general council, to heal prevailing divisions and abuses. At length the council of Constance was convened for this purpose. It was composed of 20 arch-bishops, 150 bishops, 150 other dignitaries, and 200 doctors. The Emperor Sigismund and the Pope were at its head. But what acts of reformation could be expected from men who were themselves grossly corrupt; from men whose highest interest was to have things remain just as ney were, or rather become more degenerate? Besides, had they been disposed to do according to their best ability, they could only have effected a partial reformation of a few external corruptions. The source of evil would have remained. This was the doctrine of justification by human merit; the foundation of indulgences and almost every evil in the papal world. This could only have been overturned by the true doctrine of justification through faith in the blood of Christ; and of this probably all in the council were ignorant. They did little, therefore, but condemn the writings of Wickliff, and burn Huss and Jerome, better reformers than the whole assembly. Other councils were subsequently composed for the like purpose, but were equally ineffectual. The general demand, however, for a reformation of abuses continued, and was very favorable to the interests of religion.

But notwithstanding these circumstances, favorable to a reformation, the condition of Christendom was extremely deplorable. If the Popes swayed not the sceptre which was once in their hands, they still maintained and exercised a most awful despotism over the souls and consciences of men. At the commencement of the century the chair was filled by Alexander VI., a monster in iniquity, who was continually guilty of the most execrable crimes. He was succeeded first by Pius III.; and then by Julius II., who was furious for war and bloodshed, and whose pontificate was a scene of military violence. His place was filled, in 1513, by Leo X., of the family of the Medicis; a man of literature and a promoter of learning, but a stranger to vital piety—accused even of atheism, and a man who spared no pains to uphold the wealth and grandeur of the Roman See.

This immense power, wielded by a thousand dignitaries, and holding in subjection the potentates of the earth, the Waldenses were too feeble to molest; while the Hussites, wearied by long contentions, were glad of the liberty of living and worshipping God, without being further molested or molesting others.

Of the low state of religion and of its monstrous perversions, we, in this age, can have no adequate conception. It is thus described by Frederic Myconius, a writer of that period. " The passion and satisfaction of Christ, were treated as a bare history, like the Odyssey of Homer; concerning faith, by which the righteousness of the Redeemer and eternal life are apprehended, there was the deepest silence. Christ was described as a severe judge, ready to condemn all who were destitute of the intercession of saints and of pontifical interest. In the room of Christ were substituted as saviour and intercessors, the Virgin Mary, like a pagan Diana, and other saints, who, from time to time, had been created by the Popes. Nor were men, it seems, entitled to the benefit of their prayers, except they deserved it of them by their works. What sort of works was necessary for this end was distinctly explained; not the works prescribed in the decalogue, and enjoined on all mankind, but such as enrich the priests and monks. Those who died neglecting these, were consigned to hell, or at least to purgatory, till they were redeemed from it by a satisfaction made either by themselves or their proxies. The frequent pronunciation of the Lord's prayer, and the salutation of the Virgin, and the recitations of the canonical hours, constantly engaged those who undertook to be religious. An incredible mass of ceremonial observances was every where visible, while gross wickedness was practiced under the encouragement of indulgences, by which the guilt of the crime was easily expiated. The preaching of the word was the least part of the episcopal function; rites and processions employed the bishops perpetually when engaged in religious service. The number of clergy was enormous, and their lives were most scandalous."

From this representation, we may easily perceive that an awful ignorance of religion, accompanied by the vilest superstition, pervaded all classes. The public schools of learning were filled by monks;—a class of men who had a barbarous aversion to all mental improvement, and who thought they did God service, if they locked up the faculties of youth.

Scholastic divinity, and the logic of Aristotle, filled the schools. Albertus Magnus and Thomas Aquinas, who lived in the 13th, and Duns Scotus of the 14th century, became the heads of powerful sects, called the *Scotists* and *Thomists*, who were ever disputing about the nature of the divine co-operation with the human will, the measure of divine grace essential to salvation, personal identity, and the immaculate conception of the Virgin Mary. By them philosophy was carried, it was thought, to the highest degree of perfection, but was, in truth, the most silly and unintelligible farrago. "The beautiful subtleties of sophistical syllogism, enabled the disputants to divide the hair of controverted points, which neither understood, and prove it when split, to be altar, or idem, or tertium quid; with quidditie's, and quo-ditie's and entitie's, and a profundity of like wisdom, that made an admiring audience gape, or the listening pupil stand amazed, lost in the depths of this unfathomable learning."

The best theological instruction was of so poor a character, that, when Luther rose, not a man could be found in the university of Paris, the best school of learning of the age, who could dispute with him in the Scriptures. Men preached; but their sermons were senseless unmeaning harangues upon the blessed Virgin; the merits of the saints; the efficacy of relics; the burnings of purgatory; and the utility of indulgences. If there were men of elevation in society, who read and thought, they were puffed up with a sense of their own excellence, by the Aristotelian philosophy, which was then prevalent in the schools, and which would write *foolishness* upon the doctrine of salvation by a crucified Redeemer.

The avarice of the Popes was unbounded. Desirous of maintaining the authority, grandeur, and splendor of the Roman See; they continually devised new schemes for draining Christendom of its treasures. Every ecclesiastic was required to pay *annats*, or the first year's produce of his living to the Pope. The richest benefices throughout Europe were sold, when vacant, and sometimes before, to the highest bidder. Frequent demands of free gifts were made on the clergy, and civil rulers: and extraordinary levies of tenths on ecclesiastical revenues, upon pretence of expeditions against the Turks, or some other pious purposes, never executed, were continually exacted.

But the greatest source of wealth to the pontiffs, was the sale of indulgences. This traffic was carried to awful excesses. For persuading the people, that there was an infinite treasure of merit in Christ and the saints, beyond what they needed themselves;—a treasure which was committed to the Popes, the bishops, the clergy, the Dominican and Franciscan friars, to be sold by them for money, and that whoever would purchase it, should be absolved themselves, from the greatest crimes, and deliver their friends, too, from the fires of purgatory; these crafty men had secured treasures of wealth almost unbounded. It was this abominable traffic which first opened the eyes of Martin Luther to the corruptions of popery, and roused his spirit to the work of reformation.

This wonderful man, who holds the first place in modern ecclesiastical history, and who must ever be loved and revered, as one of the greatest benefactors of mankind, was born at Isleben, in Saxony, in the year 1483. His father was a man of integrity, employed in the mines of Mansfield; but he acted like a man of enlarged mind, in giving his son a learned education. At an early period, Martin discovered uncommon powers of mind; and having passed through the ordinary studies at Madgeburg, Eisenach, and Erfurt, he commenced master of arts at the University of Erfurt, at the age of twenty-two, and devoted himself to the study of civil law. But a providential occurrence suddenly changed the whole course of his life. While walking in the fields with an intimate friend, that friend was suddenly killed by lightning. Luther viewed it as a call from heaven, to devote himself to the divine service; and he retired in 1505 into a convent of Augustinian friars. As yet he was a stranger to vital piety; and his monastic life, having the form without the power and joy of godliness, was very gloomy. But his mind was too highly cultivated for him to sit down an idle drone. The fire of genius burned within him; and had he been left to himself, and the ordinary course of monastic life, he would have found his way to the papal chair. But an invisible hand conducted him to an old Latin Bible in the library of the monastery. He seized it with avidity, and gave it a faithful perusal. Light shone in upon his understanding, and comfort dawned upon his soul. In this sacred treasury, he found the doctrine of justification by faith, the reception of which at once elevated his mind far above that scholastic philosophy and theology which were then in vogue, and of which he had become perfect master; and made his once gloomy monastery a paradise of bliss. Abandoning all other pursuits, he gave himself with incredible ardor to the study of the sacred volume; and such were his attainments in divine truth, that he was soon viewed as the most learned divine in all Germany. In 1507 he was ordained priest; and as a reward for his diligence, and astonishing attainments, he was made, in 1508, professor of philosophy and theology in the University of Wittemberg, on the Elbe, by Frederick, elector of Saxony. He also officiated as pastor of the church in Wittemberg, as the substitute of Simon Hensius, who was disabled by infirmity.

Luther is presented to us in history, as remarkably strong and healthy, and of a sanguine and bilious temperament. His eyes were piercing and full of fire; his voice was sweet and vehement, when once fairly raised; he had a stern countenance; and, though most intrepid and high spirited, he could assume the appearance of modesty and humility whenever he pleased, which, however, was not often the case. By friends and enemies, he was acknowledged as a man of great learning, and elegant taste, and pre-eminent above all others, as a popular preacher and teacher of philosophy.

His piety kept pace with his learning and popularity. In 1516 we find him thus writing to a friend. "I desire to know what your soul is doing, whether wearied at length of its own righteousness, it learns to refresh itself, and to trust in the righteousness of Christ." Remarkable language for that period.

While he was filling the highly important station, to which providence had raised him, with great credit to himself and his country, and gaining more and more knowledge of the fundamental doctrines of the Gospel, John Tetzel appeared, in the year 1517, in the neighborhood of Wittemberg, selling indulgences.* To this office that bold Dominican inquisitor

---

* According to a book called a tax book of the sacred Roman chancery, containing the exact sums demanded for the remission of sins, we find the following fees.

For simony,	10s.	6d.
For sacrilege,	10	6
For taking a false oath in a criminal case,	9	0
For robbing,	12	0
For burning a house,	12	0
For murdering a layman.	7	6
For laying violent hands on a clergyman,—	10	6

had been delegated by Albert, Archbishop of Mentz, to whom the indulgences had been sent by Leo X.

Had Tetzel been of a mild and timid spirit, the reformation might have been delayed another century; but he was a man of uncommon boldness and impudence, just calculated to rouse the indignation of Luther. He was indeed a veteran in the traffic. Ten years before, he had collected 2000 florins in the space of two days; and he boasted that by his indulgences, he had saved more souls from hell than ever St. Peter converted by his preaching. The following was one of his abominable articles of traffic. "May our Lord Jesus Christ have mercy upon thee, and absolve thee by the merits of his most holy passion. And I, by his authority, that of his Apostles Peter and Paul, and of the most holy Pope, granted and committed to me in these parts, do absolve thee first, from all ecclesiastical censures, in whatever manner they have been incurred, and then from all the sins, transgressions and excesses, how enormous soever they may be, even such as are reserved for the cognizance of the Holy See, and as far as the keys of the Holy Church extend; I remit to thee all the punishment which thou deservest in purgatory on their account; and I restore thee to the holy sacraments of the church, to the unity of the faithful, and to that innocence and purity which thou possessed at baptism; so that when thou diest, the gates of punishment shall be shut, and the gates of the paradise of delight shall be opened; and if thou shalt not die at present, this grace shall remain in full force when thou art at the point of death. In the name of the Father, and of the Son, and of the Holy Ghost." Another related to the deliverance of departed friends from the fire of purgatory; and such was the grossness of this man, that he would publicly say, 'The moment the money tinkles in the chest, your father's soul mounts out of purgatory."

The prices of these indulgences varied according to the circumstances and crimes of the purchasers. For the better sale of them, whole districts of country were farmed out to the highest bidders. These were often men of the most licentious characters, who, after they had quieted the consciences of thousands in sin, spent their nights in riot and voluptuousness. John Tetzel was a common adulterer.*

---

*That the Protestant reader may see to what extent this sale has been carried on since the reformation, in Popish countries, and how much we are indebted to Martin Luther, the following fact is added as given by

When Tetzel appeared in Saxony, vast crowds flocked from all parts of the country to purchase indulgences. The spectacle grieved the spirit of Luther, and he gently remonstrated against it from the pulpit of Wittemberg. The least opposition was sufficient to rouse the haughty spirit of Tetzel. He stormed and raged, and constructed a pile of wood, and set it on fire, to show what he would do with the man who should dare to call in question the holiness of his sales. The effect of this on Luther's mind, was to lead him to examine thoroughly the subject ; and being satisfied of the iniquity of the traffic, he came out with great boldness against it ; warned the people against trusting to any thing for salvation devised by man ; wrote to Albert, elector of Mentz, to whose jurisdiction the country was immediately subject, exposing the wickedness of the sellers of indulgences, and reproaching the sales ; and even dared to publish ninety-five theses, in which he developed his opinion concerning this iniquitous traffic and challenged its friends to defend it.

Luther, as yet, thought not of the wonderful things which ne was to accomplish. As fully as any man, he acknowledged the supremacy of the Pope, and the propriety of his granting indulgences, remitting church censures and temporal punishments ; but his mind was satisfied respecting the Pope's utter impotence to remit divine punishment, either in this or the future world. In a subsequent account of himself, he says, " I was compelled in my conscience to expose the scandalous sale of indulgences. I found myself in it alone, and as it were, by surprise. And when it became impossible for me to retreat, I made many concessions to the Pope ; not, however, in many important points; but certainly at that time, I adored him in earnest."

The boldness of Luther in doing what no one else dared to do, and what almost every one wished to have done, attracted great attention and applause throughout Germany.

Milner. " In the year 1709, the privateers of Bristol took a galleon, in which they found 500 bales of bulls, for indulgences, and 16 reams were in a bale. So that they reckon the whole came to 3,840,000, averaging in price, from 20 pence to eleven pounds." In Spain and Portugal, the traffic is still continued. In Spain, the King has the profits. In Portugal, the King and Pope go shares.

A short time since, a gentleman to ascertain the present state of things, went to the office at Naples, and for two sequins purchased a plenary remission of all sins for himself, and any two persons, whose names he should insert.

His theses spread into every city and village, and were read by all classes of people with amazing avidity. Tetzel, finding it necessary for him to do more than rage and threaten, published in opposition to Luther, one hundred and six propositions, in which he made some efforts to refute the arguments of the bold reformer. Other champions of the papal cause also came out in its defence; particularly Prierias, a Dominican friar and Inquisitor General; and Eckius, a renowned professor of divinity at Ingoldstadt. But Luther stood firm against every adversary. He had the Scriptures in his hands, and from them he was able to draw weapons of defence, which, in every contest gave him the decided advantage.

Although Luther had ventured to attack a power which appeared invincible, yet there were several circumstances occurring in that period which surprisingly favored his cause. The papal power had risen to a height which could not long be sustained. The exorbitant wealth, and dissolute manners of the clergy, had alienated from them every reflecting mind. A general demand for more than a century had been made for a council which should reform abuses. The revival of learning in the west of Europe, in consequence of the *literati* having sought refuge from Constantinople, reduced by the Turks, in Italy, France, and Germany, where they became instructors of youth in all the public seminaries of learning, and introduced a taste for the study of the ancient Greek and Roman authors; had roused the human mind to a sense of its native dignity and worth, and introduced a bold spirit of investigation into the correctness of long established notions, and an ardent desire for improvement in every art and science. The art of printing, which had been invented in Germany about the year 1440, gave the world in 1450, at Mentz, a PRINTED BIBLE; and enabled mankind to multiply copies of books to almost any extent, with amazing rapidity, and but little comparative expense. Before that period, books were written out with the pen on parchment,* which made them expensive and scarce. Had

---

* The Jews wrote the Old Testament on skins, with very great care, and connected them together and rolled them in a double roll. The Greek manuscripts were written in capital letters, and without any separation of words; thus,
BLESSEDARETHEDEADWHODIEINTHELORD.
No manuscript of the New Testament extant, can be traced higher than the fourth century. Most of the Hebrew manuscripts were written between the years 1000 and 1457. Those of an earlier period have been, for some reasons unknown, destroyed.

Luther then risen, he would have communicated his sentiments to but very few, for what he communicated must have been chiefly from the pulpit. Whatever he wrote would scarce have been read by a hundred persons. But appearing as he did, at this fortunate moment, when the discovery of this wonderful art had not only rendered the multiplication of books easy, but had raised in the world an astonishing thirst for reading, Luther's books at once filled Europe, and his opposition to the corruptions of the papacy became the subject of universal conversation. Luther himself was a Franciscan friar. Tetzel, a Dominican. These orders were bitter enemies, and it was only for Luther to imitate Paul, when he exclaimed, I am a Pharisee, the son of a Pharisee, to enlist in his favor the whole body of the Franciscans, though they had ever been firm supporters of the papal dominion.

But while these and other circumstances may be pointed out as propitious to the cause of Luther, his astonishing success must and will, by every pious mind, be ascribed to the overruling providence of God. It was the Great Head of the church, ever watchful of that which he had purchased with his own blood, who raised up this wonderful reformer, gave him his astonishing talents and ardent love of truth, preserved his life amid many dangers, and enabled him to expose the corruption of the Man of Sin, and lead forth the church from this worse than Egyptian bondage.

Leo X. the Roman pontiff, at first viewed the contest in Germany with indifference ; supposing it to be only a contest, not uncommon in that age, between a Dominican and Franciscan Monk. " Brother Martin," said he, " is a man of very fine genius, and these squabbles are the mere effusions of monastic envy." But on being fully informed of its nature and extent, he became alarmed, and summoned Luther, July 1518, to appear at Rome, within sixty days, to answer for his conduct before the Auditor of the Chamber, and Prierias, the Inquisitor General. Luther knew there would be no safety for him at Rome ; and through the earnest solicitation of his patron, Frederick the Wise, he obtained liberty to have his cause tried before Cardinal Cajetan, who was then the Pope's legate in Germany. Within sixteen days after this citation, however, he was condemned as an incorrigible heretic at Rome by the bishop of Ascoli, the Auditor of the Apostolical chamber ;—such was the sincerity of the Pope in granting him a hearing in Germany.

Having obtained a safe conduct from the Emperor, Luther appeared before Cajetan at Augsburg, in the month of October; but Cajetan was a Dominican, the avowed friend of Tetzel, and enemy of Luther. He did nothing but require Luther, in a most arrogant manner, immediately to renounce his opinions and return into the bosom of the church, and this without having one of them proved erroneous. Such an assumption of authority was not at all calculated to intimidate or move such a mind as Martin Luther's. He expressed the utmost reverence for the Pope, but declared he would never renounce opinions which he viewed as scriptural, without being convinced of his error. Cajetan immediately threatened him with the heaviest church censures; and it being evident that nothing awaited him but the severest measures, the reformer secretly withdrew from the presence of the Cardinal, and returned to Wittemberg; appealing from the Pope himself, "ill-informed, to the same Leo X. better informed."

This appeal, however, was soon evidently hopeless; for the Pope issued a special edict, commanding all his subjects "to acknowledge his power of delivering from all the punishments due to sin and transgression of every kind." This completely shut the door against all hope of reconciliation but by a direct and full renunciation of all his opinions, and Luther appealed to a General Council as superior to the Pope.

Hoping to reclaim Luther by a messenger of more mildness and cunning than Cardinal Cajetan, Leo sent Charles Miltitz, a Saxon knight, in 1519, to negotiate with him. To conciliate the elector Frederick, Miltitz carried to him the golden consecrated rose, the peculiar mark of the Pope's favor; and to gain Luther, he rebuked Tetzel with the greatest severity. The elector received the bauble, which once he desired, with indifference. With the reformer, Miltitz had several interviews, but they were fruitless, as to the great point. He persuaded Luther, however, to write a submissive letter to the Pope, and agreed with the elector to refer the whole subject to the first diet held by the new Emperor of Germany, Char¹ V. In his letter, Luther expressed a great reverence for the church of Rome; declared that his great object was to honor that church, and, though he could not renounce his opinions without being convinced he was in an error, yet he would, in future, be silent respecting indulgences, if his enemies would no longer persecute him.

Of the popularity of Luther at this period, some judgment may be formed from the following extract from one of his letters. "Charles Miltitz saw me at Altenburg, and complained that I had united the whole world to myself, and drawn it aside from the Pope ; that he had discovered this at the inns as he traveled. 'Martin,' said he, 'you are so much favored with the popular opinion, that I could not expect, with the help of 25,000 soldiers, to force you with me to Rome.'"

Soon after his conference with Miltitz, Luther was brought into a public dispute with Eckius. This learned and brilliant professor of theology, flattered himself that, in a public debate, he could silence these young reformers ; and he challenged Carolstadt, the colleague and friend of Luther, to a public dispute on the controverted points, at Leipsic. The assembly was large, and the dispute between these combatants was carried on for fourteen days ; and such were the plaudits bestowed upon Eckius, that he challenged Luther to engage in the combat. Luther accepted the challenge, and the dispute continued ten days. But Eckius was not here as triumphant as before. He found his antagonist well acquainted with the sacred Scriptures ; honest in the sacred cause ; dexterous ; eloquent, and a firm expectant of the blessing of heaven. Many were the points in debate ; but the chief one regarded the superiority of the Roman See. Luther declared it impious to maintain the divine right of the Pope to act as the vicar of Christ, though he willingly allowed him a supremacy above others, from the universal consent of the church. He was daily drawing nearer to the evangelical liberty of the Gospel of Christ ; though by slow advances. Both parties claimed the victory ; but the dispute was in general advantageous to the reformation ; for the more the corruptions of popery were discussed, the more were the minds of men enlightened, and their consciences set free. In the close of 1519, Luther began to preach and write on the administration of the sacrament in both kinds, which exceedingly exasperated his enemies. But said he, "Let us in faith and prayer commit the event to God, and we shall be safe."

While Luther was thus gaining and diffusing knowledge in Germany, and opposing the corruptions of popery, a spirit of reform similar to his own was roused in Switzerland. There the Franciscans had carried on the scandalous traffic to an awful extent, and the minds of the people were perfectly infatuated. Huldric Zuinglius, a man not inferior to Luther, dared to oppose it in the summer of 1518; and though condemned by the universities of Cologne and Louvaine, he advanced with bold and rapid steps toward a complete and thorough reformation.

The greatest scholar of the age was Erasmus. He was ordained a priest in 1492, at the age of twenty-six. The great object of his life was the revival of literature. He was extensively acquainted with the theology then universally received, and he became a most severe satirist upon all its superstitions and follies. He, by his sound reasoning, his invective and raillery, first sowed the seeds of reformation in Europe. But he had not the courage to become an open opponent of the Pope. "Every man," said he, "hath not the courage requisite to make a martyr; and I am afraid that if I were put to the trial, I should imitate St. Peter." He repressed and moderated his zeal, therefore, against the errors of popery, while he was a friend and admirer of Luther; and did more than almost any other man in promoting the study of the sacred Scriptures.

The celebrated Philip Melancthon, who became one of the most illustrious coadjutors of Luther, was at the public dispute at Leipsic. He was then twenty-three years of age; but such were his attainments in literature, that he had been made professor of Greek at Wittemberg. So fully was he convinced of the soundness of Luther's principles, that from the time of his dispute with Eckius, he entered with ardor in the cause of the reformation. Other men were present at the same disputation, who afterward became distinguished lights and guides in the cause of truth and liberty.

But one prince as yet publicly declared in favor of Luther. This was his patron, Frederic, elector of Saxony. He was a diligent searcher of the sacred Scriptures; had become much dissatisfied with the usual modes of interpretation, and with the abominations of popery; and, as far as he could, without provoking the vengeance of Rome, to whom he was still conscientiously subject, he aided Luther in his arduous work. At the death of Maximilian, the Emperor, in 1519, Frederic acted as vicar of the empire during the interregnum, and protected Lutheranism from the violent assaults of its enemies.

On the fifteenth of June, one thousand five hundred and twenty, Luther was publicly denounced by the church of Rome. Forty-one propositions from his works were condemned as heretical; all pious persons were forbidden to read his works on pain of excommunication; such as had them, were commanded to burn them; and he, himself, if he did not in sixty days recant his errors and burn his books, was to be excommunicated and delivered unto Satan for the destruction of his flesh. All secular princes were required, under pain of incurring the same censures, and of forfeiting all their dignities, to seize his person, that he might be punished as his crimes deserved.

The church of Rome had become fully satisfied that they could never reclaim him; and that the only way to save themselves was to proceed violently against him. Luther had made astonishing advances in the discovery of truth, and by almost innumerable letters, tracts, sermons, and commentaries on Scripture, had diffused his sentiments throughout Europe, and made many distinguished and powerful converts.

The papists exulted at the publication of the Pope's bull. They had been accustomed to see it terminate all controversies, and they supposed that it would for ever silence the reformer. But it had very little effect upon his mind, or his cause. It came too late to command submission in Germany. This intrepid man erected without the walls of Wittemberg an immense pile of wood; and there, in presence of the professors and students of the university, and a vast crowd of spectators, committed the papal bull to the flames, together with the volumes of the canon law, the rule of the pontifical jurisdiction.

By this public act he left the Roman communion. He denounced the Pope of Rome as the Man of Sin. He waged open war with the whole papal establishment, and exhorted all Christian rulers and people to separate from it. By this bold act the die was cast. There was henceforth no reconciliation. In less than a month after, a second bull, a bull of excommunication, was issued against him, but it was only the distant echo of thunder which had already lost its power to terrify or destroy.

Luther now resolved upon re-establishing the Church of God upon a proper basis. In the Roman church he could neither find the form nor spirit of the Gospel. He saw and felt the necessity of a church in which the papal dominion, the injunction of celibacy in the clergy, the monastic vow, the intercession of saints, auricular confession, pilgrimage and penances, and the imaginary existence of purgatory, should find no place; and in which the true doctrines of justification and acceptance with God should be properly received and applied, and Gospel discipline be duly administered. In his various schemes of reformation, he was warmly seconded by the members and professors of his own university, and by many pious and learned men scattered throughout Europe. But in the beginning of the year 1521, he was summoned to appear at the Diet of Worms.

This diet was the general assembly of the German Empire, composed of all its princes, archbishops and bishops, and many abbots, and convened by Charles V. for the purpose of checking the new religious opinions which threatened to destroy the ancient faith of Europe. No sooner was it convened, and certain formalities were settled, than the papal legates demanded an immediate procedure against Luther. But his friends plead the unreasonableness of condemning a man unheard, and the whole assembly concurred in admitting him to their presence. Frederic, however, would not consent to his appearing without a safe conduct. This the Emperor was compelled to grant. His friends, however, were very fearful of his suffering the fate of John Huss, and on his way besought him to retire to some place of safety. But said the intrepid reformer, "I am lawfully called to appear in that city, and thither will I go in the name of the Lord, though as many devils as there are tiles on the houses were there combined against me."

At Worms, Luther met with a reception which must have been gratifying to his feelings, though he feared God more than he desired the praise of man. Vast crowds gathered around him to behold the man who had so boldly attacked the corruptions of popery, and introduced a new religion. The most important characters in church and state filled his apartments, and he was conducted to the Diet by the marshall of the empire. His conduct, in the presence of that august assembly, was very becoming a man of God. He was meek and civil, but firm. When called upon to acknowledge his writings, he did it without hesitation; but he solemnly and boldly refused to renounce his opinions, unless convinced of their error from the word of God In a speech of two hours, first made in German, and then repeated in Latin, he boldly vindicated the course he had taken, and gained the applause of one half the assembly. But while the subject was in agitation, and while many efforts were making in private to reclaim the reformer, Luther received a message from the Emperor, directing him immediately to depart from Worms, and return home, because he persisted in his con*umacy, and would not return into the bosom of the church.

After he left the Diet, a decree was passed, declaring him an excommunicated, notorious heretic; and forbidding all persons, under the penalty of high treason, to receive, maintain, or protect him.

Foreseeing the storm that was bursting upon his favorite professor, Frederic provided three or four horsemen, disguised in masks, in whom he could confide, and placed them in a wood near Esinach; from whence, as he was returning home, they rushed out upon Luther, took him by force and carried him to the castle of Wartburg. There he lay concealed for ten months from the search of his implacable adversaries; and in this retreat, which he called his Patmos, he pursued his studies, and produced some works, particularly a translation of the New Testament, which were highly useful to the cause of the reformation.

The friends of Luther were exceedingly discomfited at his sudden disappearance. They were generally ready to believe that a band of assassins had waylaid and killed him. They had not the courage or ability to do much without him, and were for a period covered with gloom. Luther had friends who communicated to him the knowledge of all that transpired. Here he was told that the University of Paris, the most venerable of the learned societies of Europe, from which he had hoped much favorable to his cause, had passed a solemn censure upon his writings; and that Henry VIII., king of England, had published an answer to a treatise of his, entitled the Babylonish Captivity, and for it, had received from the Pope the title of *Defender of the Faith.* A circumstance, however, which affected him more than either of these, (for Luther was not a man who was to be overawed by monarchs or universities,) was the conduct of his own friend and partizan, Carlostadt, who had attempted to carry on the work of reformation by violence; throwing down and breaking the images of saints, and stripping the churches and public places of the various ensigns of popery Luther saw that this was no way to reform the church; that error must first be eradicated from the minds of the people, before any thing could be effected to any good purpose; and that if this was once done, images and relics, and other superstitions, would of course fall.

Safety was valuable, but his own preservation was not what the reformer sought. He felt for the good of the church, and was anxious again to be engaged in her conflicts. "I sit here," said he, in a letter to Melancthon, " in my Patmos, reflecting all the day on the wretched condition of the church. And I bemoan the hardness of my heart that I am not dissolved into tears on this account. May God have mercy upon us." And again, " For the glory of the word of God, and for the mutual confirmation of myself and others, I would much rather burn on the live coal, than live here alone, half alive and useless. If I perish, it is God's will; neither will the Gospel suffer in any degree. I hope you will succeed me, as Elisha did Elijah."

The intemperate and misguided zeal of Carlostadt brought Luther from his retreat to Wittemberg, March 1522, without the consent or knowledge of his patron and protector, Frederic. It was a happy event. Carlostadt and his party listened to his, as to a voice from heaven, and order was restored.

Luther's first business was the publication of his New Testament. This struck a heavy blow at the root of popery. It was rapidly circulated, and read with avidity by all classes throughout Germany; and it opened the eyes of men to the true doctrines of the Gospel, and enabled them at once to see clearly the corruptions of the church of Rome. He afterward applied himself, with the assistance of Melancthon, to the translation of the Old Testament, which he finished and published in 1530; a work of amazing labor.

Luther also resumed at Wittemberg, the business of preaching, in which he did much to enlighten, reform, and quiet the people of Saxony.* By his labors many souls

---

* A just idea of Luther's preaching may be learned from the following anecdote. "Luther had heard the celebrated Bucer preach a sermon, and invited him to supper. After commending the sermon, he said he could preach better than Bucer. Bucer courteously assented, saying, that by universal consent, that praise belonged to Luther. Luther then seriously replied, do not think I am vainly boasting; I am conscious of my own slender stores, nor could I preach so learned a sermon as you have done to-day; but my practice is this;—when I ascend the pulpit, I consider what is the character of my hearers, most of whom are rude

were converted and many evils were corrected in the churches. The friends of the reformation were every where animated and strengthened. Nuremberg, Frankfort, Hamburg, and other free cities of the first rank, openly embraced the principles of the reformer, and abolished the mass, and other rites of Popery. Some high princes, also, the elector of Brandenburgh, the dukes of Brunswick and Lunenburg, and prince of Anhalt, declared openly on the side of Luther, and supported his preachers in their dominions. The Gospel again was preached with great power; the word of the Lord had free course and was glorified.

CHAPTER XII.

Reformation spreads. Death of Leo X. Sacramental controversy. War of the Peasants. Death of Frederic. Decision of John. Martyrs. Diet at Spire. Luther marries. Writes, in vain, submissive letters. Publishes his Hymns. An attempt made to poison him. His conflict with Erasmus. Second Diet at Spire. The Reformers condemned, and protest. Called Protestants. Diet at Augsburg. Confession of Augsburg. League of Smallkeld. Peace of Nuremberg. Anabaptists. Reformation in England. Conference at Worms. Death of Luther. Council of Trent. Battle of Mukleberg. Interim. Peace of Religion. Reformation in Switzerland. Zuinglius. Calvin. Reformation in Holland and Scotland. John Knox. Sentiments of the Reformers. Church Government. Blessings of the Reformation.

The light of the Reformation, like that of the orient sun, soon spread over the various countries of Europe. The followers of Luther had a feeling in relation to papal Rome, similar to that which filled the breasts of the Apostles when they looked abroad and saw the whole earth given to idolatry. Their immediate duty was to enlighten man in the knowledge of the truth. Under the influence of this feeling, Olaus Petri propagated the reformed religion in Sweden soon after Luther's rupture with Rome. The Catholic priests made violent opposition to him, but his efforts were powerfully seconded by the monarch, Gustavus Vasa, who while an exile at Lubec, had learnt something of Lutheranism, and gained a favorable opinion of it as the true Gospel. Persuaded that the only way to effect a real reformation, was to enlighten the minds of the people in divine truth, he ordered Andreas, his chan-

and uninstructed people, almost Goths and Vandals, and I preach to them what I think they can understand. But you rise aloft, and soar into the clouds; so that your sermons suit the learned, but are unintelligible to our plain people. I endeavor to copy the mother, who thinks the child better fed with the simple milk of the breast, than with the most costly confections.'

cellor, with Olaus, to translate the Scriptures into the Swedish tongue; and to silence the objections of the papists, he ordered the archbishop of Upsal, also to translate them, that the two versions might be compared, and that it might be seen on which side truth lay. He also ordered a conference at Upsal, between Petri and Gallius a zealous papist, in which Petri gained the victory. For a time the situation of Sweden was critical. In no countries had the Catholics reaped greater temporal benefits from their superstitions, than in Sweden and Denmark. The revenues of the bishops were superior to that of the sovereign. They had strong castles and fortresses, and lived in the greatest luxury; while the nobility and people were in the lowest state of degradation. But they could not withstand the noble Gustavus. In 1527, he assembled the states at Westeraas, and after powerfully recommending the doctrine of the reformers, declared that he would lay down his sceptre and retire from the kingdom, if it longer continued subject to the papal dominion. Opposition was silenced; the papal empire in Sweden was overturned, and the reformed religion was publicly adopted.

In 1522, Christian II. king of Denmark, a man profligate and ambitious in the extreme, who merely wished to throw off the papal dominion, that he might subject the bishops and increase his own power, sent to Wittemberg for a preacher of the reformation. Martin Reinard accepted of the invitation, and his labors were greatly blessed. But such were the vices of the king, that the reformation was greatly retarded, and it was not until succeeding periods, under Frederic and Christian III. that it was completed.

In Hungary and Prussia, a strong desire was manifested in the same year, to receive the light of the reformation, and even to see and hear Luther himself.

In France, there was a multitude of persons, who with Margaret, queen of Navarre, sister of Francis I., at their head, as early as 1523, felt very favorably inclined towards the reformed religion, and erected several churches for a purer worship. But the reformed were exceedingly depressed by the strong arm of civil power. The French had a translation of the Bible, which had been made in 1224, by Guivers des Moulins, which was printed at Paris in 1487, and now much read; and the Psalms put into metre and sung as ballads.

While Leo X. was suffering the severest mortification of seeing the cause of the reformation advance with rapid steps he departed this life, A. D. 1522. He was succeeded in the Popedom by Adrian VI., who died the next year, and was succeeded by Clement VII. Each pursued, unremittingly, the same course for the extermination, if possible, of the new opinions, and the preservation of the papal dominion.

Could Luther and his partisans have been firmly united, their success might have been more speedy, if not ultimately greater; but how could it be expected that men, just emerging from the grossest superstitions, should have at once a full, clear, and uniform view of divine truth. In the year 1524, arose a tedious and unhappy controversy between the Reformer, and Carlostadt and Zuinglius, on the sacrament of the supper. While Luther rejected the Popish doctrine of transubstantiation as unscriptural, he still believed that, along with the bread and wine, the partakers received the real body and blood of Christ. Carlostadt, Zuinglius, and the churches in Switzerland, adopted the truly correct system, " That the body and blood of Christ were not really present in the Eucharist, and that the bread and wine were no more than external signs or symbols, designed to excite in the minds of Christians the remembrance of the sufferings and death of the divine Saviour, and of the benefits which arise from them." The firmness and obstinacy of Luther in this unfortunate contention, was as great as in his attacks upon the papacy; and friends, who had embarked together in the most important of causes, were ultimately completely severed.

A large body of peasants had rebelled in Germany, about the commencement of the reformation, against the oppressions of the feudal institutions. Their spirit of liberty reached those provinces in which the reformation was established, and immediately demanded a release from all religious domination. But the leaders of the peasants were from the lowest orders of society, and were very ignorant and fanatical. They knew not in what a reformation consisted, beyond plundering monasteries and churches, and massacreing all persons without discrimination, who upheld the old order of things. Thomas Muncer had acquired an astonishing influence over them. He, with other leaders, Stork, Stubner, and Cellory, professed to have a divine commission, and pretended to visions and revelations. Luther they utterly condemned as no reformer. All men they declared equal; and they viewed it the duty of all to live on an equality and have all things common Their seditious, leveling, demoralizing spirit, Luther utterly condemned; but it was exceedingly popular, and an immense body, under arms, filled Germany with terror; but they were routed in a pitched battle with the emperor's troops, and Muncer was taken and put to death.

This war of the peasants, which cost Germany more than 50,000 men, was unfavorable to the cause of reformation; for it gave the papists occasion to accuse the reformers of the wildest fanaticism, and led the civil powers to connect a revolution in politics with a change in religion.

On the 5th of May, 1525, Luther lost his patron, Frederic the Wise. He had been a very zealous papist; but his mind had gradually opened to the reception of divine truth; and though he had never formally broken off from the Roman church, yet he was, for many years, the protector and shield of the reformers. He was succeeded by his brother John, who at once took a decided stand in favor of the reformation, placed himself at the head of the Lutheran church; provided a new order of public worship, and placed over every congregation well qualified pastors; had the sacrament administered to the laity in the German language, and caused his new regulations to be proclaimed by heralds throughout his dominions. Such decision and boldness brought out other princes and states of Germany in favor of the same worship, discipline, and government; and also drove back all who were not heartily engaged in the cause, or who had not the boldness to wage open war with the Pope, into the bosom of the church. The line was now clearly drawn, and it was known by all parties, who belonged to the reformed, and who to the papal cause. The increase of evangelical light was great The call for preachers of the truth was unexpected from every part of Germany, and from distant places in Europe.

But a reformation was not to be effected without the shedding of blood. James Pavan was burnt alive at Paris, in 1525, for his profession of pure Christianity. A German, named Wolfangus Schuch, was condemned to the same dreadful death. One Bernard, also, and John De Becker, obtained the crown of martyrdom from the hands of the papists. An open rupture seemed unavoidable. In 1526, the Diet assembled at Spire; and the papal party endeavored to have the sentence of Worms against Luther and his adherents rigorously executed. But the German princes refused to act; declaring that points of doctrine ought to be submitted to a general council; and it was finally agreed that the emperor should be requested to assemble a general council without delay, and that in the meantime, the princes and states of the empire should be suffered to manage ecclesiastical affairs in their own dominions, as they should think most expedient, yet so as to be able to give to God and the Emperor, an account of their administration, when it should be demanded of them.

This was probably the most happy termination of the Diet, for the Lutherans, that could have taken place. For it at once put it out of the power of papists to persecute further the reformers, and gave the princes who favored the reformation an opportunity to extend their patronage to the utmost, until Charles V. should be ready to convene a general council; a period evidently far distant, for the troubled state of his immense dominions engrossed all his attentions; and the Pope, Clement VII. had entered into confederacy with Francis I. and the Venetians against that prince, and inflamed his resentment and indignation to such a degree, that Charles felt little disposition to do any thing which would injure the Lutherans, and favor the papal cause.

Soon after the death of his patron, Frederic, Luther was married to Catharine Bore, " a virtuous nun, of noble parentage." The papists reviled him for this, as a sensualist, and some of his friends thought the time for such a procedure improper; but Luther had openly opposed the celibacy of the clergy, and he said, " he thought it right to confirm, by his own example, the doctrine he had taught; for he observed many were still pusillanimous, notwithstanding the great light of the Gospel."

Being anxious, if possible, to gain his adversaries, or at least to soften their asperities, Luther wrote two submissive letters, one to Henry VIII., king of England, and the other to George, duke of Saxony, but they both replied with virulence; whereupon Luther laid down these regulations for his future conduct. " 1st, In all matters where the ministry of the word of God was not concerned, he would not only submit to his superiors, but was ready to beg pardon even of children. As a private man, he merited nothing but eternal destruction at the divine tribunal. But 2ndly, In regard to the ministry, for which he considered himself as having a commission from heaven, there was so much dignity in it, that no man, especially a tyrant, should ever find him give way, submit, or flatter. Lastly, he besought his heavenly Father to enable him to keep his resolution."

Luther was both a musician and a poet; and he circulated a small volume of hymns, containing the main points of Christian doctrine set to music, which had great effect.

An attempt was made by a Polish Jew, to poison him, but through the kind care of an overruling Providence, it entirely failed.

For a long time Luther was engaged in a contest with Erasmus. The papists had been severely lashed by him, but viewing him as still on their side, and the most able critic in Europe, both the Pope and the king of England importuned him to attack the German Reformer. Flattered by the great, Erasmus became the opponent of Luther, on the doctrines of grace; and the breach between them was very wide.

But the controversy with Zuinglius and Carlostadt, on the Sacrament, which raged with considerable violence in 1526—27, was far more lamentable.

In the favorable period that succeeded the Diet of Spire, the great reformer was very active, in company with his fellow laborers, in fixing the principles of the reformation—correcting abuses—inspiring the timid with fortitude—and extending far and wide the light of truth, the knowledge of salvation through faith in Christ.

But this period was to have a termination. The councils of princes change. The Emperor and the Pope became friends. The commotions and troubles of Europe were terminated; and the Emperor had leisure, and alas! the disposition also, to lay a heavy hand upon the reformers. He assembled another Diet at Spire, in 1529, and caused the former decree to be repealed, and every change in the doctrine, discipline or worship of the established religion, before the determination of the general council should be known, to be declared unlawful.

Such a proceeding on the part of the Emperor and his Diet, was viewed by the Protestants as iniquitous and intolerable, and designed, if not to crush the infant churches, at least to prevent their increase; and the elector of Saxony, the marquis of Brandenburgh, the landgrave of Hesse, the dukes of Lunenburgh, the prince of Anhalt, with the deputies of fourteen Imperial or free cities, solemnly protested against it, on the 19th of April, as unjust and impious. On this account they were, and from that time to this their followers have been denominated PROTESTANTS.

The legates who had the boldness to present this protest

to Charles, were put under arrest. A dark cloud seemed to hang over the affairs of the Protestants. The Emperor and Pope had many interviews at Bologna to devise measures for the extirpation of heresy. Fortunately, Charles was not disposed to accede to the violent proceedings of the Pope. He hoped to reconcile the Protestants by means of a general council. But the Pope dreaded such an assembly. General councils the Pope found factious, ungovernable, presumptuous, and promoters of free inquiry, and civil liberty. Charles, therefore, could not move him, and he proceeded to Augsburg, June, 1530, to the general Diet, resolved there to bring, if possible, all disputes to a termination. But as he could not examine, and decide without knowing the exact sentiments of the Protestants, Charles required Luther to commit to writing the chief points of his religious system. Luther presented seventeen articles of faith, formerly agreed on at Torgaw, which were called the articles of Torgaw. These at the request of the princes assembled at Augsburg, were enlarged by Melancthon, a man of the greatest learning, and the most pacific spirit among the reformers. The creed thus completed formed the famous *confession* of Augsburg.

This confession did great honor to the pen of Melancthon. It contained twenty-eight chapters, and was a fair expose of the religious opinions of the Protestants, and of the errors and abuses of the church of Rome. It was read publicly in the Diet.

Another confession was presented to the Diet, by those who adopted the opinions of Zuinglius, in relation to the eucharist.

But a decree was passed against the Lutherans, more violent than that of the Diet of Worms. It condemned their tenets, forbade any person to protect or tolerate such as taught them, enjoined a strict observance of established rites, and prohibited any further innovation, under severe penalties. All orders of men were required to assist in carrying the decree into execution.

This oppressed the feeble spirit of Melancthon, and threw him into a state of deep melancholy. But Luther was never dismayed; and he exhorted the Protestant princes, with great boldness, to unite in defence of the truths which God had revealed. His councils were obeyed, and they assembled at Smallkelde, December 16th, 1530, and formed a league of mutual defence against all aggressors, and resolved to apply for protection to the kings of France, England, and Denmark.

These kings, from enmity to Charles V., favored the Protestants, and Charles finding trouble accumulating upon him, concluded a peace with the Protestants in 1532, at Nuremberg, which amounted almost to a complete toleration of their religion. This event inspired the friends of the reformation throughout Europe, with new vigor and resolution, and excited them to press forward with great boldness, in the work of liberating mankind from spiritual despotism.

But it is an evil with which the reformers had to contend, that the human mind once roused by grand objects, especially if uninformed, is apt to become wild and irregular. The peasants who, at the beginning of the reformation, had run into such extravagances for religious liberty, were indeed subdued; but their spirit lived and raged tremendously in 1533, in Westphalia and the Netherlands. A furious rabble came to the city of Munster, pretending to a commission from heaven to destroy and overturn all civil institutions, and to establish a new republic, and committed the most horrible excesses. Their principal leaders were John Mathias, a baker, and John Boccold, a journeyman tailor. Their chief tenets were, that the office of magistracy is unnecessary; that all distinctions among men are contrary to the Gospel; that property should be held in common, and that a plurality of wives is commendable. But their more peculiar doctrine, from which they were named, related to the sacrament of baptism. They declared that it should be administered only to persons grown up to years of understanding, and should be performed not by sprinkling with water, but by immersion. Hence, as the subjects had been once baptized, they were called ANABAPTISTS.

But their reign at Munster was short. The bishop of Munster, assisted by some German princes, came against them with an armed force. In the conflict, Mathias was at first successful; and so elated was he, that he sallied forth with thirty men, declaring that he would go like Gideon, and smite the host of the ungodly. In an instant, they were all destroyed. Boccold then assumed the chief command; pretended to extraordinary revelations; marched through the streets naked, crying with a loud voice, "That the kingdom of Zion was at hand;" took to himself fourteen wives; leveled to the ground the loftiest buildings; deposed senators, and raised his officers from the lowest ranks. The blood of suspected persons flowed freely. One of his wives, expressing a doubt of his divine mission, had her head cut off with his own hands. But he was not able to maintain his dominion. On the 24th of June, 1535, the royal forces took the city, and slew most of the fanatics. Boccold was taken a prisoner, and shown through the cities of Germany. He was then brought back to Munster, and put to death in the most cruel manner. Thus ended the kingdom of Anabaptists in Germany; but their principles relating to baptism took deep root in the Low Countries, and were carried into England.

These scenes were deeply painful to Luther. "Satan," said he, "rages; we have need of your prayers. The new sectarians called Anabaptists, increase in number, and display great external appearances of strictness of life, as also great boldness in death, whether they suffer by fire or water." While he detested their turbulence and pitied their delusion, he knew that the papists looked upon them as his followers, and upon him as the grand culprit; and that such proceedings, such cries, as "No tribute, all things in common, no magistrates," must alarm every ruler in Christendom, and make each consider the extinction of Lutheranism as essential to his safety. Luther was no fanatic. He had an enlightened and noble spirit. "We differ," said he, "from these fanatics not merely in the article of baptism, but also in the general reason which they give for rejecting the baptism of infants." "It was," say they, "a practice under the papacy." "Now we do not argue in that manner. We allow that in the papacy are many good things, and all those good things we have retained."

He abhorred persecutions for religious opinions. He did not believe that errors in doctrine were to be extirpated by fire and the sword, but by the word of God. He viewed it right that false teachers should be removed from their stations; but declared that capital punishments should never be inflicted, but for sedition and tumult. He utterly disapproved, therefore, of the sanguinary proceedings against the Anabaptists, and wished that they might be reclaimed and guided by arguments from Scripture.

Another class of men arose about the same time, headed by John Agricola, a disciple of Luther, who, because of their peculiar sentiments, have been called ANTINOMIANS. Some of their peculiarities were, that the law ought not to be proposed as a rule of life; that men ought not to doubt of their faith; that God sees no sin in believers, and they are not bound to confess sin, mourn for it, or pray that it may be forgiven; that Christ became as sinful as we, and we are completely righteous as Christ; that the new covenant is not properly made with us, but with Christ for us; and that sanctification is not a proper evidence of justification.

But while Luther was disquieted with these things, a most surprising and important event occurred, which filled his heart with joy. This was the overthrow of the papal power in England.

Henry VIII., a prince of great abilities and violent passions, had come out, at the beginning of the reformation, in opposition to Luther, and obtained from the Pope the title of *Defender of the Faith*. But, like all wicked men, he cared more for the gratification of his passions than for the church of God. He was bound in marriage to his brother's widow, Catharine of Arragon, aunt to Charles V. She was a woman of but little loveliness, and by her he had no male issue. Desirous of this, and being captivated by the charms of Ann Boleyn, he applied to the Pope for a divorce, on the ground that Catharine was his brother's widow. The Pope, dreading the anger of Charles, contrived various pretexts to delay an answer to the request, and at length summoned Henry to Rome. Impatient of delay, and enraged at his final summons, Henry followed the advice of Thomas Cranmer, a secret friend of Luther, and referred the subject to the learned universities of Europe. They decided that the marriage was unlawful. Catharine was divorced, and Ann Boleyn became queen, November 14, 1532.

Henry was now completely alienated from the Pope and was determined to make the court of Rome feel the weight of his anger. He caused himself to be declared Supreme head of the church of England; suppressed the monasteries; applied their revenues to new purposes; and entirely overturned the power and authority of the Pope in his realm.

The eyes of all Europe had long been turned to a general council, as the only instrument of effecting religious peace on the continent; and the Emperor pressed the Roman pontiff to convene one. Clement at length named Mantua as the place for it, but the Germans refused to have their disputes decided in Italy.

In 1541, Charles V. appointed a conference at Worms, between Eckius, Gropper, and Pflug, on the part of the Catholics; and Melancthon, Bucer, and Pistorius, on the part of the Protestants. Here Melancthon and Eckius disputed for three days, but it was all in vain.

In 1545, the Pope with the consent of the Emperor, issued letters for the convocation of a council; and Charles endeavored to persuade the Protestants to consent to its meeting at Trent. But they were firm; the patience of the Emperor was exhausted; and, in his anger, he determined to resort to arms. The Protestants immediately took measures for defence. But while they were standing in this critical condition, and before the storm burst upon them, they were deprived of the man who had been their chief councilor, supporter, and guide. Luther died in peace at Isleben, the place of his nativity, Feb. 18, 1546, and in the 63rd year of his age.

This wonderful man was raised up by divine Providence, and endowed with suitable capacities, to be the instrument of the greatest and most important revolution ever effected on our globe. If he had faults, he had also natural and moral endowments possessed by no other man, and which qualified him to withstand the whole power of the papal dominion. His native firmness did not forsake him in his last hours. He conversed freely and fervently with his friends on the happiness reserved for good men in a future state, and fell asleep. His funeral was attended with great pomp. He left several children. His posterity have been respectable in Germany.

The papists expressed indecent joy at the news of his decease, and his friends were greatly dispirited; but both parties soon found that Luther was not dead. He lived in the hearts of his followers. He lived in the doctrines which he taught, and which were too firmly established in Europe to be destroyed.

A dark day, however, awaited the Protestants. The Emperor and Pope had mutually agreed upon their extirpation. The meeting of the council of Trent was the signal for hostilities. This famous council was convened in 1546, and was composed of 6 cardinals, 32 archbishops, 228 bishops, and a multitude of clergy. The Protestant princes in the diet at Ratisbon protested against its authority. The Emperor proscribed them at once, and marched his army against them The Protestants defended themselves with great spirit, but were defeated in battle, with much bloodshed, near Muhlberg, April 24, 1547. The elector of Saxony was taken prisoner, and the landgrave of Hesse, the other chief of the Protestant cause, was persuaded to throw himself upon the mercy of Charles.

The ruin of the Protestants seemed at hand. The Emperor required the Lutherans to submit their case to the council of Trent. Most of them yielded. A plague, however, dispersed the council and nothing was done. The prospect of re-assembling it was distant, and the Emperor caused a form of faith and worship to be drawn up, which he imposed upon both parties. This was called the *Interim*. But it pleased neither party. No sooner was it published at Rome, than the indignation of the ecclesiastics rose to the greatest height. They called the Emperor Uzzah, as touching the ark. The Protestants inveighed against it as containing the abominations of Popery, covered over with little art. Such as refused to submit to it were obliged to meet the arms of the Emperor; and as their number was considerable, his whole empire was involved in the greatest calamities.

In 1548, the principal reformers assembled at Leipsic, to form rules for the regulation of their conduct. Melancthon who had taken the place of Luther, gave it as his opinion, that the Interim might be adopted in things that did not relate to the essential points of religion, i. e. in things indifferent. A schism ensued which nearly proved fatal to their cause. Had their opponents seized the opportunity, they might have overthrown them.

In 1552, the council of Trent was again assembled. Many of the Protestants attended. But every step that was taken tended to the destruction of the Protestants, and the re-establishment of the papacy in all its terrors. Before its final close in 1563, this famous council had twenty-five sessions. In the view of the papists, it illustrated and fixed the doctrine of the Roman church, and restored the vigor of its discipline. Its decrees, with the creed of Pope Pius IV. contain a summary of the doctrines of the Roman church. It widened and rendered forever irreparable the breach between her and the Protestants. Among other things, it determined "That the books to which the designation of apocryphal is given, are of equal authority with those which were received by the Jews and primitive Christians into the sacred canon;—that the traditions handed down from the apostolic age, and preserved in the church, are entitled to as much regard as the doctrines and precepts which the inspired authors have committed to writing;— that the Latin translation of the Scriptures made or revised by St. Jerome, and known by the name of the Vulgate translation, should be read in churches and appealed to in the schools as authentic and canonical." In the name and pretended authority of the Holy Ghost, anathemas were denounced against all who denied the truth of these declarations

The Protestants, being persuaded that the Emperor, under the cloak of zeal for religion, was laboring to destroy the liberties of Germany, Maurice, elector of Saxony, emboldened by a secret alliance which he had formed with the King of France, and several of the German princes, fell suddenly, with a powerful army, upon the Emperor, while he lay at Inspruck, with only a handful of troops, and compelled him to make a treaty of peace with the Protestants, and to promise to assemble a Diet within six months, in which all difficulties should be permanently settled. The Diet, however, did not meet until 1555. It then assembled at Augsburg; and there was concluded the famous *Peace of religion*, which firmly established the reformation. In this it was provided, " That the Protestants who followed the confession of Augsburg, should be, for the future, considered as entirely exempt from the jurisdiction of the Roman pontiff, and from the authority and superintendence of the bishops; that they were left at perfect liberty to enact laws for themselves, relating to their religious sentiments, discipline and worship; that all the inhabitants of the German empire, should be allowed to judge for themselves in religious matters, and to join themselves to that church, whose doctrine and worship they thought the purest and the most consonant to the spirit of Christianity; and that all those who should injure or persecute any person under religious pretexts, and on account of their opinions, should be declared and proceeded against as public enemies of the empire, invaders of its liberty, and disturbers of its peace."

Through the bold and unremitted efforts of Zuinglius and others, the doctrines of the reformation had gained firm footing in Switzerland. Zuinglius was a man of genius. He revolted from Rome before he had any intercourse with Luther; but would never probably have dared to attack the Pope as Luther did; or, if he had, have done it as effectually. The papists early saw his greatness, and endeavored to bribe him with gold. He differed from Luther on many points, and his followers were called Sacramentarians.

In 1525, he was attacked by the Anabaptists. They declared him, as they had Luther, to be wanting in spirituality, called him the old dragon; rebaptized the people in the streets, and made rebaptization the criterion of the visible members of the church of Christ. Zuinglius confuted them with arguments in a public conference; but they became furious, and ran through the streets and cried, "Wo to Zurich! Wo to Zurich! Repent or perish;" and seemed desirous to seal their doctrine with their blood Finding them excessively riotous, the senate made their profession capital, and one or two suffered death.

The cantons of Berne and Zurich had publicly avowed the reformation. But the other five cantons declared in favor of Rome, and war ensued. Zuinglius was slain in battle 1529, aged 47. Some Catholic soldiers found him in his blood, directed him to pray to the Virgin Mary, and offered to bring him a confessor. But he made a sign of refusal. "Die, then, obstinate heretic!" said they, and pierced him through with a sword. His remains were found and burned by the Catholics.

Another distinguished luminary soon arose, shedding divine light on the Swiss churches. This was John Calvin. He was born at Noyon, in Picardy, July 10, 1509. He was educated at Paris, for the church, and obtained a benefice. But, disgusted with the superstitions of Rome, he turned to the profession of the law, in which he made rapid advances. Becoming, however, acquainted with the doctrines of the reformation, he applied himself to the study of the holy Scriptures, and resolved to renounce connection with Rome, and defend the truth. In private assemblies in Paris, he became active in illustrating and confirming the doctrines of the Bible, and was near falling a sacrifice to the Inquisition. The queen of Navarre protected him, and he escaped to Basil. There, in 1535, he published his great work, "Institutes of the Christian religion," which he dedicated to Francis I. His object was to show that the doctrines of the Reformers were founded in Scripture, and hat they ought not to be confounded with the Anabaptists of Germany.

After publishing this work, he happened to pass through Geneva, where the reformers, Farel and Viret, entreated him, by the love of souls, to remain with them, and aid in their labors. Calvin yielded; and, in 1536, became their preacher and professor of theology. But the Genevese, though reformed in name, were not in life. The severity of his doctrine and discipline raised against him a spirit of persecution, and he and his companions were expelled from the city. "Had I been," said he, "in the service of men, this would have been a poor reward; but it is well. I have served him who never fails to repay his servants whatever he has promised."

Calvin retired to Strasburg, where he established a French Reformed Church, and became professor of theology.

After two years, the Genevese earnestly desired his return, to which, after much solicitation, he consented, September 13, 1541. He immediately established a consistorial government, with power to take cognizance of all offences, and entered himself on a most arduous course of labors. Here he continued in the theological chair, until 1564, when he calmly slept in Jesus.

He was a man of great mental powers, indefatigable industry, flowing eloquence, immense learning, strict morals, and ardent piety. Besides his Institutes, he published a valuable commentary on most of the sacred Scriptures; he composed many works in favor of the reformation; carried on an extensive correspondence with all the great reformers of Europe, and exercised a watchful care over the Protestant churches, by which he was reverenced as an oracle. His writings were printed in twelve volumes, folio.

The terrors of the Inquisition compelled the nobility of the Belgic provinces in 1566, to form an association for the purpose of gaining some religious liberty. To quell their tumults, a powerful army was sent from Spain, under command of the duke of Alva. A bloody war ensued; and under the heroic conduct of the prince of Orange, both the Spanish and Roman yoke were cast off, and the reformation was completely established upon the German model, in 1578. A few Scotch nobles early conveyed the light of divine truth from Germany into their own country; but the power of the papacy prevented its spread. Two distinguished preachers, Patrick Hamilton and George Wishart were burnt alive, for opposing her corruptions. Providence, however, raised up John Knox, a man of astonishing boldness and zeal, who broke down every barrier, and gave truth free course. This great reformer was born in 1505. The writings of Jerome and Austin opened his mind to the abominations of popery, and led him to preach boldly at St. Andrews. From the arm of persecution he retired into England, and became chaplain to Edward VI. At the accession of Queen Mary, he went to the continent, and associated freely with Calvin. His enemies at home accused him of heresy, and burnt him in effigy at Edinburgh, which drew from him his "First blast of the Trumpet, against the monstrous regiment of women," meaning the queens of England and Scotland. In 1559, he returned to Scotland; and in a very short time, by the power of truth, completely overturned the papal dominion, and established the Presbyterian form of government. He died November 4th, 1572. His funeral was attended in Edinburgh, by many nobles, and by Morton the regent, who exclaimed over his grave, "*There lies he, who never feared the face of man.*"

In Ireland the affairs of religion assumed much the same character as in England.

Throughout Spain and Italy, great numbers of all ranks and orders became dissatisfied with popery, and rejoiced in the light of the reformation. In Naples, great commotions were excited by the preaching of Bernard Ochino and Peter Martyr. But the inquisition, by racks, gibbets, and other tortures, prevented any great and lasting change in the religion of those countries.

The fundamental principle of the reformers, was the sufficiency of the holy Scriptures, as a rule of faith and practice. They rejected, therefore, the authority of tradition, of Popes and councils. They believed that no man is able to make satisfaction for his sins, and that the only way of justification, is by faith in the blood of Christ. They rejected, therefore, penance, indulgences, auricular confession, masses, invocation of saints, pilgrimages, monastic vows, purgatory, and other ways of salvation devised by the church of Rome. They believed in the doctrine of the Trinity, in man's entire depravity, in predestination, in the renewing and sanctifying operations of the Holy Ghost, and in the eternal happiness of the righteous, and endless misery of the wicked. These were their leading sentiments, and have since been called the doctrines of the Reformation.

In the monarchical governments of Europe, there was but little change in the form of church order; as the diocesses and jurisdiction of archbishops and bishops corresponded with the civil divisions and ordinances, and as the episcopal government was calculated to uphold the regal. But in Switzerland and the Low Countries, where republicanism was established, a form of government extremely simple, and preserving a parity of rank, was generally adopted. Knox recommended it to his countrymen, by whom it was received, notwithstanding the power and influence of the reigning monarchy, and the English church.

The blessings of the Reformation can be duly estimated only by those who have a full view of the evils of popery, as existing in the middle ages. By it, the world was delivered from a most horrible yoke of spiritual bondage; life and immortality, as revealed in the Gospel, were brought to light, and the way was opened, that in Jesus Christ, all nations of the earth might be blessed.

CHAPTER XIII.

Modern Christendom. Roman church. Her efforts for self-preservation. Order of the Jesuits. Missionary operations and establishments. Persecution of the Protestants. Expulsion of the Moors from Spain. Massacre on St. Bartholomew's day. Edict of Nantez. Its revocation. Inquisition. Auto de fe. Downfall of popery. Reverses in the East. Disaffections in Europe. Suppression of the Jesuits. French revolution. Principles and rites of the Roman church. Character of her Popes and clergy since the Reformation. Monastic orders. Present state of popery in the world.

The reformation formed a glorious era in the history of the church and world. We no longer find one ecclesiastical power reigning supreme and universal. The Man of Sin is broken. Italy, Spain, Portugal, the Belgic Provinces under the Spanish yoke, remained papal. But Denmark, Norway, Sweden, Brandenberg, Prussia, England, Scotland. Ireland. and Holland, had become Protestant governments. Germany was about equally divided. In Switzerland, the Protestants had a little the preponderance. France was often near changing her religion, but finally became decidedly papal, though she retained in her bounds millions of Protestants.

Neither uniformity of faith nor ecclesiastical government has existed among those who have received the Scriptures as their guide. On the contrary, a great variety of religious sects has risen in the reformed churches. And if some are confident that they behold the true church descending in one to the exclusion of the rest, still the historian is bound to trace the course of all who profess to be followers of the Lord Jesus. These have been found, since the reformation, among

THE ROMAN CATHOLICS, *or* ADHERENTS TO THE POPE,
THE GREEK AND EASTERN CHURCHES, *and*
THE PROTESTANT, *or* REFORMED CHURCHES.

THE ROMAN CHURCH.

The effect of the Reformation upon the Roman pontiffs was to excite them to the greatest efforts to retain their power, and extend their dominion in the earth. They removed a few evils which had been most severely animadverted upon by the reformers, and prosecuted the most ingenious methods to strengthen the internal constitution of their falling church. Colleges and schools were established, that their youth might be more enlightened, and wield with more dexterity the weapons of controversy. But they prevented the circulation of all books which exposed the foundation of their superstitions; raised the edicts of pontiffs, and the records of oral tradition, far above the authority of the Scriptures; proclaimed the Vulgate edition of the Bible authentic; forbade the use of any other, or any interpretation of Scripture which should differ from that of the church and ancient doctors; and ordered the sacred volume to be taken away from the common people.* Finding their power and resources diminished at home, they grasped after the most amazing dominion among distant pagan nations. They suffered no opportunity, also, to pass unimproved by which they might regain what Luther and his companions had so triumphantly wrested from them.

The two great instruments which they employed to effect their purposes, were the order of the Jesuits, and the Inquisition.

The order of the Jesuits was founded in 1540, by Ignatius Loyola, a wild fanatic. Before the close of the reformation, the ancient Franciscan and Dominican orders had lost much of their influence and authority; so that the rise of some new

---

* In the French church they were never able to carry this order into execution. There the common people have ever had the Bible.

order seemed necessary to save the sinking church. Loyola, ambitious of founding one which should be more potent than any which had existed, presented his plan to Pope Paul V., and declared it revealed from heaven. Paul was afraid of the establishment, and refused his approbation, until Ignatius added to the three vows of poverty, chastity, and monastic obedience, a fourth of entire subservience to the Pope; binding the members of his order to go, without reward, in the service of religion, whithersoever the Pope should direct them. This procured, at once, the Pope's sanction, and the most ample privileges. The Jesuits were established, and in less than half a century, filled every country on the globe with their order. In 1608, they numbered 10,581. In 1710, 19,998.

Their form of government was a perfect despotism. A general of the order was appointed by the Pope for life, to whom regular reports were annually made from every branch, and to whom every individual was perfectly known, and entirely submissive. Their discipline was altogether novel. Other monks had sought the solitude of the cloister, and practiced rigorous austerities; had their peculiar habit, and appeared dead to the world. But the Jesuits were never distinguished from men of the world. They had no peculiar dress or employment. They mingled in all the active scenes of life,—were physicians, lawyers, merchants, mathematicians, musicians, painters, artists, that they might have the easier access to men of every rank and condition, and promote the purposes of the Pope without being known. Every candidate for the order was obliged to confess all the secrets of his heart, every thing relating to his temper, passions, inclinations, and life, to his superior; and was required to serve for a considerable period, and to pass through several gradations of rank before he could become a professed member. Every Jesuit was compelled to act as a spy upon the conduct of every other Jesuit. The rules of their order were hidden from strangers, and even from the greater part of their own number. They became instructors of youth in all the schools of Europe; confessors and spiritual guides to merchants, nobles, and sovereigns; they mingled in every transaction, and gave laws to empires. They established houses of trade in most parts of the world, and amassed vast treasures. And wherever they went, in whatever they were engaged, they were active missionaries of the Romish faith; being actuated by an astonishing attachment to their order and the church of Rome, and a most bitter and violent opposition to the Protestant religion. They were, for a long period, the pest of the world; and they were denounced by one state and another. But their superior knowledge, soft manners, and a morality which authorized the most atrocious crimes—treachery, robbery, murders, for the promotion of a good end, especially the good of the Roman church, they continued exceedingly popular; and the pontiffs found them of such eminent service, as to absolve them from every crime and protect them from every adversary.

The first, and by far the most distinguished of all their missionaries was Francis Xavier. In 1541, he sailed to the Portuguese settlements in India; and, in a short period baptized several thousands of the natives into the Romish faith. Meeting with such success, he prepared to go to China, and attempted the conversion of that vast empire; but was suddenly cut off, in 1552, in the 46th year of his age, and in sight of his object. Had Xavier been possessed of the true knowledge of the Gospel, thousands might have risen up and called him blessed. He no doubt had a true missionary spirit, and the best missionary habits. His labors were wonderful.

After his death, Matthew Ricci and a host of Jesuits, pressed into the regions of Siam, Tonkin, Cochin-China, and the vast empire itself. Ricci recommended himself to the Emperor by his mathematical knowledge, and obtained patronage for his religion. Converts were multiplied, and the catholic religion for a season prevailed to a great extent. The Emperor built a magnificent church for the Jesuits within the imperial precincts. Others pushed their conquests into India. On the coast of Malabar, one missionary boasted of a thousand converts baptized in a single year. Others, still more adventurous, penetrated into Japan, where they numbered, at one time, more than 600,000 Christians. In Abyssinia, also, they acquired an astonishing influence, which was retained for a season by the tortures of the Inquisition. But in South America was their greatest success. The whole of that vast continent they brought under the dominion of the Pope. In Paraguay, where perhaps they did more good than any where else, 300,000 families were said to be taught by them agriculture and the arts; to be both civilized and Christianized.

Their amazing efforts excited other monastic orders, the

Dominicans, Franciscans, and Capuchins, who found that they were, for their supineness, sinking in repute, to similar enterprises. They also induced the Popes, and others, to institute immense and splendid missionary establishments in Europe. In 1622, Pope Gregory XV. founded at Rome the magnificent college, "De propaganda fide." Its object was the propagation of the catholic religion in every quarter of the globe. Its riches were immense, and adequate to the greatest undertakings. By it a vast number of youth were educated, and sent to the pagan nations; feeble and worn out missionaries were supported, and books were published and dispersed beyond number. Its exploits are almost incredible. In 1627, another college was founded through the munificence of John Baptist Viles, a Spanish nobleman, for the education of missionaries. And in France was established in 1663, the congregation of the priests of foreign missions; and the Parisian Seminary for the missions abroad. All these sent forth legions of Jesuits and friars, to all parts of the globe.

But alas! while they put Protestant Christians to the blush, for their backwardness in heathen missions, all their labors were to but little profit. Little or no instruction did these missionaries ever give, relating to the character and love of God, to sin and holiness, and the way of salvation by Jesus Christ. Their great object was to persuade the heathen to receive and practice the religious ceremonies of the church of Rome; and this they did, to a great extent, by a compromising plan, in which they made it appear that there was no great difference between the Christian and pagan systems. They taught the Chinese that the Christian religion came from Tien, the Chinese name for God, and that there was no great difference between the worship of the saints and the virgin Mary, and the Chinese worship of their ancestors. Jesus Christ and Confucius were placed upon a level, and their religions were nearly amalgamated. The Hindoos were taught that Jesus Christ was a Brahmin, and that the Jesuits were Brahmins, sent from a distant country to reform them. The Capuchin converts in Africa were suffered to retain the abominable superstitions of their ancestors. In South America the profligate and the worthless characters of the Spaniards and Portuguese, utterly forbade any good moral influence from their instructions. Yet among such a crowd of missionaries, some few, like Xavier, may have truly sought the salvation of souls, through whose labors and prayers, some may have been gathered into the spiritual kingdom of our Lord and Saviour. If so, it has given joy in heaven.

While the Roman church was thus engaged in foreign missions, she was also deeply involved in almost uninterrupted cabals to crush the Protestants and regain her former dominion in Europe. A few amicable conferences were first held; but her genius rather led her to violence and blood. She declared that the Protestants in Germany had forfeited the privileges secured to them, in the peace of religion, by departing from the confession of Augsburg; and through the bigoted house of Austria, she made war upon them in 1618; overcame, and awfully oppressed them. The cries of the suffering affected every heart, but that of the bigot Ferdinand, who exclaimed, "I had rather see the kingdom a desert, than damned." Their cruel oppressions called forth the interposition of the noble Gustavus of Sweden. He appeared in Germany with a small army in 1629, and fell in the battle of Lutzen in 1632. But his generals persevered; till worn out with a thirty years' war, all parties agreed in the treaty of Westphalia in 1648, in which the Roman church confirmed anew to the Lutherans all their rights and privileges.

This was the last open war which the church of Rome made upon the Protestants; but in every other possible way, by bribes, by the subtleties of controversy, by the axe and the fire, she continually harrassed the men of every country. In Hungary, a violent persecution raged for ten years. In Poland, all who differed from the Pope were treated as the offscouring of the earth, for more than a century. The Waldenses were ever the objects of persecution, and were hunted in their dens and caves, and native mountains, and put to the most cruel deaths. From Spain, a million of Moors, or Saracens, descendants of the former conquerors of the country, a sober, industrious, wealthy people, nominally Christian, but strongly attached to Mahomet, were banished from the kingdom; and the church acquired immense possessions. An almost equal number of Jews were also driven out, whose estates, too, were confiscated by the Roman church. The eyes of many in that hapless country were opened upon the truth, by their connection with Germany during the reign of Charles V.; but they were silenced by racks, gibbets, and stakes. All the divines who accompanied Charles into his retirement, were immediately, upon his death, given over to the Inquisition, and committed to the flames ; which gives reason to suppose that he died a Protestant.

The Protestants in France, called Huguenots, probably from the word Huguon, a night walker, because, like the early Christians, they assembled privately in the evening ; and who were very numerous, suffered continual vexations from Francis I., before the reformation was established ; though they found a warm friend in the queen of Navarre. His successor Henry II., or probably Nero II., had them tied to a stake on the day of his inauguration, and the flame kindled at the moment he passed by, that he might see them burn. Parliament decreed that it was lawful to kill them wherever they could be found. Charles IX., as if to signalize himself still more by his ferocity, resolved upon the extirpation of the whole from his dominions. At this time, A. D. 1571, they had 2150 congregations, some of which had not less than 10,000 members. Charles laid a snare for them, by offering his sister in marriage to a Huguenot, the prince of Navarre. All the heads of the Huguenots were assembled in Paris at the nuptials ; when on the eve of St. Bartholomew's day, August 24th, 1572, at the ringing of a bell, the dreadful massacre commenced. Charles and his mother beheld it with joy, from a window. The monster himself fired upon the Huguenots, crying *kill, kill !* An unparalleled scene of horror ensued. The Catholics, like bloodhounds, rushed upon the defenceless Huguenots. Above five hundred men of distinction, and about ten thousand of inferior order, that night slept in Paris, the sleep of death. A general destruction was immediately ordered throughout France ; and a horrid carnage was soon witnessed at Rouen, Lyons, Orleans, and other cities. Sixty thousand perished, and solemn thanksgivings were rendered to God by the Catholics for the triumph, as they called it, of the church militant. It was the horrid excess of religious bigotry—the awful triumph of the Man of Sin.

As soon as possible, the Huguenots, under the prince of Conde, stood in their defence, and combated their enemies with much success. But the most terrible scenes—murders, assassinations, massacres, and all the accompaniments of a religious war, were continually witnessed ;—39 princes, 148 counts, 234 barons, 146,158 gentlemen, and 760,000 of the common people, were in about thirty years destroyed, for adopting the reformed religion.

In 1593, Henry IV. succeeded to the throne of France. He was a Huguenot. But not being able to obtain the throne, while he remained such, and imagining that if he should, his government would have no stable foundation disconnected with Rome, he made a solemn profession of popery. But he followed the feelings of his heart, in relation to the Huguenots, and in the year 1598, published the Edict of Nantez, which gave them the rights and privileges of citizenship, assured to them the liberty of worshipping God according to the dictates of their own consciences, and certain lands to support their churches and garrisons. Henry soon felt the vengeance of the papal arm; for he was assassinated in his chariot as he passed along the streets of Paris, by the fanatic Ravillac, A. D. 1610.

Tolerated by the civil power, the Huguenots, for a season, flourished greatly. But they were at variance with the government, and Cardinal Richelieu, prime minister of Lewis XIII., early adopted, and long pursued this severe maxim: "That there could be no peace in France, until the Huguenots were totally suppressed." Every method which had the least appearance of consistence with the edict of Nantez, was used for many years to carry it into effect. The Huguenots were deprived of their wealth, and strong holds, and civil privileges—were courted and frowned upon, and driven from one extremity to another, until at length, finding all these measures ineffectual, the perfidious and impolitic Lewis XIV. revoked the edict of Nantez, and ordered all the reformed churches to embrace the Romish faith. Their case was now hopeless. Their churches were razed to the ground. They were insulted by a brutal soldiery, and massacred in crowds. And though soldiers were stationed on the frontiers to prevent their escape, yet above fifty thousand fled, and sought refuge in the various Protestant countries of Europe.

Similar attempts to regain lost dominion are seen in the history of the Church of England. To this day they have not ceased, where any prospect of success has been visible.

These various efforts were not, indeed, in many countries unsuccessful. Vast foreign countries, and a great part of Europe, were held in iron bondage. A queen of Sweden, a king of Poland, a count Palatine, a duke of Brunswick, a marquis of Brandenburg, and many hundreds who had become Protestants, were brought back to the bosom of the church. And what the falling pontiffs possessed, they retained as far as they dared, by all the tortures of the Inquisition. From France, this horrid tribunal was early effectually expelled. In Rome, it was lenient, lest it should drive strangers from the city. But in Spain, Portugal, and in Goa, it was a horrid power. In the united kingdoms of Castile and Arragon, were, at one time, eighteen inquisitorial courts, having each its apostolical inquisitors, secretaries, sergeants, &c., and twenty thousand familiars, or spies and informers, dispersed through the kingdom. Persons suspected of the slightest opposition to the catholic church, were demanded at midnight by the watch of the Inquisition, dragged before the tribunal, put to the torture, condemned on the slightest evidence, shut up for life in dungeons, or strangled and burnt to death. No husband, wife, or parent, dared refuse to give up the nearest relative. Wealth in a nobleman, and beauty in a female, were sure to attract the cupidity of these horrible harpies. Their friends might never inquire into their fate.

The Auto de fe, or act of faith, has exhibited the most shocking barbarities of civilized man. On a stage erected in the public place in Madrid, the unhappy victims, having been put to the torture by infernal monks, have been tied to the stake, and burned gradually to death. The kings of Spain have sat uncovered, lower than the inquisitors, and witnessed with approbation the awful spectacle.

This horrid tribunal has almost destroyed that beautiful kingdom. All the fountains of social happiness have been broken up. The father has stood in fear of his own child. The sister of her brother. Both Spain and Portugal are sunk by it, in the grossest ignorance, and deepest wretchedness.*

But though the papal power numbered vastly more souls under its dominion after the reformation than it did before, and seemed at one time to be more formidable than ever, yet, through a series of unexpected events, it has on all sides

---

* Between the years 1452 and 1808, the whole number of victims to the inquisition on the peninsula, was as follows:
Burnt, ... 31,718
Died before execution, or escaped, . . 17,511
Punished by whipping, imprisonment, &c. 287,522

Total, 336,751
More than 1500 were burnt during the last century, but none after the year 1783. Besides these, an incredible number suffered in the Spanish possessions in America, Italy, Flanders, Goa, &c.

been weakened until its ancient power, wealth and splendor, have entirely passed away.

Its richest foreign conquests were soon lost. For failing in any good influence over the heart and conscience—and guilty themselves of fraudulent practices, and abominable dissoluteness, and often deeply immersed in civil and military affairs, exciting seditions and tumults, its emissaries rather provoked a revolt than otherwise. In China, the Jesuits and Dominicans quarrelled violently. Each appealed to the Pope. His interference excited the jealousy of the government, and imprisonment, banishment, and death, became the order of the day, until the name of Christian was almost unknown in the empire. In Japan, a still more tremendous reverse took place in 1615. The utter extermination of Christianity, root and branch, was effected in one month. Such as would not renounce it, were immediately banished or put to death. Vast multitudes of both sexes expired under the most cruel torments. The name of Christian has ever since been repeated with the utmost abhorrence. And none bearing it have been permitted to place their foot there, excepting a few Dutch merchants who had been allowed a factory in one of the extremities of the kingdom. From Abyssinia the Jesuits were forever banished, for their insolence and ambition, in 1634.

At home the catholic power was weakened by unsuccessful contests with several European governments. In 1606, Paul V. nearly lost the rich republic of Venice. Peace was made, but the Pope relinquished many of his pretensions, and the Jesuits were banished. Naples, Sardinia, Portugal, and Spain, all in their turn, withheld some immunities which had before been freely granted. But the disputes with the king of France, were the most violent and destructive. Lewis XIV. convened in 1682, a council of the Galican church, in which it was decreed, " That the power of the Pope was merely spiritual, and did not at all extend to temporalities ; that a general council was superior to the Pope ; that the power of the Pope was also limited by the canons, and that his decisions are not infallible without the consent of the church." This was a most severe blow.

But the downfall of modern popery is to be dated from the suppression of the order of the Jesuits. This great event was owing to a variety of causes, chiefly, however, to their conduct in South America. Over the immense country of Paraguay, they had established an almost independent sovereignty. The Spanish and Portuguese were excluded from it, lest they should corrupt the converts. An immense trade was wholly monopolized, and the European monarchs found themselves deprived of all revenue from that country. In 1750 a treaty was made between Spain and Portugal, in which the boundaries of the two kingdoms in South America were accurately defined. The Jesuits forbade the approach of either party into Paraguay. But an army was sent which soon broke through all resistance, and in 1758, the Jesuits were banished from the kingdom of Portugal, and soon after, from that of Spain, and their estates were confiscated. In ship loads they returned from foreign countries, and in crowds they pressed from the great peninsula, to seek some new employment from their sinking patron.

In France, they fell into disgrace, in a religious controversy. In sentiment they were Pelagians. In 1640, Jansenius published the doctrines of Augustine, concerning depravity and free grace. The publication was condemned by the Inquisition, and the Pope. But Jansenius had many followers. All united with him, who were disgusted with the Roman superstitions, and wished the promotion of vital piety. About the same time, a French translation of the New Testament was made by Quesnel, accompanied with annotations, containing the principles of Augustine. Its circulation was rapid. The Jesuits took fire, and compelled Pope Clement XI., in 1713, to issue the bull UNIGENITUS, condemning that and its notes. The Jansenists were inflamed; but Parliament confirmed the bull, and the Jansenists felt the horrors of persecution. They became enthusiastic, and pretended to supernatural succors; to revelations and miracles, and declared that to show the truth of their cause, God had ordered the bones of their dead, especially of the Abbe of Paris, to work miracles. Thousands flew to the Abbe's tomb, to behold the wonders, and the Jansenists grew popular. They exposed the moral corruptions of the Jesuits, and turned the tide against them, so that the order was abolished in France, by royal edict in 1762, and all their colleges and possessions were confiscated and sold.

Still they were upheld by the Pope, as he had felt their worth; but their cause had grown desperate, and in compliance with the universal demand, Ganganelli or Clement XIV. suppressed them entirely in all the papal countries, July 21 1773.

With the Jesuits fell the amazing power of papal Rome. But she fell into the fangs of a monster more horrible than ever stalked forth upon the bloody arena of depraved man. About the middle of the last century, a set of most ferocious infidels, headed by Voltaire, D'Alembert, Rosseau, and Frederic II. king of Prussia, resolved upon the annihilation of Christianity. Berlin was the centre of their operations; but the Gallican church was the first object of their attack. Her clergy were amazingly numerous and rich, being no less than eighteen arch-bishops, one hundred and eleven bishops, one hundred and fifty thousand priests, with a revenue of five millions sterling annually, besides three thousand and four hundred wealthy convents. But they were an easy prey. The revocation of the edict of Nantez, had driven experimental religion from the kingdom, and, with a most splendid church, the nation was given up to infidelity. Her priests themselves, from the vast increase of light, were ashamed of their tricks and pious frauds. The absurdities of indulgence, penance, and purgatory, could no longer be swallowed by a nation full of intelligence. The conspirators saw this and drew out the monster. The wealth of the church was a fine object of attack. It was soon made the property of the nation. A civil constitution was formed for the clergy, to which all were required to swear, on pain of death or banishment. The great body refused, and priest and altar were overturned, and blood once esteemed sacred, flowed to the horses' bridles. Such as could, escaped through a thousand dangers, and found an asylum in foreign countries. No tongue can tell the woes of the nation.

The revolutionary torrent overflowed the neighboring countries, and laid waste the Roman church with all her trumpery. Her priests were massacred. Her silver shrines and saints were turned into money for the payment of troops. Her bells were converted into canon, and her churches and convents, into barracks for soldiers. From the Atlantic to the Adriatic, she presented but one most appalling spectacle. She had shed the blood of saints and prophets, and God now gave her blood to drink.

The Emperor Napoleon despised the Pope, and the whole system of monkery. To secure the reverence of the people, he compelled Pius the Seventh, in 1804, to place the crown upon his head, but in less than four years after he dispossessed him of his ecclesiastical state, and reduced him to a mere cypher in the political world. The Pope issued against him and his troops a bull of excommunication, but it was the pitiable bluster of the decayed old man. The Dominicans in Spain felt his vengeance, and he there, in 1808, abolished the Inquisition. In Spain the infernal inquisition has been in part re-established,* and the Pope has sent out again some of the order of the Jesuits.

The principles of the Roman church are expressed in the decrees of the council of Trent and the confession of Pius IV.; but they have been always subject to an exposition of the Pope, who has claimed infallibility. Her rites and ceremonies have varied but little for centuries. A stranger in papal countries now feels himself transported back into the dark ages.

Her pontiffs, since the reformation, have generally sustained a better character than before. Some have been weak. Some ambitious. A few, respectable for talent and piety.

The same may be said of her clergy. Baronius and Bellarmin have been her most eminent controversialists. Father Paul of Venice, has been her most distinguished historian. Bossuet, Bourdaloue and Massillon her greatest orators.† Fenelon, archbishop of Cambray, was "the Enoch of his age." He walked with God, and by his writings did much for the promotion of piety. Pascal and Quesnel were eminent for learning and piety. The letters of Pascal first exposed the arts of the Jesuits. Many of the Jansenists appeared to be possessed of the faith and holiness of the Gospel. But the great mass of bishops have spent their

* In 1820, the inquisition of Valencia was broken open by the revolutionists, and five hundred were released from its dark and humid dungeons.

† Bossuet died in 1704, bishop of Meaux. He distinguished himself by his funeral orations in honor of the princes and great men of his age.

Such was the eloquence of Bourdaloue that on the revocation of the edict of Nantez, Lewis XIV. sent him to preach the catholic doctrines to the Protestants. He had more solidity and close reasoning than Massillon, but less imagination and less of the pathetic and persuasive. He died 1704, aged 72.

Massillon was born at Hieres, in Provence, 1663. His powers of eloquence early brought him to Paris, where he long carried captive crowded audiences. His oratory was peculiarly his own, and such his fidelity as to bring the gay court of Lewis XIV. and the monarch himself to serious reflection. "Father," said the king to him, "when I hear other preachers I go away much pleased with them, but whenever I hear you, I go away much displeased with myself." In 1717, he was made bishop of Clermont. He died 1742, aged 79.

time amid the cabals and luxuries of courts—the slaves of temporal princes ; and the lower order of priests have had little but their habit, title, and a few ceremonies to show that they had any connexion with him whose kingdom is not of this world.

Monastic orders have continued to arise. The two most famous since the reformation have been "The Fathers of the oratory of the Holy Jesus," 1613, and the monks of La Trappe, 1664. Laziness, ignorance, voluptuousness, and discord have continued to characterize all those establishments. The popularity of the Jesuits threw into the back ground the whole tribe of monks and friars. All experienced in the French revolution a tremendous overthrow.

The catholics are still very numerous in the world—probably not less than 100,000,000, an immense power if brought to act under one head. Multitudes in Asia know no other religion than that of the Pope. A large part of Europe, particularly Spain, Portugal, and Italy, are still sunk in ignorance and trammeled with superstition. In South America, too, the catholic church remains very splendid and imposing. The number of her priests, monks, temples, festivals, and idle ceremonies, is immense, and the ignorance and superstition of the people are beyond conception. But a free government must sap her foundations, or at least entirely change her character. Already the wealth and power of the priesthood are diminished, monks are ridiculed, feast days are much disregarded, the sale of indulgences is partially stopped, the Bible is getting into free circulation, and Protestants live and die undisturbed. In Great Britain and her dependencies, catholics are numerous. From the reign of queen Elizabeth they have there been guarded by the most severe enactments, and numbers have been put to death. Some of these laws have, of late, been repealed. In England there has been for two centuries no regular Romish hierarchy. The whole church is under the superintendence of the congregation *De Propagande Fide* at Rome. The clergy here are regarded as missionaries, each of the stations is called a mission, and all are included in the phrase, "The whole mission to England." The church is governed by four vicars apostolic, appointed by the Pope, with the rank of bishops. In Ireland there are bishops and priests. The catholics have six-sevenths of the population. In Canada they are sunk in the grossest ignorance.

On the United States the Pope and his cardinal have lately cast their eye as "a land of promise." Great numbers of catholics have emigrated hither from Europe, and found employment in our cities, on our canals and rail roads, or spread themselves in the valley of the Mississippi. Churches, colleges, convents, and schools, have risen in every part of the country. Their present number is two million three hundred thousand. Their principal colleges are at Baltimore, Georgetown, New Orleans, and St. Louis. Their worship here, as in Europe, is splendid and imposing. But little instruction is given, and no disposition is manifested to relax either in principles, forms, or superstitions.

CHAPTER XIV.

Greek church. Its history, doctrine, and discipline. Russian Greek church. Its establishment and separation from the Greek church. Sect of Isbranki. Efforts of Peter the Great. Doctrines and discipline. Eastern churches. Ground of their early divisions. Nestorians. Monophysites. Asiatics. Africans. Copts. Abyssinians. Armenians.

THE once happy and flourishing churches of Greece and Asia soon sunk to decay, when they had drunk the poison of Arius, and had consented with idol Rome, to bow the knee in image worship. By the Saracens they were, from time to time, awfully scourged and rooted up of heaven for their wickedness; but still they flourished in much wealth and splendor while the Byzantine Cæsars held their thrones. This rising power of the Roman pontiff excited their jealousy; and his pride and haughtiness kindled their rage. In the middle of the ninth century, Photius, the patriarch of Constantinople, was excommunicated by the Roman pontiff, for asserting that the Holy Ghost proceeded only from the Father and not from the Son. The act was resented by the Grecian emperor, and the Roman pontiff was excommunicated in turn. A breach was made between the eastern and western churches, which was soon widened by new subjects of contention, and confirmed in irreconcilable enmity. From this period is dated the rise of the Greck church; though that church embraces the primitive churches planted by the Apostles.

In numbers, wealth, and glory, the Grecian church far exceeded the spiritual dominion of the Roman See. In the tenth century, she received into her connexion the immense Russian dominions which were converted to the Christian faith. But she had a fatal enemy in the east, before whom she was rapidly consumed. One after another of her beautiful churches she beheld converted into Mahometan mosques, while their worshippers were destroyed by the sword, or converted by terrors and bribes to the religion of the Impostor. From the west the fanatical crusaders came, pouring in torrents to rescue, if possible, her lost territory. She was jealous of their design, and only submitted to what she could not resist; and while she had little cause to thank them for aid, she had reason to bewail, had her eyes been open to it, the inheritance they left,—a vast deposit of moral corruption.

In 1453, the empire of the Greeks was overthrown by the Mahometan power, and with it perished their religious establishment. For a few years, their haughty conquerors permitted something that bore the name of a religious toleration; but it is part of the religion of a Turk to treat a Christian as a dog, and the toleration was soon exchanged for a rigorous and cruel despotism. For near 400 years, the Greek church has now continued in a most deplorable bondage, until her religion is but little better than a constant succession of idle ceremonies. Why has it been thus? Eternity will unfold the mysteries of time. But let the churches which have the bright light that once shone on Asia and Greece, behold and beware.

By a defection of the Russian church in 1589, the Greek church became considerably limited in its extent. Her people are now found scattered throughout Greece and Grecian islands, Walachia, Moldavia, Sclavonia, Egypt, Nubia, Lybia, Arabia, Mesopotamia, Syria, Cilicia and Palestine. These countries are comprehended within the jurisdiction of the patriarchs of Constantinople, Alexandria, Antioch and Jerusalem. There are also branches of the Greek church in Circassia, Georgia and Mongrelia.

The boldest and most artful efforts have been repeatedly made to win the Greek church to the Roman faith, but uniformly in vain. The very youth brought from the east and educated at Rome at the greatest expense in the papal colleges, have, on their return, been the bitterest foes to the papal dominion.

The Greeks, while they pretend to acknowledge the Scriptures as the rule of their faith, have many peculiarities which distinguish them from the Catholic and Protestant churches. They receive the doctrine of the Trinity, and most of the articles of the Nicene and Athanasian creeds, but rest much upon the procession of the Holy Ghost from the Father, and not from the Son. They hold in abhorrence the supremacy and infallibility of the Pope; purgatory by fire; graven images; the celibacy of the secular clergy; and prohibition of the sacrament in both kinds;—but yet use pictures in their worship; invoke saints; have seven sacraments; believe in transubstantiation; admit prayers and services for the dead; have a fast or festival for almost every day in the year; and know of no regeneration but baptism.

Their officers are many; their convents are numerous, and their monks are all priests, who lead a very austere life. Their nunneries are few. Their patriarchs reside at Constantinople, Damascus, Cairo and Jerusalem. The patriarch of Constantinople is at the head of the church, and is chosen by twelve bishops, and confirmed by the Turkish emperor. The office, however, is generally purchased by an immense sum, of the Grand Vizier. It is a post honorable and lucrative. Its possessor has a vast jurisdiction and dominion. He not only decides controversies in the church, but administers civil justice among the members of his communion. He has the power of excommunicating any member of the Greek church, and of commanding his death, exile, or imprisonment for life. He is, in fact, the governor of the Greeks, under the Turkish emperor, and is sustained by his authority. The other patriarchs are poor and debased, as is the whole church. Without schools, without Bibles, without religious teachers, groaning for near 400 years under an iron bondage, they have sunk into the most deplorable ignorance and moral corruption. With a crowd of bishops and metropolitans, they are almost as ignorant of the true Gospel of Christ, as the benighted savage. The recent deliverance of Greece from the Mahometan yoke, and the establishment of civil and Christian liberty cannot fail to operate most favorably upon their religion and morals. Let Christians pray for those once great and distinguished churches, now in ruins and send them back the light of life

RUSSIAN GREEK CHURCH.

The immense wilds of Russia continued covered with moral darkness long after the rest of Europe had enjoyed the precious light of the Gospel. About the year 900. Methodius, and Cyril the philosopher, traveled from Greece into Moravia, where they translated some of the church service into the Sclavonian language, and converted the grand duchess Olga to the Christian faith. Christianity soon spread, and Russia became subject to the patriarch of Constantinople. Of any thing farther we know but little until 1581, when we find the Muscovites publishing the Bible in their own language. In 1589, Russia separated from the government, though not from communion of the Greek church, and an independent patriarch was established at Moscow.

About the year 1666, a sect called the *Isbraniki*, or multitude of the elect, pretending to uncommon piety and devotion, separated from the Russian church, and excited great disturbances throughout the empire. They were treated with severity, but increased, and do still remain, bound up in impenetrable secrecy.

Peter the Great resolved to be the reformer of his church, as well as of his empire. Happy had it been for Russia, had the light of the reformation dawned upon that noble mind. But he knew no other system than that in which he had been educated, and made, therefore, no change in the doctrines of the Greek church. These, however, he was resolved his people should understand; and he waged war with the ignorance of the clergy, and the gross superstition which brooded over the whole nation. He quenched the fires of persecution, and established a universal toleration of all sects and denominations excepting the catholics. He abolished the office of patriarch, putting himself at the head of the church; which, under him was to be governed by a synod; diminished the revenues of the clergy; and was once resolved to abolish the monasteries as unfriendly to population. But it was only an age of twilight; and he was induced to continue them, and to erect a magnificent monastery, in honor of Alexander Newsky; whom the Russians number among their distinguished heroes and saints. He caused the Bible to be translated, printed, and circulated, in the Sclavonian language; and had he lived in the age of Alexander, he would have placed a Bible in every family.

The Russian church has increased with the amazing increase of the nation. Happy for her had she grown in knowledge and holiness. But alas! her clergy are ignorant, and her people are without the Bible. The noble Russian Bible Society, under the excellent prince Galitzin promised to raise her from her deplorable degradation, but it has been suppressed by her tyrants, jealous for their thrones.

In her doctrine, she agrees with the Greek church; like her, receives the seven sacraments or mysteries; allows no statues or graven images, but admits pictures and invocation of saints; and is, therefore, like her and like Rome, whom she abhors, idolatrous. Her service consists of a vast number of idle ceremonies and absurd superstitions, and it is to be feared, that she is but very little elevated above the Roman catholics in acquaintance with evangelical piety. Every person is obliged, by the civil law, to partake of the sacrament once a year. An unparalleled union exists throughout the empire, in doctrine and in practice. Her clergy are very numerous, and of different orders. Her monks and nuns are about 6000 each.

Many efforts have been made by the Roman pontiff and Jesuits, to effect an union between the catholic and Russian churches, but always in vain. The Russians are very jealous of their religious independence and religious system.

The friends of truth, encouraged by the promises of God's word, are looking for some moral change throughout those immense regions. A single reign of one pious and liberal monarch may, under God, effect it. Let us rejoice that the hearts of kings are in his hands.

EASTERN CHURCHES.

It is wonderful how great results proceed from little causes, and how the human mind once turned into a particular channel, proceeds on through successive ages. In the fifth century, we saw Nestorius, a Syrian bishop of Constantinople, advancing the sentiment, that, in Christ there were two distinct natures and persons, the human and divine, and that Mary was to be called the mother of the man Jesus, and not of God. In opposition to him, Eutyches, an abbot at Constantinople, declared that these natures were so united in Christ, as to form but one nature, that of the Incarnate Word. It was an age when men were fast losing sight of the Gospel, and contending about modes and forms; and these opposite opinions threw the whole eastern world into bitter contention, and gave rise to that great division, which continues to this day among the miserable remnant of eastern churches. The followers of the former, are called Nestorians; the latter, Monophysites.

The NESTORIANS early became the chief propagators of the Gospel in the east. They enjoyed the patronage of the Persian monarch Pherazes, by whom their opponents were expelled from his kingdom, and their patriarch was established at Seleucia. They established a school at Nisibis under Barsumas, a disciple of Nestorius, from whence proceeded in the fifth and sixth centuries, a band of missionaries, who spread abroad their tenets through Egypt, Syria, Arabia, India, Tartary, and China. In the twelfth century, they won over to their faith the prince of Tartary, who was baptized John; and because he exercised the office of presbyter, was, with his successors, called Prester John. They made converts, also, of the Christians on the coast of Malabar, who, it is supposed, received the Christian faith from the Syrian Mar Thomas, in the fourth or fifth century.

They formed at one time an immense body; but dwindled away before the Saracen power, and the exasperated heathen priests and jealous Chinese Emperors. They acknowledged but one patriarch until 1551, who resided first at Bagdad and afterward at Mousul. But at this period, the papists succeeded in dividing them, and a new patriarch was consecrated by Pope Julius III., and established over the adherents to the Pope, in the city of Ormus. The great patriarch at Mousul, called Elias, has continued, however, to be acknowledged to this day, by the greater part of the Nestorians, who are scattered over Asia.

Throughout this long period they have maintained considerable purity of doctrine and worship, and kept free from the ridiculous ceremonies of the Greek and Latin churches. Of their present number, and religious character, we know but little. Probably they are very ignorant, debased, and corrupt. Dr. Buchanan visited the churches on the Malabar coast, in 1806, and found fifty-five much discouraged and distressed. Their doctrines differed but little from the doctrines of the church of England. Surely they are interesting objects for missionary effort. Towards them the English Church Missionary Society has, of late, directed its attention, and they are improving in doctrine and in morals.

The MONOPHYSITES at first received some encouragement

but were soon suppressed by the Grecian Emperors. They found, however, a father in Jacob Baradeus, an obscure monk, who died in 588, bishop of Edessa, leaving them in a flourishing state in Syria, Mesopotamia, Armenia, Egypt, Nubia, Abyssinia, and other countries. In honor of him they are, to this day, called Jacobites.

For a long period, this great body of Christians have been divided into three portions, the Asiatics, the Africans, and the Armenians.

The Asiatics are subject to the patriarch of Antioch, who, since the fifteenth century, has borne the name of Ignatius, to show the world that he is a lineal descendant of Ignatius, an early bishop of Antioch. He resides at the monastery of St. Ananias, near the city of Morden. Some of them in the seventeenth century subjected themselves to the church of Rome, but, through the influence of the Turks, were soon brought back to the dominion of Ignatius. But the condition of the whole body is miserably debased.

The Africans are divided into the Copts and the Abyssinians, and are all subject to a patriarch, who resides at Cairo.

The Copts are in number about 30,000. They reside in Egypt and Nubia; and, oppressed by the Turks, are destitute of almost every comfort of life, and are deplorably ignorant. They have a liturgy in the old Coptic tongue, which is now obsolete. Their priests understand but little of it. During their service they are continually in motion. They have many monasteries and hermitages, but are in a state of beggary.

The Abyssinians are, in every respect, superior to the Copts. We know little of their history. In the middle of the fourth century, Frumentius, it has been observed, preached among them with great success, and they were well esteemed at Rome, until they adopted the system of the Monophysites. In 1634, the learned Heyling, a Lutheran, went into Abyssinia with pious purposes, and recommending himself to the Emperor, he rose to high offices in the state. He returned to Europe for missionary aid, but perished on the way. The duke of Saxe Gotha sent one Gregory, an Abyssinian, who had resided in Europe, to succeed him; but he was shipwrecked on his voyage. One Wantsel offered to supply his place, but his conduct was villanous, and these missionary efforts ceased. The Jesuits made several attempts to bring them over to the church of Rome. The Moravians, every where else successful, have been obliged to abandon their enterprises here. The Emperor is nominally Christian, and exercises a supremacy in the church. The highest spiritual officer is the Abbuna, or bishop, appointed by the patriarch at Cairo. Their religion is a strange mixture of Judaism, Christianity, and the most debased superstition. Polygamy is common. The king has as many wives as his pretended ancestor Solomon. But the Abyssinian church acknowledges but one as the lawful wife. They pay the greatest reverence to the Virgin Mary; some even declare her to be a fourth person in the Godhead. In the number of their saints, and the strictness of their fasts, they even exceed the Roman church. About half the people can read, though they have no books excepting in the Ethiopic, which is to them a dead language. They have a great veneration for the word of God, though they have it only in an unknown tongue, and are in great darkness respecting it.

The late Abbuna was expelled for drunkenness, and the king resolving to receive no more from the Coptic church, sent an ambassador in 1827, to the Armenian church, to solicit a patriarch from them. At Cairo, he was met by two missionaries from the Church Missionary Society, who were on their way to Abyssinia, and whom he earnestly invited to accompany him home. From this circumstance much good is expected. The Abyssinians have churches in Persia, Russia, and Poland.

Great efforts have been made by the Roman pontiffs, to convert the African Monophysites to their faith, but in vain. In 1634, the Abyssinians banished forever the Jesuits from their country. They have ever displayed an astonishing attachment to the religion of their ancestors. O that they had it in its purity. Here were once some of the best churches of Christ. The north of Africa was consecrated by the prayers and watered by the tears of Cyprian, Athanasius, Tertullian, Augustine; but now it is the residence of every unclean bird and beast. But Ethiopia shall stretch out her hands to God.

The Armenians inhabit the vast country east and northeast of Syria. They differ so much from the other Monophysites in faith, discipline, and worship, as to hold no communion with them.

A church was planted among them in the fourth century, by Gregory, called the *enlightened*. This church has re mained, though their country has been laid waste and subjected to the Turks, Tartars, and Persians. A vast number of Armenian merchants have, from time to time, settled in various parts of Europe, who have remembered her with affection, and supplied her with the means of knowledge. An Armenian version of the Bible, made about the time of Chrysostom, from the Greek of the Septuagint, was printed at Amsterdam in 1664, and dispersed through the country.

The Armenian church at present embraces 42,000 individuals in the Russian provinces; 70,000 in Persia, and in Turkey 1,500,000; 100,000 reside in Constantinople. Her merchants are the bankers of the East. Her clergy are of different orders, and very numerous. Their patriarch, who resides in a monastery at Ekmiazen, near Erivan in Persia, is said to have an immense income, while his food and dress are on a level with the poorest monk. He has under him three other patriarchs and fifty archbishops. Their monastic discipline is very severe. By it all their ecclesiastics are qualified for their stations. The Sultan appoints a patriarch in Constantinople and Jerusalem, who have no share in the government of the church, and are mere instruments for enforcing his firmans, and collecting the capitation tax, for which they are responsible.

Sumptuous and unmeaning ceremonies, ridiculous traditions, lying wonders, superstitious rites, characterize this crumbling church, while her priests and bishops are sunk in the lowest ignorance and sensuality, and are treated by her enlightened merchants with the greatest contempt. The papists have made constant efforts to bring this church under their dominion, and have persuaded about 4000 in Constantinople to acknowledge the supremacy of the Pope.

A farewell letter of Mr. King, an American missionary, to the people of Syria, found its way, a few years since, to Constantinople, and produced great excitement. A council was immediately convened, consisting of all the Armenian monks, and priests, and bishops, and patriarchs, of whom several happened at that time to be in Constantinople, also of all the principal Armenians of the laity, together with the Greek patriarchs. The Bible was produced and examined relative to the truth of statements by Mr. King, and resolutions were passed reforming the convent at Jerusalem, forbidding any additions to the monks or priests for 25 years, and suppressing pilgrimages to Jerusalem, and all attendance upon the pretended miracle of the holy fire. There is evidently among them a strong tendency to a reformation. May some Luther rise and bring them to the knowledge of the truth as it is in Jesus.

The MARONITES are a sect of eastern Christians who are subject to the Pope of Rome. Their principal habitation is upon Mount Libanus. They have a patriarch who resides at a monastery on the mount. They were connected with the Monothelites until the 12th century, when they united with the Roman church on this condition, that they should retain all their ancient rites and customs, which they do to the present time. They have many monks, are very ignorant and wretched, and a great tax upon the church of Rome. There are also in the same country, Greek Roman Catholics, Armenian Roman Catholics, Syrian Roman Catholics, and Latins or Frank Roman Catholics.

CHAPTER XV.

Divisions of the Protestants. Lutherans. Their residence, rise, system of faith, liturgy, government. Persecutions. Internal commotions. Synergistical controversy Attempts at a reconciliation between them and the Calvinists. Syncretistic controversy. Degeneracy of clergy and churches. Pietistical controversy. Liberalism. Present state of religion in their churches. Swedenborgianism. Theological erudition.

WHEN the catholics saw the reformers contending about points of faith and practice, they derided them for forsaking the infallible head. But time has proved that the decisions of the Pope were of all others the most preposterous and absurd.

All would see "eye to eye," while the terrors of the inquisition were held over the least variation from fixed establishments. Such a motionless ocean, however, would breed putrefaction and death; not a social state of free inquiry. To elicit the truth which had been buried deep for ages, it was necessary for wave to dash against wave, and billow to roll over billow.

As it had been for centuries in the East, so was it now to be in the West. Those bold spirits who had bid defiance to the thunders of the Pope, and had opened the eyes of half the nations, were to be leaders or heads of vast portions of the reformed church, and to dash one against another perhaps until the millenium. To enumerate all the different sentiments advanced by the Protestants, would be almost impossible. The great mass of those who came out from the church of Rome, enlisted under Luther and Melancthon, Zuingle and Calvin.

LUTHERANS.

The followers of Luther and Melancthon have resided chiefly in the north of Germany, in Prussia, Denmark, Norway, and Sweden, They have spread also to some extent in Russia, France, Holland, North America, and the Danish West India Islands. In honor of the great Reformer, they have assumed the name of Lutherans.

The Lutherans date the rise of their church from the excommunication of Luther by the Pope ; but do not view it as completely established until the peace of Passau, 1552.

Their system of faith, is the confession of Augsburg. Its capital articles are: the sufficiency of the Scriptures as a rule of faith and practice ; justification by faith in the Son of God, and the necessity and freedom of divine grace. It was the common faith of the reformers. That which gave them distinction as a separate denomination, was the favorite opinion of Luther, that though according to the papists, the bread and wine in the sacrament are not converted into the body and blood of Christ, yet the body and blood of Christ are materially present with them, though in an incomprehensible manner. A wide breach was early made with Zuinglius and the Helvetic churches, who considered the bread and wine only as symbolical of the body and blood of Christ, broken and shed for us.

This breach was increased by a pertinacity on the part of the Lutherans, to retain in their worship some of the forms of the catholics ;—exorcism in baptism ; the use of wafers in the Lord's supper, private confession of sin ; images, incense and lighted tapers in their churches, crucifix on the altar ;—also to observe many of the festivals of the Roman church, and days of saints and martyrs.

Luther drew up for his followers, a liturgy or form of divine service, but they have not been confined to that, nor any particular form of government. In Germany the superior power is vested in a consistory, which has a president, with a distinction of rank and privilege. Denmark, Norway, and Sweden, acknowledge episcopacy ; but their bishops have not that pre-eminence which is enjoyed in England. The supreme ruler of the state is ever acknowledged as head of the church.

This portion of the reformed church has suffered no persecution since the *peace of religion*, except in 1618, when the catholics made war upon it through the bigoted house of Austria, under pretence that it had departed from the confession of Augsburg. Their sufferings for thirty years were very great, but they were relieved by the friendly interposition of Gustavus of Sweden, and in the peace of Westphalia in 1648, had all their rights and privileges secured to them.

Her internal commotions upon points of faith and practice, have often been violent. To the sacramental controversy, succeeded a dispute among her own members, upon the *Interim*, or propriety of yielding to the Emperor and church of Rome in things indifferent. The pacific spirit of Melancthon was disposed to yield points in the article of justification, and in the papal ceremonies and jurisdiction, for which Luther had most strenuously contended. He met with warm opposition from Flaccius, professor of divinity at Jena. In 1552, arose a warm controversy upon the necessity of good works; and soon after, another, called the *synergistical* controversy, upon the co-operation of the human will with divine grace in conversion.

Before the death of Melancthon, a considerable defection had taken place from the doctrines of absolute predestination, irresistible grace, and man's moral impotence, in which Luther agreed with Calvin. Men seemed to be wearied with the bold efforts, and the astonishing advancement which they had made in the discovery of truth, and, as is natural to the human mind, to repose and go backward. Some things, however, were favorable.

A large body grew dissatisfied with consubstantiation, and endeavored to extirpate it from their churches. To check their progress, a standard of doctrine was adopted by the civil and ecclesiastical authorities in 1576, at Torgau, called *The Form of Concord*, and imposed upon the churches as a term of communion. It occasioned great disturbances. Some of the churches refused to adopt it. Many of the opposers of Luther's sentiment upon the sacrament, were imprisoned. The Landgrave of Hesse, and the elector of Brandenberg, renounced Lutheranism, and embraced the communion of the Genevan church, which was a severe stroke to the Lutheran cause.

The separation which was continually widening between the followers of Luther and Calvin, filled the minds of all the Protestant world with deep concern. Many attempts were made to reconcile them. James I., king of Great Britain, interposed by an embassy, in 1915. Many conferences were held, but all in vain. The Lutherans were always unyielding.

Calixtus, professor in the University of Helmstadt, supposed that the true principles of the Gospel were retained in the Roman, Lutheran, and Calvinistic confessions, and endeavored to bring these churches together. His writings gave rise to what was called the *Syncretistic* controversy. The Lutherans heaped upon him torrents of abuse, which, as he was a man of much merit, prejudiced against them all candid and liberal minds. Had the Lutheran clergy acted out their principles in their lives, their enemies would have had but little advantage over them. But while contending violently for their doctrines, their morals were low. Through their carelessness and impotence, discipline failed, and a general degeneracy was visible in their churches before the close of the sixteenth century.

Disgusted with their strife and the grossness of their lives, a small party called *Pietists*, arose about the middle of the seventeenth century, and endeavored to revive experimental religion. Their leader was Spener. He published a book called *Pious Desires*, exhibiting the disorders of the church, and pointing out the necessity and means of reformation, which was very popular. He gained some adherents, particularly Franchius, Schadius, and Paulus, three professors of philosophy, who gave, in their colleges, an evangelical exposition of Scripture. Their *Bible Classes* were popular, and roused a spirit of opposition; tumults were excited, and the professors were brought before the public authorities, and charged no more to teach thus in the name of Jesus of Nazareth.

Persecution only strengthened and increased them. The Pietists, as they were now called in derision, were found in all the towns, villages, and cities, where Lutheranism was professed, and by the reformation which they demanded, produced a prodigious excitement. They insisted on a reform in the prevalent system of theological instruction, which was devoted almost entirely to the subtleties of controversy, neglecting the Scriptures and practical religion; demanded experimental piety in all candidates for the ministry; condemned dancing, pantomimes, and theatrical amusements, as unlawful and ruinous to the Christian, and recommended private assemblies for prayer and religious conversation. They were the Puritans of Germany. But their enemies charged them with despising philosophy and learning, and theological discussion; and derogating from the power and efficacy of the word of God, which, they said, would be as great, though it was delivered by an unregenerate minister; and with useless austerities in public, and loose practices in private meetings, so that they were publicly proceeded against by the civil authorities. But vast good followed their effort. A general revival spread over Germany. Professor Frank established an orphan house in 1705, which was remarkably blessed of heaven.

Happy had it been for the Lutheran cause, had the Pietists retained their principles and views, and enforced their demands. But it was not an age of light. They degenerated and were joined, or rather followed in subsequent periods, by enthusiasts and fanatics, who, pretending to inspirations and revelations, went through Germany and Denmark, pulling up, as they said, iniquity by the root; prophesying the downfall of Babel, i. e. the Lutheran church; terrifying the populace by fictitious visions, and introducing a mystical jargon in place of true religion.

These persons, who were of a very different character from the original Pietists, excited, for a long time, great disturbances. Some of the principal authors of delusion, were John W. Peterson, Jacob Behmen, Paul Naget, Martin Sidelius, and a host of fanatical prophets. No tongue can tell the injury they did to the cause of religion throughout Germany.

Among other consequences, the learned and refined were led to the study of a philosophical religion. They thought that in no other way could a stop be put to the progress of superstition. The science of metaphysics was brought into notice, and applied to religion by Leibnitz and Wolf. The application gave much offence to such as loved the simple doctrines of Christianity; but it was exceedingly popular in the universities. Metaphysical and mathematical demonstrations were produced of the Trinity; of the nature of Christ, and of the duration of the future punishment of the wicked. One Laurence Schmidt commenced a new translation of the Scriptures, to which he prefixed a system of theology, drawn up in geometrical order, which was to be his guide in interpreting the Scriptures. Others were exceedingly bold in the middle and at the close of the last century, in their attempts to expunge every peculiarity in the Gospel system, and give Christianity a philosophical garb. But none went to such lengths, or have been so successful as Semler, a man of great ingenuity and extensive learning. He threw aside entirely the inspiration of the Scriptures; gave rise to what is termed the doctrine of *accommodation*; denied the possibility of miracles; ridiculed the account of the creation as a philosophical fable, and of Christ, as a new mythology; and viewed what was said by Him as uttered in condescension to the ignorance and weakness of the Jews, and the writings of his apostles as little better than nonsense. His disciples have been numerous, and his system has been spread with amazing industry throughout Germany. It has almost destroyed those few churches in which were once preached the doctrines of the reformation.

But notwithstanding these great defections in the Lutheran church, a precious body of pastors and churches are found throughout Germany, Denmark, Sweden, and Norway, and a laudable zeal has recently been excited for spreading the Gospel and circulating the Scriptures and tracts in every direction. Liberalism is not adapted to the pious poor. Such choose a literal interpretation of the Augsburg confession, which still remains the standard of their faith. Nor is evangelical truth confined to these. Some eminently learned men have, of late, boldly defended the ancient faith, through whose labors liberalism has received such a check that it is evidently on the decline. Two of the original supports of the Lutheran church, the Electorate of Saxony, and the Principality of Hesse, went back at the close of the last century to the catholic faith. The efforts of the catholics to regain their lost possessions, have produced a warm spirit of animosity, and proselytism both in them and the Protestants. It has also resulted in a great union between the Lutheran and Reformed churches throughout the Prussian monarchy, in the Hessian territories, and in those of Nassau, in the Palatinate and in Baden. These churches generally retain the organization they received at the time of the reformation.

The Lutheran church has received considerable extension from the emigration of her members, at different times, to various parts of the world.

From among the Lutherans have proceeded the Moravians and the Swedenborgians, or followers of the Hon. Emanuel

Swedenborg, who pretended to visions and revelations, and founded in 1743, what he called the New Jerusalem church.

Swedenborg's theology is very mystical, and is expressed in language to which most men can attach no ideas. But it is pleasing to the visionary, and he has followers in Europe and America; though it is difficult to conceive how mankind can receive any benefit from his system.

In missionary efforts, the Lutherans have not been behind other reformed churches.

In 1717, and 1817, they commemorated their deliverance from the church of Rome.

Their learned men have been very numerous. Their princes early endowed, with great munificence, schools and universities, that their rising church might be furnished with able critics and sound theologians. Luther was a host. Melancthon was one of the greatest scholars of that or any other age. Carlostadt, Weller, Flaccius, Bucer, Westphal, Phieffer, Spener, have held a high rank. Leibnitz, Wolf, Semler, Kant, Schelling, have been extolled by the Liberals. Among the orthodox, Storr, Winer, Wahl, have recently labored with great effect.

CHAPTER XVI.

Helvetic churches Difference between Zuinglius and Calvin. Triumph of Calvinism. Its five points. Genevan Academy. Controversies with the Lutherans. Internal dissensions. Spiritual brethren and sisters. Castalio. Bolsec. Servetus. Persecutions from the Catholics. Rise of Arminianism. Synod of Dort. Decline of Calvinism in Holland, England, France, Switzerland. Disputes in Holland. Present state of the Reformed churches. Literature of the Calvinists. Distinguished men. Five points of Arminius. Persecution of his followers. Their restoration and prosperity.

The Helvetic churches, which adhered to Zuinglius in the sacramental controversy, and in his simple forms of divine worship, and which, in opposition to both the Lutheran and Catholic, assumed the title of REFORMED, received, at his death, the doctrine and discipline of Calvin. They were subjected by this act, to many changes.

Zuinglius had given unbounded power in the government of the churches to the civil magistrate. But Calvin directed that the churches should be governed by presbyteries and synods composed of clergy and laity; without bishops or any clerical subordination; leaving it to the civil magistrates only to provide for their support, and to defend them from their enemies. This form of government was called PRESBYTERIAN.

Zuinglius viewed the bread and wine in the sacrament only as symbolical of the body and blood of Christ, but Calvin, hoping to reconcile the Lutherans, acknowledged a real, though spiritual presence of Christ in the ordinance.

Zuinglius permitted all persons, regenerate and unregenerate, to partake of the supper. Calvin viewed it as improper for any to partake, who had not been born of the Spirit.

Zuinglius suffered the doctrine of divine decrees to form no part of his theology. Calvin made it an essential part of his.

Zuinglius confined the power of excommunication to the magistrate. Calvin, to the ministers and churches; but thought the magistrate should punish the dissolute.

The Swiss, however, would not at once readily accede to all Calvin's views, especially to his forms of church government. But the talents and perseverance of Calvin at length gained a triumph here, and among the reformed churches in France, Holland, Scotland, over the descendants of the Waldenses, the valleys of Piedmont, and over very many Lutheran churches in Germany, Poland, Prussia, Hungary, and Transylvania.

Among this vast collection of churches, however, which in a short time became Calvinistic, there was never a perfect uniformity of doctrine or government. The leading articles of Calvin's faith, were predestination, particular redemption, total depravity, effectual calling, and saints' perseverance. On these points he maintained,

I. "That God hath chosen a certain number of the fallen race of Adam, in Christ, before the foundation of the world, unto eternal glory, according to his immutable purpose, and of his free grace and love, without the least foresight of faith, good works, or any conditions performed by the creature, and that the rest of mankind he was pleased to pass by, and ordain to dishonor and wrath, for their sins, to the praise of his vindictive justice.

II. "That though the death of Christ be a most perfect sacrifice and satisfaction for sins of infinite value, and abundantly sufficient to expiate the sins of the whole world, and though, on this ground, the Gospel is to be preached to all mankind indiscriminately; yet it was the will of God, that Christ, by the blood of the cross, should efficaciously redeem all those, and those only, who were from eternity elected to salvation and given to him by the Father.

III. "That mankind are totally depraved in consequence of the fall of the first man, who, being their public head, his sins involved the corruption of all his posterity, and which corruption extends over the whole soul, and renders it unable to turn to God, or to do any thing truly good, and exposes it to his righteous displeasure, both in this world and that which is to come.

IV. "That all whom God hath predestinated unto eternal life, he is pleased in his appointed time effectually to call by his word and Spirit out of that state of sin and death in which they were by nature, to grace and salvation by Jesus Christ.

V. "That those whom God has effectually called and sanctified by his Spirit, shall never finally fall from a state of grace. That true believers may fall partially, and would fall totally and finally, but for the mercy and faithfulness of God, who helpeth the feet of the saints; also, that he who bestoweth the grace of perseverance, bestoweth it by means of reading and hearing the word, meditation, exhortations, threatenings and promises; but that none of these things imply the possibility of a believer's falling from a state of justification."

Calvin also taught the doctrine of three co-ordinate persons in the Godhead, in one nature, and of two natures in Jesus Christ, forming one person; of justification by faith, and of the eternal happiness of the righteous, and endless misery of the finally impenitent.

These principles were fully embodied in the catechism of *Heidelberg*, drawn up by Ursinus for the use of the church of the Palatinate in Germany, which, first under the elector Frederic III. in 1560, and afterwards under John, in 1583, embraced the discipline of Geneva. The Protestants in Holland, Poland, and Hungary, received Calvin's views of the sacrament, but not readily of predestination. The church of England became, under Edward VI., Calvinistic in doctrine, but would not renounce episcopacy. The Bohemian and Moravian brethren also received the creed of the Calvinists, while they retained their ancient government. The French and Scotch churches came entirely into Calvin's views. To the consistory of Geneva, the Scotch added a general assembly of the whole church, a tribunal to which were to be referred matters of highest moment.

Of the reformed churches, Calvin was the life and the soul. From the academy at Geneva, proceeded for many years a great number of distinguished students, who filled England,

Scotland, France, Italy, and Germany with his doctrine. He was succeeded by his colleague, Theodore Beza, who published a Latin version of the New Testament enriched with critical observations, and maintained, for many years, the high reputation of the academy.

In their early stages, these churches were engaged in violent controversies with the Lutherans. The chief point of difference regarded the Lord's Supper. They differed, also, concerning the decrees of God; the Lutherans affirming that these decrees proceeded from a previous knowledge of men's sentiments and characters, and the reformed, that they are free and unconditional, founded on the will of God;—and concerning some catholic rites and institutions—the use of images in the churches, of wafers in the supper, exorcism in baptism, private confession of sin, and clerical vestments, which the Lutherans thought proper and useful, but which the reformed condemned, on the principle that the worship of the Christian Church ought to be restored to its primitive simplicity. In these controversies, the Calvinists were generally triumphant, and brought over to their communion many Lutheran churches.

With divisions and disputes among themselves, they were much less afflicted than the Lutherans; but they were not wholly unmolested. A sect called *the spiritual brethren and sisters*, spread in Flanders, affirming that God was the sole operating cause in the mind of man, and the immediate author of all human actions; that religion consisted in an union of the spirit with God, and that those who had formed this union could not sin, do what they would. Being favored by Margaret, queen of Navarre, they gave Calvin no small trouble. At Geneva, Calvin's doctrine of decrees was openly contemned by Castalio, master of the public school, and Jerome Bolsec, a French monk. Both were banished from the city. Michael Servetus, a Spanish physician, who had written against the doctrine of the Trinity, came to Geneva in 1553 Calvin caused him to be apprehended and brought before the Senate. Being condemned as a heretic, Servetus appealed to the four Swiss churches. They approved of the sentence, and he was burnt, Oct. 27. Calvin wished to have the mode of his execution changed, but he thought the sentence should be capital. It was the opinion of the age that erroneous religious principles should be capitally punished by the civil magistrate. A miserable way of opposing and subduing error. The severity of Calvin's doctrine and discipline, (for he not only excommunicated all the flagitious from the church, but even had them punished by the magistrate and banished from the city,) roused the resentment and malignity of the libertines of Geneva, who gave him perpetual trouble.

Calvin and Beza differed some on the divine decrees, relating to the fall of man. The former held that God permitted the first man to fall into transgression without absolutely predetermining his fall; the latter, that God decreed that Adam should fall, in order that God should glorify his justice and mercy in the destruction of some, and salvation of others. Two parties were formed called Sublapsarians and Supralapsarians.

Wherever the catholics could reach them, they caused the reformed to drink to the dregs the cup of bitterness. The awful sufferings of the Huguenots in France, have passed before us. Near 80,000 were destroyed in about 30 years in that kingdom. By the revocation of the edict of Nantez, about 50,000 were driven into exile. Some fled to Holland, where they erected churches, and enjoyed religious liberty. Among these were Dumont, Dubsoc, and the eloquent Saurin.*

The most horrid scenes of violence and bloodshed were exhibited from 1660 to 1690, among the Waldenses, whom the papists persecuted with relentless fury.

The churches in Great Britain, as we shall see in subsequent chapters, suffered both from internal commotion, and the fires of papal persecution.

The church of the Palatinate passed under a Roman catholic prince, and was almost extinguished.

At the opening of the 17th century, the reformed churches were distracted by the Arminian schism. This originated with James Arminius, professor of divinity at Leyden, who rejected the whole of Calvin's system relating to predestination and grace. He was warmly upheld and applauded in his views, by many men of learning and power in Holland. He met, however, with warm opposition, especially from Gomer, his colleague. After his death, in 1609, the controversy became general, and so violent were the debates, such the tu-

---

* Saurin was born at Nismes, 1677. He left France on the revocation of the edict of Nantez and went to Geneva. There he studied with great assiduity, and then pursued for a little time a military life. Relinquishing this, he entered the ministry, and 1705 settled at the Hague. There he preached his eloquent sermons to crowded and brilliant audiences with astonishing effect. He died Dec. 30, 1730.

mults and broils, that the magistrates interfered, and the states general convened a general synod at Dort, in 1618, to consider and decide the whole controversy.

This was one of the most learned and important councils ever assembled. It was composed of the most able divines of Holland, England, Scotland, Switzerland, Bremen, Hessia, and Palatinate. At the opening of the synod, the Arminians demanded the liberty of disproving the sentiments of Calvin, especially upon reprobation, but the synod forbade them, and required them first to prove their own sentiments. This they refused to do; and for their refusal, were banished from the Assembly. Their system was then examined and condemned. The Arminians were driven from their churches and country.

But the decisions of the synod were not popular, and operated to the detriment of Calvinism. Many of the Arminians were men of learning and eloquence, and correct lives, whose sufferings excited the sympathy of the public. The authority of the synod was not universally acknowledged among the Dutch. The provinces of Friesland, Zealand, Utrecht, Guelderland, and Groningen, rejected its decisions. England threw off the doctrines of Calvin, and embraced the doctrines of Arminius. The French Protestants, finding the decisions of the synod extremely offensive to the catholics, from whom they were suffering the greatest indignities, were afraid publicly to approve of them, lest they should bring upon themselves new suffering, and gradually relaxed from the Gomarists.

The doctors of Saumur and Sedan advanced sentiments conformable to the Lutherans. John Cameron and Moses Amyraut preached the doctrine of universal redemption. De La Place came forward with a denial of the imputation of Adam's sin. Claude, Pajon, and Papin exalted the powers of human nature, rendering unnecessary the operations of the Spirit of God. By these, and other bold spirits, they were led in the course of this century to depart far from the sentiments of Calvin, and before the revocation of the edict of Nantez, the body of French Protestants had become Arminians.

The Swiss churches were seriously affected by the relaxed doctrines of the French. The academy at Geneva retained its high character for near half a century, and was the resort of students from all parts of Europe; and the churches long remained firm in the faith of the distinguished man who had so highly elevated them. But some of the pastors imbibed the principles of Amyraut and De La Place, and Geneva was numbered among the Arminians. Alarmed at the progress of the new opinions, an assembly of divines appointed John Henry Heidegger, professor of divinity at Zurich, in 1675, to construct a system of doctrine, and to add to it the other confessions of the Helvetic church. The whole was called the FORM OF CONCORD. But it occasioned great tumult, for in the next century it was imposed by the magistrates of Berne upon all professors and pastors as a rule of faith, and violently resisted, until it was abrogated. Since 1705, candidates for the ministry have been admitted upon a general declaration of faith in the Scriptures.

The Dutch Calvinists flattered themselves that they should have much peace and prosperity after the expulsion of the Arminians, but they found themselves involved in new troubles, not only with them upon their restoration, but from intestine disputes upon various points of doctrine and practice, which, for a whole century, continued to distract the United Provinces. The most important factions were the *Cocceians* and the *Voetians*. John Cocceius, Professor of divinity in the University ef Leyden, neglecting the natural and simple interpretation of Calvin, was disposed to understand the words and phrases of Scripture in every sense of which they are susceptible, and viewed the whole of the Old Testament as a mirror, in which may clearly be seen the New Testament dispensation; and every thing relating to Christ and his Apostles as types or images of future events. He considered the ten commandments not as a rule of obedience, but as a representation of the covenant of grace. With him united Des Cartes, the most famous philosopher of that period; whose leading principles were, that the man who would be a philosopher must begin his inquiries by doubting all things, even the existence of God; that the nature or essence of spirit, and even of God himself, consists in thought; that space has no real existence, is no more than the creature of fancy, and that consequently matter is without bounds. The Cocceians and Cartesians united for the purpose of delivering the theology of the day from the endless divisions and subdivisions of the peripatetical philosophy.

Their attempts met with opposition in 1639 from Voet, a theological instructor at Utrecht. He was supported by Rivet, Des Marets, Maestricht, and the greatest part of the Dutch clergy, who resolved in a public assembly to admit no one into the ministry who favored the Cartesian philosophy. The states of Holland also issued an edict, forbidding the professors to teach it in schools. But opposition rather aided than retarded the Cocceians and Cartesians. The contests between the contending parties were very violent for many years.

Other controversies arose out of attempts to simplify religion by the Cartesian philosophy, which for years agitated the United Provinces and Germany. At one time the churches were rent by a dispute on the authority of reason in matters of religion. At another on the proper generation of the Son of God, on divine decrees, original sin, and the satisfaction of Christ. Bewitched by the Cartesian philosophy, Balthazer Becher, minister of Amsterdam, got persuaded that mind could not act upon matter, unless united with it as was the soul to the body, and denied the scriptural account of the influence of the devil over mankind, and published in 1691 a work of immense labor, entitled *The World Bewitched*, which, for a time, encountered much opposition. There arose, also, about the same time, the *Verschorists* and the *Huttemists*, who perverted the doctrine of divine decrees to fatal necessity.

The Cartesian philosophy gave place to the Newtonian, and with it gradually died many of these contentions. Few new subjects of controversy engrossed the attention of the Dutch or Swiss churches in the eighteenth century. The Dutch enjoyed for some time after the revocation of the edict of Nantez, the labors of many able French divines. But these churches gradually declined, became lukewarm, and suffered with the rest of continental Europe exceedingly, from French infidelity, and the horrid wars of revolutionary France. There is in them, however, now, much of the life and power of religion.

Many of the Calvinistic churches in Germany have fallen a prey to Liberalism ; though some few remain steadfast, and Storr and others have so nobly vindicated their faith that their prospects are brightening. In some of the Swiss cantons a precious seed has remained to serve the Lord, but long since the Genevan churches degenerated from Calvinism to Arminianism, and through the poisonous infection of Rosseau and Voltaire, have now descended to the lowest degrees of Socinianism. Recent attempts to preach the doctrines of Calvin have met there with bitter persecution. The efforts of the British and Foreign Bible Society have been felt throughout

Switzerland and Germany. In Prussia the prospect is great, that not a child will hereafter grow up in ignorance of the Scriptures. The catholics are active to regain their former possessions, and their activity has compelled the reformed and Lutherans to union. The age of frivolity and arrogant philosophy seems fast passing away. The public mind is turning rapidly, in the middle and north of Europe, to serious subjects—to something which will satisfy conscience, and bring peace and consolation to ruined man.

The Protestants who have remained in France, since the revocation of the edict of Nantez, have lived in great seclusion. Their worship was interdicted by Lewis XIV.; their marriages were declared illegal, and oppression in every form laid them in the dust. From his death to the revolution, they met with milder treatment. Then every man was left to his own religion. They now number about a million and a half. For the last four years they have been rapidly increasing, especially in the south of France. Near Lyons, a number of villages have become Protestant, and some hundreds have professed to be the subjects of renewing grace. The constitution of the reformed church is Presbyterian. It is divided into 89 consistories. The Lutherans are chiefly in the north of France.

Where there is a population of a thousand, the pastors are supported by government; 295 Calvinistic, and 220 Lutheran pastors are now thus partially paid. Many others there are, who receive no pay from this source, because the population is insufficient. A handsome sum has recently been granted by government for their colleges, and the repair of their churches; 6000 members form a consistorial church.

A warm missionary spirit has lately been excited among them. The monthly concert is extensively observed, and Sabbath schools have been established. A Bible, Tract, and Missionary Society have been formed at Paris.

A remnant of the Waldenses is to be found in the valleys of Piedmont. They remain truly Protestant; but they are exceedingly oppressed by the catholics, being excluded from the military and civil employments, and the learned professions, and compelled to observe the festivals of the papists, and to abstain from work on the festival days. They number 13 parishes, comprising 13 pastors and a population of 18,000. Among them are not more than 1480 catholics.

It is remarkable and favorable, that, though the majority of the teachers and people in the reformed churches have departed far from their original standards of faith, yet those standards—the Helvetic Confession, the Heidelberg Catechism, the decisions of the Synod of Dort, and the thirty-nine articles, remain unaltered as their professed creeds.

The Calvinists have held the first rank in sacred literature. The Genevan Academy sent out a large number of able theologians. The greatness of Calvin has ever been felt and acknowledged by all his foes. Beza, as a scholar, was not much his inferior. Others who associated with them and succeeded them, shone with distinguished brightness. Oecolampadius, Bullinger, Farel, Viret, Hospinion, in the sixteenth, and the two Buxtorfs and Turrentin, in Switzerland; Gomer, Cocceius, Voet, Spanhem, De Maestricht, in Holland; Du Moullin, Daille, Claude, Basnage, Saurin, in France, in the seventeenth century; besides those in England, Scotland, and America, who will pass before us in the history of those churches.

In holiness, spirituality, purity of morals, zeal in the cause of Christ and salvation of men, the Calvinists have been surpassed by none.

ARMINIANS.

The Arminians were distinguished by their peculiar views of the five points of Calvinism. In relation to these, they believed,

I. That God, from eternity, determined to bestow salvation on those who, he foresaw, would persevere unto the end, and to inflict everlasting punishment on those who should continue in their unbelief, and resist his divine succors; so that election and reprobation are conditional.

II. That Jesus Christ, by his sufferings and death, made an atonement for the sins of all mankind, and of every individual in particular; that, however, none but those who believe in him, can be partakers of his benefits.

III. That mankind are not totally depraved, and that depravity does not come upon them by virtue of Adam's being their federal head.

IV. That the grace of God, which converts men, is not irresistible.

V. That those who are united to Christ by faith may fall from a state of grace, and finally perish.

Arminius was a pupil of Calvin, and for many years

preached his sentiments. He did not avow this creed until he had attained to the professorship of divinity at Leyden. He died in 1609, before it had much engaged the attention of the Christian world;—leaving a great reputation among his followers for penetration and piety.

After the decision of the Synod of Dort, the Arminians were treated by Maurice, prince of Holland, with great severity. Barneveldt, their most distinguished civilian, was beheaded on a scaffold. Grotius, one of the most learned men in Europe, who advocated their system, was condemned to perpetual imprisonment; but he fled, and found refuge in France. Many retired to Antwerp. A colony accepted an invitation of Frederic, duke of Holstein, and settled in his dominions, and built a town which they called Fredericstadt. Political artifice was the basis of all this religious persecution.

After the death of prince Maurice, in 1625, the Arminians were recalled from exile, and treated with great lenity and kindness. They erected churches and founded a college at Amsterdam. Episcopus, their chief advocate, was appointed their first theological professor. They soon numbered in the United Provinces, 34 congregations, and 48 pastors. The Church of England became inclined to their sentiments, through the influence of archbishop Laud, so that they number in their train some of her most distinguished prelates. A considerable portion of the Episcopal church in America, also the Wesleyan Methodists, and many Congregationalists of the last century, in New England, embraced their system.

Some of their principal writers have been, Arminius, Episcopus, Vorstius, Grotius, Limborch, Le Clerc, Wetstein, Whitby, Taylor, Fletcher. Le Clerc wrote a commentary on the Bible ; Wetstein on the New Testament.

CHAPTER XVII.

Imperfect character of the reformation in England. Cranmer made Archbishop of Canterbury. Bible translated and given to the people. Monasteries suppressed. Relics ridiculed. Catholic Rebellion. Henry VIII. excommunicated. His death. Excellent reign of Edward VI. Liturgy and articles introduced. Reign of Mary. Popish persecution. Martyrdom of John Rogers, Saunders, Hooper, Taylor, Bradford, Ridley, and Latimer. Cranmer. Darkness and distress of the period. Death of Mary and accession of Elizabeth. Restoration of the Protestants. Establishment of the English church.

The reformation in England, being little besides a transfer of supreme power from the Pope to the king, left the nation still groaning under the monstrous corruptions of popery; so that the history of this church presents a long and hard struggle between such as wished for a thorough reform, and the friends of the papacy. Henry VIII. was a monarch of violent passions. He had broken from the Pope; but he was determined to be Pope in his own dominions, and, whether right or wrong, would be obeyed. Fortunately for the cause of truth, he elevated to the See of Canterbury, Thomas Cranmer, a man of great learning and sound judgment, of a calm temper and an honest heart; whose mind rapidly opened to the doctrines of the Bible, and which, for many years, he most ably defended.

The language of Wickliff's version of the New Testament, which had been made one hundred and fifty years antecedent to this period, had become obsolete; and it was moreover a prohibited book, so that the nation were really without the Scriptures. But one William Tyndall, impressed with the immense importance of a free circulation of the Bible, in the language of the day, retired, for security, to the continent, where he translated the New Testament into English. An edition was printed at Antwerp, with short comments, and sent to England, for distribution, in 1526.* But its circulation

---

* This was the first time the Scriptures were ever printed in English "Cardinal Wolsey declaimed against the art of printing as that which would take down the honor and profit of the priesthood, by making the people as wise as they."—*Baxter.*

When the Greek and Hebrew originals were first printed, the monks declared from the pulpits, (such was the gross ignorance of the age,) "that there was a new language discovered, called Greek, of which the people should beware, since it produced all heresies, that in this language was come forth a book called the New Testament, which was now in every body's hands, and which was full of thorns and briers. And there had also now another language started up, which they called Hebrew, and that they who learned it were termed Hebrews."

was violently opposed by the papists, and prohibited by the bishops as infected with heresy; and Tonstel, bishop of London, had the edition privately purchased and publicly burnt at Cheapside. This event was far from being unfavorable; for with the money for which Tyndall sold his books, he was enabled to print, in 1534, a more correct version; and the very act of conflagration, excited great displeasure, and a spirit for reading the Scriptures, which nothing could suppress. Many who dispersed this hated book, and many who preached and avowed its doctrines, were brought before the bishop's courts, and condemned to the flames. Tyndall himself was villainously betrayed at Brussels; and first strangled at the stake and then burnt. He expired, praying, "Lord, open the king of England's eyes."

Cranmer, assisted by the new queen, Ann Boleyn, endeavored to stop the persecutions in England; but the king had written in defence of the Romish faith, and had too much pride to renounce his opinions, and was violently pressed to what he still believed to be duty, by the Duke of Norfolk, Gardiner, bishop of Winchester, and the greater part of the clergy.

Convinced that there could be no reformation without the Scriptures, Cranmer prevailed upon the king, in 1534, to order a translation of the Bible by some learned men, which should be printed and put into the hands of the people. It was a great point gained. The work was committed to nine eminent scholars; and when finished, was sent to Paris to be printed. The next year, Miles Coverdale, an associate of Tyndall, printed at Zurich the whole Bible in English; which immediately received the royal sanction, and was placed, by the king's orders, in every parish church in the kingdom. Cranmer's Bible was no sooner printed, than it was seized by the inquisitors and committed to the flames. The printers fled to London with the presses, and a few copies that were saved, where it was re-printed and offered by royal decree for sale to all the king's subjects. But so small was the number of the people that could read, that the edition of only 600 copies was not wholly sold off in three years.

The royal decree exceedingly grieved the papal clergy; but the people received the Bible with great joy. Multitudes continually flocked to the churches to hear portions of the Scriptures from those who could read.* Cranmer's heart was

---

* From one William Maldon, we have this lively picture of the times He mentions " that when the king had allowed the Bible to be set forth

filled with gladness at this "day of reformation," which he concluded was now risen in England since the light of God's word did shine over it without a cloud.

The next thing to which Cranmer directed his attention, was the suppression of the monasteries. These gave law to the learning and religion of the nation ; and while they remained, ignorance and superstition would brood over the land. Henry at once coincided with the views of Cranmer, as the monks were all his enemies, and would not acknowledge his supremacy, and he could fill his empty coffers from their vast funds. In 1535, commenced their visitation ; the object of which was to expose their iniquities. They were required to acknowledge the king's supremacy, and to pursue a holy course. In both they were condemned. Indeed their vices are not to be named. 375 of the lesser convents were dissolved. Henry acquired 10,000*l.* in plate and moveables, and a clear yearly revenue of 30,000*l.*; above 10,000 persons were cast upon the world. Pleased with the result, the profligate monarch proceeded to lay hands on the large religious houses ; the people being quieted with the declaration, that they would never again be burdened with taxes, for the revenue obtained would support 40 earls, 60 barons, 8000 knights, and 40,000 soldiers ; make provision for the poor, and support the preachers of the Gospel. All this might have been done, so immensely rich had the monks become, but Henry squandered the money among his favorites.

In the suppression of the monasteries, their relics were all brought forth, and made the objects of ridicule and scorn. Abominable frauds were exposed. A vial which was said to contain our Saviour's blood, which could be seen only by the righteous, and which had long been venerated, was exhibited

---

be read in the churches, immediately several poor men in the town of Chelmsford, in Essex, where his father lived, bought the New Testament; and on Sundays sat reading it in the lower end of the church. Many would flock about them to hear their reading ; and he, among the rest, being then but fifteen years old, came every Sunday to hear the glad and sweet tidings of the Gospel. But his father, observing it once, angrily fetched him away, and would have him say the Latin matins with him, which grieved him much. And as he returned at other times to hear the Scriptures read, his father still would fetch him away. This put him upon the thought of learning to read English, that he might read the New Testament himself, which, when he had by diligence effected, he and his father's apprentice bought a New Testament, joined their stocks together, and to conceal it, laid it under the bed of straw, and read it at convenient times."
—*Townley.*

and found to be thick and opaque on the side held to sinners, and transparent on the opposite. An image which has been a favorite object of pilgrimage, because it moved its head and feet, was taken to pieces, and its mechanism was exposed to the people in church, by the bishop of Rochester. The shrine of Becket was the most profitable in England. It received annually over 1000*l*. An immense sum at that age. Henry unsainted and unshrined him, and ordered his name to be struck from the calender and his bones to be burnt.

The Pope could not now restrain his anger. Henry was excommunicated, and his kingdom laid under an interdict; but the days of John were passed away. Henry regarded it as the idle wind.

A rebellion broke out among the papists in England. A hundred thousand collected in Yorkshire, under one Aske, and called their march the pilgrimage of grace. This encouraged risings in other parts of the country. But they were suppressed by the royal armies.

The king had filled his coffers by exterminating monasteries, relics, and images,—but he adhered rigorously to transubstantiation, and committed to the flames such as denied it. In this, Cranmer, who had not as yet gained light, coincided with him. But in 1539, to his great grief, six popish articles, establishing transubstantiation, purgatory, the celibacy of priests and auricular confession, were enacted in Parliament, and the papal cause gained a temporary triumph. Five hundred persons were committed to prison, and numbers to the flames. Cranmer came near falling a sacrifice. The king suffered him to be summoned before the council to be tried for his life, but he had a secret affection for him, and he gave him his sealed ring to present to them, should they go to extremities. This alone saved him.

At this critical moment, Henry died, A. D. 1547, cursed by the papists and abhorred by the Protestants. He was succeeded by Edward VI.; a prince only nine years of age, but remarkably mature and eminently devoted to the service of God, and the cause of the reformation. He lived but six years from this time; but he did every thing that he was able to do in so short a period, for the deliverance of his dominions from the corruptions of popery, and to bring his subjects to the knowledge of the truth. His religious principles were Calvinistic. Geneva was acknowledged as a sister church, but he adhered to the Episcopal form which had been established. He had a liturgy prepared for the people, that prayers to the saints, and lying legends, might cease; articles of religion framed, corresponding to those of Calvin; all laws and canons requiring celibacy in the clergy, repealed; auricular confession abolished; and he invited eminent reformers from the continent, particularly Martyr, Bucer, Fagius and Ochinus, to reside in his dominions, that they might aid in enlightening his people. Farther he would have proceeded if he could. In his diary, he laments "that he could not restore the primitive discipline according to his heart's desire, because several of the bishops were unwilling to it."

In his reign the doctrine of transubstantiation was fully discussed, and renounced, by Cranmer, Ridley, and Latimer, the three principal reformers. But Cranmer still thought it right to burn for heretical opinions, and had Joan of Kent, a fanatical anabaptist, brought to the flames, though Edward signed the commission with tears, saying that the archbishop must answer for it. Van Paris, a Dutchman, was afterwards burnt for being an Arian.

The reformers made merciless destruction of the wealth of churches and monasteries, and in many cases exceedingly enriched themselves. The catholics rose in many parts of the country, and threatened the entire subversion of the government, but were subdued. They had a warm friend in Mary, the sister of the king, who contrived to have mass in her house, and was a rallying point to all who were friendly to the old religion.

This violent catholic succeeded her brother. It was a mysterious providence. Edward had willed the crown to the Lady Jane Grey, a Protestant; but Mary the lawful heir, was immediately received by the people. Her mind was superstitious and melancholy. She had always hated the reformed religion, and she was resolved to bring the nation back to the church of Rome.

On the 8th of August, 1553, king Edward was buried. Cranmer read the Protestant service; but he felt it to be the burial of the reformation. The catholics throughout the kingdom, set up their forms of worship without waiting for a repeal of the laws of king Edward. Bonner, Gardiner and others, who had formerly been removed from the bishoprics, were restored. All preaching was prohibited except such as received the queen's license. The reformers were driven with great insolence from their pulpits. All the marriages of the clergy were declared null, and their children were pronounced illegitimate. Gardiner, bishop of Winchester, a man who would have held the first rank among the Spanish inquisitors, was made lord chancellor. All the laws of king Edward relating to religion, were repealed; and the ancient service was re-established. The queen expressed her desire to the Pope that England might again be received as a faithful daughter of the church, and that Cardinal Pool might be sent from Rome with legatine power.

These various proceedings taught the reformers that they had nothing to expect but death, in its most horrid forms. Many of them fled into Scotland, Switzerland, and Germany. Cranmer was advised to escape, as it was supposed that he would be the first victim; but he refused, saying it ill became him to quit the station in which providence had placed him At an early period, he and Latimer were sent to the tower. He was greatly beloved, and it was feared by many, that violence toward him would arouse the people. But the queen and his relentless enemies were bent on his destruction. Gardiner, however, fearing that Pool would succeed him in office, protracted that event as long as possible.

To strengthen herself, Mary united in marriage with Philip, son of the Emperor Charles V., sent Elizabeth, her sister, afterward queen, to prison, and brought the lady Jane Grey to the block. Jane was an eminently pious woman, of whom the world was not worthy. She rejoiced, she said, at her "approaching end, since nothing could be to her more welcome than to be delivered from that valley of misery, into that heavenly throne to which she was to be advanced." She repeated the fifty-first psalm, laid her head upon the block, and said, " Lord Jesus, into thy hand I commend my spirit."

To give the papal cause the appearance of justice and moderation, a public disputation was held at Oxford, in the spring of 1554, between the leading divines on both sides. Three questions were discussed, viz.; whether the natural body of Christ was really in the sacrament? Whether any other substance remained besides the body and blood of Christ? Whether, in the mass, there was a propitiatory sacrifice for the dead and living? Cranmer, Ridley, and Latimer, spoke for the reformed with great boldness and power. But they were declared vanquished, required to

CHAPTER 17.] QUEEN MARY'S PERSECUTION.

subscribe to the popish faith, and on refusal, were pronounced obstinate heretics, and excluded from the church.

In the succeeding summer, the bishops performed their visitations, and saw that the catholic religion was fully established. Such priests as conformed, were anointed and clothed with priestly vestments. Above twelve thousand who refused, were ejected, and the most eminent were imprisoned. In November, sanguinary laws were passed in Parliament, and persecution began.

The first martyr was John Rogers. He had been a fellow laborer of Tyndall and Coverdale, in translating the Bible, and was now prebendary of St. Paul. He had a wife and ten children with whom he wished to speak, but was not permitted. He was burned at Smithfield, Feb. 4, 1555. His wife, with her ten children, one hanging at the breast, was a spectator of the scene.

The next was Lawrence Saunders. He was burnt at Coventry. He embraced the stake, exclaiming, " welcome, cross of Christ! welcome, everlasting life!" The third was Hooper, bishop of Gloucester, the most laborious and popular preacher of the day. He had once fled from the persecution of Henry to Zurich, but returned on the accession of Edward. He had there imbibed some presbyterian principles, and refused to be consecrated in the episcopal vestments; but finally conformed. When he left Zurich, he anticipated martyrdom. "The last news of all," said he to his friends, " I shall not be able to write, for there where I shall take most pains, there you shall hear of me burned to ashes." He was again advised to flee, but refused. When he and Rogers were brought out of prison for examination, the sheriff found it difficult to conduct them through the streets, so great was the press to see them. They were men greatly beloved and respected. That the effect might be the greater, he was sent to his own diocess to be burnt there. On the 9th of February, he was bound to the stake. The fire consumed him but slowly. One hand was seen to drop off before he expired. His last words were, " Lord Jesus, receive my spirit." An immense crowd of people were witnesses of the horrid scene. He was the great father of the puritans.

The same day, Dr. Rowland Taylor was burnt at Hadley; and in the month of March, a number of others were burnt at Smithfield. The effect of these dreadful scenes was very different from what the papists expected. Gardiner supposed that two or three burnings would extirpate Protestantism from England. But the blood of the martyrs was again the seed of the church. The reformers stood firm to their cause, and gloried in their sufferings for Christ. The nation became exasperated. Philip openly disavowed them, and they were stopped for a time.

The prisons were crowded with the ablest and best men of England, and were, in fact, the best Christian schools and churches. There religious instruction was constantly imparted, and prayer and praise were offered.

In the month of June, the business of burning re-commenced. The dead body of a robber who had on the scaffold uttered something true, was condemned and burnt. John Bradford, a preacher in London, was a distinguished victim. When in prison, a recantation was sent to him; and when he had heard it, he asked for his condemnation, pricked his hand and sprinkled upon the bill his blood, bidding them carry it to the bishop, and tell him he had already sealed it with his blood. "He endured the flame as a fresh gale of wind on a hot summer's day," and exclaimed in the fire, "straight is the way, and narrow is the gate that leadeth to salvation, and few there be that find it." Through the months of July, August, and September, numbers were burnt at several places. Six were burnt in one fire in Canterbury. On the 16th of October, two distinguished victims were sacrificed at Oxford, Ridley and Latimer. The former was one of the most able and learned of English reformers; the latter was a man of great simplicity of character, of wit and boldness, who by his preaching had done more than almost any man to expose the follies of popery, and sustain the truth. When he was burnt, he was 84 years of age. He had suffered much from the cold damps of his prison, and hard treatment, and had a very decrepid appearance. He came before the council, "hat in hand, with a handkerchief bound round his head, and over it a night cap or two, with a great cap, such as townsmen used in those days, with two broad flaps to button under the chin. His dress was a gown of Bristol frieze, old and threadbare, fastened round the body with a penny leathern girdle; his Testament was suspended from his girdle by a leathern string, and his spectacles without a case, were hanging from his neck upon his breast." Ridley wrote several valuable epistles to his friends and countrymen during his imprisonment, which still remain. After his condemnation he was publicly degraded from his office. They were led out together to the place of death, which was near Baliol College. They embraced each other, and knelt and prayed. A short sermon was preached to mock them. And when the fire was brought, the venerable old man said, "Be of good courage, master Ridley, and play the man. We shall this day light such a candle, by God's grace, in England, as I trust shall never be put out." Bags of gun powder were tied about their bodies to hasten their death. Latimer soon yielded to the flames, but Ridley suffered a tedious martyrdom.

No sooner was the vengeance of the odious Gardiner glutted with the death of these excellent men, than he was called to give up his account. His last words were, "I have sinned with Peter, but I have not wept with Peter." Bonner had already been active in the bloody work, and was ready to continue it. Three were burnt at one stake in Canterbury, in November, and on the 18th of December, Philpot, archdeacon of Westminster, suffered at Smithfield. "I will pay my vows," said this excellent man, "in thee, O Smithfield." Sixty-seven had this year been burnt for their attachment to the Protestant cause.

But the great object of the queen's vengeance still remained. This was Cranmer. No sooner had this great and good man discerned the course which was to be taken, than he settled all his private affairs, that he might be prepared for the worst. His confinement was long, and no means were spared to convert him to the Romish faith. On September 12th, 1525, commissioners were sent by the queen to Oxford, to try him. Cranmer defended himself with meekness and learning. He was commanded to appear before the Pope at Rome in eighty days. This he said he would do if the queen would send him. But it was done in mockery; and before the term expired, he was degraded from his office. Clothed with vestments of rags and canvass, with a mock mitre and pall, he was publicly exhibited. The utmost efforts were again made to induce him to recant; and alas! Peter like, he finally yielded, and set his hand to a paper, renouncing the principles of the reformation, and acknowledging the authority of the papal church. The catholics triumphed in his fall. But they had no idea of sparing his life. The queen could not forgive the man who advised to Henry's divorce from her mother. A writ was issued for burning, and he was brought to St. Marie's church and placed on a platform. Cole, provost of Eaton preached a sermon in which he announced that Cranmer was to die, and magnified his conversion as the work of God, and assured him of the salvation of his soul. Cranmer discovered great confusion, and frequently shed floods of tears. When Cole had finished, he bade him disclose his faith. Cranmer prayed and addressed the people; repeated the apostles' creed, and declared his faith in the holy Scriptures. He then turned to that which troubled his conscience more than any thing else, *his recantation*—declared it was drawn from him by the fear of death; had filled his soul with the deepest sorrow, and was most bitterly repented of; and that the hand which had done it should burn first in the fire. The papists were thrown into confusion, gnashed on him with their teeth, and drew him to the stake, where Ridley and Latimer had been burned. When the fire was kindling, he stretched forth his right hand to the flame, never moving it until it was burnt away. As the flames gathered around his body, he exclaimed often, "that unworthy hand—Lord Jesus, receive my spirit." Thus died one of the greatest promoters of the reformation, March 21st, 1556, in the 67th year of his age. But it was a martyrdom most injurious to the Romish cause. It was a direct breach of promise. The sympathy of thousands was awakened by his repentance, and his calm and patient endurance of torment.

For two years more, the persecution continued with unabated fury. Bonner scorned to burn men singly and drove them in companies to the stake. The bodies of Bucer and Fagius were dug up, and with their books, were publicly burnt. But the reformers increased. They assembled together secretly for consultation and prayer. They afforded relief to those in prison, and buried the bodies of such as died there and were cast out in disgrace.

At length, to extirpate the hated religion entirely, the king and queen resolved upon the introduction of the *Inquisition*, with all its horrors. But England was happily preserved from this by the death of Mary, on the 17th of November, 1558.

The Irish Protestants escaped her vengeance through a singular providence. Their number had become great, through the energetic proceedings of George Brown, whom Henry VIII. had created archbishop of Dublin, and Mary had resolved to extirpate them by flame. But while her messenger was on his way with the bloody commission, the wife of an inkeeper, hearing him say that he had a commission which would lash the Protestants of Ireland, and being friendly to them, contrived to steal away his commission, and put in its place a pack of cards. When the commissioner arrived in Dublin, he opened his commission in presence of the public authorities, and, to his confusion, found nothing but the cards; and before he could get a renewal of the commission, the queen was dead, and God's people escaped. Queen Elizabeth was so pleased with the tale that she conferred upon the woman forty pounds a year for life.

No one can contemplate this dark period of England's history without feelings of horror at its bloody scenes, and gratitude for the blessings we enjoy. Two hundred and eighty-eight persons, including twenty clergymen, of whom five were bishops, were burnt alive; many were deprived of means of subsistence, imprisoned, tortured, scourged, placed in the most painful posture, until they expired under their accumulated sufferings. An immense amount of wealth was sacrificed, and the spirit and character of the nation was sunk very low. But it was a fiery trial, through which it seemed necessary for the nation to pass. She had given strength to the beast. Though reformed under Henry and Edward, she had not been weaned. This day of persecution made her heartily sick of popery. No one mourned the death of Mary. Every one hailed the accession of Elizabeth and the restoration of the Protestant religion.

Elizabeth had been singularly preserved from the merciless fangs of Gardiner and Bonner. She began to reign at the age of twenty-four, and governed England forty-five years, with an energy, sagacity, and prudence, of which few monarchs can boast. During her reign, Protestantism was firmly established in her dominions, and favored and supported by her in other parts of Europe.

On her way to London she was greeted by thousands, and as the bishops and clergy came around her to congratulate her, she smiled upon all, except Bonner, from whom she turned in indignation, as a man of blood. At her coronation, as she passed under a triumphal arch, an English Bible was let down into her hands, by a child representing truth, which she received with reverence, accounting it the most valuable gift that could be bestowed.

No sooner was her accession known, than all who had fled into foreign countries returned. The papists had flattered themselves that they had at least extinguished the light of the reformation; but, to their astonishment, a great body of learned and pious men came forth, who in exile or concealment, had made themselves well acquainted with the word of God. Elizabeth filled the vacant Sees with Parker, Grindall, Cox, Sands, Jewel, Parkhurst, Pilkington, and others, who proved great ornaments to the British nation. She re-established King Edward's service in all the churches, and forbade the priests to elevate the host at mass, but she would use no violence. Such papists as chose, she permitted to retire beyond the seas. Such as retired from the priest's office, she pensioned. Of these, the number was small; the papists thinking it better for their own cause to acknowledge the queen's supremacy, than refuse and quit the kingdom. Out of nine thousand and four hundred beneficed men, only fourteen bishops and one hundred and seventy-five others resigned their livings. The others remained in the church, "a miserable set of weather-cocks." The monks returned to secular life, and the nuns went to France and Spain. Bonner maintained his sullen temper, refused to submit to the queen, was committed to prison, where he died. Elizabeth was in favor of images in the churches, but so did the clergy oppose them, that she gave orders to have them all taken down. The Bible was translated anew, and published in 1571. The articles of religion received by king Edward, were revised and adopted, leaving the doctrine of the real presence untouched, and the English establishment was settled nearly upon its present form.

CHAPTER XVIII.

Troubles in the English church. Efforts of the papists to regain their lost dominion. Rise of the puritans. Acts of supremacy and uniformity. Demands of the puritans. Persecutions of the High Commission Court. The puritans separate from the establishment. Their character and principles. Conference at Hampton Court, and oppression under James I. Popish powder plot. King James' translation of the Bible. Persecutions by Laud, and overthrow of Episcopacy. Assembly of divines at Westminster. Irish massacre. Triumph of the puritans. Restoration of monarchy and Episcopacy. Severities towards the nonconformists. Efforts of infidelity. New efforts of the papists Revolution. Rise of two parties, high and low church. Bangorian controversy. Deists. Great excitement from the Methodists. Effects of the French revolution. Present state of parties. Discipline and doctrine of the church of England. Distinguished divines.

ALTHOUGH the church of England seemed, at the accession of Elizabeth, to be firmly re-established, yet she soon met with severe trials. The catholics employed every measure that human ingenuity could devise, to regain their

CHAPTER 18.]   CHURCH OF ENGLAND.   341

lost dominion. The Pope first addressed a conciliatory letter to the Queen, inviting her to the bosom of the church: and finding this in vain, excommunicated her, and absolved all her subjects from their oath of allegiance. Conspiracies were formed to set Mary, Queen of Scots, upon the throne. Elizabeth was represented as a monster of cruelty. The ladies about her were exhorted by the Jesuits to assassinate her. And finally, the whole power of Spain was brought against the kingdom. Philip, with an immense force called the Spanish Armada, came into the British Channel, with the design of taking the throne, re-establishing popery, enforcing it by all the horrors of the inquisition, and sending Elizabeth to Rome, to be treated by the Pope as he pleased. But the Armada was scattered by tempests, and the design was confounded.

Other troubles arose in her own bosom. Among the fugitives from Mary's persecution, some who took refuge at Frankfort in Germany, became attached to the Genevian forms of worship and discipline, and showed a determination to renounce entirely all the peculiar usages of the church of Rome which had been retained from politic motives, and form their practice according to the Presbyterian mode. They laid aside King Edward's service, the surplice and the responses of the liturgy. And because they considered their new worship as purer or more scriptural than their old, they were, in ridicule, called PURITANS. In the steps they had taken, they met with violent opposition from many of their brethren. Dr. Cox, who had been tutor to King Edward, disturbed their worship by answering aloud after the minister, and accused the celebrated John Knox, who was then pastor of these exiles, of enmity to the Emperor. Knox and his friends were driven from the city, and the Episcopal forms were re-established. But the Puritans received great support from the church at Geneva, and increased rapidly in numbers; and when, upon the accession of Elizabeth, they returned to their native country, it was not without strong hope that they should bring over the nation, now sick of every thing appertaining to Popery, to their views and practices. But Elizabeth was more of a papist than puritan. With her was lodged absolute power. The Parliament early passed an ACT OF SUPREMACY vesting in the crown the supreme power of all matters ecclesiastical and spiritual; giving the Queen the power to " repress all heresies, establish or repeal all canons, alter every point of discipline, and ordain or abolish any religious rite or ceremony."* They also passed an act, June 24, 1559, called the ACT OF UNIFORMITY, by which the nation was bound to submit to the liturgy and observe all the rites, ceremonies, holidays, forms, and habits of the church. The door was at once closed by this act against any reconciliation; and the more they contemplated the church service, the farther did the puritans remove from a spirit of submission.

At first they objected merely to the Episcopal vestments, the square cap, the tippet, and the surplice, which they called "conjuring garments of popery," but they soon insisted upon a parity among all the ministers of Christ, and the validity of ordination conferred by ordinary ministers as well as by bishops; they demanded the abolition of archdeacons, deans canons, and other officers not known in Scripture; refused the admission of any to communion who did not give good evidence of personal piety; denounced festivals and holidays in honor of saints; the sign of the cross, and the use of godfathers and godmothers, to the exclusion of parents, in the baptism of children; kneeling at the sacrament; bowing at the name of Jesus; confirmation of children; and prohibition of marriage at certain seasons of the year;—in a word, every custom which had been derived from the church of Rome. They also refused to acknowledge that which the bishops considered of vital importance to them, that the church of Rome was a *true* church. They looked upon the Pope as antichrist, and its whole system of doctrine and discipline as diametrically opposite to the spirit of Christianity.

The church party pleaded that the forms of religion were to be regulated by the civil government; but the puritans maintained that the power of the magistracy did not extend to these things, and if it did, that it was wrong to impose things as indispensable which were not found in Scripture, especially things that had a tendency to subject the nation again to popery. But good reasoning could avail but little at that period. The Queen availed herself of an expression in the Act of Supremacy, to establish a HIGH COMMISSION COURT, whose jurisdiction should extend over the whole kingdom, and which should be empowered to make inquiry into all offences against the ecclesiastical laws, not only by the common method of juries and witnesses, but by all other ways which

---

* Hume.

would effect their purpose. At the head of this court was the Archbishop of Canterbury. The first who was exalted by the Queen to this place was Parker, a violent opposer of the puritans. From him they received no mercy. Soon as it was known that some of the puritans officiated without the priestly garments, the London clergy were summoned before the Commission Court. The bishop's chancellor thus addressed them : " My masters, and ye ministers of London, the council's pleasure is, that ye strictly keep the unity of apparel like this man, (pointing to a Mr. Cole in uniform,) with a square cap, a scholar's gown priest-like, a tippet, and in the church a linen surplice; ye that will subscribe, write *volo*, those who will not, write *nolo*." Some attempted to remonstrate, but were silenced. Sixty-one out of a hundred subscribed to conformity, declaring it, however, against their consciences, thirty-seven chose rather to cast themselves for support upon divine providence. Persecution was now violent. A fourth part of the ministers of England were suspended. Many churches were shut up. Loathsome prisons were crowded. Heavy fines and penalties were imposed. Some worshipped God in private houses with great secrecy, but they were hunted out by the bishop's spies and informers and violently proceeded against. At length several puritans were executed, and vast multitudes were driven from their homes in great indigence to foreign countries.

Thus oppressed, and seeing no prospect of better things in the established church, a number of the puritans solemnly resolved in 1556, *" to break off from the public churches and to assemble as they had opportunity, in private houses, or elsewhere, to worship God in a manner that might not offend against the light of their consciences."* Though destitute, afflicted, tormented, they formed no small part of the nation. On a great question in Parliament, relating to alterations in their favor, there were only fifty-nine against, while fifty-eight were for them. The University of Cambridge was strong in their favor, and constantly sent out preachers, who were opposed to all prelatical usurpations. Many, too, were their friends and patrons among the nobility. But the Queen was violent in her opposition, and her unrivalled popularity enabled her to carry all her measures. She loved the pomp and splendor of the church, and she feared the spirit of liberty which she saw rising in the breast of the puritans.

Archbishop Parker died in 1575, and was succeeded by

Archbishop Grindall, who was disposed to treat the puritans with mildness. In 1583 the primacy was filled by Whitgift, who executed the laws for uniformity with the greatest rigor. Through his agency the High Commissioner Court was newly organized and became a real inquisition. In his first citation, this archbishop caused two hundred and thirty-three ministers to be suspended in his district for nonconformity. So many were at length suspended, fined, and imprisoned, that there remainded only about 3000 licensed preachers to supply 9000 parishes.

Elizabeth died March 24, 1603, in the 70th year of her age, and 40th of her reign. Amidst all the contentions for forms and ceremonies during her reign, the state of religion must have been very low. The mass of the people received but very little religious instruction. To fill the places of expelled puritans, the bishops made priests from the basest of the people. The court party ridiculed all as puritans who went twice to a place of worship on the Lord's day and spent the evening in worship or religious instruction. At one period the more zealous clergy established private religious meetings, which were called *prophesyings*, but they were totally suppressed by Archbishop Whitgift. Reverence for the Sabbath, however, gradually increased. The papists had reduced this holy day to a level with their superstitious festivals. But the morality of the day was now publicly insisted on among the English Protestants, and in 1585 a bill passed in Parliament in its favor. It was, however, rejected by the Queen, and many of her favorite clergy exclaimed against it as a restraint of Christain liberty, and eclipsing the festivals of the church. The puritans, however, and many of the church party, observed it better than it had been for ages before. In doctrine, the Episcopal church had generally been decidedly and fully Calvinistic, but in the latter part of Elizabeth's reign, the system of Arminius began to find there many advocates.

The authors of this great dissension from the English establishment, were men of excellent character, who had rendered the protestant cause the most signal services, and endured in its support the severest sufferings. One was Coverdale who was united with William Tyndall, and John Rogers, the martyr, in making the first translation of the whole Bible into English. He was silenced at the age of eighty, for nonconformity. John Fox, historian of the English martyrdoms, was another. Their sentiments were expressed in the 39 articles of the church of England, and "these," says Neal, their great historian, "they maintained to be Calvinistical and inconsistent with any other interpretation, and so did the greatest number of the conforming clergy, but as the new explication of Arminius grew into repute, the Calvinists were reckoned old fashioned divines, and at length branded with the name of doctrinal puritans." They formed on the continent an attachment to the discipline of Geneva, but they would have been satisfied with an exemption from some of the habits and ceremonies of the establishment. As oppression increased, some presented a petition to Parliament for an entire reform, and the establishment of a Presbyterian church. These, for their boldness, were committed to Newgate, 1572. This event resulted in the establishment of a regular Presbyterian church at Wandsworth, on the 20th of November of that year. Other Presbyterian churches were established during Elizabeth's reign in most parts of England, and before her death it was computed that there were in the realm about 100,000 Presbyterians. But very many of their most learned ministers and best people were driven from the country.

In 1581, a sect was formed among the puritans, by Robert Brown, and took refuge in Holland, called the Brownists. This man not only denied the church of England as a true church, but rejected Presbyterianism, and plead for Independency. He considered every Church as independent of all other churches; and pastors only as brethren privileged for a limited time to preach, and not as a superior order; and he renounced communion not only with the Episcopalians, but with the Presbyterians. The first church of Brownists was formed at London, 1592. The Brownists were much oppressed as intolerable bigots and fanatics. Brown was confined in thirty-two prisons, but before he died, he conformed to the establishment. His adherents were numerous. "I am afraid," said Sir Walter Raleigh, " there are near twenty thousand of these men; and when they are driven out of the kingdom, who shall support their wives and children ?"

Their order was improved by Mr. John Robinson, pastor of a church of Brownists in the north of England—a man of much learning and piety. From his establishment, all who followed him were called Independents; though they did not differ materially from the Brownists. Both these churches were driven by oppression into Holland, where they established themselves at Amsterdam and Leyden. A part of Mr. Robinson's church removed to New England in 1662, and settled Plymouth. The first independent church in England was formed in 1610, by Mr. Henry Jacob.

Elizabeth was succeeded by James VI., king of Scotland, who now assumed the name of James I. At his accession, the hopes of the puritans were greatly revived, for he had been educated a Scotch Presbyterian, and had said, " I thank God that I am king of the sincerest kirk in the world, sincerer than the kirk of England, whose service is an ill said mass in English, it wants nothing of the mass but the liftings," meaning the elevation of the host. On his way to London, the puritans met him, and presented him a petition called the *millenary*, because it contained the wishes of a thousand ministers. But the Episcopalians, alarmed, frowned and courted the monarch. To quiet the parties, James appointed a conference of divines at Hampton court. The disputants were appointed by the King. He had already at heart taken sides with the Episcopalians, and he showed his feelings by appointing eight bishops, and as many deacons on the one side, and only four puritans on the other. James acted as moderator, though he did little but browbeat the puritans; for, finding that puritanism was unfriendly to monarchy, he became its inveterate foe; avowing the maxim, no bishop, no king. He also renounced Calvinism, it being too puritanical, and went over with his court and bishops to the principles of Arminius. not altering, but giving an Arminian interpretation to the thirty-nine articles. He also published a declaration encouraging sports on the Lord's day, as the puritans insisted upon its sacred observance; and had a book of sports drawn up by Bishop Moreton, recommending dancing, archery, leaping, vaulting, May-games, Whitson ales, morrice games, or setting up of May-poles, and carrying rushes into the churches, &c. But of these neither papist nor puritan was to have the benefit.

Under King James, Bancroft became Archbishop of Canterbury. He brought himself into notice by asserting, in a sermon, that those only who were episcopally ordained were regular ministers. Advanced to power, he caused the puritans to feel terribly the rigor of the ecclesiastical laws. Every nonconformist was ejected from the pulpit, and every layman favoring nonconformity, was excommunicated from the church. Such persecution could no longer be borne

Many Puritan families left their native soil, and emigrated to New England and Virginia. Others were preparing to follow, but were forbidden by severe laws.

While James was thus persecuting the puritans, he and his court were threatened with a tremendous destruction from the catholics. Thirty-six barrels of gunpowder were concealed under the parliament house, with a design of blowing up the king, lords and commons, when assembled, and thus overthrowing entirely the Protestant cause. But this awful plot was happily discovered in season to prevent its execution. It occasioned new and severe measures against the catholics, and confirmed the puritans in their belief of the importance of relinquishing entirely the Romish forms and ceremonies.

In 1610, the furious Bancroft departed this life. He was succeeded by the mild and pacific Abbot, who was ever disposed to treat the puritans with lenity and kindness.

King James died, not without suspicion of poison, March 27th, 1625. One of the most important events of his reign was the formation of that translation of the sacred scriptures which is now in common use. Nine translations in English had been previously made: viz. Wickliff's New Testament in 1380; Tyndall's do. 1526—first edition of the Bible 1535; Matthew's Bible 1537; Cranmer's 1539; Geneva 1559, (the first that was printed with numerical verses,) Bishop's 1568; Rhenish Testament 1582; and Bible 1609, 1610 by the catholics. But the English language was continually changing, and many things existed in the above which were viewed as incorrect by the puritans, and they requested the king, at the Hampton court conference, to order a new translation. The king complied with their request, and appointed fifty-four of the chief divines of both universities to undertake the work, under the following regulations:—" That they keep as close as possible to the Bishop's Bible; that the names of the holy writers be retained according to vulgar use; that the old ecclesiastical words be kept, as church not to be translated congregation, &c., that the division of chapters be not altered, that when a word has divers significations, that be kept which has been most commonly used by the fathers; no marginal notes but for the explication of a Hebrew or Greek word marginal references may be set down." As some died after their appointment, only forty-seven engaged in the translation. These were divided into six companies. The first translated from Genesis to the first book of Chronicles; the second, to the prophecy of Isaiah; the third translated the four greater Prophets, with the Lamentations and twelve smaller Prophets; the fourth had the Apocrypha; the fifth had the four Gospels, the Acts and the Revelation, and the sixth, the Canonical Epistles. The whole being finished and revised by learned men from the two universities, was published by Bishop Wilson and Dr. Smith, with a dedication to king James, A. D. 1611.*

James was succeeded by his son, Charles I. This prince pursued the same policy as his father, and labored with the whole power of his kingdom to subject England, Scotland, and Ireland to his bishops, and to extirpate Puritanism and Calvinism. His primate and chief counsellor was archbishop Laud, a man who is said to have gone as far as he could go toward Rome without being a Papist, and who labored with all his might to bring the nation to receive Arminianism, and to submit to absolute despotism. But to Popery, Arminianism, and arbitrary power, the nation were hostile; and the king and archbishop found themselves involved in inextricable difficulties with Parliament. The king published a declaration like his father, encouraging sports on the Lord's day, and archbishop Laud introduced new and pompous ceremonies, that the English might be like the Gallican Church. The Lord's supper had been celebrated at a table in the midst of the house. This Laud removed, and placing an altar against the east wall, he fenced it round with a rail way. He required the people to pay great reverence on entering and leaving consecrated buildings, to bow to the altar.— Against all nonconformists, he exercised the most awful severities;† driving multitudes into exile. During twelve years of Laud's administration, four thousand emigrants passed to America. "The sun," said they, shines as pleasantly on

---

* The books of the Old and New Testaments were originally written without any division into chapters and verses. In the thirteenth century of the Christian era, Cardinal Hugo divided them into chapters for the purpose of forming a concordance. These chapters he subdivided into sections, to which he affixed the letters of the alphabet. In 1415, Nathan, a Jew, refined upon him, and divided the Old Testament into verses. These, however, were marked in no printed Bible, until 1661. But in 1551, Robert Stephens printed the New Testament, and divided it into verses which are now used. Though the division is in some respects useful, the Scriptures should always be read without any reference to it.

† One Dr. Leighton, a Puritan, was condemned in the Star Chamber, at Laud's instigation, for publishing an appeal to the Parliament against pre-

America as on England, and the sun of righteousness much more clearly. We are treated here in a manner which forfeits all claims upon our affection. The church of England has added to the ceremonies and habits of popery the only marks of antichrist which were wanting, corruption of doctrine and a bloody persecution of the saints. Let us remove whither the providence of God calls, and make that our country which will afford us what is dearer than property or life, the liberty of worshipping God in the way which appears to us most conducive to our eternal welfare."

Those that remained behind were far from being submissive. A spirit of religious liberty is not to be confined or suppressed. A sense of right, and a conviction of duty will disregard despotism, with its bars and bolts. The puritans felt that their cause was the cause of God. Their teachers were experimental, serious, learned, affectionate, and faithful. Their people were exemplary. In general they had no objection to royalty. They feared God and honored the king. But they detested hierarchy and the laws which required conformity to the episcopal rites. The severities of the High Commission Court, and the contumely and reproach of Laud, exasperated them to the highest degree. Their numbers greatly increased. Parliament and the sword of the nation passed into their hands. An assembly of divines was convened by parliament at Westminster, by whom a directory of worship was framed which superseded the prayer book, the famous Assembly's catechism was formed, and other acts were passed, destructive to the old establishment. Laud was accused of treason, and brought to the block. Episcopacy was abolished throughout the kingdom. Every thing dear to the church party was swept away. And the king himself, amazing to tell! expiated his attachment to unlimited civil and religious power on a scaffold, January 30, 1648.

lacy. When sentence was pronounced, the archbishop pulled off his cap and gave thanks. This is his own cool record of its execution: "Nov. 6. 1. He was severely whipped before he was set in the pillory. 2. Being set in the pillory, he had one of his ears cut off. 3. One side of his nose was slit up. 4. He was branded on the cheek with a red-hot iron, with the letters S. S. On that day, sen'night, his sores upon his back, ears, nose, and face, not being cured, he was whipped again at the pillory in Cheapside, cutting off the other ear, slitting the other side of his nose, and branding the other cheek." He was then imprisoned with peculiar severity for about eleven years, and when released by the Parliament, he could neither hear, see, nor walk.

Three weeks after the king's death the assembly of divines at Westminster was terminated. It had continued five years, seven months, and twenty-two days, and had had 1163 sessions. It was originally composed of ten lords, twenty commoners, and one hundred and twenty-one divines; seven only were independents. Ten of the episcopal divines who were appointed, attended, and such as did, soon withdrew, for the king, by his royal proclamation, had forbidden its convening. Richard Baxter, who knew most of them, says, those who transacted its business " were men of eminent learning, godliness, ministerial abilities, and fidelity."

The season of trouble in England was used by the Jesuits in Ireland to suppress the Protestants. Under the labors of Archbishop Usher, Bishop Babington, and others, these had flourished greatly. But the Jesuits infused into the minds of the catholics the most ferocious feelings towards them; and the moment when the troops were employed in the contest between the King and Parliament, they rose in mass, and with savage fury massacred above 200,000 Protestants. The day on which this awful scene was transacted was the 23d of October, 1641. The innocent objects of hellish rage rose from their beds in perfect ignorance of the dread design. Astonishment seized them as they beheld their nearest neighbors, with whom they had lived in friendly intercourse, approach them armed with the weapons of death; not to threaten and terrify, but deliberately to execute upon every age, sex, and condition, the most horrid assassinations. Pleas, resistance, flight, all were vain. If they escaped from one, the next catholic who met them was sure to knock out their brains or plunge a dagger in their bosom. As the power of the catholics increased, they delighted in inventing new modes of torture. Not only the weaker sex, but the very children entered into the measure, and plunged the knife into the breasts of their playmates, or the dead carcases of the massacred Protestants. Yea, the cattle of the Protestants were destroyed, as tainted by the religion of their owners, and their habitations levelled in the dust, as unfit to be occupied again by human beings. The province of Ulster, where they chiefly reeided, was nearly depopulated. Thus did they shed the blood of the saints. But in the year 1648, Cromwell subdued the catholics, and brought them into a subjection from which they have never been able to rise

The assembly of divines pulled down episcopacy without

preparing any thing as a substitute ; and the door being wide open, the country was inundated with a great variety of religious sects. In 1649, parliament declared presbyterianism the established religion of the country ; but they passed an ordinance abolishing all penal statutes for religion, and permitting every one to think and act as he pleased on the subject of religion. The Presbyterians became very lordly under their triumph, and would have established a system of religious tyranny if they could. For the principles of correct religious toleration were understood by none of that age. Every party insisted upon uniformity of worship, and upon the propriety of calling in the sword to support and enforce its own forms. They were, therefore, exceedingly grieved with this ordinance of Parliament, and still more by finding that Cromwell and the Parliament, who had grown jealous of them, now took under their patronage the Independents, and brought them up to be a large and important class of Christians.

The episcopal clergy, as might be expected, felt the heavy hand of oppression. The bishops were not only deprived of their dignities, but were, in many cases, abused : 7000 clergymen were ejected from their livings, but one fifth of the livings was reserved for the use of their suffering wives and children. Such as continued to officiate, conformed to the new establishment, but used as far as they could, the old forms of prayer, though they might not read the liturgy under severe penalties. Every thing peculiar to the old establishment, was broken down by the rude hand of violence A rage for uniformity prevailed among the Presbyterians, as much as it had in the old establishment, and painted windows, cathedral carvings, statues, organs, monuments, all, all were swept away by the besom of destruction.

As the revolution was professedly religious, every thing was done under the garb of religion. The most ambitious spirits, who could wade through seas of blood to obtain wealth and power, were found using the language of the children of God, and professing to wield the sword of Jehovah. Among all ranks was an unusual portion of religious knowledge. Prayer was the regular business of most families. The Lord's day was sacredly observed. The leading divines, Owen, Baxter, Manton, Goodwin, Howe, Poole, Bates, Flavel, have, perhaps, never been surpassed in solid learning, theological acumen, and popular eloquence. They were men who understood the Gospel, and who preached it with power. Under their preaching, thousands were convinced of sin, and converted to God. The general attention given to religion, may be learned fron the fact that the army under Cromwell, which went to subdue the catholics in Ireland, observed before their embarkation, a day of fasting and prayer. After three ministers had prayed, Cromwell and his colonels expounded scripture to the troops. Not an oath was to be heard throughout the whole camp; the soldiers spending their leisure hours in reading their Bibles, or singing psalms and religious conferences. Many, unquestionably, were held under restraint against their wills, but it was the spirit of the age that restrained them. The chaplains of the Protector, were some of the most able and faithful ministers of Jesus Christ. For his own personal religion, he stands or falls in the judgment, like the rest of men. What appear in him fanatical expressions, were the language of the day, common to him before he touched the sword of state. No man was more hated by the papists, or did more toward breaking down the spirit of superstition in England. He made provision of 10,000 pounds a year, to be used in the conversion of the heathen.

The triumph of the puritans was short. When Cromwell, their master spirit, was no more, every thing ran into confusion. The officers of the army wrested the sceptre, and in 1660 placed Charles II. upon the throne.

The tide now set as strong against the puritans, as it had before against the Episcopalians. They had hoped for better things, especially the Presbyterians, who had been active in recalling Charles, and who in fact were never much concerned in bringing his father to the block. But even their expectation perished. All the lavish promises of Charles toward them were soon forgotten. Episcopacy was fully re-established, and an observance of all its forms was most rigorously required. On St. Bartholomew's day, August 24, 1662, the act of uniformity was passed. It required every clergyman to take the following oath, on penalty of losing his cure, living or preferment.

"I, A. B., do hereby declare my unfeigned assent and consent, to all and every thing contained and prescribed in and by the book entitled the book of common prayer and administration of the sacraments, and other rites and ceremonies of the Church of England, together with the psalter or psalms of David, appointed as they are to be sung or said in churches, and the form and manner of making, ordaining, and consecra ting bishops, priests and deacons." Charles likewise decreed, that the ordination of all Presbyterians should be null and void; and that they should obtain Episcopal orders, before taking the above oath. Two thousand puritan ministers, some of them the ablest and best which ever adorned the Church of Christ, were thus at once ejected from their pulpits, and not only deprived of their ordinary support, but of the past year's remuneration, which became due shortly after.

They were moreover required to promise on oath, that they would not take arms against the king, or endeavor to effect any alteration in the church or state. If they refused, they were forever forbid coming within five miles of any city or borough where they had preached. An act called the conventicle act was also passed, forbidding any dissenters, above five in number, assembling for any other exercise in religion, than that prescribed in the liturgy of the church of England, on penalty of fine, imprisonment, or banishment.

Several denominations were at this time existing in the kingdom. Sixteen are mentioned by cotemporary writers. The Baptists and Quakers were most numerous next to the Presbyterians and Independents. All these were classed together under the general name of nonconformists, and the name of puritan was dropped. All felt the arm of oppression. The business of informers was made very lucrative. The prisons were quickly filled. The nonconformists were afraid to pray in their families, or ask a blessing on their meals, if five strangers were present. Their hardships were greater than those of the papists at the reformation, or the loyalists in the time of the civil wars. Such as could, fled to America, About 3000 died in prison, and not less than 60,000 found, in various ways, an untimely grave. Property was wrung from them to the amount of two millions sterling. In 1665, the English nation, which was daily exhibiting scenes of profligacy and oppression, was visited with the most tremendous judgments. A distressing drought, caused a murrain among the cattle. Infection was communicated to the city of London, and 100,000 people were swept off by the plague. Soon after, a large part of the city was burned to the ground. During the pestilence, the wealthy and independent inhabitants fled; some of the pulpits were deserted. Many, however, of the ejected ministers, occupied them, and visited and comforted the distressed, and were permitted to exercise their ministry without opposition. In 1672, the king granted a general declaration of indulgence, suspending the penal laws against dissenters; but the Presbyterians and Independents would have preferred further suffering, to having the Papists so greatly favored. About the same time also was passed the test act, making the Episcopal sacrament a qualification for civil offices and employments.

The churches were, at the restoration filled with their former incumbents, but the high church party were not popular with Charles, and men filled the high stations, who did not look upon Episcopacy as a divine institution, and absolutely essential, though they praised it as the best form of government and worship, and who viewed the points of controversy between Calvinists and Arminians, as of an indifferent nature, which with certain explanations, might be held, or be entirely cast away, without any spiritual detriment.

With a voluptuous monarch on the throne, and a latitudinarian clergy in the desk, vital piety rapidly declined. All who had before been unwillingly restrained by the powerful preaching of the nonconformists, now ran to the excess of wickedness, and delighted in nothing so much as reviling what they called the canting hypocrisy and fanaticism of the commonwealth. The nobles of England exchanged their sober, serious character, for one of frivolity and sin. A host of infidels, led by Hobbs, Toland, and the lords Rochester and Shaftsbury, made a bold attack, by ridicule and sophistry, upon Christianity. But the great luminaries of the age, Newton, Locke, Boyle, Tillotson, and Cudworth, threw all their influence into the opposite scale, and made them appear weak and contemptible, in the eyes of all discerning men. The excellent Robert Boyle instituted an annual course of lectures, in which the Gospel was, for a long time, most ably defended from the base and insidious attacks of these subtle enemies.

Religion continued in a state of astonishing fluctuation, and the nation soon found itself on the very point of subjection to the Roman See. Charles had been, from his exile, at heart a Papist, and would have betrayed the Protestant cause, had he dared to do it. He terminated his dissolute life, by receiving the sacrament from the hands of a popish priest, in 1684, and was succeeded by his brother, James II., a bigoted catholic.

The catholics had been closely watched in England, from

the discovery of the powder plot, but they were very numerous and powerful. In Ireland they formed the great bulk of the population. With a monarch of their own on the throne, they now felt their former dominion secured. James was not wanting in efforts to advance the cause. He filled vacant places with papists and others on whom he could rely for support. He new modeled the High Commission Court, made the infamous Jeffries one of its judges, and gave it unlimited power for searching out and punishing ecclesiastical offences. The dissenters suffered severely. The quarters of several hundred persons were seen hung up over the country. Finding opposition arise in the church, James hoped to gain the assistance of the dissenters, and courted them, and that they might be pleased, and the papists favored, he published a declaration suspending all penal laws on religion, abolishing all tests, and declaring all his subjects equally capable of employment in his service. This he required all the clergy to read from their pulpits. The Episcopalians refused. A general meeting of bishops and clergy was held in London, and a petition was framed beseeching the king not to insist upon it. It was signed by seven bishops who were soon committed to the Tower After a long trial at Westminster for rebellion they were acquitted. Only four in London read the declaration, and but about 200 in the kingdom. All the Protestants, now once more united, combined together, boldly dethroned their monarch, and forever excluded the papists from the crown. William, prince of Orange, son-in-law to James, was invited to take the throne. James saw his danger, and endeavored to quiet his disaffected subjects, but it was too late. William was received with open arms, and James fled to France.

This great event, which happened A. D. one thousand six hundred and eighty-eight, is called in English History, THE REVOLUTION. It firmly secured the liberty of the Protestants. The catholics were by a bill in Parliament forever excluded from holding any office in the nation. Episcopacy was established as the religion of the state. Free toleration was granted to all Protestant dissenters from the church of England, excepting Socinians. This is hailed by English Protestants as the most glorious epoch in their history.

From this event to the present time, the church of England has moved on with considerable uniformity, without any material alterations in her government and discipline.

Some trouble she early received from a few leading bishops, who were willing William should govern, but who refused to take the oath to him, because James was alive, and must remain until death their rightful sovereign. These were called non-jurors. They retired from their Sees into Scotland, and sunk into poverty and disgrace. Some also, from James and his party, who made a number of efforts to regain dominion.

William and Mary were invited to the throne by the most religious part of the nation, and they made early and resolute efforts to reform the morals of the people. In these they were supported by Burnet, bishop of Sarum, the famous author of the history of the reformation, and of an exposition of the thirty-nine articles. Numerous societies were formed throughout the kingdom for the suppression of vice of every description. Fifteen new bishops were constituted; Dr. Tillotson was made archbishop of Canterbury, and Dr. Sharp of York. Their learning was great, their conduct exemplary. They became preaching bishops; visited their dioceses with diligence; labored much for the instruction and reformation of the people; and produced what has been called "the golden age of Episcopacy."

The establishment became divided into two parties, the high church and the low church. The former contended for the divine right of Episcopacy, and would raise it to an absolute independence of human power. These were disposed to treat dissenters, as the nonconformists were now called, with great severity. The latter, considered Episcopacy as a mere human institution, excellent indeed, but not essential; viewed Presbyterian ordination valid, and exercised a spirit of moderation and charity toward dissenters. These had the power in their hands in the days of William, and were branded by the high church as puritanical. Violent disputes between these parties agitated the whole of the reign of Queen Anne, destroyed the religion and poisoned the social intercourse of every village. A sermon preached by Hoadly, afterwards bishop of Bangor, asserting that it was lawful, yea, a duty, to resist tyrants, threw the high church party into great rage. They were patronized by the queen, and their rage was blown into fury by one Sacheverel, a loud frothy partisan. The low church were shamefully abused, and the dissenters were treated as the offscouring of the earth. During the reign of George 1., who came to the throne in 1714, an attempt was made by archbishop Wake, to unite the English and Gallican churches, but it soon came to nought. The church of England was also agitated with the Bangorian controversy, occasioned by Hoadly, then bishop of Bangor, who declared in a sermon before the king, that Christ's kingdom was not of this world, and inveighed against the temporal power of bishops, and the regal supremacy in ecclesiastical concerns. The convocation fell upon him with violence, but he was protected by the King; and the convocation have from that period to this, only been permitted to assemble and adjourn, without transacting any business. By George, the low church party were exalted to the highest places of power and trust. When his successor came to the throne, their rivals endeavored to gain ascendancy, but were suppressed by his respect for religious liberty.

A new host of infidels led on by Bolinbroke, Collins, Tindal, Chubb, Wollaston, Hume and others, threw at this time poison into the waters of the nation, and multitudes, especially of the nobility, drank deep, and set themselves against the Lord, and against his anointed. But they were met by Butler, Chandler, and other able defenders of Christianity, in the establishment and among the dissenters. In resisting, however, the arts of infidelity, and in delivering, as they did mere moral essays, instead of the doctrines of the cross, the common people of the church of England were almost wholly neglected by her leading divines, and were fast sinking into a state of practical atheism, when those wonderful men, Whitfield and Wesley arose, and by astonishing boldness and zeal, arrested the attention of thousands on thousands to divine things. Their efforts resulted in a great increase of vital piety throughout the nation, and a dismemberment of a vast body from the establishment. Their followers were chiefly among the common people. A noble lady, however, wife of the earl of Huntingdon, became their open advocate, erected numerous chapels throughout the kingdom, for such as preached the truth with plainness and power, and opened her palace in the park, for the great and noble to hear them on Sabbath evenings.

The high church party, which had been out of favor many years from its attachment to the fallen house of Stuart, became popular upon the accession of George III., from expressing a warm attachment to the house of Hanover, and opposing the American revolution. In 1772, a body of the established clergy petitioned Parliament to be released from subscription to the articles and liturgy of the church, but were unsuccessful. The dissenters also frequently petitioned for a repeal of the test acts, but in vain. The catholics were the subjects of severe persecution. A mob, under lord George Gordon, committed in 1780, shameful outrages upon them. The French revolution was not without its demoralizing effects upon the English nation. But it produced also a greater attachment to the church, and increased the popularity of the high church party, and all who opposed the extension of civil and religious liberty. During the reign of George IV., the test act was repealed which excluded dissenters from office, and the Roman catholics gained the political liberty for which they so long struggled.

Notwithstanding the fact that Ireland has for a long time been under the domination of Protestant England, more than two-thirds of her population adhere to the Catholic Church. During the last century Protestantism lost ground in Ireland, but of late the Episcopal Church has put forth new efforts, and her writers claim that Protestantism is on the advance.

The church of England has many splendid establishments in the British colonies, in the East and West.

The reigning monarch is her temporal head, and appoints her bishops. She has two archbishops, 25 bishops, who are, all but one, peers of the realm, 60 archdeacons or bishop's deputies, 18,000 clergy, 10,500 livings, 1000 of which are in the gift of the king; a population of sixteen millions, and a revenue of three millions sterling. Her bishops have vast incomes, but the mass of her clergy are confined to an hundred pounds. The church of Ireland has two archbishops and twelve bishops; few of whom, however, reside in the country. To support these clergy, the whole nation contributes her quota in tithes and church rates.

An assembly of the clergy of England, for consultation upon ecclesiastical matters, is called a convocation. It consists of two houses. In the upper house, sit the archbishops and bishops; in the lower, the clergy, represented by their proctors, are assembled. It meets on the second day of every session of Parliament; but has not been permitted by the king, for seventy years, to transact any business, and immediately adjourns. The dean and chapter are composed of a number of canons or prebendaries, and form the bishop's court, taking cognizance of all ecclesiastical offences. The leading principle of the church of England, is the sufficiency of the Scriptures as a rule of faith and practice. Her doctrines are contained in the book of Homilies, consisting of short doctrinal discourses, and in the thirty-nine articles, which, with the three creeds and catechism, are inserted in the book of Common Prayer. The basis of her articles was laid by Cranmer, in the reign of Edward VI., and they were passed in the present state in convocation, and sanctioned by royal authority in 1562. All persons who are admitted to holy orders, must subscribe them examine. Every person who pays his tithes and taxes, is legally a member of the church in full communion. Her liturgy was composed in 1550. Her festivals are held on what are called her saints' days, and are numerous.

Her universities have retained the great principles of the reformation, while most of the universities on the continent have entirely renounced them.

This portion of the Christian church has embraced in her bosom a vast body of the faithful followers of the divine Redeemer. Many of her divines have been great ornaments to the nation, and distinguished lights in the world. Besides those noblemen who fought the battles of the reformation, the names of Usher,(a) Hall,(b) Jeremy Taylor,(c) Stillingfleet,(d) Hammond,(e) Pearson,(f) Bar-

(a) Archbishop of Armagh, in Ireland, during the reign of James and Charles I., a prelate of distinguished learning and piety. He did much to enlighten his miserable countrymen and withstand the catholics. His great work was "Annals of the Old and New Testament." He died March 21, 1655, aged 80, and was buried by Cromwell in Westminster Abbey.

(b) Bishop of Norwich. He died Sept. 8, 1656, leaving many valuable works, particularly his Meditations.

(c) Author of "Holy Living and Dying," and some much admired sermons. He died August 13, 1667, bishop of Down and Connor and Vice Chancellor of the University of Dublin.

(d) Bishop of Worcester, and author of "Origines Sacræ, or a rational account of natural and revealed religion," and many able controversial pieces against the Deists, Socinians, Papists, and Dissenters. Died March 27, 1699.

(e) Author of "a paraphrase and annotation on the books of the New Testament and a part of the Old," a work of merit. Died,1660.

(f) Bishop of Chester, author of an exposition on the creed. Died, 1686.

row,(g) Tillotson,(h) Perdeaux,(i) Pocock,(j) South,(k) Burnet,(l) Whitby,(m) Clark,(n) Berkley,(o) Butler,(p) Lowth,(q) Secker,(r) Paley,(s) Newton,(t) Scott,(u) Buchanan,(v) will ever command the veneration and love of all who delight to behold distinguished talent consecrated to the best of causes.

Patrick, Hammond, Whitby, and Scott, have been her most able commentators.

(g) Head of the English divines. He was also a great mathematician. His sermons contain the greatest number of thoughts of any in the language. He died Vice Chancellor of Trinity College, May 4, 1677, aged 47, and was buried in Westminster Abbey.

(h) Archbishop of Canterbury at the Revolution. He was born Oct. 1680, and educated among the dissenters. At the restoration of Charles II. he was promoted with other divines then called Latitudinarian. He was the most popular preacher of his day. He laid aside all the ancient technicalities of theology, and expressed himself with much simplicity and ease in the language of common sense. He introduced into England the custom of preaching by notes. His sermons are still much read and admired. Addison regarded them as affording the best standard of the English language. Died, 1694.

(i) Dean of Norwich, author of connexion between sacred and profane history. Died, 1724.

(j) Bishop of Ossory. He traveled over Palestine and the East, and published his observations, throwing much light on the sacred Scriptures. Died, 1765.

(k) A preacher of great notoriety, because of eminent learning and keen satire. His sermons are extant in 6 volumes. 8 vo. Died, 1716.

(l) Bishop of Salisbury. Author of a History of the Reformation and of a history of his own times.

(m) Author of a paraphrase and commentary on the New Testament. Died, 1726.

(n) A distinguished metaphysician. Died, 1729.

(o) Bishop of Cloyne, and author of the minute philosopher. Died, 1753.

(p) Bishop of Durham, and author of the analogy of religion, natural and revealed, to the course of nature. Died, 1752.

(q) Bishop of London, and author of Lectures on the poetry of the Hebrews, and a translation of Isaiah. Died, Nov. 1787, aged 76.

(r) Bishop of Oxford, an elegant scholar, eloquent preacher, and sound divine. Died, 1768.

(s) Author of Natural Theology, Moral Philosophy, Hoare Paulinae, Evidences of Christianity, and other very valuable works. Died, June 25, 1805, aged 61.

(t) A wonder to many. Plucked by divine grace from awful bondage to Satan, he became an eminent minister of the Gospel in London, and died, leaving many valuable works, in 1807.

(u) The most distinguished practical commentator and expositor of the sacred Scriptures. His commentary has had a most extensive circulation in England and America. His other works are in 6 vols. He died April 22, 1821, aged 75.

(v) Chaplin to the East India Company. Died, 1815.

For her many noble, pious, charitable associations, especially for the recent efforts of some of her members in the Bible, Missionary, and Tract cause, thousands and millions will rise up and call her blessed.

CHAPTER XIX.

Presbyterian Church of Scotland. First General Assembly. Established by Law Suppressed by Charles I. Re-established and prosperous during the Protectorate. Solemn league and covenant. Gains a free toleration in the Revolution. Seceders, Burghers, and Anti-Burghers. Glassites. Presbytery of relief. Scotch character. Presbyterian Discipline. Irish Presbyterian Church.
English Presbyterians and Independents. Early distinguished divines, Baxter, Owen, Flavel, Bates, Howe Number and state of the Dissenters after the revolution. Henry, Watts, Doddridge. Spread of Arianism, and decline of Presbyterians. Increase and flourishing state of the Independents.

The Presbyterian church of Scotland began to assume a regular form about the year 1560. The reformation in that country was vastly greater than in England; both as there was an entire change of religious sentiment and feeling, and also of church government. In England, the whole exterior of the Roman church remained. In Scotland, it was all abolished. " Abbeys, cathedrals, churches, libraries, records, and even the sepulchres of the dead, perished in one common ruin."

The great reformer, John Knox, had been at Geneva, the residence of Calvin; and had acquired an attachment to the presbyterian government, and a hatred of every thing pertaining to episcopacy and popery. The Scottish nobility were willing to see the dignified clergy pulled down, for they hated their persons and coveted their wealth, and the common people clapped their hands to see the reformers leveling to the dust that tremendous hierarchy which had been so oppressive.

Mary, the queen, made great efforts to re-establish the papal dominion, but her subjects had the boldness to tell her that they abhorred her religion; and even rendered it difficult for her to worship according to the education she had received, and what she declared to be the dictates of her own conscience.*

---

* The following anecdote shows the boldness of John Knox towards the queen. " After Mary had been dancing at a ball till after midnight, Knox took for his text Psalm II., ' Be wise, therefore, O ye kings,' and inveighed heavily against the vanity and wickedness of princes. The queen complained of it to him, when Knox told her that as the wicked will not come where they may be instructed and convinced of their faults, the providence

The number of Protestant clergy was for a time very small, and they were widely scattered. Knox convened them in general assembly, Dec. 20, 1560; but it was a feeble and irregular body, which affected but little. He also composed a book of discipline, which should give efficiency to their government, and he labored to get possession of the old ecclesiastical revenues; but these the nobility having once seized, would not relinquish. He met with no difficulty, however, in obtaining for his government and all its acts, the sanction of public authority, and the entire abolition of popery.

Those who had seized the estates of the popish bishops, contrived to uphold the name and semblance of the office. This occasioned violent contention. At length an act was passed in the general assembly in 1581, declaring the office of bishop to have neither foundation nor warrant in the church of God. And in 1592, the Presbyterian government was established by law.

James V. revived the office of bishop, though he had been educated in the kirk of Scotland, which he pronounced the purest church on earth; but he attached to it no ecclesiastical jurisdiction or pre-eminence, only a little revenue and a seat in Parliament. But when he ascended the English throne in 1603, and witnessed the splendor of the English church, and its devotedness to him, he became the warm friend of episcopacy, and resolved to make Scotland conform. Three Scotch bishops were consecrated at London. The Scotch clergy were commanded to receive orders from them, and the churches were compelled to submit to the episcopal ceremonies. The old Presbyterians bowed the neck with the greatest abhorrence, until Charles I. pressed them beyond what they would bear. A new liturgy was appointed to be read in all the churches, July 23, 1637. At the great church in Edinburgh

---

of God has so ordered it that they should hear of their sins and reproofs by scandalous reports;—that no doubt Herod was told that Christ called him a fox, but he was not told of the sin which he committed in cutting off John Baptist's head, to recompense the dancing of a harlot's daughter. When the ladies of the court appeared in all the elegance of dress, which Mary brought with her from France, Knox told them it was all very pleasant, if it could always last, and they could go to heaven in all that gear. But fie on that knave death, said he, which will come whether we will or not, and when he hath laid an arrest, then foul worms will be busy with that flesh, be it ever so fair and tender; and the silly soul I fear, will be so feeble that it can neither carry away with it gold, garnishing, furbishing, pearls, nor precious stones."

were assembled archbishops and bishops, and the lords of the session, and magistrates of the city. But when the dean began to read, the populace clapped their hands, and cried, "*a pope, a pope, down with antichrist,*" and greatly endangered the lives of the bishops. Other riots ensued, the flames of civil war were kindled throughout Great Britain, monarchy and episcopacy were overthrown, and presbyterianism was reestablished with new vigor, 1648.

During their struggle, the Scotch renewed in 1638, their subscription to their confession of faith, or national covenant, made soon after the formation of the general assembly, in which they condemned all Episcopal government and forms, and solemnly bound themselves to resist all innovations in religion. And in 1643 they formed with the puritans of England and Ireland, THE SOLEMN LEAGUE AND COVENANT, in which they abjured popery, and combined for mutual defence.

The Scotch Presbyterians never loved Cromwell, for he favored the Independents; and for some attempts to restore the king, they felt his vengeance; yet they flourished much during the protectorate.

At the restoration, episcopacy was re-established. Sharpe, a seceder from presbyterianism, was made archbishop of St. Andrews. An act was passed, obliging all the ministers of Scotland to receive a presentation to their livings from their lay patrons, and institution from the bishops. Two hundred churches were shut up in one day. The exiled ministers preached in conventicles and fields to great multitudes; but the king's troops were sent against them and their adherents, and the greatest severities were used to force them into the Episcopal church. Awful were the scenes that were transacted. At length, by royal indulgence, the ejected ministers were allowed to fill some of the pulpits, but this was not accepted by numbers, who, under Richard Cameron, and from him called Cameronians, fought in defence of their principles.

At the revolution, episcopacy was abolished in Scotland, and presbyterianism firmly established. The commissioners from a convention of the States, declared to the king, "That prelacy and the superiority of any office above presbyteries, is, and has been, a great and insupportable burden to this nation, and contrary to the inclinations of the generality of the people, ever since the reformation; they having reformed popery by presbytery, and that prelacy ought to be abolished."

An act was accordingly passed in the Scotch Parliament, abolishing episcopacy and the pre-eminence of any orders in the church above that of presbyters.

At the union of Scotland and England, the Scotch demanded the firm establishment of presbyterianism, as the unalterable form of government in the church of Scotland; which was granted by the Parliament of England. A clause was also inserted in the articles of union, providing that "no test or subscription should ever be imposed within the bounds of the Scotch church, contrary to their Presbyterian establishment." By these acts, the Episcopalians of England consented that Presbyterians should reign in the north, while Presbyterians also consented that episcopacy should be established in the south.

But the Scotch were soon chagrined and cast down, for as they enjoyed toleration in England, the English were resolved that the Episcopalians should enjoy the same in Scotland, and carried a bill to this purpose through the Parliament, forbidding the secular power to touch any but papists and blasphemers.

It had ever been a fundamental principle of presbyterianism, that the parishes had a right, from Scripture, to choose their own pastors; but a bill was passed in Parliament in the reign of queen Anne, entitling a lay patron to nominate the minister; thus introducing to the churches men whose chief recommendation was subserviency to some rich patron, who might be of infidel sentiments, and wounding the consciences of a large portion of the church of Scotland, and producing lasting dissentions,

In 1712 was passed in the British Parliament, the *abjuration oath*; and it was required not only of all who held offices, but of all the clergy. As it included the approbation and support of episcopacy, and prevented their seeking any further reformation, but few ministers would take it, though the refusal exposed them to a fine of five hundred pounds. This was for a long time very harrassing and distressing to the Scotch churches.

A great excitement was produced in the Scotch church in 1718, concerning a book entitled "The Marrow of Modern Divinity," which was viewed by many as heretical; and shortly after, by the opinions of professor Simpson, who was considered an Arian. But greater internal commotions were excited in 1732, by the secession of Ebenezer Erskine and a numerous body of ministers and Christians, from the com munion of the established church, because of the law of patronage. For preaching boldly against this, Mr. E. and four other ministers were deposed by the general assembly from the ministry. They then formed themselves into a distinct body, called the associated presbytery, and being popular men, and having a popular cause, they rapidly increased, and in 1745 formed three presbyteries under one synod. But they fell into a violent contention respecting the burgess oath, in some of the royal boroughs of Scotland, and split into two parties, called burghers and anti-burghers.

About the same time arose the Glassites, or Mr. Robert Glass and his followers, who plead for independency; but who united with Robert Sanderman, of England, in his peculiar views of faith,* and became a very narrow and exclusive sect.

In 1752 arose the presbytery of relief; established to afford relief to parishes which had ministers imposed on them by their patrons against their choice.

The Scotch have been a very intelligent and pious people. They have adhered remarkably to the great doctrines of the reformation. The Sabbath they have rigidly observed. To catechetical instruction they have attended more strictly than any part of the Christian church. Some of their ministers have been pious and eminently faithful men. Others have attained to high rank in the literary world. Among them may be mentioned Robert Fleming, Thomas Halyburton,† Thomas Boston,‡ J. M'Laurin, the Erskines, Dr. Robertson,§ Dr. McKnight,‖ Walker,** Campbell,†† and Dr. Blair, as some of the most distinguished. The age of George I. is commonly viewed as the period of brightest glory; for the Scotch church

---

* "That justifying faith is a mere act of the understanding, a merely speculative belief." Mr. Sanderman removed to America in 1764, and gathered a church on this principle at Danbury, Ct. Mr. Glass died at Dundee, 1773.

† A most able opponent of the Deists. He was a professor of divinity a St. Andrews.

‡ Minister of Etterick, author of "Human Nature in its Fourfold Estate;" one of the most useful books in the Christian world. Died 1732.

§ Principal of the university of Edinburgh, and author of the History of Scotland and Charles V. Died June, 1793.

‖ Author of the Harmony of the Gospels, and a new translation of the Epistles.

** An eminently evangelical minister in Edinburgh.

†† Professor of church history at St. Andrews, and author of a discourse on miracles. Died 1757.

then enjoyed great peace and quietness, had many learned men, and a great body of devoted Christians in her bosom. In 1742, a powerful and extensive revival of religion commenced and spread wide in the Scotch churches. It was a season of great solemnity and deep spirituality. The churches walked in the fear of the Lord and the comforts of the Holy Ghost. But the seceders did not favor it, being actuated too much by the spirit of secession.

The confession and catechism of the Church of Scotland are strictly Calvinistic; and the Church is governed by kirk, session, presbyteries, provincial synods and a General Assembly; but in 1843 occurred a great split on the question of patronage. Dr. Welch, Dr. Chalmers with 474 ministers withdrew and formed THE FREE CHURCH of Scotland. All the foreign missionaries went with them. In 1858 they had 71 presbyteries; 790 ministers and 886 churches; while the old General Assembly had 84 presbyteries; 1173 ministers; and 1179 churches. Every minister is assisted in the government of his own church by a body of ruling elders.

The United Presbyterian Church of Scotland had in 1858, 528 churches; 152,622 members. The Associate Presbyterians of Ireland united with it in 1858. The united original Seceders number 23 ministers.

The Presbyterian Church in Ireland formed in 1690, has undergone several changes, but has had many eminent men and much of the spirit of God. In 1858 it numbered 5 synods, 57 presbyters; 555 ministers, 514 congregations; and 600,000 members. It has a Theological Seminary at Belfast. The Reformed Church has 28 ministers.

ENGLISH DISSENTERS.

The original puritans, who were strict Presbyterians, and the Independents, who followed Brown and Robinson in their views of church government, gained a legal toleration in the revolution of sixteen hundred and eighty-eight. But as their cause had much declined from the restoration of Charles II., they entered into an union in 1690, comprised in nine articles for self-preservation, and have since been considered as one though they still differ in church government.

Their day of brightest glory was the age of Cromwell Some of their ministers were the most learned, pious, faithful and powerful men with which the church of God has ever been blessed. Among these stood pre-eminent,

RICHARD BAXTER.

He was born at Rowton, in Shropshire, Nov. 12, 1615. His father was a farmer; and, because of his low circumstances, Richard never went to a university. His mind was early impressed with the importance of securing the salvation of his soul. Under near views of eternity from ill health, he read the old puritan writers, and, with a spirit of ardent piety inflamed and directed by them, he entered at twenty-one, the service of the Episcopal church at Dudley. But disliking some things there, he became assistant to an aged minister at Brignorth. From thence he removed in 1640 to Kidderminster, where he preached the Gospel with great success. There, ignorance and profaneness had long reigned triumphant. Scarce a house was to be found in which there was family worship. When he left it in 1642, scarce one in which there was none. His labors there were interrupted by the civil wars, and he retired into a garrison and preached for two years to the Parliament soldiers. He then became chaplain in the army and followed the camp, until a dangerous illness compelled him to retire to Kidderminster, where he remained fourteen years. The act of uniformity separated him from the established church. A bishopric was offered him if he would remain, but he refused it. Forbidden to preach in public, he did good as he had opportunity, and for this he was subjected to repeated exactions, fines, imprisonment, and loss of goods. Once he lay in prison two years. The close of life he spent in London, and when no longer able to go abroad, he preached in his own hired house. He died 1691, in the 76th year of his age.

In his person Baxter was tall and thin, with a remarkable expressive countenance. To talents of the first order and ardent piety, he united an energy of character seldom found. He preached incessantly, when he could, and with great power, and he published four folios, fifty-eight quartos, forty-six octavos, and twenty-nine duodecimos, besides single sermons. His Saint's Rest and Call to the Unconverted have been the most useful of uninspired books. His last words were, "I bless God I have a well grounded assurance of my eternal happiness and great peace and comfort within."*

---

* This eminent divine felt confident he could reconcile Arminianism and

Another very distinguished divine of that period, sometimes called the oracle of the independents, was

JOHN OWEN, D. D.

He was of Welch extract and was born at Haddam, 1616. He went to the university of Oxford, but, disgusted with the superstitious rites of Archbishop Laud, he left college; and forsaken by his friends, he took refuge with the Parliament party. Here God met him by his grace, and constrained him to devote his great talents to his glory. For five years he was in deep spiritual anguish. Under his burden he went one day to hear Mr. Calamy, an eminent dissenting preacher, when a stranger entered the desk; preached from Matt. viii. 26, "Why are ye fearful, O ye of little faith;" and threw light and joy into his soul. His great learning and piety soon brought him into public notice. He accompanied Cromwell into Ireland, where he presided in the college at Dublin a year and a half. He was then made vice chancellor of the University of Oxford, a post which he filled with great ability for five years. At the restoration of Charles II. he went into retirement, and died Aug. 24, 1683, aged 67. His works are exceedingly valuable. The principal is, his Exposition of the Hebrews in four vols. folio.

JOHN FLAVEL,

Was another distinguished divine of that age, well known in the Christian world by his "Husbandry Spiritualized," his valuable sermons, and his treatise on "Keeping the Heart." He was minister of Dartmouth, but was cast out by the act of uniformity. He died 1691, aged 63.

DR. WILLIAM BATES,

Called by some, the dissenting Melancthon, died 1699, aged 73. His works were published in one volume, folio.

JOHN HOWE,

Was the domestic chaplain of Oliver Cromwell. After the restoration he was a silenced nonconformist, and became only a secret itinerating preacher. From the act of king James in

---

Calvinism. While he allowed the strict doctrine of election in regard to the saved, he supposed that others have common grace, by improving which they might obtain saving grace. He supposed, also, that a saint might possess so small a degree of saving grace as again to lose it. His system has been called Baxterianism, and has been adopted by many who were unwilling to be classed with Calvinists or Arminians.

1687, giving the dissenters full liberty of worship, he preached in Silver-street, in London, until his death in 1705, in the seventy-fifth year of his age. His works are in two folio volumes. His most celebrated pieces are, The Living Temple, his Blessedness of the Righteous, Delighting in God, and the Redeemer's tears wept over lost souls. For " greatness of talent, unfeigned piety and goodness, the true learning of a Christian divine, a thorough understanding of the Scriptures, and skill and excellence in preaching," he has been thought to excel all other men which England has produced.

These, and other dissenting divines of that age, preached without notes. Their profound, elaborate and eloquent sermons, which have been transmitted to us, were taken down by stenographers.

From the ejection of the two thousand ministers to the revolution, was a period of twenty-six years. This was, for the most part, a period of severe sufferings; and before its close, above half these servants of God had fallen asleep, and many of their congregations were scattered. The number of dissenters, however, was then great. In 1715, the number of Presbyterian, Independent, and Baptist congregations in England and Wales, was 1150. The first were double the number and size of the second. The third were few and small. Their members were chiefly merchants, manufacturers, mechanics, and farmers.

The same things which first drove the puritans from the establishment, continued to operate in favor of dissent after the revolution, and having liberty to congregate, and being shut out from all the regular places of worship, they made powerful efforts and built them meeting-houses in every part of the kingdom. Excluded from the universities by a test act, they established several seminaries for the education of ministers. From the act of uniformity to 1694, they had no public ordinations. Their ministers were set apart in secret, and often in places distant from their congregations. But now they ventured gradually to ordain in public, and in the places where the candidate was to minister. These ministers were supported by the voluntary contributions of the people. A spirit of union arose among them, and associations were formed for the promotion of the dissenting interest. Their doctrine was purely evangelical, and their manner of preaching was after the old puritan divines, plain, solemn, and pungent. Religion, of course, flourished in their churches. To public worship family devotion, private prayer, and strict morality, both Presbyterians and Independents gave great attention for many years

Henry, Watts, and Doddridge were for half a century the distinguished lights of this branch of the Christian church.

MATTHEW HENRY,

Was the son of Philip Henry, an eminent nonconformist who was ejected from the establishment. At ten years of age, he had the deepest convictions of sin, and at eleven, gave good evidence of a saving change of heart. His whole heart was, from that time, upon the ministry, which he entered at twenty-five years of age, being ordained with great privacy, May 9, 1687, at Chester. In his public services, he went nearly through the whole Bible, by way of exposition, thus forming his invaluable commentary. He afterwards removed to Hackney, near London, where he commenced the same work again, but he was removed to a better world in 1714, aged 51—declaring in his sickness, " that a life spent in the service of God, and communion with him, is the most pleasant life that any one can live in this world." He was a most able preacher as well as commentator. He wrote no farther than through the Acts of the Apostles. His work was finished by his brethren in the ministry. He published a small book on prayer, which has been a great guide and help to others.

ISAAC WATTS, D. D.,

Was born at Southampton, July 17, 1674. It is related of his mother, that while his father was immured in prison for nonconformity, she sat on the stone by the prison door, suckling her Isaac, the child of promise. At seven years of age, he composed hymns. Observing his talents, some friends offered to send him to the University; but he chose to take his lot among the dissenters, and went to one of their seminaries. At the age of nineteen, he confessed Christ. While pursuing his studies, sacred poetry much engaged his attention. The psalmody of England was early imported from France Maret and Beza first published a metrical version of the psalms which was generally sung to tunes in the reformed churches on the continent. The English protestants continued at first to chant hymns and anthems, as they had been accustomed to in the church of Rome. When they were driven to the continent by the persecution of bloody Mary, they learned the psalmody of the reformed, brought it back with them, and procured its adoption in the reign of Elizabeth. It became the psalmody of all the English churches for a century and a half. But the version of Sternhold and Hopkins, made in the reign of Henry VIII. was grating to the ear, and some of the nonconformists used the Scotch version; others, Patrick's; others, the more poetical one of Tate and Brady. But the want of one was felt, containing better poetry, and adapted more to the worship of a Christian church. On complaining of the existing psalms to his father, young Watts was desired to make better. A hymn was soon produced, which received great approbation. Others followed, until his incomparable book of psalms and hymns was produced, and this before he was two and twenty years of age.

At the age of twenty-four, he preached his first sermon, and was appointed successor to Dr. Chauncey, an Independent minister in London. But his health soon failed him, and he was laid aside for four years. Sir Thomas Abney at this period invited him into his house, and paid him the most affectionate attentions during a long period of great infirmity of thirty-six years. He often was unable to preach at all, and was always much overcome with the exercises. But he made himself eminently useful from the press, by sermons, catechism and hymns. His works are very numerous, and fill six vols. 4to. He died Nov. 25, 1748, in the 75th year of his age. On his death bed, his soul seemed, as a bystander remarked, "to be swallowed up with gratitude and joy, for the redemption of sinners by Jesus Christ." He was, in that age, is now, and will be, for ages to come, an eminent blessing to mankind, especially to the lambs of Christ's flock.

PHILIP DODDRIDGE, D. D.,

Was born in London, June 26, 1702. When an infant, he was laid out for dead; but a motion being perceived, he was carefully nursed and preserved. His parents were eminently pious, and his mother taught him the Scripture history from the Dutch tiles in the fire-place, and made deep impressions on his heart. He early lost his parents, but gained the patronage and friendship of Dr. Samuel Clark, and was trained up in a dissenting seminary for the ministry. He preached his first sermon at twenty years of age. This was the means of conversion to two persons. He soon settled over an Independent church at Kibworth, and closely applied himself to study. His favorite authors, were Tillotson, Baxter and Howe. In 1729, he opened a theological seminary. The same year he removed to Northampton, where he took the pastoral charge of a large congregation and continued his academy until 1751, when he died at Lisbon, of the consumption, in the fiftieth year of his age. For twenty-two years, he filled a great place in the religious world.

He was a man of eminent piety, a truly eloquent preacher, active in every scheme which tended to promote vital piety, an excellent sacred poet, and a tutor unwearied in his attention to a large and useful seminary. About two hundred pupils enjoyed the benefits of his instruction, of whom one hundred and twenty entered the pastoral office. His principal works are his "Lectures," "An exposition of the New Testament," "Rise and Progress of Religion in the Soul," and sermons.

Other lights were in this communion at the same period whose praise is still in the churches. Dr. Ridgley, author of a body of divinity. Dr. Evans, author of sermons on the Christian temper. Dr. Edmund Calamy, author of the Nonconformist's Memorial. Daniel Neal, author of the History of the Puritans. Moses Lowman, author of the Rationale of the ritual of the Hebrew worship. Dr. Guyse, author of a paraphrase of the New Testament. Dr. Lardner, author of "The Credibility of the Gospel History."

The Dissenters were ardent friends of the house of Hanover, and had they continued firm in their faith, and active in duty, might have prospered greatly by the side of the lukewarm and formal establishment; but in 1718, they began to be distracted by the Arian controversy. Two ministers at Exeter, were suspected of unsoundness in faith. A general controversy arose, on the subject of creeds and confessions of faith. Many thought them an infringement of liberty, and took sides against them, and against the decidedly orthodox who demanded them. These were soon suspected of error, and persecuted. Some of them took refuge from trouble in the establishment. Others became open Arians and Arminians; and as the puritans and dissenters had ever lived by the power of evangelical doctrine, the churches of such soon declined and went to decay. These were wholly Presbyterians and General Baptists. The Independents retained their ancient faith. In the deistical controversy, the dissenters lost much ground, for their preachers, dwelling almost wholly on the evidences of Christianity, and neglecting to call sinners to repentance, became dry. And as they had generally adopted the use of notes, lest they should be reputed methodistical, their manner became comparatively dull and monotonous. Mr. Whitfield and his party, with whom the independents harmonized, diffused among them for a season, much spirituality and life. But before 1760, there was a great decline in both denominations. During the life and popularity of Dr. Priestly who abhorred a middle course, the Presbyterians generally renounced their ancient discipline, and separated entirely from Independents, and called themselves rational dissenters. From Arianism, they have descended to Socinianism, and now choose to be known as Unitarians. Many of the Presbyterians in the North of England retain their orthodoxy, and are united with the Scotch. These number about 70 churches. At the end of Queen Anne's reign, the Presbyterians formed two-thirds of the dissenting interest. Now, not one twentieth part. They have not over 197 churches.

The Independents or Congregationalists, have for some years continued steadily to increase. They have at present, in England and Wales, 2400 congregations. Their ministers are evangelical and active. They have laid aside the practice of reading sermons, and preach extempore. Strict discipline is maintained in their churches. Their seminaries for the education of ministers have been distinguished, but many of them have fallen a prey to destructive errors. The most respectable, are Hackney, Airdale, Springhill, Highburg, Coward, Hoxton and Homerton. From Hoxton proceeded the lovely Spencer of Liverpool, who, having filled England with his fame by his pulpit eloquence, was suddenly called into eternity, Aug. 5, 1811, at the early age of twenty. Their ministers are supported chiefly by contribution. George I. gave one thousand pounds a year, for the maintenance of the dissenting clergy. This was afterward increased to 2000, and is still divided among them. Theological instruction is at a low ebb. Most of their academies are but apologies for a theological seminary. The Independents have entered warmly into the cause of the Bible, foreign missions, Sabbath schools, and other benevolent enterprises. Some of their best modern preachers have been Winter, Stafford, Jay, Bogue, John Pye Smith.

Many of Cromwell's army settled in Ireland, and established Presbyterian congregations. At a subsequent period, many seceders passed over from Scotland, and established about an hundred congregations in the north of Ireland. Of late, the Independents have also settled in that desolate country. Each branch of these have taken root and continue to live. King William granted their ministers 1200 pounds a year. In 1719, an act of toleration was passed in their favor.

CHAPTER XX.

Mr. Robinson's church. Its emigration to Holland and to New England. Rapid increase of the New England churches. Character of their first ministers and members. Constitution. Harvard College founded. Roger Williams. Hutchinsonian controversy. Troubles from the Baptists. Cambridge platform. Disturbances from the Quakers. Hartford controversy. Synod of 1657. Half-way covenant Synod of 1680. Witchcraft. Yale College. Saybrook platform. Great revival Sandemanian controversy. Demoralizing influence of the French and Revolutionary war. Revival of the churches. Unitarianism. Theological Institutions. Number and order of the churches and ministers. Distinguished divines.

In 1602, an independent congregation in the north of England chose Rev. John Robinson, a man of much learning and piety, to be their pastor. But scarcely had they begun to enjoy his labors, when they were subjected to fines, imprisonment, the ruin of their families and fortunes, and were compelled to flee to Holland, which at this time granted free toleration to different denominations of Protestants. The government had forbidden all such departures, and they could escape only by stealth. They secretly contracted with a captain to take them on board his ship at Boston, Lincolnshire; but the captain was treacherous, and no sooner had he received them, than he delivered them over to the civil authority; their goods were seized and they were carried back to the town, spectacles of scorn. The next spring, they agreed with a Dutch captain to take them from a spot remote from any town. The little band were collected at the appointed moment, but the vessel did not come until the next day, and much suffering was endured. At length the vessel appeared, and a boat came to the shore and received as many as it could contain. But before it returned, a company of armed horsemen appeared and seized those who remained, and the vessel weighed anchor and disappeared. As there had been no regard to families in the embarkation, great distress ensued.

Husbands were separated from wives, and parents from children. Those on the sea were tossed in a severe storm, and driven on the coast of Norway. Those that remained were treated with the greatest indignity and cruelty; were hurried from prison to prison, and officer to officer, and at last became objects of pity and public charity. Their flight was not the flight of guilt, but of humble piety from oppression and God was their helper. In process of time, they all safely reached Holland, and in 1708, Mr. Robinson saw his church established at Amsterdam, upon independent principles. Mr. Robinson's church were originally of the Brownists, who denied the church of England to be a true church. But from intercourse with the learned Dr. Ames, he adopted more enlarged views, and established his church upon better principles.

The next year the pilgrims removed to Leyden, where they acquired a comfortable subsistence, and under the care of Mr. Robinson and elder Brewster, were very prosperous. Numbers joined them from England. They had a large congregation and 300 communicants. In doctrine, they were strictly Calvinistic; in discipline, rigid; in practice, exemplary. At the end of twelve years, the magistrates declared from the seat of justice, "The English have lived among us now these twelve years, and yet we have never had one suit or action come against them."

In Holland they might have long enjoyed peace and prosperity, but their object was religion. The fathers were dropping away, and the youth were attracted by the splendor and luxuries of the Dutch. They saw that their church would soon there be merged in the world, and they resolved upon a removal to the wilds of America, where they might be freed from the oppressions, tyranny, and temptations of the old world, and perpetuate the precious blessings they enjoyed. Having obtained liberty from the Virginia company to settle at the mouth of Hudson river, and made the necessary preparations, a portion of the church with elder Brewster, embarked for America to make preparation for Mr. Robinson and the remainder, who promised soon to follow. Several individuals had sold their estates, and purchased a small vessel to take them from Holland, and hired a large one in England, which should also take a number of families from thence. The day of their departure from Holland was a day of solemn humiliation and prayer. They were removing not for the advantages of trade, but for the liberty of conscience in the worship of God, and the establishment of a Christian Church according to the apostolic pattern, and they fervently sought the blessing of heaven upon their great undertaking.

Their small vessel proving leaky, they left it in England, and all, amounting to one hundred and one, embarked together in a large ship, from Southampton, Sept. 6, 1620. Their captain being bribed by the Dutch, carried them far north of their destined haven. For two months they were tossed on the stormy ocean. On the 9th of November they saw the shores of Cape Cod, and having formed a civil government, and chosen John Carver governor, they landed at Plymouth, Dec. 11,† " with hearty praises to God who had been their *assurance* when far off on the sea."

They were, indeed, in a new world. Terrific were the dark forests, and the barbarous savages. But these they dreaded less than depraved and barbarous Europe; and here, under the kind providence of God, they planted the flourishing New England churches. Mr. Robinson, their pastor, never followed them, but died at Leyden, March, 1625, in the 50th year of his age. He was universally regarded as a great and good man, and his death was deeply lamented. His family and people goon after joined their brethren at Plymouth. For nine years, the church at Plymouth went without the ordinances, having no settled pastor. Mr. Ralph Smith was established in 1629.

As liberty of conscience could not be enjoyed in England, great numbers of her most learned orthodox, and pious people, who would not conform to the ceremonies of the established church, fled to America. On the 24th of June, 1629, three hundred people arrived at Salem. Thirty of them on the 6th of August, entered into church fellowship, forming the first church gathered in New England. Mr. Higginson, and Mr. Skelton, two nonconforming ministers, who had been silenced in England, were ordained* over them by the imposition of the hands of some of the brethren. Governor Bradford, and others, messengers from the church of Plymouth, gave them the right hand of fellowship. " They aimed to settle a reformed church, according to their apprehension of the rules of the gospel, and the pattern of the best reformed churches."

---

* " They had been ordained by bishops in England. This ordination was only to the pastoral care of that particular flock, founded on their free election."—*Prince.*

† Dec 11th, Old Style, is the same as Dec. 21st, present style, which is supposed to be the day of the landing, although the 22d has hitherto been celebrated.

CHAPTER 20.]   SETTLEMENT OF HARTFORD.   377

The next year, Gov. Winthrop arrived with a number of valuable ministers, and about 1500 people, and encamped on Charlestown hill. They first worshipped God under a large spreading tree. A day of thanksgiving was observed throughout all the settlements for God's goodness to them.

Some of these settled permanently at Charlestown and Boston; and, as their great object was the promotion of religion, they entered, August 27, into church covenant, and chose Mr. Wilson, a man of distinguished piety and zeal, who had been minister in Sudbury, England, to be their pastor. This church embraced the governor, deputy governor, and other men of distinction. Others scattered about, forming nine or ten villages, and establishing as many churches. One company settled Watertown, with Mr. Philips for their pastor. Another settled Roxbury, and chose the famous John Elliot, and Mr. Weld, for their pastors. Another, and a very excellent company, which had been formed into a Congregational church in England, under Mr. Wareham and Mr. Maverick, and which came over about the same time, settled Dorchester. Three years after, another valuable company came over under Mr. Hooker and Mr. Stone, and settled Newton, now Cambridge. Mr. Hooker had been a preacher at Chelmsford, and was silenced for nonconformity, and obliged to flee to Holland. But he was a man of such pulpit talents, that many who viewed him as their spiritual father, were ready to follow him to the ends of the earth. They invited him to go with them to America. Some of them preceded him and formed their settlement, and when he arrived, he embraced them with open arms, saying, "Now I live if ye stand fast in the Lord."

As the numbers of the planters increased, the churches at Dorchester, Watertown and Newton, resolved to remove to the fertile valleys of the Connecticut. About the beginning of June, 1636, Mr. Hooker and Mr. Stone, with an hundred men, women, and children, left Newton, and traveled with the greatest difficulty over an hundred miles of trackless wilderness, to Hartford. They drove about 160 cattle, which afforded them sustenance, and carried their arms and utensils. They were about a fortnight in the wilderness. Mr. Wareham also removed with his church and settled Windsor. The church at Watertown removed to Wethersfield, but Mr. Philips did not go with them, and they chose Mr. Henry

Smith their pastor. The places left vacant were soon filled by new emigrants and able ministers.

In 1637, Rev. John Davenport, an eminent Christian and a learned divine, who had preached with great celebrity in London, but had become obnoxious to the ruling party, and fled to Holland, came over with Mr. Eaton and Mr. Hopkins, two pious and wealthy merchants of London; and with a few families from Massachusetts, settled New Haven. Their republic was eminently Christian. About the same time, settlements were formed on the Piscataqua, and a church was gathered at Exeter.

Ninety-four ministers had now passed from England to Massachusetts, and 21,200 people. Of the ministers, 27 had returned, and 36 had died.

These early emigrants, endured almost incredible hardships, from famine, disease, and the barbarous tribes of Indians, but as they looked around them, they were compelled to exclaim, "What hath God wrought!" In a very few years, this waste, howling wilderness had become a fruitful field, and the habitations of savage cruelty had become vocal with the high praises of God. In 1650 there were about forty churches in New England, over which had been settled above eighty ministers, and 7,750 communicants.

Both ministers and people, were, as a body, eminently pious. Many of the ministers were distinguished in England, for literature and pulpit talent. "They were men," says Neal, "of great sobriety and virtue, plain, serious, affectionate preachers, exactly conformable to the doctrine of the church of England, and took a great deal of pains to promote a reformation of manners in their several parishes." Among the emigrants, they were abundant in preaching, prayer, catechising, and visiting from house to house; and such was the fidelity, and such the excellent character of the emigrants, that religion exceedingly flourished, and intemperance, profaneness, Sabbath breaking, and other gross immoralities, were for a long time unknown in the community.

Like the church at Leyden, they all aimed at independence. They viewed every church as completely organized, when it had a pastor, teacher, elder and deacons. The pastor was a practical and experimental, and the teacher, a doctrinal, preacher. The elder assisted the pastor in discipline, and was ordained like the ministers. The deacons were to distribute the elements and provide for the poor. If a pastor and teacher could not both be supported, the pastor performed the duties of both, and was strictly confined to one congregation.

Synods or general councils, were acknowledged by them as ordinances of Christ, and valuable as advisory bodies, but without judicial power. They confined the right of choosing ministers, and exercising discipline, entirely to the churches, which, for this reason, were called Congregational churches.

Early provision was made for the support of ministers and schools, and the supply of every family with a Bible, and religious books and catechisms. And that ministers might be raised up from among the youth, a college was founded at Newton, now Cambridge, in 1638, and called Harvard College, after the Rev. John Harvard, of Charlestown, who left it a handsome legacy. With this institution a press was connected, and there a new version of the Psalms was formed and printed, to supplant the miserable rhymes of Sternhold and Hopkins.

Between the civil and religious community, subsisted the most perfect harmony. The leading civilians emigrated, not for any worldly emolument, but for the express purpose of enjoying the ministrations of their exiled pastors. And the pastors looked upon them with great tenderness and affection, as their spiritual children, who had left the comforts and pleasures of their native land, to hear from them the word of life, and aid in building up the church in its primitive purity. No church could be gathered without liberty from those in authority; and what was, no doubt, a very erroneous principle, and proved, in its operation, very injurious to the country, none could be chosen to the magistracy, or vote for a magistrate, who was not a member of a church. Possessed of Christian benevolence, these devoted men made early, and not unsuccessful efforts toward the conversion of the heathen tribes around them.*

But they soon found that this was not their rest. Discord among brethren, difficulties between pastors and churches, and trouble from different denominations, early taught them that there was no perfection in this land of promise.

Rev. Roger Williams, one of the ministers of Salem, refused to hold communion with the church of Boston, because its members would not make a confession of guilt for having

---

* See Chapter xxi.

communed with the Episcopal church while they remained in England. He also taught that the magistrates ought not to punish breaches of the Sabbath, or any disturbance of the worship of God; and that there should be a public toleration of all religions. For these things, which occasioned great commotion, he was banished as a disturber of the church and commonwealth. He afterward formed a settlement at Providence in Rhode Island, renounced his baptism, was rebaptized by Mr. Ezekiel Holyman, then proceeded to rebaptize him, and ten others, and thus formed the first Baptist church in New England.

But a far greater source of trouble was a Mrs. Ann Hutchinson, a violent Antinomian. She maintained, "That the person of the Holy Ghost dwells in a justified person; that no degrees of sanctification furnish any evidence of justification; that all the ministers, but Mr. Cotton, preached the covenant of works, and that they could not preach the covenant of grace, because they had not the seal of the spirit." She gave public lectures, had crowded audiences, and gained many proselytes. The whole colony was agitated and thrown into parties, which styled each other Antinomians and Legalists. Such was the extent of the controversy, that a synod was called at Cambridge, in 1637, consisting of all the ministers in the country, and of messengers from the churches. The Rev. Peter Bulkley, of Concord, and the Rev. Thomas Hooker, of Hartford, were chosen moderators, and the synod sat three weeks. Eighty-two opinions were condemned as erroneous, with considerable unanimity; and, by the general court at their next session, Mrs. H. was banished from the jurisdiction. She was excommunicated also from the church and removed to Rhode Island; but it was long before the effects of the controversy ceased. These things broke down in some degree vital piety; but the wars with the Indians did more, for they took the people away from the means of grace and excited a spirit of revenge, cruelty, and conquest.

In 1642, Messrs. Cotton of Boston, Hooker of Hartford, and Davenport of New Haven, received an invitation to sit in the assembly of divines, at Westminster, England, to settle the faith of the church, but they declined attending.

The next year several persons arrived at Boston, and endeavored to establish the Presbyterian government under the authority of that assembly; but the ministers and churches were too firm for them in their principles of independency.

Several Anabaptists spread in Massachusetts, and contemned the civil and ecclesiastical authorities. A severe law was passed against them in 1644. An adherence to their principles was punished by banishment. So little did the puritans understand the rights, for which they themselves had contended.

Hitherto, nothing had been done towards settling an uniform scheme of ecclesiastical discipline, and as the churches were fast increasing, and errors of faith and practice began to multiply, the general court of Massachusetts called a synod, which met at Cambridge, 1646, to attend to this business. Many objected to this step, fearing that it would lead to persecution. But it was generally agreed to, and a full representation was made of the churches of New England. The synod protracted its sessions by adjournments for two years, when it adopted the platform of church discipline, called the Cambridge Platform, and recommended it with the Westminster confession of faith to the churches. This platform recognized the distinction between pastor and teacher, and the existence in the church of ruling elders; it declared the visible church to consist of saints and the children of such as were holy; required of every communicant repentance toward God, and faith in Christ; directed every church to ordain its own officers, and to ordain them by imposition of the hands of brethren if no elders or ministers could be procured, and required all to pursue a course of rigid separation from all excommunicated persons. It referred to synods and councils, controversies of faith and practice, but gave them no disciplinary power. With the ecclesiastical laws, it formed the religious constitution of the colonies. About thirty years after, it was confirmed by another synod at Boston. The churches of Connecticut, made it their religious constitution for sixty years, until the adoption of the Saybrook Platform.

The Churches had felt themselves disturbed by the Anabaptists, but they were much more so afterwards by the Quakers. George Fox had come to Rhode Island and published his sentiments. Numbers also arrived in Boston. They were accused of being "open seducers from the Trinity; from the holy scriptures as a rule of life, and open enemies to the government as established in the hands of any, but men of their own principles." They were guilty of improper practices and much disturbance of public worship.

The Quakers of that day, whether excited by a new born zeal, or by the opposition they met with, were certainly different in their deportment, from the unassuming, quiet, and well ordered society of Friends, which we now have in our midst. If they were guilty of offences, they suffered severely for them, and a penalty of £100 was laid upon any master of a vessel who should bring one of them into the country.

The Puritans of New England regarded the Quakers, not only as schismatics, but as disturbers of civil society. Neither of the parties were guiltless, the Quakers were too heedless of the proprieties of life, and the Puritans were too severe in their punishments, and we believe it is generally admitted that the penalty of death was utterly disproportioned to any offence, ever attributed to the then new sect.

While the first ministers and settlers of Connecticut remained, their churches had great peace and harmony. But when they were removed, a generation arose with very different sentiments relating to church membership. A dispute commenced in Hartford soon after the death of the excellent Hooker, between Mr. Stone and elder Goodwin, upon " some nice points of congregationalism," which threw the whole colony into a flame. The worldly and unprincipled took advantage of the convulsed state of things to bring forward their complaints against the rigidity of the churches. They thought it unreasonable that persons of regular lives should be excluded from the communion, though they gave no evidence of experimental religion, and from the privilege of having their children baptized if they acknowledged their covenant. They also viewed it as a grievance that church members alone should have a vote in the choice of pastors. These points were argued throughout Connecticut with great warmth. Some were actuated in their support by worldly principles. According to the constitution of church and state, they were, while out of the church, entirely excluded from all the honors and offices in the state, even from the freedom of election, and to be free, they must either join the church, or alter the prevalent system. Others were actuated by a zeal for God, but not according to knowledge. These were chiefly among the aged. They saw their grand children growing up without baptism. Their children were men of sober, regular lives, but made no pretensions to personal piety. These they viewed as members of the visible church, in consequence of their baptism, and these they thought might, with propriety, own their covenant and have their children baptized, so that the church might be perpetuated. But many viewed it as highly dangerous thus to bring the world into the church, and violently opposed the innovation.

A number of councils sat in vain upon the disputed subject. At length, in 1657, all the difficulties were referred to a council composed of the principal ministers of New England, at Boston. These presented answers to twenty-one questions. They declared, "That it was the duty of those who come to years of discretion, baptized in their infancy, to own the covenant; that it is the duty of the church to call them to this; that if they refuse, or are scandalous in any other way, they may be censured by the church. If they understand the grounds of religion and are not scandalous, and solemnly own the covenant, giving up themselves and their children to the Lord, baptism may not be denied to their children." This decision introduced into the churches what has since been termed *the half way* covenant, and constituted such as had been baptized in infancy, voters in the election of a pastor. Such was the result of the mistaken attempt to amalgamate the church and the world.

But the churches in Connecticut were not quieted. Many viewed the decision as destructive to the interests of religion, and a violation of the fundamental principles of congregationalism. The ferment in the church at Hartford, was also high. In 1659, a council composed of elders and messengers from Boston and its vicinity met there, and labored a long time to conciliate the parties. But the conflict only ceased with the removal and death of some of the principal actors. It was indeed terrible. "From the fire of the altar," said Mather, "there issued thunderings, and lightnings, and earthquakes, through the whole colony."

In Massachusetts, a synod was called to reconsider the decision of the Boston council. It was warmly opposed by several leading ministers, especially by President Chauncey and Mr. Increase Mather, but the controversy had assumed a political character. A large body of the people were cut off from all honors and offices, and the privileges of freemen, and such was the clamor from them, that a majority of the synod confirmed the decision. This synod also gave their opinion in favor of a consociation of the churches, but nothing was done to establish it.

The churches in Massachusetts generally adopted the practice recommended, and one of the results of it was, that viewing unconverted men who entered into an external covenant with God, as fit to bring their children to baptism, many pastors viewed them as fit to come to the Lord's table. This was the case especially with the Rev. Solomon Stoddard, of Northampton, who contended with great zeal that the supper was a converting ordinance, and that a moral life was the only requisite for admittance. His influence was very extensive.

But the pious part of the community in Connecticut were so opposed to it, that the Legislature passed an act endeavoring to enforce it, and convened another council in 1667, to sanction it. It was not adopted by a single church for thirty-nine years after, i. e. until almost a whole generation had passed away. The church at Hartford first introduced it, in 1696. The covenant was signed by most of the young people in the congregation. Other churches gradually came into the same practice. It was wholly discontinued in the State about the close of the 18th century.

The ministers and churches of New Haven colony were unanimous in opposition to it.

Both the Connecticut and New Haven churches continued their former strict practice of admitting members to their communion, and would not suffer any but church members to vote in the choice of pastors. The churches throughout New England were also very strict in their examination of candidates for the ministry; requiring of them a knowledge of the three learned languages, a knowledge of doctrinal and practical theology, and ability to defend them, and satisfactory evidence of personal piety.

In 1672, a synod assembled at Boston, called the Reforming synod. The colonies had been greatly distressed with various calamities, and the pious community were anxious to know their sins and duties. The results of the synod were very happy in unfolding the provoking sins of the age, and leading the people to repentance.

The first settlers of Plymouth had adopted, while in Holland, the doctrinal articles of the church of England, and the confession of the French reformed churches, which was the confession of Calvin; and the synod of 1648 had recommended to the churches the Westminster confesssion of faith; but it was thought advisable for the churches publicly and solemnly to adopt one as their own. Accordingly, this reformed synod adopted, May 12, 1680, the Savoy confession, composed by a convention of congregational divines, at a public building in London, called the Savoy, which differed in nothing essential from the Westminster confession, which was adopted in 1648. They chose thus to unite with European churches, that they might not only with one heart, but with one mouth, glorify God, and our Lord Jesus Christ.

Blessed with great purity of doctrine and excellent religious instruction, the New England churches had been remarkably free from superstition. But at the close of the 17th century, a cloud came over them producing the most deplorable consequences. Two children in the house of the Rev. Samuel Paris, of Salem village, were in the year 1692 affected with some unusual distemper. The physician declared that "*they were under an evil hand.*" A report spread that they were bewitched. An Indian woman privately made experiments to find out the witch. The children, hearing of her experiment, complained of her as tormenting them, and visible, though not present. They would be dumb and choked, and declare that pins were thrust into their flesh. Others soon complained of similar sufferings, and accused various persons of the sin of witchcraft. The public commotion was tremendous. Councils were called. Fasts were held. The Legislature appointed a fast through the colony, that the Lord might rebuke satan. The accused were imprisoned; tried before the civil magistrates, and shocking to relate, nineteen were, between March and September, publicly executed. And these were such only as plead not guilty. All who confessed themselves guilty of witchcraft, and many there who did this to save their lives, were acquitted. "Terrible was the day. Every man was suspicious of his neighbor. Business was interrupted. Many people fled from their dwellings. Terror was in every countenance—distress in every heart." Before winter, there was an entire change of public opinion. All were sensible that it was an awful delusion in the public mind. And those who had been active in condemning, confessed their error, and sought forgiveness from the public.

Witchcraft was universally believed in Europe until the sixteenth century, and very generally until after the phrenzy at Salem. King James wrote a book to teach his people the reality of witchcraft, and the duty of punishing it with the greatest severity, and the great Sir Matthew Hale condemned to death two women for this supposed crime. The religious community had been taught by the Mosaic writings, that a " witch ought not to live." Let us spare our condemnation of them, and be grateful that we have more light, and clearer views on this awful subject. During this early period, the churches of New England were blessed with signal outpourings of the Holy Spirit. The years 1637, 1679, 1683, 1696, and 1704, were memorable for the visitations of grace. At the commencement of the 18th century, there were in New England one hundred and fifty churches, thirty of which were Indian, with Indian pastors.

Harvard College had become flourishing; but that the Connecticut churches might be supplied with a learned ministry, with less expense than sending their sons there, they in 1700 laid the foundation of Yale College.

In 1703, the trustees of this institution invited all the ministers of Connecticut to meet with the churches in a general consociation, for the adoption of an uniform system of faith, after the example of the synod in Boston, in 1680. The proposal was acceded to, and the Westminster and Savoy confessions were adopted. But as there was no authoritative bond of union among the ministers and churches, and as one was much needed, a convention of ministers and delegates met in 1708, at Saybrook, which adopted a system of discipline and church fellowship. called the Saybrook Platform. This was recognized by the Legislature as the religious constitution of the colony. It established district associations, a general annual association of ministers, composed of delegates from the district associations, and a consociation of ministers and churches, a perpetual council in each district composed of ministers and lay delegates, to which all difficulties might be referred, and whose decision should be final.

In 1725, the convention of ministers at Boston, petitioned the general court to call a general synod; but it was the opinion of the leading civilians, that it could not be done without an order from the king, and the thing was relinquished. No synod has since been known in these Congregational churches, and no public body has adopted any other confession of faith, or system of church government, than those adopted by the above synod.

By the settlement of Rhode Island, New Hampshire, Maine and Vermont, the bounds of Congregationalism became much enlarged. The Congregational churches in these States adopted in general, the same faith and government as the mother churches. None, however, but Connecticut, in all New England, became consociated.

About the year 1737, commenced a very general, powerful, and happy revival of religion throughout New England. An extraordinary zeal was excited in the ministers of the churches. They addressed crowded audiences in the demonstration of the Spirit, and with power. The doctrines of the reformation were presented in their native simplicity Men were taught their entire depravity, the necessity of regeneration by the Holy Spirit, the duty of immediate submission to God, of evangelical repentance and faith in Christ, and holy obedience. Converts were exceedingly multiplied. Religion was, in many places, almost the only subject of thought and conversation. Vast multitudes united themselves to the Christian Church, who, through life, adorned the doctrine of God their Saviour.

This work found a great promoter in Massachusetts, in the Rev. Jonathan Edwards of Northampton, one of the greatest divines of the Christian Church, who preached incessantly with great power, and who exposed with wonderful skill in his writings, all the arts of the adversary to mislead, delude, and destroy by error and false religion, the souls of men. In Connecticut, it was promoted by the ministry of Bellamy, Wheelock,* Pomeroy, and others; but, unfortunately, a class of fanatics arose in that State, who made great disturbances, and finally separated from their brethren, as holier than they. These formed a new and distinct community of churches, called *Separates.* They are now nearly extinct.

Throughout New England, the work found warm opposers, both among ministers and churches, who made loud clamors against the wildness and fanaticism which appeared, and in such a world of depravity as this, is apt to hover around and attach itself, in some measure, to revivals of religion.

The good effects of that work of grace were long felt; yea, are felt to this day. They would have been vastly greater

---

* This eminent divine made great efforts to educate Indian youth, and establish an Indian charity school at Lebanon. In 1769, he removed his school to Hanover, N. H., and founded Dartmouth College. He had 40 Indian youth under his care; 20 of them, however, returned to savage life. One, Sampson Occum, became a preacher of some distinction, and acted as a missionary among his brethren. . He went to England, where he was viewed as a great curiosity.

had the churches listened to the faithful warnings of Edwards, and avoided the gross errors which prevailed; and had they educated their sons, the numerous youth who were called into the kingdom of Christ for the Gospel ministry. An army of able warriors might then have been sent into the field. But the churches saw not the price put into their hands. The warnings from the watch tower were disregarded; their youth, ignorant of truth, ran wild; errors and corruptions increased, and a long night of darkness succeeded. Such ministers and churches as opposed the revival, triumphed at every unhappy result, and became more decidedly Arminian in sentiment than they were before.

In the French war, which commenced in 1755, the inhabitants of New England mingled for the first time with foreigners. These were men who were disposed to ridicule their reverence for God, their respect for the Sabbath, their unhesitating belief in revelation, their abhorrence of profanity and sensuality; and men who naturally had a great influence over them as officers from the mother country. The association was very destructive to the piety and morals, especially of the youth of New England.

The churches engaged in controversy with the Sandemanians, or followers of Mr. Robert Sandeman, who came into this country about 1760, and established churches at Boston, and Danbury, Connecticut. His peculiar sentiments were, "That justifying faith is no more than a simple belief of the truth, or the divine testimony passively received, and that this divine testimony is in itself sufficient ground of hope to those who believe it without any thing wrought in us or done by us to give it a particular direction to ourselves." He adopted also some peculiar rites and ceremonies. This controversy naturally increased the Arminian spirit that was rapidly growing in the country.

The Revolutionary War engrossed the supreme attention of every individual. Had it been attended only with the ordinary consequences of war, it must have been exceedingly destructive to the interests of vital piety. War always lays waste the morals of a nation, and hardens the heart and sears the conscience of depraved man. In the Revolutionary war, the clergy took an active part. It was the constant subject of prayer and preaching, especially on all public occasions. Many forsook their charges, and became chaplains in the army. All the worst passions of man were brought into exercise by the introduction and depreciation of paper currency. But a greater evil than all was, the nation was brought into alliance with the French, and prepared to drink deep of the intoxicating cup of French infidelity The country was filled with the friends, and deluged with the writings of Voltaire, Rosseau, D'Alembert, and Diderot. An immense edition of Paine's Age of Reason was printed in Paris, and sent to America to be given away or sold for a few pence a copy. Many were the secret friends of the new philosophy, and not a few in the high places became its open advocates. Secret societies were forming in the country with similar views to the Illuminati in Europe, and Christianity seemed in danger of being overthrown in this precious land, as it had been in France. But an able clergy remained in her churches, who only needed to be aroused to a sense of danger. They were soon found to be neither unfaithful, timid, nor weak. Among the bold assailants upon the destroying monster, stood pre-eminent Dr. Dwight, President of Yale College. The churches were roused and became watchful and prayerful. Men of intellect in the various walks of life were convinced of the danger to which they had been exposed, and turned in abhorrence from the vile seducers to the word of God. The Spirit of grace began to descend upon various parts of New England. A series of revivals almost unparalleled for purity and power, rapidly succeeded one another. Many Colleges were remarkably blessed. A numerous body of learned, experimental Christians, entered the ministry, under whose labors accompanied with signal outpourings of the Holy Spirit, the orthodox churches of New England have risen to a state of prosperity, which calls for the warmest expressions of gratitude and praise. Their number of communicants is far greater now than at any former period. Still, however, many great and alarming evils exist. Many places, where were once flourishing churches, have become waste. In others, where the Gospel is preached, it is supported with great reluctance. In all, profanity, Sabbath-breaking, intemperance, and unbelief, are shamefully prevalent. Powerful efforts have of late been made by means of domestic Missionary societies, to reclaim waste places, and, by means of moral societies, to reform the community.

In Massachusetts, the clergy and churches which were Arminian, have, with the university of Cambridge, recently become Unitarian. A few have united with them in other parts of New England. With the exception of these, the Congregationalists generally, closely adhere to the doctrines of the Reformation. If there is any one point of doctrine by which they may be characterized, it is the distinction between man's natural and moral ability to obey the law of God and receive the Gospel of Christ. Viewing him as possessed of all his original natural faculties, they consider him as under obligation to do all that God requires of him, and guilty for not doing it. They call upon him immediately to make to himself a new heart and follow Christ. At the same time they view him as totally averse to the service of Christ, and made actively and cheerfully obedient only by the power of the Holy Spirit operating by the truth. No ministers therefore are more full believers in personal election, and more active in the use of means that revivals may be promoted, sinners be gathered in, and the world be converted to God.

The New England churches are supplied with well educated and pious ministers, and have handsome houses for public worship. The office of teacher as distinct from pastor, and of ruling elder, is entirely extinct. In almost every county, the ministers meet twice a year in association for mutual improvement; to consider and improve the state of religion in their bounds, and to examine and licence candidates for the ministry. They also appoint delegates who, in each State, meet annually in General Association or Convention. These public bodies are represented by delegates in each other's assembly, and are very harmonious. They have a similar connexion with the General Assembly of the Presbyterian church. Their communicants number about 200,000.

There are many Congregational churches in New York and Ohio, composed chiefly of emigrants from New England.

The Congregationalists were early distinguished for efforts to christianize the Indians, and have, of late, been very active in sending the Gospel to the new settlements and to pagan nations.

A valuable Theological Seminary was established at Andover, Mass. in 1808, through the princely munificence of a few individuals. It has four professorships, one of Sacred Rhetoric, one of Christian Theology, one of Ecclesiastical History, and one of Sacred Literature.

Its course of instruction extends through three years. The average number of its students is about 140. A theological school is also connected with Yale College and with Harvard

University. One is established also at Bangor, Maine. A Theological Seminary was also established in East Windsor, Conn. in 1834.

The state of literature in New England has ever been very respectable; and in no part of the Christian Church have the doctrines of the Gospel been so well understood by the great mass of her ordinary members. Catechetical instruction has been thoroughly pursued. Sabbath schools and Bible classes are now in powerful operation. And the orthodox clergy have considered it a great part of their business, continually to explain and defend the great doctrines of natural and revealed religion.

The distinguished lights of these churches have been numerous. Cotton,(a) Hooker,(b) Davenport,(c) the two Mathers,(d) Shepherd,(e) Chauncey,(f) Willard,(g) Wadsworth,(h) and Colman,(i) shone conspicuous in their early periods. Of a later age have been the two Presidents Edwards,(k) and Doctors Bellamy,(l) Hopkins,(m) La-

---

(a) Mr. Cotton died, Dec. 23, 1652. Before coming to Boston, he had been a very eminent minister in Boston, Eng. He was a great scholar and an eloquent man, but was strangely deluded by Mrs. Hutchinson.

(b) Mr. Hooker died at Hartford, July 6, 1647, ag. 61. Dr. Ames declared that he never met with Mr. Hooker's equal, either in preaching or disputation.

(c) At the close of life, Mr. D. removed to Boston, and became pastor of the first church. He died March 15, 1670, ag. 73.

(d) Increase and Cotton, father and son. The first was sixty-two years minister in Boston, and president of Harvard College, a man of great learning and extensive usefulness. He died in 1723, ag. 84; the second succeeded him in the pastoral office. He was a prodigy of learning and eminently pious. His publications amount to 382. Among them was an ecclesiastical history of New England.

(e) Minister of Cambridge. Author of "parable of the ten virgins illustrated."

(f) (g) (h) Presidents of Harvard College.
(i) Minister in Boston. Died Aug. 29, 1747, ag. 73.
(k) Father and son. The former was born at Windsor, Conn., 1703, educated at Yale College, and settled in the ministry at Northampton. He died in the presidency of Princeton College, March 22, 1758, ag. 54. He was the most acute metaphysician and distinguished divine of that age, and perhaps any other. His works are published in 8 vols. 8 vo The latter was some years minister at New Haven, and died in the presidency of Union College, Aug. 1, 1801, ag. 56, but little inferior as a theologian to his father.

(l) Minister of Bethlehem, Ct. A very powerful preacher and able instructor in theology. A large number of young men were fitted by him for the ministry. He died March 9, 1790, ag. 71.

(m) Minister of Newport, R. I., author of a System of Divinity. He was

throp,(*n*) Dwight,(*o*) Strong,(*p*) Trumbull,(*q*) Backus,(*r*) Smalley,(*s*) Emmons.(*t*) Beecher.

CHAPTER XXI.

Episcopal, Presbyterian, Dutch, Associate Reformed, German Lutheran, and reformed churches in the United States.

THE State of Virginia was settled for purposes of worldly emolument. The emigrants from England, who took possession of that favored soil, with few exceptions, fled not from their country for the enjoyment of religious liberty. They were Episcopalians, high in favor with the governing party in England. Planted in America, they took bold and decisive measures to establish and maintain their own worship. As early as 1621, we find the Virginia company setting apart in each of the boroughs, an hundred acres of land for a glebe, and two hundred pounds sterling to be raised as a standing, and certain revenue, out of the profits of each parish to make a living. There were at this time five ministers in the colony. In 1633, the Legislature passed severe laws against all secta-

---

supposed to carry the principles of Calvin farther than any other writer. His leading principle was, that holiness consists in disinterested benevolence, and sin in selfishness. Such as coincided with him have been called Hopkinsians. Died, Dec. 20, 1803, aged 83.

(*n*) Minister of West Springfield, author of a number of volumes of popular sermons.

(*o*) President of Yale College. He was born at Northampton, 1752, educated at Yale College and settled in the ministry at Greenfield, Ct. In 1795, he removed to New Haven, where he died in the presidency, Feb. 11, 1817, aged 65. He was one of the greatest and most excellent and useful men in the Church of Christ. His theological lectures delivered to the college students, have been published since his death in 4 vols. 8 vo.

(*p*) Minister in Hartford, Ct. A sound theologian and most solemn and penetrating preacher of the Gospel. Died, Dec. 25, 1816, aged 68. Author of benevolence and misery, or the future punishment of the wicked vindicated

(*q*) Minister in North Haven, Ct., an excellent divine, and author of history of Connecticut.

(*r*) Minister in Somers, Ct. and head of a large theological school. Died, 1803.

(*s*) Minister in Berlin, Ct. A man of great logical powers, who contributed more than any one of his age, to the progress of theological science. Died, 1820, aged 86.

(*t*) Minister of Franklin, Mass. Died 1839, aged 90. Author of several volumes of sermons.

ries, which drove numbers of Independents and Presbyterians from their colony, and prevented others from settling. Some pious people there, however, earnestly desired some ministers from the eastern churches; and three were sent to them from Boston in 1642 ; but by the law of the State, such as would not conform to the ceremonies of the church of England, were required to depart on a certain day, and they returned in a few months. A Congregational church six years after, had increased to the number of 101 persons ; but its pastors were obliged to depart, and it was dispersed. During the triumph of the puritans in England, multitudes of Episcopalians came to this colony for the enjoyment of church privileges, and on the restoration of Charles II., the church became very prosperous. It received the support of the Legislature ; handsome churches were built ; glebes were laid out, and vestries appointed ; ministers, who had received their ordination from England, were inducted by the governor; all others were prohibited from preaching on pain of suspension or banishment. The English in general, who settled the other southern States, were of the same order, excepting the settlers of Maryland, who were Roman catholics. Those that were puritans, found the best asylum in New England.

In 1693, Mr. James Blair founded in Virginia, under a charter from queen Mary, William and Mary College, and served as president of it fifty years.

The first Episcopal society in Boston was formed in 1686, when Sir Edmund Andross assumed the government of the colony. To encourage the emigration of Episcopal clergymen from England, Sir Edmund pronounced no marriages valid, unless celebrated according to the rites of the church of England. The old south church was demanded and used for the Episcopal service. In 1688, a church was built in Tremont street, and called the king's chapel.

To Connecticut, Episcopacy was introduced in the year 1706. Some of the people of Stratford had been educated in the doctrines and practices of the church of England, and being dissatisfied with the rigid doctrines and discipline of the puritans, invited Mr. Muirson, a church missionary at Rye, N. Y. to labor among them. Mr. M. came and baptized five and twenty. He made several successive visits ; and in 1722, Mr. Pigot was appointed by the Society for propagating the Gospel in foreign parts, missionary at Stratford. He had twenty communicants, and one hundred and fifty hearers.

Soon after the establishment of Yale College, a number of new and learned works on the Arminian and prelatical controversy, were presented to its library. These were read with avidity by President Cutler, Rev. Mr. Johnson of West Haven, and Rev. Mr. Wetmore of North Haven, who became converts to Arminianism and Episcopacy. They all resigned their respective charges, and went to England in 1722, and obtained orders. President Cutler became rector of Christ's Church in Boston, where he remained until his death, August 17, 1765. Mr. Johnson became rector of Christ's Church in Stratford, where he remained until 1754 when he was elected President of Columbia College in New York. Mr. Wetmore was stationed as a missionary at Rye. In a few years a number of persons in the county of Fairfield, adopted the Episcopal worship; and for some time a warm controversy was carried on between Mr. Johnson, Mr. Wetmore, Mr. Beach, and Mr. Carver, on the one side, and Mr. Hobart, Mr. Graham, Mr. Dickinson, and Mr. Foxcraft on the other.

At the commencement of the Revolutionary War, the whole number of Episcopal clergymen to the north and east of Maryland, did not exceed eighty; and these, with the exception of those settled in Boston, Newport, New York and Philadelphia, derived the greater part of their subsistence from the society established in England for the propagation of the Gospel in foreign parts. In Maryland and Virginia they were more numerous, and had legal establishments for their support.

The governors of the provinces had an inducement to patronize the Episcopal order, as it would have given them popularity in the mother country; but, on the other hand, many grants would have been very obnoxious to the Presbyterians and Independents, who composed the great body of the people. The largest grant ever made, was of land to Trinity Church in New York, which was at the time inconsiderable in itself, but has been ultimately of immense value, from the extension of the city.

The church labored under great disadvantages from the distance by which it was separated from England. The bishop of London was the diocesan of the Episcopal churches in America, and his inspection was unavoidably very imperfect, and his authority not much regarded. In Maryland, the civil law forbade his interference, except in the business of ordination. How unworthy soever an officer might be, he could not there depose him. Every candidate for the ministry was obliged to go to England for orders, which was often very difficult, and always expensive.

Applications were often made to the mother church for an Episcopate here; but the applications were warmly opposed, from the fear that bishops here would assume the same spiritual authority they had exercised in England, and interfere with the original design of the greater part of the colonists in coming to the country.

During the revolutionary contest, all intercourse with the mother church was entirely suspended. No candidates were able to obtain orders, and the parishes which were, from time to time, deprived of their ministers by death, remained vacant. Many ministers attached to the British government, were unwilling to omit in the liturgy, as they were required to do, the prayer for the king, and ceased officiating. Most of the Episcopal churches, therefore, were entirely closed.

Upon the establishment of the American government, the Episcopal churches found it necessary for them to form some social compact, for the purpose of taking care of some charitable funds which they had held under the British governors, and promoting their general welfare. A meeting was held of a few clergymen in the middle States, at Brunswick, (N. J.) May 14, 1784. This was adjourned to a more general meeting at New York, in October, where the basis was laid of a future ecclesiastical government.

On the 27th of September, 1785, a convention of clerical and lay deputies from the middle and southern States, met in Philadelphia. The eastern churches were not represented, as they had adopted measures to procure for themselves a bishop. The convention made such alterations in the Book of Common Prayer, as should adapt it to the federal government. They next proceeded to the subject of obtaining a bishop. The Rev. Samuel Seabury, D. D. had returned to Connecticut from England, consecrated to the bishop's office, not by the bishops of England, but by the nonjuring bishops of Scotland, who had broken from the State in the revolution of 1688. But they preferred, if possible, receiving a consecration from the presiding prelates in England; and finding some encouragement, they made application, which was favorably received. An act of Parliament was obtained for consecrating for America; and the Rev. Samuel Provost, D D., rector of Trinity Church in New York, and the Rev. William White, D. D., rector of Christ's Church, and St. Peter's, in Philadelphia, being recommended by the Episcopal convention, were consecrated as bishops, Feb. 4, 1787, by the archbishop of Canterbury, in the chapel of the archi-episcopal palace of Lambeth. The Rev. Dr. Griffith, of Virginia, was at the same time recommended, but was unable to go to England, and soon died. Soon after, however, the Rev. James Madison, D. D. of Virginia, was elected in his stead, and went to England, and received consecration. Immediately on the return of these new bishops, they took charge of their dioceses, which extended over the States in which they resided, and proceeded to give orders, and to ordain bishops for several States in the Union.

To perpetuate their body, the convention of Philadelphia framed an ecclesiastical constitution; in which it was provided, that there should be a triennial convention from the bishops, clergy, and churches of each State, that the different orders of clergy should be accountable only to the ecclesiastical authority in the State to which they should respectively belong; and that the engagement previous to ordination should be a declaration of belief in the holy Scriptures, and a promise of conformity to the doctrine and worship of the church.

In the triennial convention in 1789, an union was formed between the eastern and southern churches. Bishop Seabury was acknowledged; the liturgy was revised, and the Book of Common Prayer was established in its present form.

The Episcopalians had, 1858, in the United States 31 dioceses, 39 bishops, 1995 churches, and 1979 clergymen. Their bishops have been their most distinguished men. They can also boast of the two Johnsons, father and son, successive presidents of Columbia College; two of the most learned men America has produced.

They have five colleges under their direction, one in Virginia, two in New York, one in Connecticut, and one in Ohio; and four theological seminaries, one in the city of New York, one at Alexandria, D. C., one at Gambier, Ohio, and one at Lexington, Ky.

PRESBYTERIAN CHURCH.

The Presbyterian church in the United States, was originally composed of a few strict Presbyterians from Scotland

and Ireland, and some Congregationalists from New England and South Britain. These were scattered through the Middle States for nearly half a century, with but few ministers and no bond of union, and in Virginia in particular, oppressed by Episcopacy. The first Presbyterian churches duly organized were the first Presbyterian church in Philadelphia, and the church in Snow hill in Maryland. Which of these is the oldest it is difficult to determine. In 1704, the first presbytery was organized. And in 1716, a synod was formed, called the synod of Philadelphia, consisting of the presbyteries of Philadelphia, New Castle, Snow hill, and Long Island. But in this body thus organized, there was not perfect harmony. The old Presbyterians were in favor of strict Presbyterianism, and were great advocates for a learned ministry. The Congregationalists cared but little about rigid forms, and were willing to receive men into the ministry who were eminently pious, though they might be without great learning. In 1729, the synod passed the *adopting* measure by which the Westminster confession of faith was adopted as the standard of the churches, and every minister was bound to subscribe to it, on his entrance into the ministry; but the Congregationalists were not cordial in it, and for many years contention ran very high. The two parties were called the old side and new side, and sometimes new lights. These were more attached to experimental religion than the old side; and when Mr. Whitfield went through the country, such was their attachment to him and his preaching, and such the aversion expressed by the old side, that a rent was made, and the synod of New York was established by the new side, in opposition to the synod of Philadelphia. The leading divines in this separation were the Tennents* Blairs, Dickinsons, Piersons, Woodbridge, Dr. Finley, and Mr. Burr. The Thompsons, Dr. Allison, and Robert Cross, headed the old side. But they were men in whom was the spirit of piety and love, and soon grew ashamed and weary of contention. In 1758,

---

* Gilbert and William, brothers. The first was minister of Philadelphia, a man of large stature, grave aspect, and powerful in persuading men by the terrors of the Lord. He succeeded Mr. Whitfield in his labors, in Boston, 1741. His preaching there was exceedingly blessed. Above 2000 anxious sinners applied to their minister for guidance during his ministry. He died 1754.

The second was minister of Freehold, N. J., and was the means of advancing the cause of religion in a very remarkable degree in New Jersey.

a union was happily formed, and the two synods moved forward in much harmony. Gaining in strength and importance they commenced in 1785, a revision of their standards, and in 1786, resolved that the two synods be divided into three or more synods, out of which shall be composed a general assembly of the Presbyterian church. This assembly was first convened at Philadelphia, in 1789. From that period, the Presbyterian church has moved on, not without internal contention, but with prosperity and success, until she numbers within her bounds, (including both old and new school,) 3516 ministers, 4254 churches, and 350,366 communicants scattered through the Middle, Southern, and Western States. The whole government of the Presbyterian church is by presbyterial judicatories; from the lowest, a session, through presbyteries of a second and third gradation to a fourth and last. Her doctrine and discipline are strictly Calvinistic. Her clergy have been pious, learned and active. Frequent outpourings of the Holy Spirit have refreshed her in all her borders. For the instruction of her youth, a college was founded in 1746, at Elizabethtown, in 1747, removed to New York, and in 1757, to Princeton, N. J., which has to this day maintained a high standing. With this was connected, in 1812, a Theological Seminary. This has 5 professors, and usually about 113 students.

Similar seminaries have been established in various places: the most important are those in New York city, in Auburn, N. Y., and in Alleghany city, Pa.

As early as 1766, the synod of New York and Philadelphia instituted missions to the destitute. After the formation of the general assembly, they were managed by that body until 1802, when a standing committee of missions was appointed.

The general assembly, composed of clerical and lay delegates, met annually in May at Philadelphia, enjoying great harmony and fellowship, until 1837; when two great parties, styled the old school and the new school, divided and formed two distinct general assemblies. Both meet in May, and are about equal in number.

Besides those above mentioned, the Presbyterian church counts, among her distinguished lights, President Davies,* Witherspoon,† and Dr. Rodgers.‡

---

* Rev. Samuel Davies was one of the most eloquent and useful ministers of the Christian Church. A very powerful revival of religion having commenced in Hanover county, Virginia, the seat of Episcopacy, in 1748, ap-

CUMBERLAND PRESBYTERIANS.

In 1810, a body of Presbyterians in Kentucky and Tennessee, separated from the General Assembly of the Presbyterian church, and formed an independent body, called the Cumberland Presbytery. The ground of separation was a difference of opinion concerning the proper qualifications for the ministry; they considering it advisable to put into the sacred office men of piety, though destitute of a liberal education. They use the confession and discipline of the Presbyterian church, though they deny predestination. They commenced with nine preachers, and had, 1858, about 588 ministers, 580 congregations, and 100,000 communicants. Their preachers itinerate; with them originated camp meetings, which they continue. They labor and pray much for revivals, which have been frequent among them.

DUTCH CHURCH.

The Dutch Reformed church was first established in New York, in 1693, exactly according to the pattern of the reformed churches in Holland. From that period until 1737, nothing worthy of record transpired, excepting that the doctrines of the reformation were preached by learned ministers from Holland, in purity and power, and the ordinances of the Gospel were regularly administered to a serious and devout people.

In 1737, some incipient steps were taken toward forming

---

plication was made to the synod of New York, for aid. Mr. Tennent and Mr. Finley first visited that region. They were succeeded by Mr. Whitfield, and then by Mr. Davies, who was ordained to the ministry there, in 1748. In seven years, he had 300 communicants. In 1759, he was chosen to the presidency of Princeton College, which office he filled until his death, Feb. 4, 1761, aged 36. Three volumes of his sermons are printed.

† Dr. Witherspoon was, for some years, minister of Paisly, in Scotland, where he was highly esteemed as an able and pious divine. He was the leader of the orthodox party in Scotland. Upon invitation, he removed to New Jersey, and became president of Princeton College in 1768. He was also an eminent politician, and was appointed member of Congress. He was one of the signers of the Declaration of Independence. He closed his life in the service of the college and country, Nov. 15, 1794, aged 72. His works are in 4 vols. 8vo.

‡ Dr. Rodgers was the father of presbyterianism in the city of New York. He was converted under the preaching of Whitfield, and first settled in Delaware, in 1749. In 1761, he removed to Wall street church, in New York, where he remained until his death, May 7, 1811, aged 83, full of usefulness and honor.

a *Cœtus*, an assembly of ministers and elders, to be subordinate to the classes of Amsterdam; but such a body was not fully established until 1747. It then met at New York. It was the first judicatory in the American branch.

As the churches increased, they had need of many ministers. These they had generally received from the schools in Holland. Such of their own youth as desired the ministry were obliged to repair to the mother country for instruction and ordination. This was found to be both difficult and expensive; and in 1754, a plan was proposed to change the *Cœtus* into an independent *Classis*, which should have the power of ordaining. It met the approbation of the major part; but some that were peculiarly partial to the mother church violently opposed it. A schism ensued, which for many years destroyed the peace and prosperity of this part of Zion. Those who had long been united in the tenderest bonds, became bitter foes. Churches which were one in sentiment and name, refused communion; and ministers ceased entirely from all ministerial intercourse. The *Conferentie* men, as the opposers to independence were called, viewed no man as fit to dispense to them divine truth, or break the bread of life, who had not been educated and ordained in Holland. As those who were willing to emigrate naturally adhered to those with whom they were so popular, the Cœtus party laid, in 1770, the foundation of a college at New Brunswick, N. J., which was called Queen's College, where they might educate their sons for the ministry.

In May, 1766, Mr. John H. Livingston, of New York, a young man of much promise, went to Holland to pursue his theological studies. He had viewed with grief the dissensions of the American church, and now exerted himself to effect, if possible, a radical cure. To the leading divines in Holland, he represented the deplorable effects of the controversy, and the importance of their having in America, the power of ordination; and he finally obtained a vote in their supreme judicatory, empowering the *Classis* of Amsterdam to settle the concerns of the American church.

On his return to New York in 1770, he took charge of a church in the city, and soon prevailed upon the consistory to call a general meeting of the Dutch churches. They met in New York in 1771. All felt tired of contention, and without much delay, a plan of pacification, proposed by the Classis of Amsterdam, was unceremoniously agreed to. Joy reigned throughout the long distracted churches; and, forgetting the past unhappy contentions, they moved forward with much harmony and strength in building up the walls of Jerusalem.

From that period to the present, there has been probably less change in that than in any portion of the Christian Church. Queen's college, which had declined, has been lately revived. In 1784, a theological school was established. Doctor Livingston was made the first theological professor. In 1810 it was united to Queen's college, New Brunswick, and removed thither.

The Dutch churches, particularly in New York and Albany, are large and wealthy. They subscribe the canons of Dordrecht. Their ministers are required once on the Sabbath to expound the catechism. They have about 271 ministers, 279 churches, 31,214 communicants, with a population of 450,000. Their principal divines have been Doctors Laidlie,* Livingston,† Westerlo,‡ Romeyn,§ Hardenburgh, and Abeel.

ASSOCIATE REFORMED CHURCH.

About the middle of the last century, a number of the Scotch seceders emigrated to America, and as they had here nothing to do with the Burgess oath, which had been a source of contention, the Burgher and Anti-Burgher ministers formed a coalition, and joined in a general synod, called the synod of New York and Pennsylvania, and received the name of the Associate Reformed church. They have been favored with two very distinguished divines, the Drs. John Mason, father and son, ministers of the church in New York.

GERMAN CHURCHES.

The emigrants from Germany to America settled chiefly

---

*Minister in New York. He was originally settled in a church at Flushing, Zealand. Came to New York in 1763, and died in 1778. He was the first who preached in the Dutch church in English.

† Dr. L. was both pastor of the Dutch church in New York, and from 1784 professor of theology. In 1810, he resigned his pastoral relation, and removed to Queen's college with this theological school, and took charge of the whole institution. He died Jan. 29, 1825, aged 80, highly esteemed throughout the American churches.

‡ Minister in Albany.

§ Minister in Schenectady, a man of extensive learning, a professor of theology in the Reformed Dutch church, and one of the principal founders of Union college.

in Pennsylvania, in 1741. The greater part of these were Lutherans. But there were numbers of the Reformed These two have always been separate churches, though they differ but little in their doctrines and church government. The Lutherans in general no longer contend for the old views of the eucharist, and the majority of the Reformed believe with the Lutherans in general atonement. In many places they have jointly erected houses of worship, worshipping in them alternately, and having separate ministers. The subject of union has often been discussed, and is ardently desired by many on both sides. A hymn book has been printed for the joint use of both churches.

The government of both is substantially Presbyterian. The Lutherans border most on Independence. Their General synod is viewed rather as an advisory council. The Lutherans adopt as their standard of faith, the Augsburg confession The Reformed, the Heidleberg catechism. The number of Lutheran congregations in the United States, is 1,604, that of the ministers is 663. They have suffered much from the want of learned ministers. To remedy the evil, a theological seminary was erected at Gettysburg, Pa., and a professor of Christian theology, inducted May 5, 1826. They have one also at Harwich, N. Y. The German Reformed have a seminary at Carlisle, Pa.

CHAPTER XXII.

Unitarians. Anabaptists or Mennonites. English Baptists, General and Particular American Baptists. Free Willers. Seventh day Baptists. Quakers. Shakers.

THE Unitarians are properly all those who reject the doctrine of three coequal persons in the Godhead, and suppose Jesus Christ to be a created being.

Their numbers we have seen to be very great in the time of Arius. During the long reign of the Roman church, they were not known to have any being. But in the earliest periods of the reformation, some were found in Switzerland, Germany, and Poland, publicly denying the divinity of Christ, and endeavoring to establish a system of religion which should consist wholly of practical piety. They were among different sects and classes, and unable to embody themselves and become a regular denomination. In 1532, Michael Servetus published seven books, " concerning the errors that are contained in the doctrine of the Trinity," and, under the ancient sanguinary code of Frederic II., which required heretics to be put to death, was burned at Geneva. His notions concerning the Supreme Being are said to have been very obscure and chimerical. He agreed with the Anabaptists in censuring infant baptism. Such as denied the doctrine of the Trinity, were, for some time after, called Servetians.

In 1562, died at Zurich, Lælius Socinus, of the illustrious family of Sozzini, in Tuscany. He was a man of genius and learning, and becoming disgusted with popery, he traveled through the reformed countries to make himself acquainted with the system of the reformers; but finding no satisfaction, he formed a system of his own, which he communicated secretly to a few learned men. This system might have expired with him, had it not been drawn from his papers and published by his nephew, Faustus, for certain Unitarians who were scattered throughout Poland. Its fundamental principle was, "That Scripture is to be investigated and explained by human reason, and that no doctrine is to be acknowledged by us which is not level to human comprehension." He not only rejected, therefore, the doctrine of the Trinity, but supposed that Jesus Christ was a mere man, and that the Holy Ghost is nothing but the power of the Father, who alone is God. He discarded, also, the distinguishing doctrines of the reformers: original sin, predestination, propitiation for sin by the death of Christ; and viewed Jesus only as an inspired preacher of righteousness, who died an example of heroism, setting a seal to his doctrine by his blood. He viewed the future punishment of the wicked, disciplinary, to be succeeded by annihilation, if it did not bring them to repentance. His moral system chiefly regarded the external actions and duties of life; so that whoever was externally virtuous, was to be received as a Christian. He also denied the plenary inspiration of the Scriptures.

Such as adopted this system, have since been called Socinians. Through the exertions of its patrons it was received by multitudes, especially in the higher ranks in Poland. Several flourishing Unitarian congregations had been planted in Cracow, Lublin, Pinczow, Lauk, and Smila. In 1572, their ministers translated the Bible into Polish, and in 1574, they had drawn up a summary of religious doctrine. These Faustus soon drew over to his peculiar views, and they permitted him to revise their catechism and confession of faith, which has from that period been called the catechism of Racow, and considered as the true confession of the party.

In 1563, the doctrine of Socinus was introduced into Transylvania, and received by vast numbers. Its supporters endeavored also to introduce it into Hungary and Austria, but met with a repulse from the catholics and Lutherans. Joseph Siemineus built for their use the city of Racow. There they set up a press and printed many books and tracts, which they dispersed with great zeal through many countries. They also sent several missionaries, men of high birth, learning, and eloquence, into many parts of Europe, but without much success. A small congregation was gathered at Dantzic, and a few embraced Socinianism in Holland and England.

At Racow and Lublin they erected seminaries of learning; and gave themselves much to the pursuits of human science. About 1580, they fell into dissension relating to the dignity of Christ's nature and character, the personality of the Holy Ghost, and infant baptism. Two popular sects arose, one called Budneans, who refused rendering any worship to Christ; and the other Farnovians, who inclined to Arianism.

The Socinians continued to flourish and increase until about the year 1638, when, having excited against them the indignation of the catholics, the government demolished the academy at Racow, banished the professors, destroyed their printing house, and shut up their churches. But this was only the forerunner of a tremendous act of the Diet of Warsaw in 1658, by which all Socinians were forever banished from the country, and capital punishments were denounced against all who should adopt their sentiments or harbor their persons.

The fate of the exiles was very severe. They were dispersed with the loss of every thing dear to them through various countries of Europe, but could no where gain protection so as to form an united settlement and establish their worship. Through the exertions of Stanislaus, a Polish knight, they for a time enjoyed the patronage of Frederic III., king of Denmark, but they were soon deprived of that through the opposition of the clergy. Numbers fled to England, but dispersed themselves among the reigning sects as they could do it and retain their principles. These, however, generally adopted the Arian and Semi-Arian system. One independent congregation only existed in London during the protectorship of Cromwell, which received the doctrine of Socinus.

Early in the eighteenth century the Unitarian controversy was revived in England by Mr. Whiston, professor of mathematics in the University of Cambridge, who supported the Arian system to the loss of his chair. He was followed by Dr. Samuel Clarke, who, however, rather maintained a difference of rank than nature between the Father, Son, and Holy Ghost. He was opposed in his peculiar views by Dr. Waterland. About 1720, Arianism began to spread in the Presbyterian and general Baptist churches, which it ultimately almost wholly engrossed. But it is now supplanted by Socinianism, principally through the labors of Dr. Lardner, Dr. Priestly, Mr. Lindly, Gilbert Wakefield, and Mr. Belsham. All the Unitarian churches do not amount to 100, and these are small. A seminary has for some time existed at Hackney for the education of Unitarian ministers. In Germany and Switzerland, unitarianism has of late prevailed very extensively. The Unitarians of Germany have surpassed all others in their low views of revelation, and the character of the Gospel of Christ, rejecting inspiration and miracles, and treating the whole history of Jesus as little better than pagan mythology. In 1794, Dr. Priestly, meeting with much opposition and persecution in England, removed to America. By his conversation and writings he gained some adherents; and a few congregations were formed in the Middle States. This eminent man died in 1801.

During the present century Unitarianism has gained a triumph in the eastern part of New England. Many of the wealthiest congregations with their ministers renounced the doctrine of the Trinity and the other doctrines of the reformation. Some became Arians, others simple Humanitarians. The Calvinistic doctrines were viewed by them as scholastic chimeras. An able controversy was for a period sustained between Dr. Worcester, Professor Stuart, and Woods, on the one side, and Dr. Channing and Professor Ware on the other.

Most of the students from the Theological Institution connected with Harvard University are Unitarians.

In the United States, the Unitarians have about 350 ministers, 300 societies, and a membership of more than 300,000

ANABAPTISTS.

The leading principle which had actuated the Anabaptists in Germany, took deep root in the breasts of the multitude throughout the North and West of Europe. This was, "That the kingdom of Christ, or the visible Church he had established upon the earth, was an assembly of true and real saints, and ought, therefore, to be inaccessible to the wicked and unrighteous, and also exempt from all those institutions which human prudence suggests, to oppose the progress of iniquity, or to correct and reform transgressors." It had led the Anabaptists to the exclusion of magistrates, the abolition of war, the prohibition of oaths, rejection of infant baptism, contempt of all human science, to false miracles, visions, prophecies, and other extravagancies, until it had brought upon them the civil arm, and caused their suppression.

But in the year 1535, Menno Simon, a man of extraordinary activity and perseverance, who had been a popish priest, united himself to their miserable remnant, and, for twenty-five years, continually traveled through East and West Friesland, Holland, Guelderland, Brabant, and Westphalia, preaching to them, and laboring to form them into one regular community. His labors were successful. They united around him, viewed him as their common father, and after him were called

MENNONITES.

Menno retained all the leading principles of the German Anabaptists, but he drew up a form of discipline which suppressed fanaticism, and gave his community an appearance not dissimilar to that of the Lutheran and Reformed churches. That their form of doctrine might be entirely Scriptural, it was drawn in Scriptural language; but so much did the Mennonites trust to the extraordinary directions of the Holy Spirit, that they cared but little about any formula, or instructing their people in any of the great truths of religion. They early fell into violent dissension on points of discipline, and suddenly their church was divided into two great parties, the austere and the lenient. The former were disposed to excommunicate all open transgressors, even such as varied from established rules in their dress, without warning from the church, and from all intercourse with their wives, husbands, brothers, sisters, and relations, and avoid them as they would the plague. The latter were for treating offenders with lenity and moderation. The rigid party were sub-divided on other points, but they soon dwindled to a small number. These were called Flandrians, while the moderate were called Waterlandrians, from the places where they resided. Both parties, however, uniting in the principle that sanctity of manners is the test of the true church, went far beyond other denominations in austerities, and would admit none to their communion but such as exhibited the greatest gravity and simplicity in their looks, gestures, and clothing, and practiced the greatest abstemiousness in their lives. Learning and philosophy, too, they both considered as the pest of the church. The most ignorant man was viewed as proper for a religious teacher as any other, if he had the teachings of the spirit. On this point, however, the Waterlandrians were less bigoted than the others, and established a public seminary at Amsterdam.

The Mennonites first gained a legal toleration in the United Provinces in 1572. They did not, however, enjoy undisturbed tranquillity until 1626, when, by the publications of a *confession of faith*, they cleared themselves from public opprobrium. In 1630, a general conference of all the Mennonites in Germany, Flanders, and Friesland, was held at Amsterdam, when they entered into bonds of fraternal union, each retaining their own peculiarities. In 1649, the conference was renewed, and many of the severities of Menno were mitigated. A few of them came to England in the reign of Henry VIII., but they suffered much persecution from the government, and were banished by Queen Elizabeth to Holland.

BAPTISTS.

In 1608, the sentiments of the Mennonites began again to spread in England. A few imbibing them, separated from the Independents, and established a communion of their own, and, renouncing their former baptism, sent over one of their number to Holland, to be immersed by the Dutch Anabaptists, that he might be qualified to administer the ordinance in England. From this they soon spread and became numerous.

They rejected the name of Anabaptists, because they would not allow that any baptized by them had been baptized before, and assumed the name of Baptists; declared themselves the only true church of Christ, and claimed a direct descent from Christ and his apostles, through the Waldenses. Like the Mennonites, they viewed believing adults as the only proper subjects of baptism; and immersion as the only proper mode. None, therefore, but those who had been immersed upon a profession of saving faith, would they allow to belong to the church of Christ, and to be proper subjects of communion. They early fell into contention upon points of doctrine, and split in 1611, into two great parties, called the *particular* and the *general* Baptists. The particular Baptists are Calvinists, and the general, Arminians. The former have ever been by far the most numerous. Some of both parties have recently admitted those who have been baptized in infancy to the Lord's Supper. Some, also, of both parties, observe the seventh day as the Sabbath, from an apprehension that Christ never abrogated the Jewish Sabbath. These are called Seventh-day Baptists.

During the reign of the High Commission Court and Star Chamber, many of the Baptists suffered severely. Cromwell extended protection and patronage to them, and they increased considerably during the protectorate. But they met, at that period, with much perplexity and trouble, from the Quakers, who violently opposed all water baptism. By the act of uniformity in 1662, they suffered with other non-conformists, and were ejected from their pulpits; and subsequently were subjected to vexations, imprisonments, loss of goods, and of life. Among those who suffered severely, of this denomination, was the celebrated

JOHN BUNYAN.

He was the son of a tinker, born 1628. In early life, he was infamous for the most daring impiety. Thrice was he snatched from the jaws of death; but the divine mercies he only abused to sin. Fortunately he married the daughter of a pious man, whose only portion was two books, "the Practice of Piety," and "the Plain Man's Pathway to Heaven." These books brought conversion to his heart; and submitting himself to God, he entered into the communion of the Baptist Church, at Bedford, in his 27th year, and soon became an active and powerful preacher of the gospel. He established himself at Bedford, and was active in forming numerous churches around him. At the restoration, he was seized and thrown into prison, where he lay twelve years. But there he was not idle. He maintained himself and family, by making long tagged thread laces ; and there wrote that most wonderful book, "The Pilgrim's Progress." After he regained his liberty, he traveled through England, to comfort and establish his brethren. A meeting house was built for him at Bedford ; but he often preached in London, where he attracted vast crowds. He died August 31, 1688, aged 60 years. He was a man of deep humility and gentleness. His industry is to be seen in his two folio volumes. His Pilgrim's Progress has been translated into various languages, and has been printed more times than any book excepting the Bible. Until the middle of the 18th century, the Baptists never admitted psalmody into their worship, considering it a human ordinance. It was then introduced by some, and a violent controversy ensued.

At the revolution in 1688, the Baptists, with the other dissenters, gained a legal toleration ; and in the next year, delegates from upwards of an hundred churches, met in London, to inquire into the state of the churches, and adopt measures for their prosperity. By this assembly, was published the confession of faith, known as the century confession. It continued its annual sessions a few years. At this period there were in England and Wales, about 300 churches, though many of them were small and without pastors.

Their increase in the last century was small. Of the Particular Baptists, there were in 1768, 217 churches ; in 1790, 312 ; in 1798, 361. In Wales, there were about 80 churches. In Ireland, but 8 or 10. In Scotland, but a few, and these have been Sandemanians, who have had no fellowship with the English Baptists. The general Baptists have about an hundred churches in Great Britain. They are generally Arminian and Unitarian.

In 1793, the Particular Baptists formed a missionary society, and sent Messrs. Thomas, Carey, and Marshman, to India, who, under God, have done wonders.

The assembly of 1689, laid the foundation of a Baptist academy, at Bristol, for the education of ministers. This has been very flourishing. Another was founded near London, in 1810.

From the opposition to human science and human aid, in building up the cause of Christ, the English Baptists have had but few learned men, and have produced but few valuable works. Gill,* the Rylands,† Stennets,‡ Pearce,§ Fuller,‖ Ward,¶ Hall,** and Foster,†† Particular Baptists, have been ornaments to the Christian church. The ministers among the General Baptists, have usually been men of more learning than among the Particulars, though no individuals have excelled them. In foreign missionary operations they have been surpassed by none.

The Baptists came to New England soon after its settlement. Roger Williams, who left his congregational church in Salem and contended with the government and churches in Massachusetts, on points of discipline, established himself at Providence, with no particular church order, in 1639. In a short time he and his people renounced infant baptism and were baptized according to the views of the Baptists. This church was the first Baptist church in America. A Baptist church was gathered in Charlestown, Mass. 1665, in New Jersey in 1688, in South Carolina in 1690, in Groton, Ct. 1705. In the first century, seventeen churches were gathered. Nine of them were in New England. In the next forty years twenty more were established. After the great revival in 1741, arose many separate churches all over New England. Several of these became Baptist, so that in 1790 they numbered above 800 churches. But a destroying blast came over them through the influence of Elhanan Winchester, who preached among them the doctrine of universal restoration. With the increase of the country this denomination also has rapidly increased, and have now in the United States about 11600 churches, and 7141 ministers. They are chiefly in the Western and Southern States. In the early period of their

---

* Dr. Gill was pastor. first of the Baptist church in Kittering, and afterwards in London. He was a great scholar and an high Calvinist. He wrote an exposition of the Bible, in 9 vols. folio, and a body of divinity, in 3 vols. 4to. He died Oct. 13, 1771.

† Father and Son. Both ministers at Northampton. The latter became head of the Baptists' academy at Bristol.

‡ Father and Son. Both ministers at Exeter, of excellent character and distinguished abilities.

§ Minister of Birmingham, a man of ardent piety, and warm missionary spirit. Died Oct. 1799, aged 33.

‖ Minister at Kittering. One of the most able and excellent men of any communion.

¶ Late missionary to India. He inspected the printing press at Serampore. His labors were immense.

** Robert Hall, perhaps the greatest preacher that England has produced
†† An exceedingly able writer ; author of several valuable works.

history the Baptists in New England and Virginia were much molested on account of their peculiarities. From Massachusetts they were at one time banished.

The Baptists in the United States are generally particular and Calvinistic. As a body they are serious and very regular. Many of their churches have enjoyed precious revivals. Their ministers have not generally been distinguished for learning, but some have been highly respectable, particularly Mr. Gano,* Dr. Manning,† Dr. Stillman,‡ Dr. Furman,§ and Dr. Baldwin.‖ They have a college at Providence, R. I.,—a literary and theological institution at Waterville, Maine—another at Washington city, a theological school near Boston, and one in the State of New York. They liberally support foreign missions.

After the French war a number of families removed from New England and settled in Nova Scotia and New Brunswick. Some were Baptists, who laid the foundation of churches there. But they have never prevailed much there until within a few years. In Upper and Lower Canada there are but few of this order. In the West Indies they have some churches.

THE ARMINIAN BAPTISTS

Are in America few in number. They are called Freewillers. They date their rise in 1780, through the activity of Elder Randall, of New Durham. They are most numerous in New England and Canada. They have 1252 churches, 1082 ministers, 56,452 communicants.

---

* Mr. Gano, was pastor of the Gold street church, New York, twenty-five years. At the close of life he removed to Kentucky, where he died in 1804, aged 77, leaving behind him a very high reputation as a laborious, faithful minister of Christ.

† Dr. Manning was, during his life, considered as the most learned man among the American Baptists. He received his education at Nassau Hall, New Jersey; preached in several places with reputation, and then settled at Warren, R. I., where he opened a Latin school. In 1765, he obtained a charter of incorporation for Rhode Island college, of which he was chosen president. When that institution was placed at Providence, he removed there and performed the duties of the presidency, and preached to the Baptist church for twenty-five years. He was sent by Rhode Island to the old Congress. He died, greatly lamented, July 29, 1791, aged 53.

‡ Dr. Stillman was born in Philadelphia, 1737. After preaching in various places, he was settled in Boston in 1765, where he continued greatly beloved and respected, until his death, March 113, 807, in the 70th year of his age. He was a truly eloquent preacher and good man. His publications were many.

§ Minister in Charleston, S. C.
‖ Minister in Boston

A body of men styling themselves Christians, a species of Unitarians, coalesce with them on the subject of Freewill and immersion. They have 607 churches and 498 ministers.

SEVENTH DAY BAPTISTS

Have been known in England about 200 years, but have never been numerous. They first appeared in Newport, Rhode Island, and formed a church in 1671. This church has continued to the present time. A more flourishing one existed at Hopkinton. Several were in connexion, and some have been planted in the State of New York. They conceived that it was an anti-christian power that changed the Sabbath from the seventh day to the first. They have 70 ministers, 60 churches, and 6000 communicants.

Other small sects of Baptists exist in America, as the Rodgerene Baptists in Connecticut; the Keithian Baptists, a sect of Quakers; Tunker Baptists, or dippers, and Mennonites in Pennsylvania, and at the West. There are also Six Principle Baptists, with twenty-five churches. Free Communion Baptists, who have two conferences in New York. The General Baptists have in Kentucky eight churches.

QUAKERS OR FRIENDS.

In that great revolution of religious opinion in England which first gave every one, excepting the old standing order, free toleration, and advanced a Cromwell to the throne, it might be expected, from the natural tendency of the human mind to extremes, that some would go in their speculations and demands as far beyond all that those with whom they differed would approve, as would balance the restraints under which they had before been held. Among those who thus went beyond all reformers, was George Fox, who was born at Drayton, 1624, and educated a shoemaker and grazier Discontented with these employments, he led a wandering life, frequented much the company of religious and devout persons, and in 1647 became a preacher. He found nothing in the religion of the times that pleased him. Christians were, in his view, worldly and licentious. The modes of worship were established by law. The clergy were ordained over particular parishes, and paid for preaching. These things, as well as the drunkenness, injustice and profanity of the age, were the subjects of his severe animadversion.

Against the commonly received doctrine, that the Scripture is able to make us wise unto salvation, and that ministers should be qualified for their office by suitable degrees of learning, he asserted that the light of Christ, let in upon the heart, was the only means of salvation, and a sufficient qualification for the ministry. At Nottingham, "he went away," says his biographer, "to the steeple house where the priest took for his text, 'We have a more sure word of prophecy, whereunto ye do well that ye take heed, as unto a light that shineth in a dark place, until the day dawn, and the day star arise in your hearts.' And he told the people this was the Scripture by which they were to try all doctrines, opinions, and religions. George Fox hearing this, felt such mighty power, and godly zeal working in him, that he was made to cry out, O no : It is not the Scripture, but it is the Holy Spirit by which the holy men of God gave forth the Scriptures, whereby opinions, religions, and judgments are to be tried. That it was which led into all truth, and gave the knowledge thereof. He thus speaking, the officers came and took him away, and put him into a filthy prison." After his release, he traveled through England, Ireland, Scotland, Holland, Germany, the American colonies, and the West Indies, calling upon men to disregard the ordinary forms of religion, and attend to that divine light which is in all men. Several times more he was imprisoned as a disturber of the peace, and of public worship.

Fox had many adherents who were called Quakers, as some say, because he once told one of the judges to tremble at the word of the Lord, or as others affirm, from certain distortions in their worship. In these, Fox, assisted by Robert Barclay, George Keith and Samuel Fisher, formed a regular system of doctrine and discipline. He died in London in 1690. And though William Penn said of him, "He was a man that God endowed with a clear and wonderful depth ; a discerner of others' spirits, and very much a master of his own ; of an innocent life, meek, contented, modest, steady, tender," yet it is evident from his history, that he had no small portion of fanaticism, and that he broached sentiments which must have appeared to men at that period, as utterly subversive of civil and religious order and decorum.

These sentiments many of his followers fully acted out creating great disturbances, and they were severely chastised by the magistracy. Of these disturbances, however, they acquit themselves as the guilty cause, since they only pursued the course pointed out by the light that was in them, and would have nothing to do with the established forms of presbyterianism or episcopacy, and refused to take oaths to the magistracy, or pay tithes, or engage in war. The tumults were occasioned by those who would not let them pursue their own course. But the ministers viewed this course as destructive of all true religion, and the magistrates as subversive of civil government; and the Quakers were imprisoned, fined, and whipped, sometimes for their tenets, but more frequently for their obstinacy. Cromwell was disposed to suppress them; but the more he learned of their character, the more disposed he was to let them alone, but he did not put a stop to the persecutions.

The Friends have not increased for a considerable period in England. The number of their congregations is about 396. Population 40,000. They are found chiefly in the counties of York, Lancaster, Cumberland and Kent. Their peculiar dress and phraseology, have, to a considerable extent, been laid aside, especially by the wealthy.

King Charles II. and James, oppressed them, and made severe laws against their meetings for worship, chiefly because they would not take the oath of allegiance. Had the value of their *affirmation* been understood, as it now is, they might have been spared much tedious imprisonment, and been found as faithful, peaceable subjects as those who took the oath.

In 1656, a few female Quakers came to New England, and practised conduct which they said was required of them by the Divine will, and pointed out by the light within them, but which the civil magistrates viewed as inconsistent with civil and religious order; and they were punished with stripes and banishment. In 1658, four were put to death. But they interceded with Charles II. and obtained a mandamus to stop these severities.

In 1672, Charles released four hundred from prison, who had refused to conform to the church of England, to take the oath of allegiance and pay tithes; but at the king's decease, fifteen hundred were still confined for what was considered outrageous conduct. Their imprisonments were long and severe, and many of them died without regaining their liberty. They enjoyed no peace in Great Britain until the revolution. Their affirmation is there now taken in civil courts, except in criminal cases.

In 1680, William Penn received from Charles II. a grant of

that fertile territory which now forms the State of Pennsylvania, as a reward for the eminent services of his father, who was a vice admiral in the British navy. Penn was a shrewd, intelligent, active man, and improved his grant to the greatest advantage. He carried with him a large number of Friends from England and founded a city of remarkable regularity and beauty, which, for the harmony that prevailed among them, he called Philadelphia; and a State which has arisen to the first rank in the Union. Here they became a large and respectable community. The first law in Massachusetts exempting the Quakers from taxation for the support of the congregational ministry, was passed in 1734. During the Revolutionary war, they were involved in great distresses because they refused to join the army. Many large estates were sacrificed to pay fines imposed upon them.

In America they have between five and six hundred congregations, and over two hundred thousand people.

The Friends have ever maintained many doctrines in common with the reformed churches, but they view every man as furnished with a measure of the Holy Spirit, or as they call it, of the light of Christ, which is a rule of duty superior to the Holy Scriptures, and which requires only to be brought into exercise in silence and meditation. They reject a regular Gospel ministry, viewing every person, male and female, as a suitable religious teacher, who is influenced by the Spirit, to speak in a public meeting. They reject, also, the Sabbath, singing, outward ordinances, baptism, and the Lord's supper, giving them all a spiritual interpretation. They have no family worship, and no audible religious service at meals. They consider outward forms as hindrances to true spiritual worship, and think their most precious meetings to be those in which they have perfect silence and communion with God. They practice abstemiousness in living, renounce amusements, forms of politeness, and respect of persons, lest these things should cloud the divine light. They view the common name of the months and days of the week as relics of paganism, and substitute the ordinal numbers.* They refuse to take an oath, to engage in war, to give titles, to pay outward homage, and are uniform and plain in their dress.† A drunken

---
* In this they were not at first peculiar. The Independents and Baptists did the same.

† They adopted what was the plain dress in 1650, and this they have never altered.

Quaker is seldom seen. Their government is sustained in monthly, quarterly, and yearly meetings, and is a kind of presbyterianism.

Of late, there has been an extensive and serious division among them on points of doctrine; one party has struggled for a considerable degree of orthodoxy and spirituality, while the other has been upholding Socinianism. They are now completely separated under the names of the Orthodox and Hicksites.

The SHAKERS are a sect formed in England by one James Wadley; but their prime leader was Ann Lee. This woman claimed the gift of languages, of healing, of discovering the secrets of the heart, being actuated by the invisible power of God, sinless perfection, and immediate communication with heaven. In 1774, she emigrated with her followers to America. They have one large establishment at New Lebanon, N. Y., and fifteen or twenty others in various States. Their number. exceeds four thousand. They view Ann as the elect lady, who travails for the whole world, and by and through whom alone any blessing can be obtained. They derive their name from a heavy dancing and shuddering in their worship. They reject matrimony—are celebrated for their neatness and worldly thrift; but consider the Scriptures as obsolete, and really have so little among them of the Gospel of Christ, as to render it questionable whether they should find a place in the history of the church.

CHAPTER XXIII.

Moravians. History and Discipline. Methodists. Early labors of Wesley and Whitfield. Their separation. Methodist Episcopal Church. Their order, discipline, and increase in Europe and America. Whitfieldian Methodists. Associated Methodists Wesleyan Methodists. Lady Huntingdon. Universalists and others.

THE Moravians and Bohemians were first converted to the Christian faith in the ninth century, and united in communion with the Greek church. In process of time, they submitted to the Romans. But animated by the labors and example of John Huss and Jerome, they, in the fifteenth century, renounced the papal dominion. In the time of the reformation they were called the United Brethren, and formed friendly correspondence with Luther and the principal reformers But in a civil war in 1620, they were exceedingly distressed, and scattered throughout Europe.

MORAVIANS.

In 1722, a small remnant of them were conducted by Christian David, a brother, from Fulnech in Moravia, to Upper Lusatia, where they put themselves under the protection of Nicholas Lewis, Count of Zinzendorf, and built a village which they called Hutberg and Hernhut, or Watch-hill. The count showed them much kindness, and being a zealous Lutheran, endeavored to gather them into the Lutheran Church. But he failed and became himself a convert to their faith and discipline. In 1735, he was consecrated one of their bishops, and became their spiritual father and great benefactor. He died at Hernhut in 1660, aged 60. He is viewed by the Moravians as one of the greatest and best of men, though he is represented by many as fanatical in his preaching.

Hernhut the Moravians have held as the centre of their vast operations in the heathen world. A few have fixed their residence in London and Amsterdam. They profess to adhere to the Augsburg confession of faith, which was drawn up by Luther and Melancthon in 1530. But they have some peculiar views, and a very peculiar government. They know but little of the points which divide Calvinists and Arminians, and speak almost constantly of the Redeemer. They have several congregations, which meet by deputies once in seven years in a general synod, for the superintendence of the congregations and missions. All questions of importance are determined by lot, i. e. as they suppose, by the Lord. A subordinate body is appointed at the close of the session, on whom devolves the chief management of the institution. This is called *The elder's conference of the unity*, and consists of thirteen elders, who are divided into four departments. 1st. The mission department, which superintends the missionary concerns. 2d. The helper's department, which watches over the principles and morals of the congregation. 3d. The servant's department, which superintends the domestic concerns. 4th. The overseer's department, which looks to the maintenance of the constitution and discipline of the brethren. The power of this elder's conference is very extensive. Every servant in the unity is appointed or removed by it at its pleasure. Bishops and ministers are alike subject with the people.

Each congregation also has a conference of elders for its own government, which is divided into five departments. They have economies or choir houses, where they live together in community; the single men and single women apart, under the superintendence of elderly persons. They take peculiar care in the education of their children. They marry only in their own communion. In the plainness of their dress they strongly resemble the Friends. They have ever been devoted to foreign missions, and have set a most noble example to all other denominations of Christians. In America they have 33 ministers, 24 congregations, and 5745 members.

The Moravians have bishops, ministers, deacons, and deaconesses: but their bishops are superior to the ministers only in the power of ordination, and can ordain none but such as are designated by the elder's conference.

METHODISTS.

The revolution in England in 1688, had given such toleration to the various protestant churches, that care for self-preservation was supplanted by a worldly spirit, and infidelity entered and overflowed, and threatened to sweep Christianity from the kingdom. At this period, when not merely vital piety was the subject of ridicule, but the learned divines of the nation found it difficult to defend the outworks of Christianity, the Methodists arose, producing a prodigious religious excitement, especially among the common people throughout England and America.

This sect may be traced to Mr. John Wesley. That extraordinary man was born 1703. He received his education at Oxford university, and in 1725, while a tutor there, was ordained to the ministry in the established church. Being deeply impressed with the subject of religion, he conversed with a friend on the means of improvement, who told him that "he must find companions, or make them;—that the Bible knew nothing of a solitary religion." This led him to associate with him in 1729, his brother Charles, Mr. Morgan and Mr. Kirkham, and a few years after, Messrs. Ingham, Hervey, Broughton, and George Whitfield, then in his 18th year—all students in college. Their meetings for religious improvement were so regularly attended by them, and so methodical did they become in all things, as to be called by the licentious students, methodists and the godly club. This society continued about five years, and rendered itself very popular with many by its religious and charitable efforts, while, by others, it was calumniated and abused. But none of the members seem to have known much of the religion of the gospel

Whitfield pursued the course of a pharisee, and by ascetic austerities nearly brought himself to the grave, while Wesley directing his attention to the inner man, but not knowing there was an Holy Ghost, labored at his great work, "the recovery," as he expressed it, "of that single intention and pure affection which was in Christ Jesus."

The popularity of these young Methodists, induced some of the trustees of the new colony of Georgia, to invite the Wesleys to go thither, and preach to the Indians. With this request they complied, and sailed in 1735, in company with some Moravian missionaries from Germany, whose humble faith and holy joy, even in the storm, showed John that notwithstanding his ardent pursuit of inward holiness, he was yet a stranger to vital piety. Charles returned the next year to England. John remained three years, but without effecting much good.

Whitfield early turned from his austerities to the Gospel scheme of justification by faith, and by studying closely Paul's Epistles, and Henry's Commentary, entered fully into the views of Calvin. In 1736, at the age of twenty-one, he commenced preaching the Gospel with a popularity unknown before or since by any man in England. To a rich curacy he was invited in London; but on Mr. Wesley's return, he chose to take his place, and embarked for Georgia in 1738. On his voyage he became instrumental of a thorough reformation in the ship's crew. At Georgia he established an orphan house; which led him to travel through New England to procure assistance for it, and where he preached with wonderful power and success. For the same purpose he re-crossed the ocean and was received with the most enthusiastic applause by thousands of hearers. From many of the pulpits of the establishment he was shut, as an enthusiast, and to this circumstance may be traced the formation of a new sect. For he now found it necessary to set up for himself, to effect any good. "I thought," said he, "it might be doing the service of my Creator, who had a mountain for his pulpit, and the heavens for his sounding board; and who, when his Gospel was refused by the Jews, sent his servants into the highways and hedges." He accordingly went among the poor colliers near Bristol, and preached on a mountain in the open air, often to twenty thousand people, and with the greatest success. "His first discovery of their being affected was," he observed, "in the white gutters made by their tears, which plentifully run down their black cheeks as they came out of the coal pits. Several hundreds of them were soon brought under deep convictions, which, as the event proved, ended in a sound and thorough conversion. The change was visible to all, though numbers chose to impute it to any thing rather than to the finger of God. As the scene was quite new, and I had just begun to be an extemporary preacher, it often occasioned many inward conflicts. Sometimes when twenty thousand people were before me, I had not, in my apprehension, a word to say. But I was never totally deserted, and frequently, (for to deny it would be lying against God,) so assisted, that I knew by happy experience, what our Lord meant by saying, 'he that believeth in me, out of his belly shall flow rivers of living waters.' The open firmament above me, the prospect of the adjacent fields, with the sight of thousands on thousands, some in coaches, some on horseback, and some in trees, and at times all affected and drenched in tears together, to which was sometimes added the solemnity of the approaching evening, was almost too much for me, and quite overcame me."

From Bristol he went into Wales, where he again preached to admiring thousands; and from thence to London, where in Moorfields, and on Kensington common, he addressed the most astonishing assemblages of people on the subject of salvation. After this, he revisited America, and left the field to Wesley.

That extraordinary man, on his return to England, learned, he said, (what he least of all suspected,) that he who went to America to convert others, was never himself converted to God. On his voyage out, he had formed a favorable opinion of the piety of the Moravians, and meeting with a band of them soon after his return, in London, he conversed much with them, adopted their peculiar views of true faith, as a belief that our sins are pardoned, accompanied with constant dominion over sin; and, in one of their assemblies, gained, as he thought, an assurance of their forgiveness of all his sins, and everlasting peace. Desirous of visiting the place where this favorite people lived, he went into Germany, to the settlement of the Moravians. He returned to London in 1738, and began to preach with great zeal and success. The multitudes who gathered around him were not equal to those which followed Whitfield; but the impressions and outcries exceeded any thing which had been witnessed.

Mr. Whitfield returned again to England, in 1741, after a still more popular and successful tour through North America than before. But alas! with Wesley he was no longer to co-operate. These two men were found to be possessed of very different systems of theology. Whitfield had preached and printed in favor of election, and Wesley in favor of universal redemption and christian perfection. Their different views were communicated to their hearers, and two great parties were at once formed. Whitfield preached once for Wesley, and no more. "You and I," said he, "preach a different Gospel." Both continued to labor with astonishing success, and became the heads of large and powerful sects.

THE METHODIST EPISCOPAL CHURCH.

Mr. Wesley at once found himself at the head of an immense body of people, all in the church of England, as he himself was, yet looking to him as their spiritual guide. Leave them to the ministers of the establishment he could not, for they excluded him from their pulpits, and reviled him as an enthusiast. Nor could he expect preachers from the learned universities, for they would neither supply present exigencies, nor meet his views, nor be ever sufficient in number. Whitfield had set him the example of raising up lay preachers. And he now thought it his duty to put any man into the ministry who desired the office, provided he gave evidence of piety, had a good understanding, and clear utterance, and was successful in converting souls. Numerous men possessing these qualifications, he sent from the most ordinary employments of society, into various parts of the kingdom, and such was the credit of his name, and to such a degree did they adopt his dispassionate manner, and "infantile simplicity," that wherever they came, they were received, supported, and listened to, with the greatest deference.

Their fundamental principles were, in the liturgy, homilies and articles of the church of England, but to these they gave a broad Arminian interpretation. Against personal election, the point on which Mr. Wesley broke with Mr. Whitfield, and the saint's certain perseverance, they were violent. They also maintained that perfection is attainable in this life. In his views of faith, their great leader coincided, as has been remarked, with the Moravians; considering it, as he said, "not only a divine evidence or conviction that God was in Christ reconciling the world unto himself, but a sure trust and confidence that Christ died for my sins, that he loved me, and gave himself for me. And the moment a penitent sinner believes this, God pardons and absolves him: and as soon as his pardon or justification is witnessed to him by the Holy Ghost, he is saved."

As the mass of preachers and converts grew, it became unwieldy, and Mr. Wesley called all his preachers to an annual conference. This conference first met in 1744.

In this conference a general view was taken of doctrine, discipline and moral conduct. The whole kingdom was divided into circuits. Fifteen or twenty societies which lay around some principal towns formed a circuit. In each circuit was stationed two, three, or four preachers, according to its extent and importance, who were to labor in it for one year. The eldest was called the assistant or superintendent, who directed the labors of his associates. Each, having his place assigned him, was to begin a progressive motion round the circuit; perpetually traveling and preaching, as the superintendent directed. Each therefore had his daily work before him, and knew where his brethren were laboring. They were to have no regard for any other sect or people, but to preach in their place to all who would hear them, and gather into their society all who would join them.

The days of bloody persecution for religious dissent had passed away. The puritans had fought the battle, and gained a general toleration of all religions. The Methodists therefore grew up without opposition from government. Indeed when their meetings were threatened, as they often were by the mob, the government usually protected them.

From England they soon passed to Ireland, America, the Indies, Africa, and the continent of Europe, maintaining every where, as far as possible, the same system.

Mr. Wesley lived to see the 88th year of his age, and 65th of his ministry He died March 2, 1791. He maintained to the day of his death a perfect ascendency over the vast body that had adhered to him. He was remarkably neat in his person, exact in his habits, simple in his style of speaking and writing; a man of great ardor; confident, bold, and of unparalleled diligence. He is supposed to have traveled near 300,000 miles, and to have preached more than 40,000 sermons. He presided at forty-seven annual conferences.

After his death his followers were much divided on points of government. Wesley had ever closely adhered to the church of England. He did not permit his traveling preachers to preach in church hours, or administer baptism or the Lord's supper, but directed all his people to attend the church worship, and receive the ordinances from the hands of the regular clergy. At his decease, many united in publishing a declaration that they would adhere to his system, but others revolted and established a new connection in which they had preaching in church hours, and the ordinances administered by their own preachers, and in which also the people had a voice in the temporal concerns of the societies, and the election of church officers.

The Methodists under the care of the British and Irish conferences, which includes all excepting those in the United States, are about 400,000. Their traveling preachers, about 1500.

A seminary was established by Mr. Wesley at Kingswood, for the education of the children of preachers.

The first Wesleyan Theological Institution for the improvement of junior preachers, was established in 1834. The great names in their history are Wm. Wesley, Richard Watson, and Dr. Adam Clarke. Their missionary operations have been carried on with great system and energy.

A few Methodists came to New York from Ireland in 1766, and through the labors of a Mr. Embury, so increased, that they erected a meeting house in John street in 1768. The next year two preachers were sent over by Mr. Wesley from England. And in 1771, came over Francis Asbury and Richard Wright. Thomas Rankin was also sent over by Wesley to take the general superintendence of the American churches. Through the exertions of these and other zealous laborers, the number of the Methodists was soon greatly increased, and in 1773 a regular conference was held in Philadelphia.

Until the close of the Revolutionary war, the system of Methodism was according to the plan of Wesley. The preachers were not empowered to administer ordinances, and the people were obliged to go to other churches. As the United States had now become independent of Great Britain, Wesley determined to make the American churches independent; and sent Dr. Thomas Coke, commissioned as a superintendent or bishop, to constitute the American churches independent; to raise Mr. Asbury to the same office, and to ordain preachers and elders. He arrived in 1784, and on the 25th of Dec., consecrated Mr. Asbury to the office of bishop. The number of members in America then, was 14,988, and of preachers 83. Universal satisfaction was expressed at the procedure; and the general cause was revived and strengthened. Bishop Asbury imitated Wesley in his diligence and labor, and a vast increase of numbers was soon gained to the Methodist cause.

The Methodist church in the United States, like that in Great Britain, is Episcopal. Its clergy consist of bishops, presiding elders, elders, deacons, and an unordained order of licensed preachers. Its preachers are also divided into itinerant and local, or such as travel at the discretion of the ecclesiastical authorities, and such as perform duty only as opportunity offers. Its great ecclesiastical authority, is the general conference. Previous to 1808, it met annually. It was then agreed on account of the extent of the country, that there should be several annual conferences in the United States, and one general conference of delegates from these subordinates; in the ratio of one delegate for every 21 itinerant preachers, which should meet once in four years. The general conference elects bishops and makes rules and regulations for the church. On some points, however, it can legislate only by the joint recommendation of all the annual conferences, and by a vote of two thirds of the general conference. In the United States, there are fifty-one annual conferences, consisting of all the traveling preachers in full connection, and no others. They perpetuate themselves by the election of their own members, and hold the exclusive right of sitting in judgment on the character and conduct of their members. No itinerant preacher can make any appeal from their decision, except to the general conference.

The bishops, who are eight in number, ordain elders and deacons, preside in the conferences, appoint presiding elders, assign to every preacher the circuit or station in which he shall labor, for a term not exceeding two years in succession, and take the general oversight of the spiritual and temporal concerns of the church.

There is a presiding elder to each particular district, whose business it is to preside at each quarterly conference meeting within his district; exhorters and preachers are licensed at the quarterly conference meeting, but when the quarterly meeting is not in session, the presiding elder or a preacher can license exhorters, subject to the decision of the next meeting.

The traveling preachers are appointed to their stations by the bishop; they remove and appoint the class-leaders, and nominate the stewards, subject to the decision of the quarterly meeting; their stipend is regular, and ordinarily sufficient.

The superannuated clergy are supported from the profits of a book concern, under the patronage of the denomination, and the regular contributions of the people. The Wesleyans in America maintain sentiments similar to those in England. They value highly Adam Clarke's Commentary on the Bible. They have class meetings, band meetings, love feasts, quarterly meetings for communion, and camp meetings. They have a college at Middletown, Ct.; at Carlisle and Meadville, Pa.; at Boydton, Va.; at La Grange, Ala.; at Augusta, Ky.; at Lebanon, Ill.; at Green Castle, Ind.; at Delaware, Ohio; at Lima, N. Y.; and at Appleton, Wis.

They have in the United States eight bishops, fifty-one conferences, 6,034 traveling preachers, 9,677 local preachers, and 1,250,000 members, North and South.

No denomination is so well organized for increase. But a diversity of opinion has manifested itself on the subject of episcopal government. Some wish to change the government now confined to the traveling preacher and ultimately centering in the bishops, so as to give the local preachers and private members a voice. These have seceded from the main body, and are called THE ASSOCIATED or PROTESTANT METHODISTS. They have 740 ministers, and 64,313 communicants.

In 1843 the connection of "*Wesleyan Methodists*" was formed, composed chiefly of seceders from the Methodist Episcopal Church, who were dissatisfied with that church in consequence of its connection with slavery and its form of government. They already number 600 ministers, and 20,000 communicants. They have no Bishops, and will not admit slaveholders to their communion.

WHITFIELDIAN OR CALVINISTIC METHODISTS.

After his separation from Mr. Wesley, Mr. Whitfield continued to go through England, Scotland, and America, melting thousands by his eloquence. Fourteen times he crossed the Atlantic, and finally died in the midst of his labors, at Newburyport, Mass., September 30, 1770, aged 55.

Mr. Whitfield never marshaled his followers into a distinct sect as did Mr. Wesley. He ever remained in communion with the church of England, though he commonly engaged in extemporaneous prayer. After the death of Whitfield, the Calvinistic Methodists formed a union, but have never been reduced to much order. In England there are about eighty places of worship, and in Wales three hundred and fifty. The preachers in Wales are chiefly itinerant.

SWEDENBORGIANS.

The Swedenborgians derive their names from Emmanuel Swedenborg, a man of great learning and ability, who lived in the seventeenth century. He received the Scriptures as a divine revelation, but claimed that they contained an *inner meaning* in addition to their more palpable interpretation, which inner meaning may be said to bear the same resemblance to external interpretation that the soul does to the body. Swedenborg did not put forth this view as a mere theory, but claimed to be informed of the truth of his utterances through direct communications from the spiritual world. His followers receive his teachings as a new revelation, not denying or in any way invalidating, but developing and unfolding the true meaning of the inspired writings.

The great mass of the Christian world, while they admit the piety, learning, and genius of Swedenborg, believe that his claims, while honestly asserted on his part, are the result of a diseased imagination.

His followers hold that Christ was God incarnate, but do not believe in a tri-personal Deity, or in what is called the orthodox view of the atonement. As a class, they are intelligent and correct in their conduct.

The Swedenborgians have in the United States 42 churches, 50 ministers, and 8,000 communicants.

UNIVERSALISTS.

The doctrine that all mankind will, through the merits of Christ, finally be admitted into the Kingdom of Heaven, is the distinguishing feature in the creed of the Universalist denomination. Origen, in the third century, entertained some views of this nature, but none of the reformers, unless it be the Socinians, adopted it. The first open advocate of any importance in modern times, of Universalism, was Dr. Chauncey, of Boston. He considered that Christ died for all men and that it was the purpose of God that all should finally be saved, and that in this state or another, all would be reduced by God to a willing subjection to his moral government. These sentiments he advanced in an anonymous volume, published in London in 1784. Dr. Jonathan Edwards of New Haven, wrote a reply.

In England similar sentiments were advanced by James Relly, one of the preachers of Mr. Whitfield. He believed in strict imputation, and extended it to all mankind ; supposing that through the death of Christ, all were perfectly restored to the divine favor.

He rejected water-baptism and the sacrament. Numbers adhered to him.

Mr. Murray, an English Universalist, emigrated to America before the revolution, and established some congregations, and the Universalists now number 1234 churches and 700 ministers.

With but few exceptions, the Universalists are Unitarian in sentiment. Baptism and the Sacrament are generally adhered to by them.

In 1831 a portion separated from the rest, taking the name of UNIVERSAL RESTORATIONISTS ; maintaining future, but denying endless punishment. They have about 30 ministers and about 3000 members. Another branch contend for the final annihilation of the wicked. They are called Annihilationists.

CHRISTIANS.

The Christians, emphasizing the first syllable, are a somewhat numerous body both in England and America. They have come out from Baptists, Methodists and Presbyterians. They are Unitarians in sentiment ; but they reject all creeds ; and yet hold to Christ as a divine Saviour. They have been a people singularly by themselves, having no fellowship with others and very proselyting. They have a Theological school at Meadville, Pa., and have both in England and America about 1800 ministers, and 140,000 members.

IRVINGITES.

The Irvingites date back to 1836 in America. They consider themselves as the Holy Catholic and Apostolic Church, having the Apostolate, the prophetic office and the gift of tongues. The Apostles are the highest order. All others are subject to them. They have a liturgical service.

In 1810, Rev. Thomas Campbell of the secession Church, North of Ireland, and his son Alexander at Bush Run, Pa.; Baptists, became the founders of a denomination which has been numerous in America, and the source of no little trouble to those who differed from them. They opposed all creeds, and much confounded Regeneration, Conversion and Baptism. In fact, they made not faith, but baptism the remitting ordinance of the gospel. To whosoever was baptized, their sins were remitted, and though regeneration and conversion were assumed, yet remission through baptism, became the leading doctrine, and great attraction into the church. From 1813 to 1828 they were connected with the Baptists; then came a schism. They were much engaged in controversy in 1820, 1823 and 1830. In 1858 they numbered 2000 churches, 2000 ministers and 350,000 members.

MORMONS.—LATTER DAY SAINTS.

This extraordinary denomination, affirming that God has a material body, claiming the gift of tongues and prophecy, and sanctioning and practising polygamy, originated with Joseph Smith of Sharon, Vt., the translator of certain golden plates which were said to have been found at Nephi in Ohio, and deciphered through white stones. The translation was published as THE BOOK OF MORMONS. A church was founded April 6, 1830. In its organization were three high priests, eighteen apostles, seventy elders. It soon extended to Europe, whence many converts emigrated to America. A magnificent temple was erected at Nauvoo city, which place in 1842 numbered 10,000 people. In 1846 the Mormons were compelled to flee to Utah, the great Salt Lake. They number 60,000 in America, 30,000 in Europe, and many in other parts of world. They receive the Bible with the Apochrypha and Book of Mormon, all as inspired. Conflicts with the Government and the encroachments of miners and others have given them much disturbance. Of late there has been a schism in the Mormon ranks. The seceding party declare against polygamy, and content themselves with one wife each.

PERFECTIONISTS.

The Perfectionists have not formed a distinct sect or denomination with a form of church government, though various societies have been formed, and some distinguished preachers have advocated the doctrine of sinless perfection in this life. Pres. Finney and Prof. Mahan at Oberlin, viewing man as capable of obeying the whole law of God, and therefore under obligation to do it, felt that they could not deny but that, in some cases, it might be done. Others have felt confident that they had attained to an entire freedom from all sin. More numerous are those who believe in a second conversion, and in living a much higher life, with more light, more joy, greater nearness to God, and greater foretastes of heaven.

MILLERITES.

Were the followers of Wm. Miller of Low Hampton, N. Y., who, in 1833, began preaching that the end of the world was near, as early as 1843. Miller by preaching and the wide diffusion of a paper called the Advent Herald produced great excitement. As many as 20,000 imbibed his views, and many began to lay aside all their worldly business. When 1843 was passed, they fixed upon 1847. As their predictions failed of fulfilment, they lost their power. They called themselves Adventists.

CHAPTER XXIV.

Protestant Missions. Neglected by the reformers. First attended to by the puritans in North America. Eliot. Mayhews. Brainard. Danish missions. Swartz. Hans Egede. Moravian missions. Wesleyan Methodist missions. Baptist. London, Edinburgh, Church Missionary Society. Buchanan. Martyn. American Board. Bible, Tract, and Education societies. Concluding Remarks.

WE have traced the Christian Church down through eighteen hundred years, and seen her engrossing the attention of but a small part of the human race. In the mean time, far the greater part of mankind have been totally ignorant of her existence; while myriads who have known her, have united in treating her with contumely and scorn. The last command of Christ was felt in all its proper authority by the Apostles and first Christians, and the Gospel received under their efforts, an amazing extension. The ten heathen persecutions in some measure broke the spirit of the followers of the Lamb, and the patronage of Constantine corrupted their principles; and when the world had broken into the church, she was then engaged for centuries in building up a temporal kingdom, forgetful of the spiritual wants and woes of the heathen. The eighth century was an "age of missionaries," and twilight shone upon the north of Europe, through the apostolic labors of Boniface, Willebrod, Villehad, Llefewyn, and others; but Mahometanism soon destroyed the churches in the East, and "gross darkness" covered those in the West. When Luther broke the power of the Roman hierarchy, and wrested from its dominions the fairest States of Europe, a prodigious effort was made by the prostrate power to regain what it had lost at home, from among pagan nations. We have sufficiently noticed its missionary proceedings.

The reformers were too much engaged in the immense revolution which they were effecting at home, to think much of those who were bowing to idols in distant lands. Their geographical knowledge, too, was small; and their intercourse with pagans almost as little as with the inhabitants of another planet. As commerce opened to the view of Europe the numberless tribes of men, they formed an acquaintance with their spiritual wants, and when they saw, they pitied The love of Christ was not a cold, inactive principle in their breasts. Their operations, however, were slow and small. Centuries rolled away, and little was done. And even now, protestant nations have reason to blush and be ashamed, in view of their diminutive operations in the conversion of the world.

The 16th century presents us with but two feeble efforts of the protestants among the heathen; one, of the Swedes among the Laplanders, to whom they gave the New Testament, the other, of fourteen students from Geneva, who went to the Indians of South America, but soon perished.

In the 17th century, when the greatest efforts might have been expected, as the protestant churches had become firmly established, wealthy and numerous, was almost equally barren of incidents, excepting with the Dutch, and the band of emigrants to North America.

The former carried with them the Gospel in their widely extended commerce in the East. Had they pursued a course of thorough instruction, the good they had done would have been incalculably great, and India might now have presented some of the fairest churches of Cnristendom. But they baptized, and admitted to the profession of Christianity, every individual who could repeat the Lord's prayer, the ten commandments, a morning and evening prayer, and say grace before and after meals. In 1688, 180,364 of the inhabitants of Jaffnapatam had thus received Christianity. In the city of Batavia, a church was opened, and 100,000 persons were thus brought into its connexion. Numerous churches were also collected in like manner in Sumatra, Timor, Celebes, and the Molucca Islands, which the Dutch were careful to furnish with the Bible in their own language. But what could be expected of Christians thus formed, without a change of heart? They must have been then, as the remnant of them are now, mere pagans, with a nominal profession of the religion of Jesus.

A more spiritual and evangelical work was attempted and carried on in the latter part of the century, by the emigrants to North America. About twenty nations of Indians came under the influence of the English colonists. These Indians were polytheists. Like most pagans, they believed in two superior deities, good and evil, Kitchhan and Hobbamok. Their priests, called powaws, were supposed to have much secret communication with them. They had no temples, excepting in the country of the Narragansetts, where was one. They were much subjected to the delusions of witchcraft. Their powaws pretended to perform wonders, and inflicted upon themselves the most horrible severities. The Indians had some notions of another life, and happiness or misery, according as they were good or bad. Their ignorance and wickedness early excited the compassion of the pious Puritans. The heart of the Rev. John Eliot, who had emigrated from England in 1631, and settled at Roxbury, was particularly affected. The wretchedness of the heathen, the design of emigration, the seal of the colony, on which was pictured a poor Indian with a label in his mouth, "Come over and help us," pressed him to do something. He saw in them many things resembling Jewish customs, and thought they might be descendants of the dispersed Israelites, concerning whom there was a promise of conversion. The Indians had no written language, but Mr. Eliot soon learned their barbarous dialect, and preached with great success. The sachems and powaws became alarmed, lest they should lose all their influence over the people, and threatened to kill him if he did not desist. But he did not fear them, and always said to them, "I am about the work of the great God, and my God is with me; so that I neither fear you, nor all the sachems in the country. I will go on, and do you touch me if you dare." It was his custom to take care of his own flock and go on a missionary tour once a fortnight, through various parts of Massachusets and Plymouth, preaching Christ. His fatigue and dangers were great, but he never sunk before them. "I have not," he says in a letter, "been dry night or day, from the third day of the week unto the sixth; but so traveled; and at night pull off my boots, wring my stockings, and on with them again and so continue. But God steps in and helps. I have considered the word of God, 1 Tim. ii. 3; 'endure hardness as a good soldier of Jesus Christ.'"

In 1660, an Indian church was formed at Natick, and numbers were admitted to the Lord's table, who had stood as catecumens or been propounded ten years. These abandoned polygamy, drunkenness, and other sins. Other churches were soon after formed in other places. And that they might be built up in a most holy faith, Mr. Eliot translated and published in their language the whole Bible,* perhaps the greatest labor ever performed by any man. The whole was written with one pen. He also composed and translated a primer, grammar, singing psalms, the practice of piety, and Baxter's call to the unconverted. He might well remark, "prayers and pains will do any thing."

This wonderful man, whose firmness, zeal, benevolence and perseverance were almost unparalleled, lived to see six respectable churches, and twenty-four Indian preachers laboring successfully as missionaries of the cross. He rested from his labors May 20, 1690, aged 86. He has well been called the APOSTLE OF THE INDIANS.

The Mayhews also deserve to be had in everlasting remembrance for their long continued and successful labors on Martha's Vineyard. For a century and a half, this family devoted themselves to the conversion of the heathen. In 1652, 282 gave evidence of conversion and were received into the Christian church. Eight of them were powaws. At a subsequent period, of 180 families, only two remained heathen. By Experience

---

* The longest word is in Mark i. 40: Wuttappesittukgussunnoohwchtunkquoh.

Mayhew, the Psalms, and John, were translated into their language.

Others among the first settlers of New England, entered into the same field of labors with much success. The character of their converts is very interesting and dear to all the lovers of experimental religion, and shows that man in his most savage state, can be brought to the knowledge of God and may taste the joys of salvation. The wars with the colonists soon interrupted all efforts to evangelize the Indians, and drove them from New England.

David Brainard distinguished himself in the middle of the last century, by his zeal for the conversion of the American Indians. At Crosweeksung, N. J., he witnessed a signal outpouring of the Spirit upon the nations of the forest. Multitudes seemed to be convinced of sin and to submit themselves to God. Thirty he saw seated at the table of Christ. Mr. Brainard early fell a prey to a feeble constitution and severe hardships. He died at Northampton, Oct. 9, 1747, aged 29. He is considered as one of the most pious of later missionaries, and as having given the great spring to modern missionary enterprise.

Laudable efforts were also made to enlighten and convert the Stockbridge Indians, by Mr. Sergeant and President Edwards; and also afterwards to convey the gospel to the Oneidas and Senecas, by Mr. S. Kirkland.

The first of the modern European nations, that seriously engaged in converting the heathen were the Danes. Messrs. Zeingenbalg and Plutsche were sent by Frederic IV. to the Malabar coast in India, in 1705. They early translated the four Gospels into the Malabar tongue, and subsequently the whole Bible. At the end of twenty-four years the number of the baptized amounted to 8000, and but ten missionaries were in the field.

In 1750, Swartz engaged in this mission, and remained in it forty-eight years. He was a rare missionary of the cross. His influence over the heathen, especially over those in exalted stations, was probably unparalleled. The Rajah of Tanjore, made him his counselor, and when he died, committed to him the care of his son. When Swartz died, the reigning Rajah made great lamentation over him, covered his body with a gold cloth, and erected a monument to his memory. More than two thousand were converted by him to the faith of Christ. Other valuable men have entered into his labors, and not less than 80,000 of all casts have here received Christianity.

In 1708, the attention of the Danes was turned toward Greenland. That country was settled in the middle of the ninth century. About the eleventh, it was enlightened by the Gospel, but for three hundred years, it had been entirely secluded from the continent. Hans Egede, a clergyman of Norway, fancying that his countrymen were still there, resolved to visit them; and, under the patronage of the king of Denmark, sailed with his family in 1721, for that inhospitable region. The old colony was extinct. The country barren; the inhabitants barbarous. A set of jugglers called Angehoks controlled their spirits. But amid the unparalleled distress from polar winters, pestilence, famines, and a barbarous people, the mission has continued, and by the assistance of the Moravians, paganism is nearly abolished in the country.

The efforts of the Danes arrested the attention of the Moravians, and in 1732 they entered into the same labors. And though only about 600 in number; poor exiles; without literature, wealth, or patronage, they have made themselves known in every clime. Every Moravian is a missionary in his feelings, and stands ready to go to the ends of the earth, when directed by the elder's conference. Their first station was among the blacks in the West Indies. Their next on the icy shores of Greenland. They have planted themselves among the Indians of America, the Hottentots of Africa, and the hordes of Tartary, and supported themselves by the hardest toil. They have now about thirty stations, and employ 170 laborers, including females, and number 30,000 converts. They are a wonderful people. The history of their missions is full of interest.

The Methodists have, from the very first, considered themselves as engaged in a kind of mission throughout Christendom; and, until of late, have turned their attention but little to heathen lands.

In 1786, Dr. Coke, a Wesleyan Methodist, engaged on his own responsibility, and without patronage, in a mission, chiefly among the blacks of the West Indies. He was followed in his labors, by a number of active missionaries, who collected societies, and who now number about 25,000 in their connection. They have had to contend with violent opposition from the slave-holders, and from the regular established clergy. Both of these have had the government on their side, and very severe laws have been passed from time to time, against all who in this manner, accounted irregular, preached the Gospel, and collected assemblies of the blacks. Both the preachers and their converts, have been imprisoned, and severely chastised, and some most disgraceful and cruel scenes have been acted.

In 1814, that enterprising man, Dr. Coke, sailed from England with seven other missionaries for the island of Ceylon. Dr. Coke died on his passage. His surviving brethren established themselves at Colombo, where they have since labored with fidelity and success. Their number has been since considerably reinforced. Their Church members exceed 300.

The Methodists have since planted stations at Australia, Sierra Leone, South Africa, and Bombay.

A Wesleyan missionary society was formed at London, Dec. 1, 1814, which raised in 1821, 137,444 dollars. It supports 148 missionaries.

The Wesleyans in North America, have stations among a number of the Indian tribes.

The attention of the Baptists was first directed to the subject of missions about the year 1784. But no system of operation was set in motion until 1792, when the Rev. Mr. Carey of Leicester, in England, who had borne the wants of the heathen much on his heart, having preached a sermon before his association, in which he exhorted them to *Expect great things*, and *Attempt great things*, a SOCIETY was formed, and 13*l*. 2*s*. 6*d*. was subscribed to send the Gospel to the heathen. Which way to direct their attention they knew not. Providentially their views were turned to India, by Mr. Thomas, a surgeon, who had resided there, and had his compassion excited for the myriads there, in Pagan darkness; and he, with Mr. Carey, were designated and solemnly set apart for that field of labor. They arrived in Calcutta with their families, November, 1793.

They took their station amid hundreds of millions, who have for centuries been subject to the grossest idolatry, and most debasing superstitions. The mythology of the Hindoos has taught them the existence of a Supreme Being, but has shut him out from all concern with the world; excepting as he has created three principal deities, called Brahma,

Vishnou, and Seva, to whom he has committed its creation, government, and preservation. These are worshipped, especially the second, who is supposed to have had nine incarnations, all of which are represented by various images. Besides these, the Hindoos have inferior gods and goddesses, amounting to 230,000.000. Every family has its household god, which is placed at the entrance of their dwelling Their images are made of brass, wood, and stone, and though said to be mere images, are worshipped by the mass of the people as gods. They worship also the heavenly bodies; their spiritual guides; the cow; the Ganges, which has on its banks three millions of sacred places, annually visited by millions of people. The country is filled with temples. The most sacred of their religious establishments is the temple or car of Juggernaut, an horrid idol, which has been visited annually by millions for worship, and to which vast multitudes have sacrificed their lives.

Their whole system of worship is most cruel, debasing, and polluting. Horrid self-tortures are daily practised and applauded. Innumerable infants are destroyed. Widows are compelled to be burned on the funeral piles of their husbands. No morality is taught or known among these vast myriads of the human family. They are perfect fatalists, and have no belief in man's accountableness. After death, the soul is supposed to pass into some other body, or to a bird or beast.

Their divisions into casts, renders them almost impenetrable by the preachers of the Gospel. These casts are different degrees or orders in society. Of these, there are two Brahmins, or priests, and the Soodra, or common people, but each of these has many divisions and sub-divisions. Every man is obliged to follow exactly the business of his father. Each line of business is a cast. All social intercourse between the casts is forbidden. If a person eats or marries with one of another cast, or interferes with his employment, he loses cast, which is a calamity worse than death. He is deprived of his property; forsaken of his friends; treated every where as a vile outcast, and left to drag out a most miserable existence in famine and disgrace. But cast he must lose, who eats with a missionary or listens to the Gospel.

Throughout India, the education of all but the Brahmins, is very limited. The myriads of females are never taught by them, to read, and are considered as a grade below the cow.

Among such a people did these two Baptist brethren throw themselves, a drop in the ocean, but a drop with which the ocean would not assimilate, and losing their friends, they came near perishing for want of sustenance. They hired themselves to an indigo factory, and there began their labor. In 1796, they were joined by Mr. Fountain, and in 1799, by Messrs. Marshman, Grant, and Brunsdon, with their wives, and Mr. Ward and Miss Tidd. The whole fixed the seat of their labors at Serampore. They threw all their property and the fruits of their labor into a common stock. Some of them have fallen asleep. But some have lived to see the Bible translated either in whole, or in part, into forty-three different languages, each spoken by millions of people, and issued from their press and circulated among the people, and to behold numerous missionary stations established by their European brethren in various parts of India; above 1000 natives converted to Christianity, who have renounced cast and been baptized, and several preaching with much success to their countrymen, the everlasting Gospel. With every missionary station is connected large schools, in which vast numbers of children are educated in the principles of Christianity. Such operations, persevered in, must and will undermine and overthrow even the gigantic system of Hindoo superstition.

The Baptists in America were first excited to this all important subject, by two missionaries in India, of the American Board, Judson and Rice, who left the service in which they were engaged, in consequence of a change of sentiment on the subject of baptism. The Baptists at Serampore had made an unsuccessful attempt to establish a mission at Burmah. Mr. Judson directed his attention to that country, and Mr. Rice returned to America to seek patronage. Through his influence, an American BAPTIST MISSIONARY BOARD was formed at Philadelphia, in 1814, by delegates from eleven States, and handsome collections were made in most of the Baptist churches. Mr. Judson, accompanied by Dr. Price, a physician, remained for some time at Rangoon, a solitary laborer.

In 1816, the Board sent Mr. Hough and wife to his aid, and subsequently Mrs. Wade and Boardman.

The Burmese are civilized like the Hindoos; but are debased and bloody pagans; chiefly followers of Boodhu. The prospects of the missionaries have ever been discouraging. Mr. Judson translated the New Testament into the language of the Burmese. The Baptist Board has also established stations in Africa and among the North American Indians, which have been much prospered.

The zeal with which the Baptists in England engaged in missions in England, excited a number of dissenters and members of the establishment to unite, Sept. 22, 1795, in the formation of the splendid LONDON MISSIONARY SOCIETY.

Its attention was first directed to the South Sea Islands. A ship called the Duff, commanded by Captain Wilson, was prepared, and thirty persons sailed, August 10, 1796, from London. Some were left on the Friendly Islands, in a partially civilized community: but were soon, through adverse providences, part destroyed, and part compelled to flee to New Holland. The remainder landed at Otaheite amid the most deplorable ruins of the fall. There where the eye witnessed a fertile soil, salubrious climate, and delightful scenery, it also beheld the most awful moral desolation, accompanied with no mental cultivation or refinement of manners, and connected with a religion which sanctified every crime—a *taboo* system, the most horrid; the offering of human sacrifices to the most foolish and absurd idols ever imposed by Satan upon mankind.

Fifteen years they toiled amid worse than Egyptian darkness. At length, light began to dawn. In 1813, Pomare the king, was impressed by the Gospel, and soon renounced his idol gods. His people followed him. For years the Sun of righteousness has now shone upon the island; and 12,000 adults have been taught to read; 3000 children are in schools; 28 houses of worship have been erected, and are filled Sabbath after Sabbath, by worshippers of Jehovah; idolatry and superstition have passed away; peace has succeeded to the most cruel and desolating wars, a missionary spirit is excited, and eighteen natives have entered the field of labor, through whose instrumentality two churches have been formed on distant islands, and 5000 taught to read. A nation was born born in a day. It brought millenium nigh.

The London society have establishments also in other parts of the globe. In 1798, Dr. Vanderkemp, a learned and skilful physician, whose name is precious in missionary annals, with Mr. Kicherer, was sent to the Hotentots and Bushmen of Africa, through whose instrumentality, together with that of successive laborers, some thousands have come to the knowledge of Christ. Fifteen stations, 25 missionaries, and some native preachers are now under the care of the society, in the South of Africa. To the East and West Indies the Society have also sent forth able heralds of salvation, who are active in dispelling the thick darkness which veils the human mind in those regions. Among its laborers, no one deserved greater commendation than Mr. Morrison, who had compiled a Chinese grammar and dictionary; translated the Scriptures into the Chinese language; and circulated above 150,000 pamphlets and tracts. The Chinese are pagans, though not so gross as the Hindoos. They are worshippers of the god Foe.

In 1801, a missionary seminary was established at Gosport, in England, under the care of Dr. Bogue.

In 1796, the Scotch came forward with their usual zeal in religion, and formed the EDINBURGH MISSIONARY SOCIETY. They first directed their attention to the Sosoo country in Africa. But being unsuccessful, they turned to Tartary, where they have had three stations, and the prospect of doing great good by circulating Bibles and tracts in the Tartary language, through the immense regions of Tartary, Persia and China.

Until the commencement of the 19th century, the immense church establishment of England remained a stranger to foreign missions. A society was indeed formed in 1647, "for the propagation of the Gospel in foreign parts," which received the sanction of parliament, and the patronage of different princes, but had done little excepting in British provinces. In 1800, was formed the noble CHURCH MISSIONARY SOCIETY.

Its first missionaries were sent to Western Africa—awfully debased by the slave trade, where, after conflicting with many most distressing evils, their stations are flourishing. But the immense British dominions in Asia, have been the chief object of attention. There, their operations have been generously supported and blessed. A recent effort to teach females to read, who have for centuries been totally neglected as incapable of it, has been very successful and promises to effect the greatest changes in India.

In 1814, an establishment was formed under the Rev. Henry Marsden, at New Zealand, among a people barbarous in the extreme, and continually engaged in the most ferocious contests. This society had 45 stations, 296 schools, 440 teachers and laborers, and 14,000 scholars. It had a flourishing missionary seminary at Islington.

Two Britons, though employed by no missionary society will be held in lasting remembrance for their labors among the heathen. The first, Claudius Buchanan, D. D., one of the Chaplains to the East India Company at Bengal, was for a course of years indefatigable in his labors in ascertaining the state of the moral and religious world in the East, and in rousing the attention of his countrymen at home to its spiritual desolations. He died in England, Feb. 9, 1815. The other, Henry Martyn, who was excited to devote his life to the heathen by reading the life of David Brainard, gained the chaplaincy to the East India Company. He reached Dinapore, Nov. 1806, and having learned the Hindostanee, he translated into it the liturgy and the New Testament. From India he traveled into Persia; boldly disputed with the Mahometan doctors; translated the New Testament into the Persian, and produced a prodigious excitement in that kingdom. He was cut off at Tocat by a fever, in the midst of usefulness, Aug. 16, 1812, aged 31. "While some shall delight to gaze upon the splendid sepulchre of Xavier, and others choose rather to ponder over the granite stone which covers all that is mortal of Swartz, there will not be wanting those who will think of the humble and unfrequented grave of Henry Martyn, and be led to imitate those works of mercy which have followed him into the world of light and love."

The friends of missions in Germany have of late been directing their efforts towards the southern provinces of the Russian empire, where German colonists are planted through the Crimea and Georgia—even to the borders of Persia. Their object is to revive religion among their countrymen, to awaken into life the ancient Greek Church, and ultimately to carry their conquests into the territories of Mahomet.

The spirit of Missions which once burned in the breasts of Eliot, the Mayhews, and Brainard, had become nearly extinct in the American churches as they advanced in age and increased in riches, and for a considerable period no sympathy seemed to have been felt for the nations sitting in the region and shadow of death. In 1787, a society was formed in Boston, for propagating the Gospel among the Indians and others in North America; but little, however, was ever effected by it. This was followed by the institution of the New York Missionary Society, in 1796—the Connecticut, in 1798—the Massachusetts, in 1799—and the New Jersey, in 1801—all valuable institutions; but their efforts were chiefly directed to the relief of the destitute in the New Settlements. The General Assembly of the Presbyterian Church have also for some years had annual collections for missions.

Soon after the opening of the present century, that spirit again burst forth and will continue, it is hoped, to burn, until the kingdoms of this world are all become the kingdoms of our Lord and of his Christ. That great institution, THE AMERICAN BOARD OF COMMISSIONERS FOR FOREIGN MISSIONS, was formed in 1810. A generous legacy of 30,000 dollars was received from a lady; others threw their gifts into the Lord's treasury, and five beloved missionaries, Judson, Hall, Newell, Nott and Rice, were ordained and sent with their wives to India.* Much perplexity attended them on their arrival. The government ordered them to return. Mr. Newell, in endeavoring to plant himself in the Isle of France, was called to see his lovely wife close her eyes in death. Mrs. Judson and Rice unexpectedly avowed a change on the subject of baptism, and withdrew from the services of the Board. After many trials, Newell, Hall, and Nott, commenced labor at Bombay.

June 21, 1815, a new mission was fitted out for the East. Four missionaries were sent to Ceylon. Nor were the Board unmindful of the wants of the heathen on their own continent. They sent Mr. Kingsbury, in 1817, to the Cherokee country, by whom a foundation was laid for extensive establishments, both among the Cherokees and Choctaws. In 1820, a large and valuable mission was sent to the Sandwich Islands, in the Pacific Ocean. The religion and morals there were not dissimilar to those of the Society Islanders, though, through a wonderful providence, just before the arrival of the missionaries, they had renounced all their idol gods. The next year, the attention of the Board was directed to the countries about the Mediterranean Sea, particularly Jerusalem and the Holy Land, and two missionaries were sent out to explore, and establish a mission.

The zeal and success of the Board roused to action the friends of Christ in New York and its vicinity; and in 1818, they formed a society, denominated the United Foreign

---

* The beloved Samuel J. Mills was devoted to the same mission, but was detained at home by Providence, and became a great instrument in exciting the American Churches to the formation of some of the noblest institutions of the age. He died on a passage from Africa, June 16, 1818, aged 34, whither he had been in the service of the Colonization Society, which lay near

Missionary Society. Two large establishments were made by them among the Osage Indians. Missionaries were also sent by them to the Indians in New York, to the Michigan Territory, and in Ohio, and to the colored people of Hayti. But in the summer of 1826, an union was formed between this society and the American board, and these stations were transferred to the care of the board.

Since its institution, the American board has been blessed with a constantly increasing patronage from the American churches; and though it has been called to weep over the early extinction of many of the bright lights which it has planted in regions of darkness, yet it has had the happiness to find others, burning with equal brightness, to place in their stead, and to behold all dispelling, to an amazing extent, the thick darkness of paganism.

In Bombay, Newell, Nichols, Frost, Hall, and others, have successively fallen before the king of terrors. But through the labors of these men and their companions, the New Testament, and some part of the Old, have been faithfully translated and printed in the vernacular tongue of twelve millions of people, and more than a million Christian publications have been put into circulation, and many children have been taught to read and know something of the true God, and of Jesus Christ. A chapel has been erected at Bombay. This mission " has struck its roots deep in the native soil."

On Ceylon, God has remarkably poured out his Spirit, and the mission church contains not less than 500 native members who give great evidence of sound piety. Some have become preachers of the Gospel.

Southern and Western Africa have been blessed with the light of the Gospel sent forth by this noble institution.

At the American stations, Brainard, Eliot, and Mayhew, (named after the distinguished friends of the heathen in former times) some of the natives exhibited bright examples of piety and benevolence. The children in numerous schools, have showed much intelligence and industry. But the removal of the Indians to the west of the Mississippi, has broken up these missionary labors.

The success of the Sandwich Island mission, has been similar to that of the London mission to Otaheite without its delay and awful trials. These isles truly " waited for His law." And when it was published they submissively received it. Thousands of people have been brought under the instruction of native teachers who have been taught by the missionaries. The native language has been reduced to writing; Bibles, and books, and tracts, have been printed and vast multitudes of the people are able to read. During the winter of 1839, in an outpouring of the Spirit, more than 10,000 were added to the churches of Christ. Immense churches have been erected which are thronged with worshippers. The Spirit has been poured out upon various places, and thousands have erected the family altar. Chiefs, of great influence, have publicly professed the religion of Christ. Whole villages once given to drunkenness, theft and murder, have become sober and honest. The Sabbath is generally sacredly observed. They are now a Christian nation.

The Palestine mission was early deprived by death, of two beloved missionaries, Parsons and Fisk; but no small degree of evangelical light has shone upon that part of benighted Asia. Since the establishment of the mission, more than 35,000,000 pages have been issued from the press in Western Asia.

The Board have continued to extend their operations until now in 1864 they have 20 missions, 112 stations, 211 outstations, 154 ordained missionaries, 36 native pastors, 154 churches, 22,952 church members, 9,634 pupils in schools. The receipts are now annually from 4 to 500,000 dollars. In 1857, the Dutch churches withdrew from the Board and established a Foreign Mission for themselves. In their work they have been active and successful.

In 1846 was established the American Missionary Association on an Anti-Slavery basis. Its first missions were in the Mendi country, Africa. Its income is large and its missions are successful.

In 1849 was established The American and Foreign Christian Union. Its object was the evangelization of Roman Catholic countries. It has 125 laborers and expends annually about 75,000 dollars.

In 1843 the Old School Presbyterian Church established a Board of Foreign Missions which has been very prosperous and successful, chiefly in Northern India; having had 10 missions and 20 to 30 missionaries in the field. Some have fallen martyrs before the cruel heathen.

On the 20th of May, 1823, the PROTESTANT EPISCOPAL

MISSIONARY SOCIETY IN THE UNITED STATES, was formed at Philadelphia. Auxiliary societies have been established and preparations made for active co-operation with other societies in bringing men to the knowledge of salvation.

As the people of God in America have looked abroad, they have felt a new spirit arising in their breasts toward their own country. In May, 1826, THE AMERICAN HOME MISSIONARY SOCIETY was formed at New York. It designed to concentrate the operations of all the domestic missionary societies in the United States.

Amid the benevolent efforts of Christians toward the pagan nations, the children of Israel scattered among every nation have not been forgotten. Mr. Wolf, a converted Jew, made the most laudable efforts in Europe and Asia, to search out and convert his brethren, and large societies have been formed in Great Britain and America, which have sent among them missionaries and tracts, and instituted schools for their children.

If this zeal for Missions which we have been contemplating and which has, for the last fifty ·years especially, swelled the song of heaven, has constituted a new era in the church, no less has the powerful operation of a sister spirit which has carried forth the Bible to every nation.

In 1803, a Mr. Charles, minister in Wales, went to London to obtain if possible, some Welsh Bibles for the destitute poor in that country. His affecting representations and appeals excited numbers to unite, March 7, 1804, in the formation of that now magnificent institution,

THE BRITISH AND FOREIGN BIBLE SOCIETY.

The great object of this society from its commencement has been, the circulation of the Scriptures, without note or comment, in the principal living languages. Its early and unrivaled popularity, the vastness of its exertions and its blessed results, are, and ever must be, objects of wonder and lively gratitude. It has issued from its depository in fifty-two years, above 30 millions of copies of the Scriptures, and assisted in disseminating or translating the Bible in one hundred and fifty-seven different languages and dialects. Its expenditures had been above four millions sterling.

While it has been thus active in supplying the spiritual wants of the vast family of man, it has excited Christians in different parts of the world to go and do likewise. Noble societies have been formed in Switzerland, Ireland, Russia,

Prussia, Norway, Denmark, Sweden, North America, Holland, Germany, Paris—also in Asia and Africa, which by their numerous auxiliaries, are rapidly filling the earth with the word of life. About 3,000 are now in active operation, whose annual receipts are many millions.

In this age of benevolence, have also arisen the industrious TRACT SOCIETIES, which are fast filling the world with little heralds of salvation. The first was instituted in 1799 in London, which has issued from its depository 80 millions of tracts, in forty-two different languages. The American Tract Society was formed at Boston, 1814. In 1825, it became auxiliary to the National Tract Society formed at New York. These institutions have also sent forth millions of publications for the spiritual instruction of mankind. In 1817, the Methodists, with a like commendable zeal, formed at New York the Methodist Tract Society, which has been active in the cause.

In 1822, the Reformed Dutch church, established under the auspices of the general synod, the R. D. C. Missionary Society, whose operations have been chiefly domestic. The Evangelical, Lutheran, and German Reformed churches have each missions connected with their respective synods.

To supply the great demand which exists for preachers of the Gospel, a society was formed in Boston, N. E., Aug. 29, 1815, called the AMERICAN EDUCATION SOCIETY, whose object is the education of pious young men for the Gospel ministry. This society has, during its existence, rendered itself eminently serviceable to the church, and promises, by its permanent funds, to continue to do so to the end of time. About 700 of its beneficiaries have passed through their course of education, and devoted themselves to the promotion of the cause of Christ.

Toward the close of the last century, the attention of the church was directed to her children and youth. Schools were established in Great Britain on the Lord's day, through the agency of Robert Raikes, for the instruction of the ignorant poor in divine things. The churches in America and other parts of the world saw their utility and followed the example. In Great Britain and Ireland 700,000 youth are now receiving instruction in 6,000 schools, from more than 50,000 teachers. In the United States, about 2,000,000. In the whole world more than two and a half millions.

The seamen, who have in all ages been deplorably destitute of religious instruction, have also of late received great attention from the pious and benevolent. Places of worship have been prepared in some of the principal seaports in the Christian world; preaching has been afforded, and some thousands have been converted to the Lord.

In 1826 was formed at Boston the American Temperance Society, to arrest the progress of a vice which was sweeping 30,000 annually to an untimely grave, and most lamentably marring the purity of the churches. Millions in this country have enlisted under its banner, and millions in other countries have totally abjured the use of all intoxicating drinks.

That the divine blessing may descend on all these efforts for the redemption of the world, a concert for prayer has been for some time very extensively observed on the first Monday in every month throughout the Christian world, and by missionaries and converts to Christianity, in heathen lands. Concerts for prayer are also extensively held for particular objects; as Sabbath schools, Education Societies, Colleges, &c.

We have briefly contemplated the operations of the Protestant world for the enlargement of the Redeemer's kingdom. By these the great Captain of salvation is going forth conquering and to conquer. How beautiful are his feet upon the mountains! The church is moving rapidly toward millennial glories. Forgetting, in a measure, the contentions and sectarian animosities, which have, in past ages, engrossed her, she is with apostolic benevolence and zeal, carrying the light of life to "the old wastes, the desolations of many generations." Who is not grateful that he lives in this age? that he stands on this spot between the living and the dead? Who, in this moment of holy enterprise, of lofty exploit, will not pray, with greatest earnestness, Thy kingdom come? Who will not consecrate to Messiah's triumphs over pagan darkness and idolatry, Mahometan imposture, and popish superstition, his time, his talents, his possessions, his influence?

"BEHOLD THE TABERNACLE OF GOD IS WITH MEN; AND HE WILL DWELL WITH THEM; AND THEY SHALL BE HIS PEOPLE; AND GOD HIMSELF SHALL BE WITH THEM AND BE THEIR GOD. AND GOD SHALL WIPE AWAY ALL TEARS FROM THEIR EYES; AND THERE SHALL BE NO MORE DEATH, NEITHER SORROW NOR CRYING, NEITHER SHALL THERE BE ANY MORE PAIN, FOR THE FORMER THINGS ARE PASSED AWAY."

APPENDIX.

HISTORY OF THE JEWS FROM THE DESTRUCTION OF JERUSALEM TO THE PRESENT TIME.

A Coin struck at Rome after the destruction of Jerusalem by Titus, representing the conquered country—she that was full of people, sitting a widow, solitary and weeping.

No mind can contemplate the ancient history of the children of Israel, the chosen people of God, without feeling a strong desire to trace their course subsequent to their excision from the church, for their unbelief, and to know something of their present state and future prospects. In this place can be presented only a brief view of their RESIDENCE, GOVERNMENT, RELIGION, LEARNING AND LEARNED MEN, THE FATE OF THEIR BELOVED CITY AND COUNTRY, THEIR FALSE CHRISTS, PERSECUTIONS, AND SUFFERINGS, NUMBERS AT VARIOUS PERIODS AND COUNTRIES, EMPLOYMENT, ATTEMPTS FOR THEIR CONVERSION, PRESENT STATE AND PROSPECTS.

THEIR RESIDENCE.

The Jews have been scattered, as Moses declared they would be, among all people, from one end of heaven to the other. When the Roman general, Titus, in the year of our Lord 72, had destroyed Jerusalem, and ploughed up its foundations, all the lands in Judea were ordered to be sold, and such oppressive acts were passed, that only a few who felt an attachment to their land, which could not be destroyed, remained to die amidst its desolations. Multitudes retired to Egypt and the islands of the Adriatic; great numbers fled to Persia and Babylon; and many took refuge in Italy and the western part of the Roman Empire. From that day to this, they have been found, when suffered by civil governments, in every region of civilized man.

GOVERNMENT.

It was predicted that the sceptre should not depart from Judah, nor a lawgiver from between his feet, until Shiloh should come. The Jews, with few exceptions, governed themselves until Christ came, and then the government departed from them, and they have now, for 1800 years, without a moment of independent sovereignty, been subject to others. They have, excepting in the United States, served their enemies in every land, and had an iron yoke of bondage put upon their necks. They could not, however, well long remain as a separate body, without some internal organization, and soon after their dispersion, they divided into two great branches, the eastern and western, and chose distinguished leaders to be their guides. The head of the eastern Jews was styled the Prince of the Captivity. His residence was at Babylon or Bagdat. The head of the western, the Patriarch. He resided at Tiberias. These chiefs were of the Levitical race; and being excluded from the royal dignity, and confined to religious concerns, they never became alarming to the Romans, As the Sanhedrim could meet in no place but Jerusalem it became extinct at the destruction of the city, but tribunals called houses of judgment, for the decision of religious disputes, were afterwards erected.

In the year 429, the office of Patriarch was abolished by imperial law, to the great grief of the western Jews. They were, in consequence of this, left solely under the direction of the chiefs of the synagogues, whom they called primates. The Princes of the Captivity were splendid and powerful, but they were totally extinct, in 1039, when the Jews were banished from the East. In the Ottoman empire, the Jews are subject to a chief of their own nation, called Cochan Pasca, whose power over them is very absolute.

Every Jewish Church is at present governed by a presiding Rabbi. Two or three of these Rabbis form a tribunal termed Beth Din, the house of justice, for settling religious, and sometimes civil dispute.

RELIGION.

To their religion the Jews have adhered with an inflexible obstinacy. Such parts of their worship as were necessarily confined to Jerusalem, particularly sacrifices, have ceased; but as closely as they could, in their dispersed state, they have adhered to the Mosaic dispensation. They have continued to read the law in their synagogues, with a variety of prayers: to repeat blessings and praises to God, on all special occasions, to avoid swearing, and to treat the name of God with the greatest reverence; to abstain from meats prohibited by the Levitical law; to teach their children the law of Moses, to venerate the Sabbath, which they have viewed as commencing an hour before sunset on Friday; to practice circumcision, and to observe the passover, feast of pentecost, of trumpets, of tabernacles, of purim, and the great day of expiation. They have also had many festivals not appointed by the law of Moses.

Since the destruction of Jerusalem, they have had no High Priest. A rabbi or priest continues to preside in the synagogue worship, and occasionally preaches and marries. He is not confined to the tribe of Levi. The members of that tribe are now considered as laymen, yet they have some little deference paid them in the Synagogue service.

The Jews in their dispersion have rigidly adhered to a few great articles of faith; the unity of God; the inspiration and ever binding power of the law of Moses; the future appearance of the Messiah; the resurrection of the dead; and future retribution. They have supposed that Christ will be a great temporal prince, will restore the Jews to their native land, and will subdue all nations before him and the house of Judah. As the prophets have predicted his mean condition and sufferings, they have supposed that there will be two Messiahs, Ban Ephraim. a person of low and mean con-

APPENDIX. 449

dition of the tribe of Ephraim ; and Ban David, a prince of great power and glory, of the tribe of Judah.

The Jews have acknowledged a two-fold law of God ; the five books of Moses, and oral tradition. The oral tradition was, in their view, first delivered by God to Moses, and by Moses to the leaders of the Jews after him. The number of these traditions was constantly increasing, and had become, in the time of our Saviour, the chief objects of attention in the Jewish schools.

About the middle of the second century, rabbi Judah reduced all these traditions of the commentaries which had been made on them, to one book, called the *Misna*. This was soon received by the Jews as a sacred book, and of equal authority with the written law. A commentary was written on the Misna by Jochanan, soon after it was formed, and called the Jerusalem Talmud, because it was composed for the Jews who remained in Judea.

In the East, Rabbi Asce began to collect in the fifth century, the sayings, debates, and decisions of the rabbis, for 300 years, into 35 books. The work was compiled in about a century, and styled the Talmud of Babylon. For it the Jews entertain the highest veneration, and view it as of divine authority.

About the sixth century, the attention of the Jews was turned to the Scriptures. They much feared, as they had lost their existence as a nation, that they should lose their sacred books. To prevent this, a number of learned men composed a work, in which they first fixed the true reading of the Hebrew text by vowels and accents, and then numbered, not only the chapters and sections, but even the verses, words and letters of the Old Testament. This is called the Masora, the hedge and fence of the law, and is "the most stupendous monument in the whole history of literature, of minute and persevering labor."

After the invention of printing, the Jews carefully printed several Hebrew bibles in folio, and quarto, and lexicons and concordances. Cardinal Hugo, in 1240, had divided the Scriptures into chapters. But in 1445, Mordecai Nathan, a rabbi, refined upon him, and divided the chapters into verses, but they were never marked in any printed Hebrew copy, until 1661. Most of the Hebrew manuscripts extant, were written between 1000, and 1457. One very fine copy of the Pentateuch is on 40 skins, written in 153 columns, about twenty-two inches deep, and five broad, each column containing 63 lines. These skins are connected together and rolled up.

Some new sects have come from time to time appeared among the Jews, but the Pharisees have ever formed the bulk of the nation. A few Caraites, who reject the traditions, and are Jewish Protestants, remain. A colony of these are on the Crimea. The Sadducees, as a sect, are nearly extinct. But there are many real Sadducees, that is, Infidels, among the Jews; men who reject all belief in revelation, and moral accountability, and any Saviour A party has recently sprung up in Germany, who despise both the Talmud and the Old Testament. They are little better than deists. The New Testament is read extensively.

LEARNING AND LEARNED MEN.

The Jews have never been a literary people. Rabbinical knowledge is all that has been esteemed by them of any value, and from this they have feared the study of Geek and Roman classics would wean their youth. In the twelfth century, however, a constellation of learned men appeared in

Europe, who were an honor to the nation. The chief of these were Nathan Ben Jechiel, Abram Ben Ezra, a commentator on the Old Testament; Moses Maimonides, master of many eastern languages, a distinguished physician, and an able defender of the Mosaic institution; Isaac Jarki, called by the Jews, Prince of Commentators, and the family of the Kimskis, distinguished for Hebrew learning. In a knowledge of the Scriptures, the Jewish Rabbis always excelled the Roman and English priests in the dark ages. Poland has in modern times, been the chief seat of Jewish literature. A famous Jewish school existed at Cracow in the sixteenth century, to which youth were sent from all parts of Europe. At Lessen, in Germany, a college was established in 1801, where Hebrew youth were taught the languages and sciences.

FATE OF THEIR BELOVED CITY AND COUNTRY.

About fifty years after the destruction of Jerusalem, the emperor Adrian sent a colony to rebuild it in the Roman style, and called it Ælia Capitolina, which excited a rebellion of the Jews under Barchobebas, the false Messiah, but they were subdued with a terrible slaughter, and the city was finished, and all Jews were prohibited from entering it, or looking at it, upon pain of death. To prevent further disturbance, Adrian destroyed all that remained of the ancient city, and as he could not change the face of nature, he profaned every place held sacred; erected a theatre with the stones of the temple to Jupiter on the site of the Jewish temple, and placed a hog of marble upon the gates of the city. For centuries, the Jews durst not creep over the rubbish to bewail their city, without bribing the guards.

About the commencement of the fourth century, the emperor Constantine restored to the city its ancient name, and enlarged and adorned it; and soon after, Julian, designing to root out Christianity from the earth, favored the Jews, and offered to rebuild their temple. The Jews were at once raised to a pitch of enthusiasm. They brought forth immense wealth, and concentrated it for the purpose. Spades and pickaxes of silver were provided by the rich, and the women showed their zeal by removing the rubbish in their mantles of silk. But a terrible earthquake, and fiery appearances, compelled them to abandon the undertaking.

In the year 613, Chosroes, the Persian monarch, took Jerusalem, and delivered it into the hands of the Jews, who pillaged the Christian temples, and put 90,000 Christian prisoners to death. It was soon after retaken by Heraclius, the Greek emperor, but retained only a short period, for in the year 636, the Saracens took it, and by command of Omar, on the ground where Solomon's temple stood, was erected a Mahometan mosque. The inhabitants were allowed their religion, but were not permitted to ride upon saddles, or to bear arms. The holy and beloved city now remained subject to the caliphs, about 400 years.

In 1099, the city was taken by the crusaders, and as the Jews were successors of those who crucified the Saviour, they were most inhumanly put to death.

In 1189, it was retaken by the Turks, and by them it has been held in subjection, together with the whole of Palestine, to the present time.

FALSE CHRISTS.

Christ told his disciples that there should be false Christs, and false prophets, who should show great signs and wonders; insomuch, that, if it were possible, they would deceive the very elect. But none attracted much regard, until A. D. 132, when one arose calling himself Barchobebas, or son of a star, the person predicted by Balaam. He excited his countrymen to rebellion against the Romans, and promised them a full restoration to former glory The Rabbi Akibha became his fore-runner, and publicly anointed him as the Messiah and King of the Jews, putting a diadem on his head. 200,000 Jews were soon collected around this impostor, in the field, who fell with fury upon both heathens and Christians. They gained at first, some advantage over the imperial army ; but in a short period, they were all scattered or slain by the forces of Adrian. Barchobebas and his precursor, with 580,000 Jews, fell by the sword ; besides vast multitudes who perished by famine and pestilence. Such of the Jews as survived, were sold as slaves, and dispersed over the earth.

Others in succeeding periods claimed the like homage, but the twelfth century was the most prolific. One then appeared in France ; another in Persia ; another in Spain ; a fourth in Fez, who pretended to work miracles ; a fifth beyond the Euphrates, who drew prodigious multitudes after him ; two others in Persia, and one in Moravia. All these impostors were put to death, and drew indescribable calamities upon the Jews in various parts of the world.

But none, since Barchobebas, ever imposed so far upon the Jews, or became so distinguished as Zabathia Tzevi, who appeared at Smyrna in 1666. He was adored as the first born of God. 400 prophets prophesied of his glories. The Jews every where prepared to follow him to the Holy Land. But interfering with the rights of the Grand Seignior, he was taken, and being shown the stake, he turned Turk.

The last impostor that has collected many followers, was Mordecai, a German, in 1682. In 1650, a great council was convened upon the plains of Egeda, in Hungary, to consider whether the Messiah had come. 300 Rabbis were present. Some were perplexed with the Christian miracles, but the majority agreed that he had been retarded by their sins.

PERSECUTIONS AND SUFFERINGS.

In the 28th of Deuteronomy, Moses declared to the Israelites that if they forsook God, they should endure sufferings such as no nation had ever known. Some of these were brought upon them in the first captivity, and in the wars of the Maccabees. But since they crucified the Lord of glory, they have awfully realized the whole.

Eleven hundred thousand perished in the destruction of Jerusalem. 580,000 fell with Barchobebas. Such as survived were sold as slaves into Egypt, and forbidden, on pain of death, even to look at their beloved city. Sapor, king of Persia, becoming jealous of them, violently persecuted them, A. D. 200, throughout his dominions. When the Roman empire became Christian, the Jews were universally abhorred as the persecutors of Christ, and all intercourse with Christians was publicly forbidden. If any Jew married a Christian, or circumcised a slave, he was put to death. Mahomet flattered them for a season, so that they began to view him as the Messiah ; but he became their inveterate foe, and turned his arms against them as a people accursed of God; slew vast multitudes ; drove them into exile ; confiscated their estates, and compelled all who remained to pay the most exorbitant tribute.

In the East, a law was passed in 760, constituting such Jews as embraced the Mahometan faith, sole heirs of the property of the whole family, which induced numerous youth to renounce Judaism. In 849, the eastern

Jews were compelled by the Mahometans to wear a cord or sash around their waist, as a disgraceful mark, were expelled from all offices which they had enjoyed, and prohibited the use of horses, and compelled to ride on asses with iron stirrups. These marks of infamy have continued in all Mahometan countries to the present day.

By the disputes respecting image worship, they were involved in new trouble in the eighth century, in the West. Such as would not bow to the cross and images, were subjected to the greatest vexations.

In 763, the Jews aided the Saracens in their encroachments upon France, which excited the rage of Charlemagne. He determined to destroy them, but commuted their punishment, and their chiefs only suffered death. The Jews of Thoulouse, were condemned to receive a box on the ear thrice a year at the gates of the churches, and to pay a perpetual fine of thirteen pounds of wax. In other cities they were made liable to other insults. At Beziers, in Languedoc, the populace threw stones at them with impunity from Palm Sunday to the Tuesday on Easter week.

In Egypt the Jews suffered persecutions about 1037, from the Caliph Haben. And in 1039, they were all banished from the East by the Sultan Cajens, who resolved upon their total extirpation. Multitudes of them passed into Africa and Spain. The princes of the captivity became totally extinct.

In 1055, an effort was made by the Jews in Spain to convert the Mahometans to the Jewish faith, which so incensed the king of Grenada, that 100,000 families were reduced to the greatest extremities.

During the eleventh and twelfth centuries, the Jews suffered the greatest indignities from the crusaders, who trampled upon them, extorted their money, and put them to death, on their march to and from the holy land, as the crucifiers of the Lord of glory. In the first crusade, 1500 were massacred at Strasburg; 1300 at Mayence. 12,000 were slain in Batavia. Women at Trevers, seeing the crusaders approach, killed their children, preferring to send them, as they said, to Abraham's bosom, to having them fall into the hands of the crusaders. Basil, Trevers, Coblentz, and Cologn, became human shambles. When Jerusalem was taken, all the Jews were inhumanly murdered. It is difficult to tell who were hated most, the Saracens in the East, or the Jews in the West. The public cry through Europe was, "Let us exterminate the descendants of those who crucified Jesus Christ, and let the name of Israel be no more remembered."

In England, the Jews who, by usury, had attained to great wealth, were, in 1188, assessed at the then enormous sums of £60,000, and in 1189, when Richard I. ascended the throne, the mob fell upon them, and put multitudes to death. At York, the mob assembled to inflict upon them similar barbarities. The Jews shut themselves up in a castle; and being closely besieged, rather than fall into the hands of the English, they set fire to the castle, and 500 were burnt after killing their wives and children These persecutions induced the wealthiest of them to leave the kingdom. Subsequent monarchs invited them back, but only to plunder them. The whole of their property was often claimed by the kings, and extorted by the greatest cruelties. King John compelled them to wear a disgraceful badge on their garments. He ordered the whole of them, women and men, to be imprisoned and tormented until they should pay 66,000 marks. From Henry III. they purchased an edict to preserve them from the outrages of the crusaders. Some of the archbishops and bishops forbade any one's selling them provisions, on pain of excommunication. They were often accused of the foulest crimes, and, though not found guilty, were compelled to pay the most enormous fines. Such was their oppression, that in 1254, they requested to depart from England, but it was not granted. 700 were massacred in London, 1262, by the barons, to please the Londoners. King Edward I. passed many severe enactments against them, and drew from them several hundred thousand pounds. In 1287, he ordered all the Jews in the kingdom to be imprisoned, and 280 to be executed in London, besides vast numbers in other cities; and in 1290, he ordered them all to be banished from the kingdom, never to return upon pain of death. He seized their whole property, scarcely allowing them sufficient to bear their expenses into other lands; the number expelled was 16,511. From this time they were shut out of England for 350 years.

In France they met with no better treatment. In 1182, Philip, the August, banished them, and confiscated their estates. He soon recalled them to exact money, as he said, to carry on the crusades. Under Lewis IX. they were forbidden to change their abode without leave of their feudal lord, and were sold with the land on which they dwelt; and if a Jew became a convert to Christianity, the whole of his property was confiscated to the use of his lord. The disgraceful badge he compelled them to wear on their garments, and forbade all intercourse with Christians.

In the year 1238, they were accused of sacrificing some Christian children, and using their blood at the passover. A violent persecution ensued, and 2500 Jews were put to death by the most cruel tortures. Soon after, they were all banished by Lewis from his dominions.

The next year a decree of banishment was passed, and rigorously executed in Brittany, and all their debtors were exonerated; and in 1240, the council of Lyons requested all Christian princes to compel them to pay all the money they had gained by usury, to the crusaders.

Again they were recalled to France in 1295, by Philip the Bold, to revive commerce, but no sooner did they accumulate great wealth, than they were expelled by Philip the Fair, in 1300, and stripped of all their treasures. In 1314, they were again recalled, upon condition of paying a heavy tax, but were allowed to remain in the kingdom only twelve years. In 1320, they were violently persecuted by the shepherds, who collected in a body to march to Jerusalem; many were put to death. In 1339 they were accused of having poisoned all the rivers, wells, and reservoirs of water. The populace fell upon them without formality, and executed upon numbers the greatest cruelties. By Philip the Tall, they were then again banished from the kingdom, and took refuge in Lombardy. In 1360 they purchased their return by an exorbitant sum, but scarce had they become re-established, when they were, in 1380, universally pillaged, and nearly destroyed. In the reign of Charles VI., an act was passed for the final expulsion of the Jews from France. An inventory was taken then of all their effects. From this last exile, in 1394, they commence the date of their years. They retired chiefly into Germany.

The sufferings of the Jews in Spain from the crusaders, were probably greater than in any part of Europe. Their own writers indeed, view them greater than their people were ever called to suffer since the destruction of Jerusalem. In Spain, too, they were accused of poisoning the rivers and wells, and 15,000 were in consequence put to death. In 1396 the inhabitants of Seville and Cordova were exasperated against them by the preaching of Mortin, an archdeacon, and a violent persecution arose, which spread through various cities, so that many populous synagogues became deserted.

APPENDIX.

In 1413 about 25,000 Spanish Jews professedly embraced Christianity, but it was chiefly to avoid severe treatment, and they were found secretly practicing Jewish rites. The officers of the Inquisition were ordered narrowly to watch them, and bring the delinquents to punishment. The result was terrible; 2000 were put to death, many were long imprisoned, and such as had their liberty, were compelled to wear two red crosses on their garments, to show that they had escaped from the flames. 17,000 returned to the bosom of the papal church.

In 1492, Ferdinand and Isabella issued a fatal edict, which banished all the Jews in four months from Spain. Seventy thousand families, or eight hundred thousand persons, pursuant to this decree, left that beautiful kingdom, amidst the greatest distress and suffering. Vast multitudes perished on their way to foreign countries. Such as reached them were in the deepest distress, and many perished from famine and disease, before they could find a settled abode. Portugal was esteemed the most fortunate asylum. But none could reach it without paying eight golden ducats to King John, and promising to quit his dominions at a limited time. His successor had some compassion on them, but was compelled by an alliance with Ferdinand, to compel them to depart. Wishing, however, to save them, he resolved to convert them to Christianity, and assembling them at Lisbon, with the promise of ships, he commanded all the children to be separated from their parents, that they might be taught Christianity. The utmost distress ensued. Many parents killed their children rather than release them, and many assumed the name of Christians; but being insincere, they fell a prey to the inquisition. But few left the country.

In Germany, the Jews were accused of more and greater crimes than in other countries, and when accused, they were treated with great cruelty, by the exasperated populace. 12,000 were killed at Mentz, on a charge of poisoning the fountains. In 1350, Lewis, king of Hungary, banished them all from his dominions. The Jews at Spira, of every age and sex, were murdered for insulting a priest. In the year 1400, on an accusation of poisoning the rivers and fountains, all were banished from the German empire, who would not receive baptism.

In 1434 the council of Basil prohibited all Christians from employing the Jews in any business whatever, forbade the Jews residing near any church, or in the inside of any city, and compelled them to wear a particular habit, and lose all sums lent on sacred book.

In the year 1454, Lewis, the duke of Bavaria, banished them from his dominions, and confiscated their estates. In the East the Jews were persecuted in the middle ages with as much severity as in the West. In the thirteenth century, they were at one time all obliged to leave the Babylonian territories or adopt the Mahometan religion. By the invasion of the Tartars, in 1291, they were driven from place to place, and robbed of their possessions. And during the wars of Tamerlane, in 1500, all their schools were broken up—their learned men were destroyed, and the whole people exceedingly impoverished. In Persia they suffered in 1666, under Shaw Abbas II., a general massacre for three years. All, without distinction of age or sex, were destroyed without pity, who would not renounce their religion.

Africa, too, presents us the astonishing fulfilment of prophecy respecting this wretched people. In some parts of it, indeed, they have for a time exceedingly flourished. In Ethiopia, they long had great tranquility, but attempting in 960, to seize the throne of Abyssinia, they were reduced to the lowest extremities, and in 1600, they were on the very brink of ruin. In Egypt, too, they have been greatly prospered. At Cairo, they have formed all the customs of the city, so that no goods have ever passed to the city on their Sabbath, and they have had 30 synagogues; but they have always been free plunder for every dominant party. In Morocco, too, they have found refuge, when expelled from other countries, but the lowest classes of the Moors have ever felt at liberty to pillage and insult them, because the Koran and the judge are always against them. At Fez, a day is appointed for the payment of their tribute. No sooner is it paid, than the populace strike and insult them. The Negroes in the interior have been found treating them also in the most contemptuous manner, calling them dogs.

The Reformation freed the Jews from many sufferings in Europe, to which they had been exposed by the papists, but Luther advised Christian princes not to receive them into their dominions. The emperor Rodolphus, wishing to drive them from Hungary, imposed an enormous tax upon them, which he supposed they would be unable to pay. In Moravia, a severe persecution commenced in 1574 In Poland, they enjoyed, in the sixteenth century, greater privileges than were ever allotted them in any of the European States. The kings farmed to them the royal demesnes: but their prosperity excited discontent; and severe enactments were passed against them. In the city of Nuremberg, they were not permitted to walk without a guide. At Augsburg, they were suffered to enter only at the price of a florin for every hour they wished to remain. In Frankfort, where they numbered 30,000, they were plundered and ridiculed, and shut up in one long narrow street, which was closed upon them at both ends, every night, during divine service among Christians. In Prague, where they filled a third part of the city, they were exposed to the greatest insults, and confined to the most degrading employments.

By the popes in the sixteenth century, they were treated with great severity. Pius V. expelled them in 1569, from every part of his dominions, except Rome and Ancona. There he suffered them to remain, he said, to remind the people of Christ's suffering, or that they might he converted. The Jews offered Charles V. 800,000 crowns of gold, if he would suffer them to return to Spain; but their offer was rejected. In Spain and Portugal they lived only by dissimulating. Outwardly they were good Catholics, while they secretly practised the Mosaic rites, and if at any time they were discovered, they were at once put to the tortures of the Inquisition. The sufferings of the Jews in that horrid tribunal for three centuries, were beyond all description.

After being shut out of England 350 years, the Jews made powerful efforts for restoration, in the revolution under Cromwell. The protector favored them, but so violent was the public prejudice against them, that no public act could be obtained. Similar efforts, but equally unsuccessful have since been made.

Their gradual settlement, however, has been connived at by the rulers, but they are to this day aliens in the law. In 1753, a bill naturalizing them, passed in Parliament, but the very next year it was repealed; such was the public indignation.

In Holland, the Jews had much comparative perplexity. But there, at some periods, they have been excluded from every lucrative and honorable employment, and from the arts and professions. A fine of 1000 florins was laid on him who found the least fault with the government. And no Jew could purchase meat of any but the public butchers, on penalty of being scourged.

In the Ottoman empire they have ever been treated with the utmost contempt. They pay a tax for the privilege of worshipping in their own way.

In their ancient city of Jerusalem, they have for 1900 years received nothing but oppression, ignominy and reproach. Sometimes they have for ages been entirely excluded from it, and not suffered to look at it from the distant mountains. And when permitted to reside there, have exhibited the most affecting spectacle of human wretchedness.

EFFORTS FOR THEIR CONVERSION.

The Apostles, made great efforts for the conversion of the Jews, and were eminently successful. 3000 were converted on the day of Pentecost. But after the destruction of Jerusalem, they were so hardened in opposition to Christ, and such objects of general detestation, that they were for a long period left to total blindness, by God and man.

In the year 428, some infant efforts were made by the bishop of Minorca, to convert the Jews in that island. A similar effort was made in 606 in the isle of Cyprus; but neither were very successful. In 1250, Raymond de Penneforte exerted himself to this effect in Spain. In 1411, Pope Benedict XIII. appointed a public conference; Jerome, a converted Jew, reasoned with his brethren out of the Scriptures, and 4 or 5000 were said to be converted. 25,000 Jews renounced their religion in Spain in 1413; but it was merely for safety. They secretly observed the Jewish rites. In 1690 Esdras Edgardus, a converted Jew at Hamburg, made the most successful efforts recorded since the days of the Apostles. Gregory XIII. ordered a sermon to be preached every week at Rome, for their conversion, and compelled one third of the Israelites in the city to be present.

In the year 1800, the Missionary Society in London zealously engaged in the conversion of the Jews, and were afterwards much aided in their designs by Joseph Frey, a converted Jew, who became a preacher of the Gospel of considerable celebrity. And in 1809, a society was formed in London, consisting of fifteen different denominations, until 1815, when it fell into the hands of the establishment, whose special object was the conversion of the Jews. Of this society Mr. Frey was made president, and he preached often to his brethren. Hundreds attended on his preaching, some of whom were converted. Some thousands of pounds have been expended in instructing Hebrew children, and printing and circulating Hebrew Bibles and tracts. A seminary was founded in 1821, for the education of the Jewish youth for the ministry. Thirty have gone forth to preach the Gospel to their brethren in Asia.

In 1819, a society was formed in Edinburgh for the conversion of the Jews; another has been established in Glasgow, and several on the continent.

In 1820 was formed the American Society for meliorating the condition of the Jews. Many auxiliary and several independent societies have since risen up in various parts of the United States, through the agency of the Rev. Mr. Frey the converted Jew.

But the greatest effort made by any individual of modern times, has been made by Joseph Wolf, a converted Jew—a man of astonishing talents and most noble spirit, who has visited his brethren in Europe and Asia, and addressed them with great power and effect.

APPENDIX.

NUMBERS.

The number of Jews in the world and in various countries at different periods is an interesting subject, but never can be ascertained with much accuracy. At the time of the destruction of Jerusalem, they probably numbered not far from three millions. This number has varied much in different ages and countries, according to the opportunity given them for increase. For the first 1200 years, they were far more numerous in the East than in the West. But in the tenth century, their numbers were greatly diminished there by the invasion of the Tartars and persecutions of the Persians. In Palestine, their number has always been small. When they were banished from Spain in 1492, there were in that kingdom 70,000 families. In 1619, there were in the province of Fez, 80,000. In the Ecclesiastical State they have numbered an hundred synagogues, nine of which were in Rome. Their present number is probably between three and four millions. In the Ottoman empire it is supposed that there are a million. At Constantinople, 80,000. At Aleppo, 5,000. Jerusalem 3,000. In China, India, and Persia, 300,000. Of the white and black Jews at Cochin, 16,000. In Ethiopia, 100,000. In Morocco, Fez, and Algiers, 400,000. In Poland, 300,000. England, 20,000. Holland, 60,000. France, 20,000. The United States, 50,000.

EMPLOYMENT.

As the Jews were, at the destruction of Jerusalem, dispossessed of their lands, and driven into foreign countries, they were compelled to resort to commerce for support. And having ever been in expectation of returning to Judea upon a sudden summons, they have never purchased, to much extent, any territory, nor engaged largely in agricultural employments; but have been the brokers and bankers of others. Their commercial pursuits were much promoted in the fifth century by the invasion of the northern nations, who had an abhorrence of commerce, and suffered it all to be transferred to a people whom they viewed with ignominy and contempt. In England, they were for a long time the chief conductors of foreign trade, and wrought most of the gold and silver ornaments for the churches. In the Ottoman empire they obtained the privilege of selling wine, because it was supposed that they would strictly regard the Jewish law which forbade their making any mixture. In Egypt and Morocco, they have ever formed the customs, coined the money, and conducted all foreign commerce. In most parts of the world, and in every age, they have accumulated great wealth. In Europe and America they are now generally brokers, dealers in clothes, watches, jewels, and a number of young people are teachers of children.

PRESENT STATE.

In Great Britain the Jews are not known in law, but they are connived at and valued for their enterprise. They have the free exercise of their worship, and the opportunity to acquire, and ability to hold property to any extent. Their literature is respectable. They have five synagogues in London. Population, 14,000.

In Holland the Jews are numerous, wealthy, and respectable.

In Spain they are not known as Jews; but are numerous in every class of society, even among priests and inquisitors as good Catholics.

In Portugal, they are in the same manner obliged to dissemble. The Spanish and Portuguese Jews claim their descent from a colony of the tribe of Judah, sent into Spain at the Babylonish captivity, and will have no intercourse with the German Jews. They are in every respect superior to the German Jews, and vie with other Europeans in refinement and intelligence. They have separate synagogues wherever they reside.

In Germany and Prussia, most of the vexatious statutes of former ages have been repealed, and the Jews are living in quiet. At Frankfort, however, they are subject to many humiliating restrictions.

From Russia, they were formerly excluded, but they have been united to it by the union of countries in which they resided, and favorable edicts have been passed by the Emperor. A colony of Caraite, or Protestant Jews, who adhere closely to the Scriptures, are on the Crimea. Poland has been their chief seat in modern ages. There are now in that country from 2 to 300,000, enjoying great privileges.

In Sweden and Denmark, they have a good degree of liberty.

In France, from whence they were expelled in 1304, and where only a few for centuries were known at Metz and Bordeaux, their situation since the revolution has been highly gratifying. In 1791, all who would take the civic oath were admitted to the rank of citizens. This act first gave them a country in Europe. The emperor Napoleon convened an assembly of them in Paris, May 30th, 1806, that he might learn their principles, and the next year the Grand Sanhedrim, composed according to the ancient custom of seventy members, for the establishment of a civil and religious polity. A synagogue and a consistory were established in every department.

In Paris, the Jews had in 1812, a consistory, and three grand Rabbis, and are improving in literature and agriculture.

In the Ottoman empire, the Jews are still numerous, but less affluent and more ignorant than in Europe. For a heavy tax to the Porte, they have the liberty of their own worship. They all wear beards, and are distinguished by their dress. Their priests are much respected. " In Jerusalem, their ancient city, they are, as a people, the objects of universal contempt; who suffer the most wanton outrages without a murmur; who endure wounds and blows without a sigh; who, when the sacrifice of their life is demanded, unhesitatingly stretch forth their necks to the sabre. If a member of the community thus cruelly proscribed and abused, happens to die, his companion buries him clandestinely during the night, in the valley of Jehosaphat, within the purlieus of the Temple of Solomon. Enter their habitation, and you find them in the most abject, squalid misery, and, for the most part, occupied in reading a mysterious book to their children, with whom again it becomes a manual for the instruction of future generations. The legitimate masters of Judea should be seen as they are in their own land, slaves and strangers—awaiting, under the most cruel and oppressive of all despotisms, a king who is to work their deliverance."

In China, the Jews have existed for many centuries in considerable numbers. They have their synagogues, but so far conform to the Chinese customs and worship, and are so peaceable as to meet with but little persecution.

In India, the Jews are numerous. Dr. Buchanan, who visited that country in 1806 and 8, found their residence about a mile distant from Cochin, called Jewstown. They were divided into two classes, the Jerusalem, or white Jews, and the ancient, or black Jews. The former came into India soon after the destruction of Jerusalem. The latter had a tradition that their ancestors came thither soon after the Babylonish captivity. Their complexion differs much from the white Jews, and they are viewed by them as an inferior race. From these, Dr. B. obtained a manuscript copy of the

APPENDIX. 459

Pentateuch, handed down from their ancestors, which differs but little from the European copies.

In South America and the West Indies, the situation of the Jews is favorable to the accumulation of wealth, and the practice of their religion.

In the United States, the Jews enjoy perfect freedom. But few have settled in New England. A synagogue has existed for half a century at Newport, R. I. In New York are 17 congregations; in Philadelphia, two; in Charleston, S. C., one very large, on the Portuguese customs; in Richmond, one.

PROSPECTS.

The prospects of the Jews are brightening. Their condition is rapidly meliorating in all parts of the Christian world. The extension of civil liberty and rational Christianity, and the efforts making for their illumination and conversion, are fast placing them on the same footing with other nations, and bringing them into the kingdom of God.

From the sure promise of Jehovah, we learn that the branches of the olive tree, which were broken off, shall be grafted in again. And if the trump of the prophecy does not give an uncertain sound, the time is not far distant when the Jews will every where bow to the yoke of Jesus Christ, and enjoy the liberty and blessedness of the children of God.

The Jews, especially the Portuguese Jews, believe that they shall yet all be restored to the holy land, where, under the dominion of Messiah, they shall become an independent and glorious nation. Many Christian writers, also, believe in their literal restoration to the promised land, and the re-establishment for a season, of their temple worship. In support of these opinions, the following passages are adduced. Deut. xxx. 5. Ezekiel xxxvi. 23—32, xxxvii. 19—28. Isaiah xi. 10—16. Jeremiah xxiii. 6—8. Isaiah lxvi. 20. Amos ix. 14, 15. Joel iii. 1. Hosea i. 10, 11. Romans xi. Others give all these passages a spiritual interpretation, and say they will be fulfilled in the conversion of this ancient people of God to the Christian faith.

An interesting inquiry relates to the ten tribes, which were scattered abroad at the Babylonish captivity, and which never returned to the Holy Land. Are they in existence? If they are, where are they to be found? Some suppose that they are entirely lost among the nations. Others, that they are still in existence, because their entire extinction would be inconsistent with the promise of God, and render impossible the fulfilment of prophecy. But where are they to be found? Some suppose that they are the Jews in China, who have a tradition that their ancestors settled that country 1000 years before Christ. Sir William Jones supposed that they were the nations of the Affghans in Persia, who had generally mingled with the Mahometans. Dr. Buchanan thought he found them among the black Jews near Cochin, who had copies of the books of the old Testament, written before the captivity, but none after. Manassas Ben Israel, in a work styled "The Hope of Israel," attempted to prove that the American Indians are the descendants of the ten tribes. This was also the opinion of Eliot, the Apostle of the Indians, and has been since strongly advocated by Mr. Adair, for many years a trader among the Indians, by the Hon. Elias Boudinot and the Rev. Ethan Smith. These writers flatter themselves that they can find among the Indians something like the Hebrew festivals, fasts, and religious rites, the Jewish prophets, priests, and cities of refuge; the basis of the Hebrew language; many Hebrew words; something of the theocracy, or divine government of Israel; the doctrine of the divine unity; the Jewish division into tribes; phylacteries, or ancient Hebrew writings, and various traditions, unaccountable on any supposition but this, that they descended from Israel. It is not necessary however, to seek for the ten tribes in such obscurity. They did not indeed return to Palestine, the Holy Land, but remained, scattered in all the 127 provinces of the vast empire of Ahasuerus. There, and in other parts of the world, they were in the days of the Apostles. Paul, in his speech to King Agrippa, affirmed that the twelve tribes were then existing, and serving God day and night, in expectation of the promise made to the fathers. To the twelve tribes scattered abroad, James directed his epistle; so that there is no small reason to suppose that by far the greater part of the Jews now in the world, are descendants of the ten tribes.

The preservation of the Jews through eighteen hundred years of awful suffering and disgrace, "a reproach and a by-word" among all nations, "a bush burning with fire, yet not consumed," is a most wonderful fulfilment of prophecy, and of course affords incontestible evidence of the truth of the Bible. He who can contemplate it and be an infidel, must renounce all claim to a candid and considerate mind.

TABLE *of the Inhabitants of the world, according to Religion, from different authorities.*

	Malte Brun.	Hassel.	Adams.
Catholics,	116 millions.	122 millions.	80 millions.
Greek Church,	70 "	74 "	30 "
Protestants,	42 "	44 "	65 "
Total of Christians,	228 "	240 "	175 "
Jews,	4 or 5 "	5 "	2¼ "
Mahometans,	100 "	120 "	140 "
Votaries of Brahmanism,	60 "	80 "	"
Votaries of Shahmanism, and the religion of the Grand Lama,	50 "	90 "	"
Of the religion of Budhoo, Fo, &c.	100 "	100 "	"
Various other Pagans,	100 "	72 "	"
Total of the Pagans,	330 "	342 "	482 "
Total of Inhabitants of the Globe.	653 "	707 "	800 "

TABLE *of Christian denominations.*

Denominations.	Number and Countries.	
Catholics,	100,000,000.	Southern and Middle Europe.
	Do.	Spain, Portugal, and Italy, exclusively.
	Do.	France, Austria, Poland, Belgium, and Ireland, almost entirely, and a large part of the German States. Switzerland has 700,000. England 500,000.
Greek Church,	34,000,000.	Russia and Greece. 3½ millions in Austria.
Protestants,	42,000,000.	Northwest of Europe.
Lutherans,	Sweden, Norway, Denmark,	5 millions.
	Russia,	2½ "
	Germany, Lutherans and Reformed,	15 "
	(Prussia, 6 m. Austria, 3 m. German states, 6 m.)	"
Other Protestants,	Great Britain,	14 "
	Holland,	2 "
	Switzerland,	1 "
	France.	3 "

The remainder of the population of Europe consists of Jews, scattered through all parts; Mahometans in Turkey, and southern Russia, and a few Pagans in Russia.

APPENDIX.

CREEDS OF THE WORLD.

BY DR. DIETERICI OF BERLIN.

Christians,	335,000,000
Jews,	5,000,000
Buddhists, Chinese, Japanese,	600,000,000
Mohammedans,	160,000,000
Pagans,	200,000,000
	1,300,000,000
Roman Catholics,	170,000,000
Protestants,	80,000,000
Greek Christians,	76,000,000

PRINCIPAL AMERICAN MISSIONS.

AMERICAN BOARD, 1864. FIFTY-FIFTH YEAR.

Receipts, $531,985.67
Expenditures, 522,414.38
Missions, 22
Stations, 111 Out-stations, 213
Laborers.
Ordained missionaries, 150, Others, 918. 1068
Churches gathered, 166
Communicants, 23,647
Pupils in Schools, 10,317

AMERICAN BAPTIST, 1864. FIFTIETH YEAR.

Receipts, $135,525.25
Expenditures, $135,019.68
Missions, 19
Stations in the Asiatic, 15. Out-stations, 400, 415
Stations and Out in the French and German, 1,100
Laborers.
Missionaries, 40 Male, 36 Female, 50 Native and other, 542. Total 688
Churches, 469
Members, 35,000

PROTESTANT EPISCOPAL, 1864. TWENTY-NINTH YEAR.

Receipts, $143,539.76
Expenditures, $136,063.96
Missions, Domestic, 2 Bishops, 104 Preachers.
Missions, Foreign, 5
Missionaries and Teachers, 86
Communicants,

Presbyterian Board, 1864. Twenty-ninth year.

Receipts, ... $222,337.18
Expenditures, ... $221,609.93
Missions, ... 10
Stations, . . , . . . 62
Laborers.—65 Ministers, 85 American and 123 Native Teachers.
Communicants, ... 961
Scholars. 4,910

Methodist Episcopal Church, 1864. Forty-fifth year.

Receipts, ... $429,768.75
Expenditures, ... $362,031.16
Foreign Missions, ... 7
Missionaries, ... 129
Members, ... 6,122
Domestic Missions, ... 5
Missionaries, , ... 304
Members, ... 30,174

Dutch Reformed B. of For. Missions, 1864. Thirty-second year.

Receipts, ... $35,391.81
Missions, ... 13
Missionaries 16, Native Helpers, 27. . . 43
Communicants, ... 553

American Missionary Association, 1864. Eighteenth year.

Receipts, ... $95,395.83
Expenditures, ... $96,076.03
Missionaries and Teachers among Freedmen, . 288
Clothing received for Missions and Freedmen, . . $44,341.00

American Home Missionary Society, 1864. Thirty-eighth year.

Receipts, ... $230,967.81
Total for 38 years, ... $4,372,588.48
Expenditures, ... $149,325.58
Missionaries sustained, ... 756
Congregations and Missionary Districts, . . 1,518
Sabbath School and Bible Class Scholars. . . . 55,200
Whole Number of additions to Churches in 38 years, . 178,832

American and Foreign Christian Union, 1864. Fiftieth year.

Receipts, ... $72,758.11
Expenditures, ... $69,584.11
Home Field. Foreign Field. 13 Countries.

Presbyterian (N. S.) Home Missions, 1864. Third year.

Receipts, ... , $61,709.87
Churches contributing, ... 897
Missionaries employed, ... 297
17 Churches organized, 36 edifices built, 675 converts.

APPENDIX. 463

RELIGIOUS DENOMINATIONS IN THE UNITED STATES.

NAMES.	Churches.	Ministers.	Communicants.
Roman Catholics,	2,585	2,235	2,343,000
Protestant Episcopalians,	2,110	2,073	135,767
Presbyterians, Old School,	3,491	2,578	279,600
Presbyterians, New School,	1,543	1,558	137,989
Cumberland Presbyterians,	1,163	927	84,249
Dutch Reformed,	410	400	50,304
German Reformed,		365	80,000
Evangelical Lutherans,	1,441	792	146,082
Moravians,	28	24	6,000
Methodist Episcopal (North and South,).	9,742	8,205	928,320
Methodist Protestant Church,	1,200	2,000	90,000
Wesleyan Methodists,		400	40,000
Mennonites,	400	250	36,280
Orthodox Congregationalists,	2,676	2,531	257,634
Unitarian Congregationalists,	261	291	30,000
Universalists,	932	693	600,000
Swedenborgians,	57	50	8,000
Regular Baptists,	12,186	7,609	934,620
Seventh-Day Baptists,	60	70	6,567
Free-Will Baptists,	1,297	1,095	55,676
Reformed Baptists, (Campbellites,)	2,000	1,500	350,000
Christian Baptists, (Unitarians,)		1,897	140,000
Anti-Mission Baptists,	1,720	825	58,000
Quakers,	550		100,000

A TABLE *exhibiting some of the most important versions of the Holy Scriptures.*

The Septuagint, a Greek version of the Old Testament, made by some Jews in Egypt, about 286 years before the Christian era.
The Syrian version, made early in the second century.
Two Egyptian versions, made about the same time.
The Ethiopic or Abyssinian version of the Old Testament, made about the second; and of the New, made about the fourth.
The Armenian version, made about the close of the fourth.
The Latin vulgate, made by Jerome, about the close of the fourth ; adopted as the true, by the Roman Church.
Several Arabic translations made between the seventh and the tenth centuries.
The Gothic version, made about the fifth century.
The Sclavonic or old Russian translation, made by Cyril and Methodius, in the ninth century.
The Anglo-Saxon version, made from the Latin in the eighth and ninth centuries.   A. D.
The German, made by Martin Luther, ... 1534
The English, by Tindall and Coverdale, ... 1535
The French, by Olivetan, ... 1535
The Swedish, by Olaus Petri, ... 1541
The Danish, by Pallaudius, ... 1550
The Dutch, ... 1560
The Italian, by Antonio, ... 1562
The Spanish, by Cassiodorus de Reyna, ... 1569
The Welsh, ... 1598
The Icelandic, by Thorlach, ... 1584
The Polish, ... 1596
The American Indian, by Eliot, ... 1663
The Turkish Testament, ... 1666

The Irish Bible, ... 1685
The Tamul, by the Danish missionaries, ... 2723
The Portuguese, ... 1748
The Bengalee Testament, by the Baptist missionaries, ... 1801
The Orissa Bible,   do.   do.   do.   1809
The Sanscrit Bible.   do.   do.   do.   1811
The Chinese Bible, by Dr. Morrison, ... 1815
The Arabic Testament, by Henry Martyn, ... 1816
The Persian,   do.   do.   1816
The Otaheitan Testament, by the English missionaries, . . . 1818
The Cingalese,   do.   do.   do.   . . . 1820
The Burnese, by Dr. Judson,   , ... 1834
The Armeno Turkish, by Dr. Goodell, ... 1841
The Nestorian, by Dr. Perkins, ... 1849
The Armenian, by Adger and Riggs, ... 1855
The Chinese, by Bridgman & Culberson, ... 1851
The Arabic, by Drs. Smith & Vandyke, ... 1864

CHRONOLOGICAL TABLE.

Before Christ.
4004. The Creation. Fall of man.
3017. Translation of Enoch.
2348. The Deluge.
1998. Death of Noah.
1996. Abraham born.
1897. Circumcision instituted.
       Jewish Church commences.
       Sodom and Gomorrah destroyed.
1872. Isaac offered.
1706. Jacob goes into Egypt.
1491. Israel delivered from Egyptian bondage.
       Law given. Mosaic ritual formed.
1451. Israel enter Canaan.
1444. Tabernacle of Shiloh.
1122. Samson dies with the Philistines.
1075. Monarchy establish'd in Israel.
1004. Dedication of the Temple.
975. Division of the ten tribes into two kingdoms.
588. Babylonish captivity. Jerusalem destroyed.
536. Return of the Jews from captivity.
515. Dedication of the 2d Temple.
458. Esther, Queen of the Jews.
       Ezra sent to Judea.
409. Close of the Old Testament.

Before Christ.
332. Alexander visits Jerusalem.
251. Death of Simon the Just.
166. Wars of the Maccabees.
63. Jerusalem taken by Pompey.
19. Herod repairs the Temple.
4. Birth of Jesus Christ.
A. D. 4 years before the Christian era.
29. Jesus baptized.
31. Death of John the Baptist.
33. Crucifixion of Christ.
    Day of Pentecost.
34. Death of Stephen.
35. Conversion of Saul.
39. Gospel preached to the Gentiles.
52. Council at Jerusalem.
64. Rome burnt by Nero.
    — First heathen persecution.
70. Destruction of Jerusalem by Titus.
135. Barchobebas, the false Messiah. 580,000 Jews destroyed.
177. Persecutions at Lyons and Vienne.
324. Roman empire becomes Christian.
324. Rise of Arianism.
    Council of Nice.
363. Vain attempt of Julian to rebuild Jerusalem

APPENDIX. 465

A. D.
496. Baptism of Clovis.
606. Popery and Mahometanism.
622. The Hegira.
726. Controversy about Images.
751. Pope a temporal power.
1096. First crusade to the Holy Land.
1099. Jerusalem taken by crusaders
1308. Pope's removal to Avignon.
1324. Wickliff.
1414. Council of Constance.
1415. John Huss burnt.
1444. Invention of Printing.
1492. America discovered.
1517. The reformation in Germany.
1529. Reformers called Protestants
1534. Reformation in England.
1535. Order of the Jesuits.
1545. Council of Trent.
1550. Era of English Puritans.
1555. Persecution by Mary.
1560. Reformation in Scotland.
1572. Massacre of St. Bartholomew.
1592. Presbyterianism established in Scotland.
1618. Synod of Dort.
1620. Landing of the Pilgrims at Plymouth.
1638. Solemn league and covenant in Scotland.
1648. Cambridge Platform.
1662. Act of uniformity.
1688. Revolution in England.
1708. Saybrook Platform.
1729. Rise of Methodism.
1742. Great revival in New England.
1792. Baptist Missionary Society in England.

A. D.
1804. British and Foreign Bible Society.
1810. American Board for Foreign Missions.
1814. Tract Society in Boston.
1816. American Education Society.
" American Peace Society.
" American Bible Society.
1817. American Colonization Society.
" Methodist Tract Society.
1820. Society for ameliorating the condition of the Jews.
1822. Reformed Dutch Church Mission Society.
1824. American Sun. School Union.
1825. American Tract Society.
" Prison Discipline Society.
1826. American Temperance Society at Boston.
" American Home Missionary Society.
1827. American Seamens' Friend Society.
1832. Baptist Home Mission Soc.
1833. American Anti-Slavery Soc.
1836. American and Foreign Bible Society, Baptist.
1837. American Temp. Union.
1843. Society for Collegiate and Theological Education.
1846. American Missionary Association.
1849. American and Foreign Christian Union.
1857. Foreign Mission Dutch Ref. Church.
1858. New York State Inebriate Asylum.

CHRONOLOGICAL REGAL TABLES.

KINGS OF THE JEWS.

	B. C.
1. Saul,	1095
2. David and Ishbosheth,	1055
3. David alone,	1047
4. Solomon,	1015
5. Division of the kingdom.	975

KINGS OF JUDAH.
TWO TRIBES

	B. C.
1. Rehoboam,	975
2. Abijam,	958
3. Asa,	955
4. Jehosaphat,	914
5. Jehoram,	889
6. Ahaziah,	885
7. Athaliah,	884
8. Joash,	878
9. Amaziah,	838
10. Azariah or Uzziah,	810
11. Jotham,	758
12. Ahaz,	742

	B. C.		B. C
13. Hezekiah,	727	6. Omri,	929
14. Manasseh,	698	7. Ahab,	917
15. Amon,	643	8. Ahaziah,	897
16. Josiah,	640	9. Jehoram,	896
17. Jehoahaz,	610	10. Jehu,	884
18. Jehoakim,	610	11. Jehoahaz,	856
19. Jehoakim,	599	12. Joash,	841
20. Zedekiah,	599	13. Jeroboam II.,	825
21. Nebuchadnezzar destroyed		Interregnum 11½ years,	784
Jerusalem.	588	14. Zecheriah,	773
		15. Shallum,	772
KINGS OF ISRAEL.		16. Menahem,	772
TEN TRIBES.		17. Pekahiah,	761
	B. C.	18. Pekah,	759
1. Jeroboam I.,	975	19. Hoshea,	730
2. Nadab,	954	Salmaneser, king of Assyria,	
3. Baasha,	953	destroyed the kingdom of	
4. Elah,	930	Israel,	721
5. Zimri,	929		

EXPLANATION OF THE CHART.

This Chart exhibits to view all periods of time. The perpendicular lines represent centuries. On the top of the Chart is given the Christian era On the bottom the era of the world. The first perpendicular line on the left, gives the fourth year of the world, and the 4000th before Christ. The second the 104th year of the world, and the 3039th before Christ. The history of the church is given near the top. The first 2100 years presents the church in an unembodied state. The next 1900, the Jewish Church. The next 1800, the Christian Church. A little below is the record of remarkable events. Thus, the Call of Abraham was 1922 before Christ. Jerusalem was destroyed 70 years after Christ. The horizontal lines under the names of individuals, represent the length of their lives, the figures the time of their birth and death, counting on the Christian era. Adam was born the first year of the world, or 4004 years before Christ. He lived 930 years, and therefore died 3074 before Christ. Abraham was born 1996 before Christ, and died 1821. Mahomet was born 571 after Christ, and died A. D. 632. Dwight was born A. D. 1752, and died 1817 By subtraction the length of the life is at once given. And by looking to the bottom of the chart, it may, by a moment's calculation, be seen in what year of the world each event occurred, or individual was born. Thus, the Passover was instituted A. M. 3513. Christ was born A. M. 4004. Luther A. M. 5187. Edwards, 5707.

| 4 | 13 | 900 | 1000 | 11 | 12 | 13 | 14 | 15 | 16 | 17 | 18 |

Eastern Churches
54 Greek Church
93 Bernadines
Church
56 Augustines
13 Dominicans
71 Carmelites
6 Franciscans
10 Jesuits
40 Jansenists
16 Reformed or Presbyterians
17 Lutherans
57 Moravians
7 Hussites
50 Independents
60 Waldenses
69 Wickliffites
54 Ch. of England
25 Baptists
29 Methodists
16 Socinians

Judges

Columbus
42 — 6
Charles V
56
Francis I.
49 — 47
Henry VIII
41 47 Cromwell
50 58
Louis XII
5
Leo X
75 — 57
Wickliff
21 84
Bellarmin
42 21
Huss
L. Socinus
Bevenger
2
35
74 65 Erasmus 25 62
Jerome 67 35 63 Massillon
42
Baconius
16
Lanfranc
39
Luther
25 10
Sourin
17 — 30
Owen
Calvin 16 34
9
64 Baxter
Peter the Hermit
Zwinglius 15 31
27 51
Howe
40 5
Melancthon
Bates
9 60 26 95
Anselm
Bucer
Sherlock
34 9
51
73 64
Beckel
Beza
Scott
19 4
60 5 Henry 46 21
Langton
Cranmer 62 11 Newton
23
50 56 25 7
Carolstadt
Edwards
Kempis 11 33 33
Jepthath
20 71 Servetus Brainard
73
13 17
Sampson
53
Dwight
Savanorola Laud 52 15
Eli
72 41
0 15
Tillotson
Sam
27 94 Ward
Wessalia
Pool Swarts
51
B.Bacon 19 84
11 79 24 95
Ruth
11 93
Prideaux
Xavier 13 60
52 Wesley
Eliot 5 91
40
1 Whitfield
11 70

| 27 | 28 | 29 | | 500-4 | 51 | 52 | 53 | 54 | 55 | 56 | 57 | 58 |

www.ingramcontent.com/pod-product-compliance
Lightning Source LLC
Chambersburg PA
CBHW022136300426
44115CB00006B/215